Cultural Crisis and Social Memory

ANTHROPOLOGY OF ASIA SERIES

Series Editor: Grant Evans, *University of Hong Kong*

Asia today is one of the most dynamic regions of the world. The previously predominant image of 'timeless peasants' has given way to the image of fast-paced business people, mass consumerism and high-rise urban conglomerations. Yet much discourse remains entrenched in the polarities of 'East vs. West', 'Tradition vs Change'. This series hopes to provide a forum for anthropological studies which break with such polarities. It will publish titles dealing with cosmopolitanism, cultural identity, representations, arts and performance. The complexities of urban Asia, its elites, its political rituals, and its families will also be explored.

Dangerous Blood, Refined Souls
Death Rituals among the Chinese in Singapore
Tong Chee Kiong

Folk Art Potters of Japan
Beyond an Anthropology of Aesthetics
Brian Moeran

Hong Kong
The Anthropology of a Chinese Metropolis
Edited by Grant Evans and Maria Tam

Anthropology and Colonialism in Asia and Oceania
Jan van Bremen and Akitoshi Shimizu

Japanese Bosses, Chinese Workers
Power and Control in a Hong Kong Megastore
Wong Heung Wah

The Legend of the Golden Boat
Regulation, Trade and Traders in the Borderlands of Laos,
Thailand, China and Burma
Andrew Walker

Cultural Crisis and Social Memory
Modernity and Identity in Thailand and Laos
Edited by Shigeharu Tanabe and Charles F. Keyes

Cultural Crisis and Social Memory

Modernity and Identity in Thailand and Laos

Edited by

Shigeharu Tanabe and
Charles F. Keyes

UNIVERSITY OF HAWAI'I PRESS
HONOLULU

Published in North America by
University of Hawai'i Press
2840 Kolowalu Street
Honolulu, Hawai'i 96822

First published in the United Kingdom
by RoutledgeCurzon
11 New Fetter Lane
London EC4P 4EE
England

Printed in Great Britain

Library of Congress Cataloguing-in-Publication Data

Cultural crisis and social memory : politics of the past in the Thai world
/ edited by
Shigeharu Tanabe and Charles F. Keyes.
        p. cm. – (Anthropology of Asia series)
    Includes bibliographical references and index.
    ISBN 0-8248-2603-5 (alk. paper)
    1. Thailand–Civilization. 2. Laos–Civilization. 3.
Thailand–Politics and government.
    4. Laos–Politics and government. 5. Memory–Social
aspects–Thailand. 6.
    Memory–Social aspects–Laos. I. Tanabe, Shigeharu. II. Keyes,
Charles F. III. Series.

DS568 .C84 2002
959.3–dc21   2001050754

Contents

Acknowledgements

This book derives from the Sixth International Conference on Thai Studies held in October 1996 in Chiang Mai, Thailand. At the conference, a panel entitled 'Social Memory, Ritual, and History' was organised under the broader theme of 'Cultural Crisis and the Thai Capitalist Transformation' by Anan Ganjanapan, Yos Santasombat and Tanabe. We are grateful to the joint convenors of this panel, which marked new steps to a multidisciplinary agenda on social memory and modernity in Thai studies with a large attendance. Among those who took a prominent part in the panel, but could not contribute to this collection, we would particularly like to thank Gehan Wijeyewardene, Andrew Turton, Ing-Britt Trankell, Hong Lysa, Yoko Hayami, Yasmin Saikia, and other participants. The panel in the conference was made possible by financial support, particularly from the Japan Foundation, the Toyota Foundation and the Ford Foundation.

Following the conference, Keyes joined Tanabe in editing a volume, in which ten of those who had presented papers at the panel were invited to submit revised versions for inclusion. In addition to these ten, Tanabe also agreed to include a paper he had delivered as a conference lecture. We worked together during a three month period from October 1997 to January 1998 while Keyes was on leave from the University of Washington as a Visiting Professor at the National Museum of Ethnology, Osaka. The editorial work continued until the period when Tanabe had been invited to teach at the Department of Sociology and Anthropology, Chiang Mai University from July 2000. The editors are grateful to these institutions for providing opportunities that enabled us both to undertake a collective enterprise with the authors to revise their original papers and to think through some of the broader theoretical and historical issues that relate to the subject of this volume.

We are grateful to two anonymous readers of an earlier version of the book for their comments and suggestions. Finally, our gratitude goes to

ACKNOWLEDGEMENTS

Grant Evans, General Editor of the 'Anthropology of Asia' series, and to
Geoffrey Walton for his help in copy-editing at the final stage.

Shigeharu Tanabe
Chiang Mai

Charles F. Keyes
Seattle

List of Illustrations

List of Contributors

Grant Evans is Reader in Anthropology at the University of Hong Kong. His numerous publications include *The Politics of Ritual and Remembrance: Laos since 1975* (Silkworm Books, University of Hawaii Press, Allen and Unwin, 1998); *Lao Peasants under Socialism and Post-socialism* (Silkworm Books, 1995); and with Kelvin Rowley *Red Brotherhood at War: Cambodia, Vietnam and Laos since 1975* (Verso, London, 1990, revised edition). He also edited *Lao Culture and Society* (Silkworm Books, 1998). He is General Editor of the 'Anthropology of Asia' series for Curzon Press.

Masato Fukushima is Associate Professor of Anthropology at the University of Tokyo. He is the author of *The Anatomy of Tacit Knowledge: the interface between cognition and society* (Kaneko-shobo, in press, in Japanese) and the editor of *Constructing Body Socially* (Hitsuji-shobo, 1995, in Japanese). In addition to his numerous articles on religion and ritual practice in Indonesia, he published 'Another meaning of meditation: on the Santi Asoke movement in Thailand' in *Tai Culture* (1999).

Kyonosuke Hirai is Research Fellow at the National Museum of Ethnology, Osaka. He obtained his PhD at the London School of Economics in 1998 for a thesis titled 'Women, family and factory work in Northern Thailand: an anthropological study of a Japanese factory and its workers' villages'. His recent English articles include 'Making up the home: modern consumption of Northern Thai factory women' in *Tai Culture* (1999) and 'A practice approach to the Japanese company: loyalty, harmony and incentives' in *Asian Review* (1995).

Kasian Tejapira is Assistant Professor of Political Science at Thammasat University in Bangkok. He is the author of numerous academic publications and a dozen books in both Thai and English. He is also a noted columnist and was formerly a radical activist and guerrilla fighter in the forests of Northeastern Thailand.

Charles F. Keyes is Professor of Anthropology and International Studies at the University of Washington. He is the author of *The Golden Peninsula: culture and adaptation in mainland Southeast Asia* (reissued, University of Hawaii Press, 1995); *Thailand: Buddhist kingdom as modern nation-state* (Westview, 1987); and numerous articles, including 'Cultural diversity and national identity in Thailand' in Michael Brown and Sunait Ganguly (eds.) *Government Policies and Ethnic Relations in Asia and the Pacific* (MIT Press, 1998); 'Moral authority of the sangha and modernity in Thailand: sexual scandals, sectarian dissent, and political resistance' in Sulak Sivaraksa, et al *Socially Engaged Buddhism for the New Millennium: essays in honor of the Ven. Phra Dhammapitaka (Bhikkhu P.A. Payutto) on his 60th Birthday Anniversary* (Sathira-Nagapradipa Foundation and Foundation for Children, 1999); and 'A princess in a peoples' republic: a new phase in the construction of the Lao nation' in Andrew Turton (ed.) *Civility and Savagery* (Curzon, 2000). He has edited *Ethnic Change* (University of Washington Press 1981) and co-edited (with E. Valentine Daniel) *Karma: an anthropological inquiry* (University of California Press, 1983) and (with Laurel Kendall and Helen Hardacre) *Asian Visions of Authority: religion and the modern states of East and Southeast Asia* (University of Hawaii Press, 1994).

Rosalind C. Morris is Associate Professor of Anthropology and Director of the Institute for Research on Women and Gender at Columbia University. She is the author of *In the Place of Origins: modernity and its mediums in Northern Thailand* (Duke University Press, 2000), and is currently editing a volume on the histories of the mass media in East and South East Asia.

Ryoko Nishii is Associate Professor at the Institute for the Study of Languages and Cultures of Asia and Africa (ILCAA), Tokyo University of Foreign Studies. She obtained her PhD from the Graduate University of Advanced Studies. She has carried out fieldwork in the border areas between Thailand and Malaysia where Muslims and Buddhists are co-resident. This research has resulted in several publications in Japanese and English, the latest of which is 'Emergence and transformation of peripheral ethnicity: Sam Sam on the Thai-Malaysian border' in Andrew Turton (ed.) *Civility and Savagery* (Curzon, 2000).

Shigeharu Tanabe is Professor of Anthropology at the National Museum of Ethnology and the School of Cultural and Social Studies, Graduate University of Advanced Studies, Japan. He is the author of *Ecology and Practical Technology: peasant farming systems in Thailand* (White Lotus, 1994) and of *Wearing the Yellow Robe, Wearing the Black Garb: a story of a peasant leader in Northern Thailand* (Sangsan, 1986, in Thai). His most recent articles include 'Memories displaced by ritual: cognitive processes in the spirit cults of Northern Thailand' in *Bulletin of the National Museum of*

Ethnology (2000) and 'Autochthony and the *Inthakhin* Cult of Chiang Mai' in Andrew Turton (ed.) *Civility and Savagery* (Curzon 2000). He edited *Anthropology of Practical Religion: the world of Theravada Buddhism* (Kyoto University Press, 1993, in Japanese) and *Religious Renewal in Asia: politics of religious experience* (Kyoto University Press, 1995, in Japanese), and co-edited with Andrew Turton *History and Peasant Consciousness in South East Asia* (National Museum of Ethnology, 1984).

Nicola Tannenbaum is Associate Professor of Anthropology at Lehigh University. She is the author of *Who Can Compete against the World: power-protection and Buddhism in Shan worldview* (Association for Asian Studies, 1995). She co-edited with Cornelia Kammerer, *Merit and Blessing in Mainland Southeast Asia in Comparative Perspective* and *Founders' Cults in Southeast Asia: ancestors, agriculture, and polity*, (both Yale University Southeast Asia Program Monograph Series, 1996, and in press).

Nicholas Tapp is Senior Fellow in the Department of Anthropology, Research School of Pacific and Asian Studies, The Australian National University. He is the author of *Sovereignty and Rebellion: the White Hmong of Northern Thailand* (Oxford University Press, 1989) and with Chien Chiao co-edited *Ethnicity and Ethnic Groups in China* (The Chinese University of Hong Kong, 1989). His forthcoming book, *Reconstructions* (Brill, 2001), deals with the Hmong of Sichuan, China.

Thongchai Winichakul is Associate Professor of History and Southeast Asian Studies at University of Wisconsin-Madison. His first book, *Siam Mapped: a history of the geo-body of a nation* (University of Hawaii Press, 1994) received the Harry J. Benda Prize from the Association for Asian Studies in 1995. He also published several articles on Thai history and historiography: among them, 'The changing landscape of the past: new histories in Thailand since 1973' in *Journal of Southeast Asian Studies* (1995); 'The quest for 'siwilai': the geographical discourse of civilizational thinking in the late 19th and early 20th century Siam' in *Journal of Asian Studies* (2000); and 'The others within: the ethno-spatial differentiation of Siamese subjects, 1885–1910' in Andrew Turton (ed.) *Civility and Savagery* (Curzon, 2000); and numerous articles in Thai.

Introduction

Shigeharu Tanabe and Charles F. Keyes

The authors of this volume seek to contribute to the study of the ways in which the remembrance of the past is situated in wider contexts that are influenced by the politics of the present. These contexts range from the politics of the nation, situated in regional and global milieux, to the practices of everyday life in the localities where people actually live. Our main examples come from the practices and politics found in the rapidly transforming social and cultural realities of Thailand and Laos. Both countries, particularly in the two decades since the 1970s, have been undergoing radical social and economic changes. While Thailand has travelled down the road to industrialisation, neighbouring Laos experienced a communist revolution in 1975 and only since the late 1980s has been attempting, under the guidance of the communist party, to follow a reformist path to development. Increasingly influenced by globalised economic and social institutions, both countries, however, have come to face crises that have made people insecure in the present and anxious about the future.

The recent economic development in Thailand, which most chapters in this volume address, has brought with it a major crisis of cultural identity. Change has eroded the hierarchical socio-political order that had emerged in the 1970s, and authoritarian elements, most notably representatives of the military, have not been able to re-impose that order on society. The declining influence of the Buddhist sangha, one of the primary institutions on which the traditional order was based, is another contributory factor to, and symptom of, the decomposition of the familiar order. Major changes in the roles of women, in large part, but not solely, due to the revolution in fertility control since the 1960s, have also produced a sense of cultural crisis that has been given an added and tragic twist by the outbreak of the HIV/AIDS pandemic in the late 1980s. Since mid-1997, this crisis has been further deepened by economic recession. Region-wide deterioration of the economy has spread gloom over South

1

East Asian and East Asian countries. In Thailand in particular, the sharp contraction of the economy has intensified for many the sense of crisis in their lives.

Concern at the extent of the cultural crisis was reflected at the Sixth International Conference on Thai Studies held in October 1996 in Chiang Mai. At the conference a session entitled 'Social memory, ritual, and history' was organised and jointly convened by Anan Ganjanapan and Yos Santasombat, both at Chiang Mai University, and Shigeharu Tanabe under the broader theme of 'Cultural crisis and the Thai capitalist transformation'. In this multidisciplinary session, which placed special emphasis on the recent cultural crisis and the capitalist transformation in Thailand, most of the papers, and much of the discussion, probed various acts of remembering and types of social memory, such as those that are embodied in ritual practice, monuments and statuary, oral history, contested discourses, and in the formation of persistent local and postmodern identities.

In dealing with these issues, the discussion was also extended to cases in Laos, as illustrated in some chapters of this volume. This is because although the two countries have had very divergent histories since the late nineteenth century, many in both countries share social memories of a premodern past. Some of the identity crises in both countries today are centred on how 'Lao' and 'Thai' nations are to be distinguished.

This is a book about social memory in the milieu of cultural crises of modernity in Thailand and Laos. In this introduction, we try to explicate the ways in which social memory constructed by the people works in entering modernity, that in turn causes fundamental ruptures with their past, and cultural crises that have been experienced in various ways in their lives. It also gives some thought to how in these crises they constitute their cultural, social, or individual identities, particularly focusing on the theoretical issues of identification and their relevance to distinct historical processes in Thailand and Laos.

Social memory

Remembering as a socially constructed process

Early twentieth century, Maurice Halbwachs (1925, 1951), a faithful disciple of Émile Durkheim, employed the notion of 'collective memory'. He believed that collective memory shapes a persistent framework that is constituted by the members of a social group, such as the family, religious groups, or social classes, by particular words and images that arise out of the process of remembering. The collective memory is thus seen as a common stock of knowledge that is retained by a social group, from which the individual members repeatedly and almost automatically draw their own way of recalling. We should then note that Halbwachs' idea of collective memory explains only the nature of the social determination of recollection; it fails to deal with the processes whereby the social group itself retains and recalls its past. Such a Durkheimian framework, that stresses the social determination of individual perception, thinking, and action is unable to support the connection of individual experience with social memory, or the imaginative reconstruction of the past.

A more plausible formulation was put forwards early in the twentieth century by Frederick Bartlett, a Cambridge psychologist. Bartlett maintained that human experience constantly and continuously reshapes recollection. After a variety of experiments on remembering a story, Bartlett concluded that what the test subjects remembered of the story was never reproductive. Rather, their recollections were strongly and evidently constructive or reconstructive, and much was actively inferred from their own cultural and social environment. His experiments furthermore demonstrated the prominent features of rationalisation: the subjects made sense of the tale by trying to adapt the story more readily and satisfactorily to the contexts in which they lived (1932: 93–94).[1] In this way, Bartlett, not surprisingly, had already opened up an anthropological perspective on the social construction of remembering, and thus opened a vista over a landscape that was dominated by the Durkheimian tradition.[2] Thus Bartlett sees memory as culturally constructed on the one hand, and also indicates, on the other, that recalling the past experiences involves sensory, personal processes which enable a series of semantic reconstructions of meanings.[3]

In this volume, the authors are concerned with various aspects of the social processes of remembering, which can be lumped under the heading of socially constructed memory, or social memory. Events in the past, whether remembered or forgotten, are never passive entities. Rather, they are reconstructed through inherently social activities evolved in the milieu of cultural conduct and invention. The implications of Bartlett's formulation are also consonant with the processes of collective remembering and remembering together, in which people share memories of events, recalling them together or commemorating them, all the while reconstructing and reinterpreting features of the past. Social memory is, as James Fentress and Chris Wickham (1992: 25) put it, an expression of collective experience, giving a group a sense of its past, and defining its aspirations for the present and the future. In doing so, social memory, as a way of knowing the past, is imaginatively shared by a social group, such as a family or ethnic group, and provides a basis for its identity and an instrument for shaping ideas and emotions that affect the actions and practices of its members.

Social memory as embodied memory

Following the work of Bourdieu (1977), Connerton (1989), and Stoller (1995), we recognise that the body of the individual is often a repository for memories of past experiences even when the individual is not consciously aware of it being so. Bourdieu (see also 1990) in particular has systematically explored how such everyday practices as those carried out in a house, in the exchange of gifts, and in ritual serve to reproduce and transmit social memory in embodied forms. Bourdieu offers the concept of *habitus* – 'a system of durable, transposable *dispositions*' (Bourdieu 1977: 72) – for what we are terming social memory. By internalising and incorporating into the body the objective structures of the surrounding society, conventional practices are continually reproduced by *habitus*, and can be thus harmonised with other members' practices without intentional effort, and orchestrated without a conductor. The accumulated memory, or a set of dispositions, that can reproduce an almost infinite number of embodied practices is, as Bourdieu (1977: 87) puts it, preserved only in the person, not possessed in economic terms or exchanged as in cases of things. It is transmitted only through the practical imitation of what other persons do, without requiring the use of language or conceptual representation.[4]

For Bourdieu social memory is purely and simply a *social fact*. The irrefutably naturalised past is moulded in what he termed the *doxic* mode,[5] consequently the way in which individual subjects voluntarily recall and articulate their past events and experiences is of little account. Thus Bourdieu is able to elaborate a sociological theory of memory that accommodates tacit knowledge and the associated embodied practices in everyday life. On the other hand, he largely ignores the processes by which individual experiences and interactions are able to significantly affect and constantly reshape socially located memory.[6] Our contention is that embodied practices are reproduced and transmitted through Bourdieusian *habitus*, but not all socially constructed remembering activities can be reduced to objective structures.

Social memory as articulate memory

Rather than simply the meanings, representations, or symbols, social memory is a means of transmission and wider preservation of what is recalled by individuals. What is recalled in the individual mind is articulated in visual images or in semantic terms that, externalised and thus offered as communication, may be transmitted to and preserved by other people. Fentress and Wickham (1992: 47) have contended that 'a memory can be social only if it is capable of being transmitted, and, to be transmitted, a memory must first be articulated'. As embodied memory is articulated, when it is acted out, in terms of gesture, bodily movement and other performative acts through *habitus*, a variety of forms of remembering in social context may also be articulated in part by linguistic forms. This is not to say, however, that social memory is always semantically constructed. Social practices involving remembering activities range from everyday conversations dealing with past experiences, recitation of, and listening to narratives, to joint recollection in commemoration ceremonies. These practices construct semantically organised meanings that nearly always accompany the particular sensory images and that arouse emotions among participants.

Nishii's ethnographic account in this volume (chapter 9) gives an example of joint recollection at the funeral of a young man, born in a Buddhist family, but married to a Muslim woman. The activities of the Muslims were initially remembered individually in different ways, but gradually a discourse about the death that reconciled these differences was constructed. No such common discourse has emerged, as Thongchai Winichakul shows in this volume (chapter 10), about the events of the '6 October 1976 massacre' at Thammasat University in Bangkok. To the contrary, these memories remain contested and unsettled. For many individuals involved, directly or indirectly, the incident has been remembered as a traumatic past that causes intense emotions, pain and fear that suggest post-traumatic stress disorder (cf. Young 1997). Memory can, in extreme cases, become so abstract as to lose its linkage with actual experience. Such disembodied symbols and concepts become linked instead in abstract ways to a wider semantic field and discourse (Fentress and Wickham 1992: 29). This decontextualised and disembodied form of memory occurs not only in literate societies, where knowledge is most strongly articulated in textualised forms, but also in oral social contexts, where abstract knowledge tends to be preserved in stories about the past (Fentress and Wickham 1992: 10–11), as is exemplified in the Hmong moral narratives discussed by Tapp in this volume (chapter 3).

Both individual remembering and social memory share this composite form of semantic organisation and sensory imagery. When an individual subject, or a group of people, recalls the past through social practices, however, the semantic representations and visual images in their memory become more conceptualised. The conceptualisation of images in those constructing processes of memory, such as sequences of conversation and commemoration ceremonies, occurs in such a way as to make what is recalled more readily transmitted, and later more readily recalled by the recipients of the communication. Hence, the process usually reduces, and sometimes even displaces, the personal and intricate details of the images to make what is recalled more schematic and conceptual (Tanabe 2000). In this way, the collective images and meanings constructed in social practices tend to be highly conceptualised, being increasingly decontextualised from what has been experienced in the past. Consequently, this conceptualisation of meaning and image naturally comes to provide material that is open to argument and contestation.

The conceptualisation that occurs is not limited only to everyday and ritualised communicative interactions, but extends to the world of material objects that surround us in social life. Material culture – ranging from religious and other monuments such as Buddhist stupas, tombs, and statuary to houses and consumer goods – always provides a basis for constructing the past (Evans 1998; Keyes 1975; Bloch 1971; Bloch 1998; Turton 1978; Carsten and Hugh-Johns 1995; Feeley-Harnik 1991; Küchler and Melion 1991). Monuments and statuary themselves are placed in an articulate and conceptualised form with a status comparable to texts, though rather in an abridged form, in order to commemorate a particular person or event. Yet, because of their inevitably conceptualised and reified nature, monuments and statuary have to remain ambiguous and even fetishistic. The original intentions behind the placement of these types of artefacts are also subject to forgetting, and they may be transformed into rather impoverished cultural symbols to be utilised for tourism promotion, thus becoming detached from the original nationalist or socialist conceptions inscribed in them. Such volatile meanings are illustrated in the ethnographic analysis of the fate of statues in Laos by Grant Evans in this volume (chapter 6), and elsewhere (Evans 1998). Predicated on the nature of fetishisation, the articulation and conceptualisation of social memory that is said to be embodied material culture also becomes subject to popular interpretation, and to the hermeneutics of intellectuals in the society.

Having said something about the psychological and cultural processes involved in individual remembering and social memory, we intend to explore in the next section how this remembrance of the past is situated in the wider contexts of modernity in the Thai and Lao worlds.

Crises of modernity in the Thai and Lao worlds

Crises of modernity

Modernity has everywhere rendered identifications with the past problematic, and the construction of social memory is often a socially contested process. New cultural discourses and social institutions that emerged first in the West, and then spread throughout the world, generated fundamental discontinuities with all types of traditional order (Giddens 1990: 3). In modernity, contradiction is to be accepted as intrinsic. Modernity gives rise to the increasingly fragmentary, fleeting and uncertain nature of modern life and, at the same time, to new possibilities that may be expressed as political liberation in the public sphere, and the feeling of freedom in mass consumption. As Georg Simmel (1978) contended early in the twentieth century, the rupture of the present from the past, a fundamental condition of modernity, inevitably leads to contradiction between the desire for abstract rationality and the resistant desire to retain particular values and elements previously assured. The negative and positive consequences simultaneously become embedded in the mind and body of the people in modernity. Thus, in this critical and crushing transition, modernity can no longer borrow its models from another epoch but must forge its naturalness from the conditions of modernity that the people experience themselves (Habermas 1987: 5–7; also see Miller 1994: 61–62). Modernity, in other words, entails an irrevocable rupture with a *habitus* rooted in an unquestioned cosmology (see, in this regard, Anderson 1991: 36; also see Werblowsky 1976: 14 and Kasaba 1997: 19).

We maintain that the ways of being in the world that are characteristically modern have been generated through four analytically distinct processes – the use of rationalised and secularised knowledge in place of understandings derived from religion and magic; orientation of economic action with reference to demands generated in a globalised market instead of to subsistence needs; acceptance of the political authority of those representing a nation-state rather than of those whose status is determined by a hierarchy of personal relationships; and construction of one's identity as a person with reference to diverse messages and images transmitted through mass media, in contrast to the highly redundant meanings ascribed to the ancestors transmitted primarily through ritual. While each of these processes have been made central to one or another theory of modernity, we take our lead from Giddens (1990, 1991) in treating them together. These processes as manifest in Thailand and Laos have their roots in the West, but they have not unfolded in the same way as they did in the West. Modernity always has a distinctive character depending on the specific social and historical contexts in which it develops.[7]

Here we present only a very schematic version of our approach as the basis for examining the processes of modernisation in the Thai and Lao worlds. It should be emphasised that the four processes do not necessarily follow in the sequence in which we discuss them, and in actual situations the four are often inextricably intertwined. Nonetheless, it is important, we believe, to distinguish them analytically in order to understand why, as the chapters in this volume demonstrate, the shaping of social memory has become so wrought by contention, ambiguity, uncertainty, and contingency in modernity in the worlds of the Thai and the Lao.

The chapters in this book offer interpretations of a number of different crises of modernity in which peoples in Thailand and Laos have questioned, or have been compelled to question, or have sought to resolve questions, about social memories of the past that are taken as central to their identity. Although crises of modernity are found today in both Thailand and Laos, the relationship to modernity is very different in the two countries. Laos today is still very much in the process of becoming modern, while Thailand, by contrast, began the fundamental transformations associated with modernity over a century ago. Yet our schematic account of the modernisation relevant to the two countries gives, we hope, some basic understanding of how social memory is recalled and used in their lives faced with modernity.

Secularisation and disenchantment

Secularisation and demystification of the world are recognised as being among the fundamental processes of modernity.[8] By secularisation, we mean the clear separation of religious from other institutions of society, and by demystification we mean that many aspects of life that once had been understood in religious or magico-religious ways now became understood in commonsensical ones. Secularisation and demystification, as is now well-recognised (see, for example, the essays in Keyes, Kendall and Hardacre 1994), have not led to the demise of religion. Rather, while they have entailed the detachment of much human experience from direct linkages to religious absolutes, they have, at the same time, led many to a much sharper awareness of the limits of commonsensical knowledge.

Most peoples living in the Siamese empire, which throughout the nineteenth century encompassed all of what would later become Thailand and Laos, understood their world with reference to Buddhist cosmology. In the period between 1824–1851, a monk who would later become King Mongkut, began to challenge this perspective, and his challenge would eventually lay the groundwork for the radical disenchantment of the Thai-Lao world.[9]

Mongkut, who was greatly influenced by Western scientific knowledge, proposed that not all of the conditions of existence (*dhamma*; Thai, *tham*) needed to be explained with reference to religious truths embodied in Buddhist cosmology. There were, he maintained, many such conditions which were 'natural' (*thammachat*, from Pali, *dhamma-jati*, lit. the 'given essences') that could be understood through common sense or, more deeply, through science.

Mongkut's project as a monk was also to attempt to answer the question of what it means to be a Buddhist. The question stemmed initially from Mongkut's awareness of the divergence of ritual practices from the scriptural sources he had studied. The question would later become, as encounters between Thai and foreigners increased, what does it mean to be a Buddhist in a religiously pluralistic world? The reflexive question regarding the self in the context of real or possible choices of what the self might be lies, as Giddens (1991: 5) has emphasised, at the root of being modern.

Mongkut's ideas would subsequently be adopted not only by leading members of the Siamese *sangha*, or Buddhist clergy, but would also become the foundations for a system of secular education that would be implemented throughout Thailand in the first decades of the twentieth century. Those educated in this system came to see themselves as belonging to a 'new era' (*samai mai*), a term that became the equivalent of 'modern' in both Thai and Lao.

Mongkut's reform movement in the sangha, known under the name of Thammayut-nikai (*Dhammayuti-nikaya*), the order of 'righteousness', also found a significant following among Lao monks. Because French colonialists carved a new domain they called Laos out of what had been a part of the Siamese empire, Buddhist reforms did not have the direct impact on secularisation among the peoples of Laos that they had on the peoples of Thailand. The French actually showed very little interest in creating an educational system other than for a very small elite.[10] Because more people continued to be educated in monastic schools, the new ideas emanating from Thailand did, however, have some impact. A few men who would go on to be leaders of the Lao nationalist movement were educated in this system. These leaders would prove to be relatively impotent in comparison to other leaders who took their modern secularist perspective from Marxist-Leninism. Even these leaders, however, have had very limited success, since taking control of the whole country in 1975, in implementing educational reforms even when – as has been the case since the mid-1980s – they have combined Marxist-Leninism with reformist Buddhism. Even into the late 1990s, there remain many Lao who still understand their world with reference to premodern worldviews.[11]

In both Thailand and Laos, upland peoples, of whom the Hmong discussed in Tapp's chapter are a major example, have been the most remote from the influences of a secularising elite. Even upland peoples have, nonetheless, often found themselves confronting a crisis of identity as they become increasingly integrated into a global market economy, and into the nation-states under whose jurisdiction they now live. Such uplanders have, in many instances, even begun to become consumers of mass media.

Although secularisation has proceeded much further among urban Thai than any other people in the two countries, many still turn to practitioners, such as the spirit mediums discussed in this volume in the chapters by Tanabe and Morris, who offer non-rational or non-scientific methods to confront modern experiences. As these cases demonstrate, the processes of modernity generate new uncertainties, tensions, and suffering that cannot be addressed adequately with modern perspectives. For those urban people who consult spirit mediums, the crisis of modernity is often very personal.

Incorporation into a global market economy

Incorporation into a globalised market system constitutes the second process of modernity. The expansion of the global market has entailed, in

9

Karl Polanyi's (1957) terms, the 'liberation' of land, labour and capital from the nexus of kinship. People have turned to production for the market instead of production primarily for domestic consumption, or to meet the demands of local lords. Concomitantly, people have increasingly turned to the market to purchase goods rather than produce them themselves. Associated with the turn toward the market as the primary institution shaping economic life, social life has been re-oriented towards practical, means-ends relationships rather than with reference to the authority of tradition, which was much more pronounced in the premodern period.[12] This process has been significantly facilitated for those who have already undergone secularisation and demystification.

Between the early 1960s to July 1997, when Thailand became engulfed in a financial and then more general economic crisis, Thailand had enjoyed one of the fastest growing economies in the world.[13] Beginning in the 1970s, almost everyone in the country, with rare exceptions, mainly among upland peoples, was realising significant income from selling products or labour, and was using this income to purchase increasing amounts of consumer goods. Increased dependence on cash income and on purchasing products from the market led in turn to a significant rise in economic differences within the population. Although the severe economic crisis that developed following the devaluation of the *baht*, the Thai currency, in mid-1997 has greatly dampened the consumer economy, it has not undone, nor can it undo, the fundamental reorientation of people in Thailand toward the market economy.

The situation in Laos has been radically different to that of Thailand. Even into the 1990s, much, perhaps most, of the populace were still engaged in production primarily for subsistence rather than for the market. The limited penetration of a market economy in Laos is a consequence of a poor infrastructure inherited from the colonial period, the highly destructive and disruptive civil war from 1954 to 1975, and the resistance of the ruling Communist Party to foreign investment and capitalist development even since the adoption of a more open economic policy in the mid-1980s.[14] Where modernisation of the Lao economy has occurred – in the capital city of Vientiane and areas near the Mekong – it has been primarily because of the extension of the Thai economy into Laos.

Integration of peoples into modern nation-states

The third process of modernity entails the integration of peoples into modern nation-states. The modern state is characterised by the deployment of a number of new 'technologies of power' that has made administration more effective and more intrusive into everyday life.[15] These technologies include a bureaucracy organized along functional lines, and subject to rationalised systems of rules and regulations; a military that is also functionally organised, and whose members are technically trained; a system of compulsory education predicated on a common curriculum for all in a country; the systematic keeping of records on the citizens of the state through compulsory registration of 'vital statistics', censuses, surveys, and applied research; the systematic and legal demarcation of land within the borders of a state through mapping, cadastral surveys, and registration of titles and of land transactions; and the regulation of communications through licensing and monitoring.

The modern state has everywhere been conceived of as legitimated by the authority of a 'people' who constitute a 'nation'. The power of particular states has been deployed through schooling, public ceremonies, elections, and other means to disseminate and instil in the citizenry a sense of personal identity with a national heritage, that is, with a selected past. The self-conscious 'invention' of national traditions makes the modern nation different from premodern communities, such as those based on religion in which tradition was a given.[16]

The modern nation-states of both Thailand and Laos emerged from the premodern empire of Siam. The transformation began with the expansion of British and French colonialism in the nineteenth century, particularly in its second half. By its end, the Siamese court in Bangkok had been compelled to cede many of its former vassals and dependencies to the two colonial powers.

In order to prevent further dismemberment, the Siamese court in the last decade of the nineteenth century instituted radical governmental reforms that resulted in the creation of a modern state that would later be known as Thailand. These reforms included the establishment of a uniform system of administration over the whole of the country, instead of a system of mixed centralised and feudal governance, and also the rationalisation of the fiscal, bureaucratic and military functions of the government. These reforms were undertaken within a territory – a 'geo-body' in Thongchai Winichakul's (1994) term – whose boundaries had been established by new methods of mapping, and had been recognised internationally through treaties with neighbouring (colonial) powers.[17]

Although the government of King Chulalongkorn was able to suppress all opposition to these changes, the resistance that occurred was indicative of the fact that those who were now deemed to be citizens of the Siamese state did not necessarily share a common identity with that state.[18] During the early twentieth century, a number of institutions were established that were designed to promote a new national culture, or *chat Thai*.[19] Through these institutions almost everyone in the kingdom eventually came to identify with a nation predicated on three pillars (*lak*): *chat*, defined primarily in terms of competence in the national language and identification with the nation manifest in certain key symbols and national history; *satsana*, religion, that for the vast majority is equated with

Buddhism; and *phra maha kasat*, monarchy. These remain emotionally compelling to this day for many Thai people even as the social memories on which they are based have come to be contested, as chapters by Evans, Thongchai, and Keyes in this volume demonstrate.

In marked contrast to the situation in Thailand, the Lao state has been very weak since it emerged from its colonial chrysalis, and nation-building still remains at the beginning of the twenty-first century an incomplete project.[20] The territory that would be included within a Lao geo-body was brought under French control in a succession of treaties Siam was compelled to sign between 1893 and 1910. Initially, these territories were subsumed within the new French-created Indochina, but by the 1930s the effort to transform all those living within this domain into 'Indochinese' was abandoned. The French then began to encourage the development of a distinct Lao identity to counter continued Thai efforts to reclaim the 'lost' territories of the Siamese empire.

French promotion of a distinct Laos identity was, however, quite limited. The colonial government invested very little in transportation, communication and, above all, education in French Laos. Moreover, the colonial government employed many more Vietnamese than Lao in the administration of French Laos. As a consequence, by the end of the colonial era in 1954, there were very few people indigenous to Laos who were competent to govern an independent state (see Deuve 1984). Moreover, this small elite was deeply divided over the premises on which a Lao nation might be built.

These divisions were markedly intensified by the support outside forces provided for the different groups. From the mid 1950s through the mid 1970s, Laos became a battleground with local factions backed by an extraordinary amount of weaponry, as well as troops from Vietnam, China, and the Soviet Union on the one side, and from Thailand and the United States on the other, all contending for control of territory.

The communist-led government that finally assumed control of the whole of Laos in 1975 has faced insurmountable problems in creating either a modern state or a nation (see Stuart-Fox 1986, 1996 and Evans 1988, 1990, 1998). The government has had very few resources to draw on to build an economic infrastructure that had never been attempted during the colonial era. State-building has also been significantly impeded by the dominance of an ideologically rigid party. Although compelled by the collapse of the Soviet Union and East European communist regimes to look to the capitalist world for some assistance, the party has sought to remain in control of the economy, and has thrown roadblocks in the way of capitalist investment. The Lao economy proved to be particularly vulnerable following the Asian economic crisis that began in 1997. Early in 2000, Laos was ranked the tenth poorest country in the world.

The Lao government has also failed to create a viable national culture with which even many ethnic Lao, who form the majority of the population, can identify (see Evans 1998 and Evans in this volume). The decision of the government to abolish the Lao monarchy, and the subsequent death of the king and crown prince in a prison camp, deprived the country of a unifying symbol of monarchy comparable to that of Thailand. A cult of the revolution, meanwhile, has singularly failed to capture the imagination of many in the country. Although the Lao government makes use of Buddhist monks to promote a national system of education, Buddhism has not become a pillar of Lao nationalism, because the leadership of the government still adheres to Marxist-Leninism, and because only about half the population of Laos is Buddhist. The government has succeeded in extending compulsory education, which uses a standardised written and spoken Lao as the means of instruction, and gives students a common story about their national heritage in many parts of the country, but the effectiveness of such education has been severely hampered by the lack of well-trained teachers and the limited contexts in which school learning is useful. A weak education system combined with strong competition to the limited state-controlled media by TV and radio programming beamed from Thailand has undermined the efforts to instill a sense of identity with Lao national history and to ensure competence in the national language. As Evans' chapter in this volume demonstrates, the crises of modernity faced in Laos, in contrast to those in Thailand, turn less on the contesting of the pasts among peoples who already live in a modern nation-state than on the failure of the small elite in Laos to create a state strong enough to make any past hegemonic.

Mediated modernity

The final process of modernity relates to the choice of cultural identity made possible through the expansion of the mass media. Modern mass media are traceable to two sources – the invention of moveable type that made possible the production of printed materials that could be widely circulated, and the invention of electronics that has made possible the movement of messages exceedingly rapidly over vast distances.[21] What the telegraph and subsequently other electronic means of communication made possible was the juxtaposition of stories that happened at the same time, but occurred in places very distant from one another. Electronic communications have rapidly expanded with the subsequent invention of the telephone, the radio, television, the computer, and the liberation of many media from earthly transmission brought about by satellites. Today, almost everywhere in the world people are in daily contact with images and stories that originate in very different milieux than those in which they live and work. The mass media make it possible, thus, for social memories to be shared by peoples living in places very distant in space or time. It is with reference to these images and stories that people, living in what a century ago would have been very remote and isolated worlds, can nowadays imagine themselves as different persons living in very different worlds from their parents, or even their peers.

Until the middle of the nineteenth century, the only books known in the Thai and Lao worlds were hand-written manuscripts used primarily for transmission of religious teachings, or implementation of governance or, to a much lesser extent, by performers of folk operas and other entertainments. Print media was introduced to Siam in the mid-nineteenth century by Western missionaries (Winship 1986). Although missionaries made few converts, their efforts to promote their message through printed materials made a profound impression on the Siamese elite. The use of moveable type in Thai for promulgations and bureaucratic reports began what would become a revolution in communications.

From the end of the nineteenth century onwards, a publishing industry began to develop in Thailand which within a few decades was producing a variety of books and periodicals. Until well after World War II, however, printed materials were read only by a small elite. As average educational levels increased, transportation improved, and incomes increased, a popular press developed.

Electronic media were to have a much more widespread influence than print media on the populace of Thailand. Electronic communication began with the introduction of the telegraph and telephone, but it was not until the radio began to be widely used in the 1930s that electronic media began to have a significant impact. Radio listening significantly expanded after World War II, and by the early 1960s, there were few people throughout the country who did not listen to a radio for several hours a day, often while they worked in the fields.

Film viewing, which prior to World War II had been restricted to the elite, also began to draw larger popular audiences in the 1960s. Films began to lose popularity in the 1970s, as television became more accessible, both when sets became much less expensive relative to incomes and programming was significantly expanded. By the 1980s, television sets were owned by even relatively poor villagers living in remote communities, and television viewing had supplanted many traditional forms of entertainment. Television audiences in the 1990s have a significant range of programming to choose from, with Thai-made soap operas and Thai boxing matches being the most popular. All viewers are also exposed to numerous advertisements that promote a variety of material goods associated with being modern.[22]

The significant expansion of the media in Thailand has offered people not only in its cities but also in its villages a variety of very different ways of conceiving of the self. Popular TV and film actors and musical performers have for many, especially younger people, become far more charismatic than Buddhist monks, the traditional embodiments of charisma. Of particular note, popular culture in Thailand today emphasises sexuality detached from moral constraints. This emphasis finds strong reinforcement in advertisements in malls and other stores, in commercials and soap operas on TV, in stories, ads, and images in popular magazines, and even daily newspapers, and in the numerous popular beauty contests that began in the 1930s.

With the marked rise in incomes and the concomitant expansion of a consumer economy in which goods and services from diverse sources have become available, it has become increasingly possible for people in Thailand to turn away from identities rooted in localised religiously-based cultures, and toward ones of very disparate and often contradictory origins. Because Thai governments have lost their once strong control that enabled them to use the media to promote hegemonic domination, the media also make possible the expression of different images of the polity. In short, the media in Thailand have fostered the emergence of diverse identities, and the concomitant tensions and conflicts that such diversity engenders.

In Laos, the only really significant influence of modern media is in the areas near the Mekong River, where TV broadcasts from Thailand are widely watched. Outside of Vientiane and some other towns near the Mekong, there is very little penetration of any mass media. No government in Laos has had the resources to invest in expansion of either print or electronic media. The communist-led government that has held power since 1975 has also imposed very strict controls on the content of all media and on the sale of publications in Thai, which can be read relatively easily by those literate in Lao. The government has been notably unsuccessful in sponsoring radio and TV programming in Lao to compete with that coming from Thailand. People living in the North and Northeast of Laos, away from the Mekong valley, sometimes listen to radio broadcasting or, more rarely, watch TV programming from China or Vietnam rather than to that from Laos or Thailand. Many Hmong are also known to listen to radio broadcasts in Hmong that come from Chiang Mai in Northern Thailand, or from an evangelical Christian station with a powerful transmitter located in the Philippines.

Although there is almost no concrete information available to assess the impact of media messages in Laos, it is clear that the strong competition to state-sponsored media from media located in Thailand and elsewhere has significantly undermined efforts on the part of the government to create a national culture shared by both ethnic Lao and other peoples living in the country. Indeed, among many ethnic Lao living near the Mekong, modern mass media have contributed to an identity with modern Thailand rather than with a still far from modern Laos.

Modernity and politics of the past

Albeit in different ways and at different times, the dominance of elites that have adopted Western conceptions of modernity, the influences of globalised economic institutions, the intrusion into everyday life of institutions of the nation-state, and the spread of mass media have led peoples throughout the world to become self-conscious, and often insecure about who they are and how they relate to others. It is this unmooring of identities from what were long taken as the givens of life embedded in practices, which Bourdieu (1977, 1990) has termed *habitus*, that has given rise to what we refer to as crises of modernity. The processes associated with modernity not only generate tensions with the pre-existing givens of social life but often also create tensions between contending 'certainties' that are proffered to replace these older givens. Although crises of modernity from time to time become acute and reach climactic conclusions, the latter do not resolve in any absolute or final way the underlying tensions. On the contrary, each climactic event generates social memories that serve to fuel new crises. In Thailand crises of modernity have erupted in every sphere of life, especially in the post-World War II period. Many of these crises have stemmed from the deep uncertainty among various groups about the legitimacy of the power wielded by those who govern the country. Such questioning of political authority has its origins in the political reforms instituted at the end of the nineteenth century.

In the premodern Siamese empire, almost everyone accepted the idea that the right to rule was a consequence of 'having merit' (*mi bun barami*), that is, a legacy of very positive *karma* from a previous existence. The most accepted sign of having the merit that legitimated political authority was coronation as a king. The initial reforms of King Chulalongkorn were understood by many, perhaps most, as an assertion that he had superior merit to all other local kings and lords in the empire. Resistance to this assertion of ultimate authority was manifest in the numerous millenarian movements in the early twentieth century that coalesced around men who claimed to have greater merit.[23] The failure of these movements served to confirm the superior moral qualities of the Siamese monarch.

Such neo-traditional political crises gave way to a very modern one when King Prajadhipok was compelled by the promoters of the 1932 revolution to accept that his authority was not absolute, but was subordinate to a constitution. Thai political history since 1932 can be understood as a series of crises centred on who has the right to exercise legitimate power in place of, or in the name of, a monarch. For two decades following the 1932 revolution, there was no active king living in the country. When King Bhumipol Adulyadej returned to the country in 1950, the situation radically changed. The young king quickly gained popular recognition for being an exceptional 'man of merit'. Capitalising on the restored charisma of the monarchy, Field Marshal Sarit Thanarat overthrew the government led by Field Marshal Phibun Songkhram, who had dominated Thai politics for much of the period since 1932 and who sought to place himself above the monarchy.

Since 1957, no government in Thailand has been able to claim legitimacy unless it is publicly approved by the king. From 1957 until the early 1970s, the king publicly sanctioned a political system in which actual power was held by military dictators accountable to no one. When, in October 1973, the military rulers used excessive force to suppress protests led by students against the blatant misuse of power for personal gain by the military rulers – protests which attracted wide support in Bangkok – the king very dramatically intervened. The king's 'request' on 14 October 1973 – a day that has entered Thai social memory as *sipsi tula*, 'the fourteenth of October' – that the military rulers resign and go into exile represented, in a very real sense, a reversal of the 1932 revolution. The monarch had re-emerged as the sole arbiter of legitimate power.

This reversal became very problematic for many when, on 6 October 1976, the king recognised the installation of the right-wing government that emerged following the bloody suppression of renewed student protests. The remembering of *hok tula*, the 'sixth of October' as Thongchai's chapter in this volume demonstrates, continues to be the source of a persistent crisis of authority. In the wake of *hok tula*, 6 October 1976, so many people joined a Communist-led insurrection that there appeared to be a total collapse of a national consensus regarding the legitimate basis of power. The Communist Party, which followed a rigid Maoist line, failed, however, to offer a vision of an alternative political order, not only for those whose support it sought, but also for many who had initially joined the insurrection. When, in 1980, a new military leadership offered amnesty to those who had joined the insurrection, the Communist challenge totally collapsed.

The 1980 amnesty had the effect of sanctioning competition between a number of quite diverse groups for political power. When business interests, represented by political parties, succeeded in gaining significant power at the expense of the military, the military attempted in 1991 to reassert its dominance. Following mass protests in May 1992, and particularly the violence that ensued when the military attempted to suppress the protests with excessive force, the king once again intervened. This time, however, intervention did not re-establish the ultimate authority of the monarchy, but marked the beginning of a new political crisis.

In the post-1992 period, the political parties representing business interests gained control of the government, but found their authority challenged not only by the old guard, now more evident in the civil service than in the military, but also by 'new social movements' (Baker 2000). During the 1990s in Thailand, previously disenfranchised groups of farmers, fishermen, and urban labourers have staged many protests, some quite large, against actions taken by governmental agencies. These groups have found organisational leadership in the now numerous non-governmental organisations (NGOs), and have received the backing of academics and some elements of the press.

By the mid-1990s, these protests, coupled with growing, albeit not publicly voiced, concern about the role of the monarchy once an ageing and ailing King Bhumipol is no longer present, stimulated an intense debate about whether or not there could be 'good governance' (*thammarat*) in Thailand within the framework of a 'civil society' (*pracha sangkhom*) (see Thirayuth Boonmi 1998). This debate became especially intense in 1997 when the Assembly of the Poor (*Samatcha khon con*) – a loose assemblage of farmers and their NGO supporters – staged a 99-day protest in Bangkok in February–May. When the baht collapsed in July, there was widespread recognition that Thailand faced a profound crisis. This crisis led not only to the collapse of one government and the emergence of a new one, but, much more significantly, to the adoption of a new constitution – the most liberal one in Thai history. The new constitution is at once a charter for a contemporary civil society and an evocation of the memory of the 1932 revolution. Both memory and charter continue to be challenged by powerful elements, thereby perpetuating a crisis of political authority.

Rapid development – economic growth and adoption of technological innovations – has been another source of the crises of modernity experienced by people in Thailand. The economic boom in Thailand, that continued over nearly four decades before July 1997, has made possible a pluralism of lifestyles. These have increasingly spread to rural Thailand from Bangkok and other urban centres where they were originally manifest. While even as recently as the 1950s over 80 per cent of the population held occupational identities as farmers, by the 1990s, many of the 60 per cent who still lived in villages had had some significant experience working in a non-agricultural occupation. Those Thai who have grown up in urban settings are quite unfamiliar with the temporal modes of living associated with rice cultivation that for so long were taken for granted by most of the populaion. By the 1990s, village society was differentiated by occupation, wealth, and lifestyles that were without precedent. In this changing world, as Hirai (chapter 7) and Kasian (chapter 8) show, many people came to conceive of their identities with reference to the material goods they could obtain.

The most profound change in lifestyle is manifest in the diversity of gender identities that emerged, beginning in the 1960s. In that decade, new technologies of birth control began to become available. So many Thai women made use of these new technologies in the 1960s and 1970s that Thailand underwent the most dramatic drop in fertility of any country in the world. The revolution in fertility, what Giddens (1991: 219) has termed the 'end of reproduction as fate', has made it possible for women to choose identities other than the one most valued in traditional culture, that of being a mother (see, for example, Bencha Yoddumnern-Attig 1992; Mills 1995, 1997; Morris 1994; and Prangtip Daorueng 1998).

For men, sexuality disassociated from reproduction became far more prevalent with the marked increases in cash income that came about during the boom years from the 1960s through the 1990s, and the concomitant marked expansion of sexual services for sale associated initially with Thailand's role in the American war in Vietnam. The once rather unusual role of the man, who accentuates, in an inversion of Buddhist values, the pursuit of desire, became commonplace. Beginning in the 1960s, some men also began to openly identify themselves as 'gay', in contrast not only to traditional male roles, but even to the role of the *kathoei* or transvestite that existed in premodern society (Jackson 1995).

The patterns of promiscuous sexuality, associated primarily with prostitution, became the source of yet a new crisis in the 1980s. The rapid expansion of HIV infections, especially as the strain of the virus dominant in Thailand is spread primarily through heterosexual transmission (Van Landingham and Grandjean 1994), led by the 1990s to a marked increase in the number of people with full-blown AIDS. Such people are the source of intense drain on both official and unofficial health services, as well as on the emotional energies of relatives and friends (cf. Tanabe 1999b; Brummelhuis and Herdt 1995).

The social suffering that can be traced to development is manifest not only in the HIV/AIDS crisis, but also in a marked increase in pollution, environmental degradation, and industrial and automobile accidents. While, in premodern times, most Thai would have found Buddhism to be a refuge to turn to when confronted with suffering, recent sectarian conflicts, scandals involving monks, and the materialist orientation of many monks has made the sangha, the Buddhist monkhood, an increasingly problematic source of moral authority for many people (see Keyes 1999). As Tanabe (chapter 2) and Morris (chapter 3) discuss in their chapters, urban people increasingly turn to spirit mediums when faced with the uncertainties and social suffering associated with modernity in Thailand.[24]

The endemic crises of modernity in Thailand are experienced as more or less intense by different people depending on their particular circumstances. There are none, however, who in the early twenty-first century are immune to such crises and most find their experiences render problematic relationships that were once taken as certitudes in the past.

Laos, in contrast to Thailand, has never really emerged from the first crisis of modernity, namely the creation of a modern nation-state. This has remained the case even since 1975, when the Lao Peoples Revolutionary Party succeeded in establishing the first post-colonial government that could claim to have authority throughout the territory of Laos. As Evans (in this volume and in Evans 1998) shows, the Party has yet to succeed in making the premises on which it bases its power hegemonic for a large proportion of the population. Many in Laos continue to see themselves with reference to local, not national traditions. Some in Laos draw on memories of a royal past to challenge the authority of the Party while others, especially among the upland Hmong, resist the regime by recalling the tribal autonomy that was fostered by Americans and Thai during the War in Indochina. With the exception of a very small urban elite, the Lao who have truly entered the modern world are those among the over ten per cent of the population who fled the country and resettled in North America, France, and Australia. The models which these 'overseas Lao' and neighbouring Thailand offer to people still living in Laos have become the primary source of tension for many living in a country that is still betwixt and between the modern and premodern world.

Politics of identity

Contested past and identity

Collectively, the essays in this volume try to demonstrate that modernity does not have a single face, one that is uniform when it is fully realised around the globe. Instead, they demonstrate that while processes of modernity may have common characteristics, human agency always leads to diverse expressions of identity shaped by the distinctive politics of the past. On these grounds, we give some theoretical consideration to social and individual identifications, particularly those concerned with the past constructed in crises of modernity. None of the features of social memory are themselves by any means free from power relations, pre-existing discursive formations, and the effects of strongly influential forces, including new types of behaviour evolving out of ever-growing consumerism, in which most social practices of remembering are situated in modernity.

Any attempt to locate social memory within relations of power and domination poses questions as to how remembering subjects collectively constitute themselves in relation to the past; hence our inquiries into the concept of identity. In this formulation, individuals come to identify with some collective past in order to know who they are in the present. This point directly relates to many of the contributions in this volume that highlight, in a variety of ways, social memory that is being created in the context of the recently emerging cultural and social crises of modernity. It should then be noted that the faculty by which individuals recall and identify a particular past event or experience is not the same as that which impels personal remembering (cf. Bloch 1998). Many writers in the social sciences have pointed out that voluntary and collective activities to identify

20

the past are undertaken so as not to forget the past, in an effort to secure the past for the present and future, thus using the past to shape who we are in the present (Bellah et al 1985; Middleton and Edwards 1990a; Tonkin 1992). Constitutive narratives are persistently retold among the group, making a very real contribution to the formation of a 'community of memory', which leads to the construction of its identity and integrity. Identity formation in modern social sciences is, however, somewhat more complexly conceived of, when we look closely at the processes by which people attempt to anchor their identities by reference to the past through remembering.

Acts of specifying the significance of events in the past often evoke contradictory and contesting identity formation among people involved with, or receiving, the specification. Most commemorative activities, and other collective rituals, promulgate immutable and irrefutable aspects of the past. These may serve as sources of legitimacy for codes of conduct or morality, but they also give rise to alternative memories or interpretations of the past as refutable and manipulable. Most commemorative rituals, nonetheless, intentionally confirm limited and one-sided significance by defining what should and should not be remembered of past events, thereby rendering mute alternative interpretations of the past. This causes tensions in times of rapid transformation of modernity: particularly, in recent years, as the wider world has impinged on peripheral areas in the process of globalisation. The effects of this, and the accompanying extension of the influence of the organs of nation-states on the practices of the people, are described in the contributions of Tapp (chapter 3), in his account of Hmong discourses on morality, and of Morris (chapter 2), in her analysis of commodification in the culture of the Khon Müang in Northern Thailand.

Contested identity often arises in opposition to nationalist and socialist projects that assert an immutable and legitimate past by presenting discourses and images constructed from arbitrarily selected past events. Social memories generated around nationalist discourses, statues, and monuments are often completely detached from the actual experience of the event by the individuals involved in it; nor do they necessarily even connect with the articulated remembering of others (cf. Anderson 1991: 204–205). These memories are also different from those that are sustained by ritual practices, such as funeral rites, ancestral spirit cults, and so on, which have been preserved in local communities and continually recalled as embodied memory through re-enactment, often accompanied by the retelling of narratives (cf. Tanabe 2000a). Nationalist attempts to construct social memories detached from both individual and communal processes invoke an all-inclusive and unitary identity without any internal differentiation. This, too, is a process that involves the social construction of memory: one which has been much in evidence in the dominating discourses that have been employed to buttress authority in many South

East Asian nation-states. On the other hand, the nationalist construction of social memory has been confronted with alternative 'popular' memories. Recalled, individually or collectively, these feature prominently in the crises of modernity that have accompanied the disruption of 'traditional' authority in recent decades, as we have already illustrated.

As we have already noted, the individual remembering of a subject is distinct from the processes that produce would-be dominant social memory. Yet, simply reducing the individual responses to a dominating social memory to an aggregated form of 'popular' or 'counter' memory, and thus ignoring its genesis, would be misleading. When Foucault (1977c: 195–196; 1980: 81–82) speaks of a return of 'subjugated popular knowledge', or le savoir des gens, which has hitherto been hidden under the edifices of centralised knowledge and discourses, he envisages the construction of differentiated forms of the subject, as opposed to the binary contested field of identity to which modern social theories and identity politics have so obsessively adhered. As he (Foucault 1997: 290, 298–299) explicitly suggests, the identity of a subject is never a substance; rather it is something that is constantly remade and reshaped depending on the diverse life circumstances of the subject, ranging from sexual relationships and governance by family members to political actions. This Foucauldian shift, where the conception of identity is taken out of the contested field of identity, can be seen to be of greater significance when we look at individual practices in the context of the transformations in modernity. Whether in urban settings, or in marginalised minority communities, the strategic and manipulative practices of individual subjects come into prominence in coping with the increasing insecurity and uncertainty of life circumstances, as illustrated by Tanabe in the cases of HIV/AIDS self-help groups in Northern Thailand (Tanabe 1999a, 1999b).

Consequently, in so far as they are socially located and constituted activities, identifications of the self that the subject makes are open-ended in an incessantly reconstituting process. Individuals constantly attempt to come to terms with the world by struggling with, resisting, or negotiating collective memories in processes such as the commemorative rituals of small communities, or in confrontation with more powerful discursive and emotional formations such as nationalist discourses. These 'practices of freedom', to use Foucault's term, should be distinguished from those predicated on the putatively free and selective actions of individuals within a field bounded by structural constraints, such as that recurrently conceptualised in anthropological 'transactionalism' and sociological 'action theory' (cf. Kapferer 1976; Ortner 1984), or in 'rational choice' theory that dominates other social sciences. Rather, freedom is practised in the form of strategic and manipulative interactions in a field populated by other individuals, and patterned with normative and regulative rules, and under the influence of dominating discourses. It is under these conditions, inherently embedded in the modern, that the subject is continually reconstituted.

Tanabe, Morris, Hirai and Kasian in this volume, if from different viewpoints, account for these processes, focusing on spirit-mediumship, consumption among villagers and the urban populace in Thailand. As Hirai (chapter 7) and Kasian (chapter 8) show, the rise of consumerism led to the possibility of people defining their identities with reference to goods and services that could be purchased from a global supermarket. Even if consumerism never wholly supplants other foci in shaping identities, it does make possible a much wider variety of choices of identity based on lifestyle and fashion than had ever existed before. The cultural dissonance intrinsic in modernity increasingly gives rise to anxiety, or passive, or even active, resistance in response to abstract rationality, regulative rules and bureaucracy. Conversely, however, people manage to find out their sense of identity by relying on the same ground of modernity, and using it as their instrument to continually reconstitute their subjects (cf. Miller 1994: 74). In the next section, we look more closely at the processes of appropriation that make possible the reconstituting of subjects in the contexts of power relations.

Appropriation and forgetting

One of the significant features of strategic practices associated with the politics of the past involves appropriating, and thus potentially transforming, the power relations that are continually moulded in rituals, dominating narratives, and discourses of 'cultural tradition', as illustrated by many writers in this volume. We define appropriation as a process of making one's own the messages embodied in these cultural practices. As Ricouer (1981: 143; also see pp. 18–19) says, 'What I appropriate is a proposed world. The latter is not *behind* the text, as a hidden intention would be, but *in front of* it, as that which the work unfolds, discovers, reveals'. A proposed world, as Keyes (1991: 90) notes, opens up 'the possibility of relationships that may be established in the future'. Subjects are not bound by the intentions of those who create and promulgate a message; rather they make use of the meanings they derive from the message – which may well be only a part of the whole – for their own expedient benefit. In other words, while the subject may continually remake one's identity with reference to the past, this process is not the straightforward and involuntary internalisation of the past that Bourdieu and Connerton seem to propose. Rather appropriating practices are shaped by what the subject finds in the public recollection of the past that is relevant for the constituting of one's own self.[25] The subject acts 'tactically' (Certeau 1984: xix, 35–37), continuously manipulating messages to turn them into opportunities for one's own profit, even against the intention of those who created the messages in the first place. In authoritarian societies, individuals may even rework the message in the form of what James Scott calls 'hidden transcripts' (1990: 1–16; also see Tanabe 1984) in order to resist domination.

At the micro-level, the act of appropriating practices reconstitutes what one is – in the present in everyday conversational settings, in which one's own past is created and revised through rhetorical skill and argument against the dominating discourses (Middleton and Edwards 1990b). This kind of pragmatics in everyday practice is not confined only to conversational remembering. Appropriation is also at work in ritual and other associated embodied practices. These practices are stable and difficult to change in the short term because they are publicly stipulated, and preserved in, and acted out through, the actor's body. Yet, when we look at the pragmatic aspects of ritual, for example, during a curing session of a spirit cult that involves a spirit medium and a client, we see that the actors can manipulatively make use of the situation, so as to justify the client's present state through interactions that involve accepting or eliminating past recollections (chapter 1). Contemporary spirit cults, with their recently evolved divining and even therapeutic rituals, seem prominently to focus on the interactive relations between the individual practitioner and client. As Lambek and Tanabe remark, memory here is more inter-subjective and dialogical than exclusively individual (Lambek 1996: 239; Tanabe 1999a: 102–104).

The practice of appropriation, through the creation, revision or recapturing the past as one's own, is associated with the cultural politics of identification. At the opposite extreme is what is often called 'organised forgetting', a voluntary or involuntary eradication of what has happened, and could be recalled from the past (see Trouillot 1995). In a general sense, forgetting is inevitably involved in every individual act of remembering and constructing social memory, but organised forgetting often relates to particular forms of ban and suppression under discursive and non-discursive domination. Numerous instances of the large-scale manipulation of the past by totalitarian governments have been recorded in modern history. In Thailand, as argued by Thongchai in chapter 10, there is indubitable historical evidence of an organised attempt to consign to oblivion the 6 October 1976 massacre in Bangkok. The massacre and its aftermath remain a major critical issue of modernity in Thailand.

Organised forgetting is certainly a focal point of 'identity politics' in crises of modernity, whether national, ethnic, local or gender related, yet, it is arguably an issue in the cultural politics of the past in everyday life, as well. As we have noted before, while an act of remembering involves forgetting through continual reconstruction, social memory also undergoes a process of conceptualisation when what is recalled is articulated and represented in the forms of dominating narratives, folk-tales, or statuary (cf. Anderson 1991; Carsten 1995). In fact, Bourdieu's notion of embodied practice also illustrates the ways in which all practices are produced infinitely from *habitus*, as transposable dispositions integrate past experiences: practices produced as such persist as organised forgetting in the form of *doxa*, a world of tradition experienced as a 'natural world' and taken for granted (1977: 83, 164). Thus, in wider contexts, what is generically called 'tradition' (*carit prapheni* in Thai or *hitkòng* in Lao) involves a normative, and consequently legitimate, forgetting, by assuming a set of beliefs and practices that are handed down from the past, i.e. a *traditum*, and taken for granted. In the recent capitalist transformation, however, some traditions, for example, the 'Lao' traditions of Northeastern Thailand and the Lanna traditions of Northern Thailand, have begun to be less taken for granted and frequently held up to public scrutiny and debate. Modernity changes the status of traditions and makes them objects that can be talked about and strategically manipulated. In this volume, Morris (chapter 2) discusses this, and also the way in which traditions can virtually engender the discourses of themselves in the society (also see Morris 2000).

The rapid expansion of the capitalist economy in Thailand has also led to certain cultural practices, including many Buddhist rituals and spirit cults, being commodified and thus becoming, to different degrees, objects of mass consumption in the same market place as industrial goods and services, as Tanabe (1991, 2000b) illustrates in a variety of spirit cults in Chiang Mai. Those who 'consume' such practices for healing or divination or even, as is often the case, for entertainment engage them in a very different way than did the participants in the traditional forms from which these practices are derived. Whereas participants in traditional rituals became co-producers, along with other participants of kin groups or local communities, the clients of contemporary practices are often radically alienated from these collectivities. These clients appropriate the meanings of these practices in accord with their own subjective agendas (Miller 1987: 175–176; 1995). Such de-contextualisation of ritual practices undermines their traditional givenness, their naturalised foundations; at the same time, their re-contextualisation makes it possible for many people to appropriate from them meanings to confront actively the contradictions of modernity. The remembering and silencing of the past which takes place in many contemporary cultural practises in Thailand provides clear evidence that their relationship to authority is far more diverse than would be expected if they were viewed solely, as many would do, as tools of domination.

The contributions

In the first part of this book entitled 'Embodied Memories in Cultural Crisis: Spirit Possession and Ritual', Tanabe (chapter 1), Morris (chapter 2), and Tapp (chapter 3) show how the past is compellingly and powerfully embodied in ritual and spirit mediumship. The cases they explore, as well as that examined by Keyes (chapter 6), demonstrate that ritual and spirit mediumship have taken on new significance with people who are confronting radical changes brought about by modernity. The urbanised people of Chiang Mai, among whom both Tanabe and Morris have worked, face crises in their everyday lives that are very much a product of their living in a modern world.

Both Tanabe and Morris pay attention to the dramatic surge in professional spirit mediumship in Northern Thailand, particularly in the city of Chiang Mai, during the past three or four decades. This indicates a remarkable shift in the practices of the people from more legitimate, orthodox Buddhist and other 'traditional' practices, which have hitherto been nurtured within the modern nation-state. Tanabe focuses on the personhood of the Khon Müang (or Northern Tai) in Chiang Mai, that has been maintained through the embodied techniques and social memory concerned with stabilisation of the mind-body relationship. Tanabe argues that in professional spirit cults the permeable interaction and negotiation enacted between the medium and the client enables the latter, mostly lower and middle class peoples, to appropriate their transforming life circumstances and contexts, and to recover stability of mind-body relations. On the other hand, spirit mediums, who themselves had entered this profession after a prolonged period of suffering, have reconstituted their selves and appropriated available diverse knowledge and practices hitherto rather monopolised by male ritual practitioners. Thus Tanabe reveals the ways in which embodied memory and practices in the spirit cults enable the newcomers and lower class peoples to reconstitute themselves in response to anxiety, insecurity and contingency in the current transformation.

Whilst Tanabe puts forwards a micro-level analysis of the social construction of memory and practices in spirit cults, Morris in chapter 2 looks at spirit mediumship differently (also see Morris 2000). Rather than focusing on local discursive aspects, she examines spirit cults with reference to the wider economy of representation shaped by the Buddhist orthodoxy that has buttressed the nation-state. For Morris, the ritualised and magical practices of spirit mediumship propose a new relationship to the past – one expressed in a discourse of 'traditionalism' – that many find appealing because of their particular experiences of alienation associated with living in modernity. The discourse of traditionalism, now encompassing ritualism, is however challenged again by another more radical 'ritual libertinage' featuring fire-walking and other acts of extreme asceticism, where display value has come to supersede exchange value in the on-going consumerism involving the people in Northern Thailand. Together, the papers by Tanabe and Morris clearly demonstrate that individuals can, and do, derive very different meanings from the 'same' cultural practices. Moreover, the very 'sameness' is quite problematic as the conditions of modernity generate desires for improvisations, and even inventions of 'tradition'.

Although the upland dwelling Hmong in Northern Thailand among whom Tapp worked might, at first blush, be considered to be a marginal people for whom 'authentic' tradition is still significant, a second look at the Hmong shows that these people are not isolated from conditions of modernity and the globalised environments. Avoiding a sharp distinction between embodied social memory and history, Tapp contends that social memory is a kind of 'organised forgetting' of the past, constantly reinventing the past, as historical reconstruction does. In his investigation of Hmong morality, he found that under the impact of urbanisation the boundaries hitherto maintained between self, community, and the world have been 'ex-ploded'. While behaviour traditionally seen as only appropriate beyond their social space is now universalised among the Hmong, the essential bases of their core morality, strongly linked with Confucian notions of filial piety and humility, remain intact and actively preserved through verbal propriety in their daily life. Thus Tapp sees that the Hmong social memory has been continuously reshaped by reaffirming traditional moral values and, at the same time, by organised forgetting as the core experience of modernity.

The chapters in the second part, 'Nationalist Monuments: Competing Social Memories', are concerned with concrete forms of memorialising persons whose lives have been situated within nationalist or ethnic narratives. The monuments discussed by Keyes (chapter 4), Tannenbaum (chapter 5), and Evans (chapter 6) have had very different roles in promoting social memory to most monuments of the premodern world, such as the ubiquitous images of the Buddha or stupas that serve as 'reminders' (cedi, from Pali, ceitya) of him, and that are found throughout Thailand and Laos.[26] Reminders of the Buddha embody myths not about origins of communities but about timeless truths for all those who are wise enough to turn towards them. Modern monuments, such as those discussed in the chapters included here, are meant to remind those who view them of particular individuals who worked or sacrificed to help create or preserve the heritage of a national, ethnic or religious community.[27]

Monuments are inherently inchoate and 'speak' only when audiences collect around them at commemorative events or festivals, at which time their stories are vested with an aura of authority. The voices heard, however, may not all convey the same message. The role accorded, for example, by Thai nationalist leaders at official holidays to an equestrian statue of King Chulalongkorn (see chapter 6) that stands near the seats of power in Bangkok, is not the same as that conveyed by spirit mediums who literally speak in the voice of the king who died in 1910. Similar, but more pronounced, tensions are also associated with the monument to Suranari, an early nineteenth century woman, in the Northeastern Thai city of Khorat (Nakhon Ratchasima). This monument has become a site at which different views of the past are strongly contested (see chapter 4).

Monuments may also remain as reminders of pasts that a current government may deny or denigrate, as is the case of the one to King Srisavang Vong in Luang Prabang, Laos (chapter 6). Yet other monuments scarcely speak at all. The monument to Phaya Sihanatraja, the recently remembered founder of the remote province of Maehongson in North-western Thailand (chapter 5), appears to attract little attention from locals or outsiders. Even more puzzling is the monument to Kaysone Phomvihane, the man who led the revolution that created the Lao Peoples Democratic Republic (chapter 6). This monument is hidden away and receives attention primarily from high-ranking members of the party rather than the general public. Monuments can also be 'silenced'. During the colonial period, French authorities erected in a central plaza in Vientiane a statue to Auguste Pavie, the Frenchman most responsible for creating French Laos. After independence, student protesters succeeded in casting the monument into the Mekong River. The monument was subsequently recovered by the French embassy and moved to within the confines of the embassy, where it remains to this day. In short, the past that a monument is supposed to memorialise when it is first erected may not remain the same past that the monument evokes to subsequent audiences that participate in commemorative events at the monument.

The chapters subsumed in the third part under the rubric of 'Commoditisation and Consumer Identities' concern peoples in Thailand who have found compelling significance for their contemporary identity in goods that have, at best, only very shallow histories, and little or no connection to premodern Thai culture. The significant increases in disposable wealth that the economic boom produced in Thailand made it possible for some people to accentuate, in the presentation of self, their association with purchased goods, whose value derives from the market rather than from tradition. As Hirai shows, in chapter 7, about women in a village in Northern Thailand who have taken up work in a modern factory, even a traditional practice such as a housewarming rite can be made to serve as an occasion for the conspicuous display of consumer goods purchased with money earned through their new occupations.

In chapter 8, Kasian argues that at least some among the urban middle class in Bangkok have gone further, and severed all emotional connection with symbols of the past rooted in premodern Thai culture in favour of defining their identities with reference to consumer goods, whose high monetary (and concomitant cultural) value has been determined by the global economy. Although Kasian's argument, that 'the exclusive power of Thainess as a signifier to refer to only Thai things [has been] loosened' through the push to acquire consumer goods of non-Thai origins (at least in labelling), may be overstated, (especially in light of the decline in consumerism since the economic crisis of 1997 began), he has certainly shown how participation in a global economy has rendered problematic the relationship between being Thai and being modern for many in Thailand.

The chapters in the fourth part, 'Remembering, Social Memory, and History', explore how personal remembering of events relates to the social memory that is constructed around such events. In chapter 9, Nishii discusses the death of a young man from a Southern Thai Buddhist family married to a Southern Thai Muslim woman. The shock of his premature death is rendered even more emotionally fraught when the Muslim wife and the Buddhist mother contest with each other over who should have the right to choose which religious rites should be followed; burial or cremation. Despite the freshness of memories of pain and conflict, Nishii shows that mother and daughter-in-law are subsequently able to emphasise the shared positive memories they have of the son and husband. Although a very particular case, Nishii's chapter suggests that, at least in some instances, deeply disturbing memories can be set aside in favour of memories that promote positive and reconciliatory social relations.

Emotionally disturbing memories may, however, continue to haunt those who hold them. In chapter 10, Thongchai is himself haunted by his own personal remembering as he attempts to explore how the events of *hok tula*, referring to the 6th of October 1976, when a student movement was brutally repressed by military forces in Thailand, has entered into both social memory and history. Thongchai was a student leader at the time and his own personal memories provide a poignant counterpoint to his effort to write as full and detailed an historical account of the events as he can do on the basis of available sources. Moreover, he has also played a key role (including his presentation of earlier versions of his paper in Thailand in 1996) in the efforts to shape the social memory of the events for those who look back to the events as a significant watershed in recent Thai political history. In discussions with the editors, he has talked about the great difficulty he has faced in handling the interplay between remembering, social memory, and history, demonstrating the extent to which caution must be exercised in any effort to determine what is 'true' about the past.

Finally, in an epilogue to the book, Fukushima (chapter 11 in the fifth part) offers some reflections on social memory based on his reading of the papers as presented at the conference at which he was a discussant. He redirects our attention back to the psychological origins of memory, and the relationship of remembering to social memory. Fukushima notes that there are three theoretical stances adopted by the authors in the volume: one focuses on how memory is embodied; the second is how memory is constructed through mediation and re-mediation; and the third concerns the political use and abuse of social memory. Fukushima envisages a synthesis of the first two micro-level approaches with the latter macro-level one in order to identify the processes that together 'co-construct' memory.

Together, the chapters in this volume explore how the past has been evoked, or forgotten, or suppressed by peoples in Thailand and Laos as they have confronted a variety of problematic experiences in worlds significantly reshaped by modernity. Although comparable processes by which social memory is constructed and identities asserted or contested are to be found in all other societies, as the cases presented here demonstrate, understanding of these processes always must be grounded in the particular situations in which they are manifest. It is also hoped that our attempt will shed light on the ways in which many social scientists, as well as the contributors to this volume, try to understand the experiences of remembering, and their transformations in the wider social and cultural settings of modernity.

Notes

1 One of the important concepts developed in Bartlett's theory of remembering is 'schema', which refers to an active organisation of past reactions, or of past experiences, that must always be supposed to be operating in any well-adapted organic response (1932: 201). As to the recent conceptualisation of schema, also see Neisser (1976), D'Andrade (1994) and Tanabe (2000).

2 Relatively few anthropologists in earlier generations paid due attention to the social processes of remembering of the peoples they studied: exceptions being Evans-Pritchard (1940) on the Nuer in Africa, and Bateson (1958) on the analysis of Iatmul mnemonic performances in New Guinea.

3 Bartlett (1923) eventually abandoned his earlier social constructivist position moving closer to cognitive psychology (cf. Douglas 1986; Shotter 1990).

4 Yet, in extreme cases – for instance, of Goffmanesque 'total institutions' such as prisons, asylums, monasteries, the armed forces, and the like – details of dress, posture, and manners of body and language become most significant in the process of the making of new men, where the body itself is treated as the expression of memory (Bourdieu 1977: 94; Goffman 1961: 41).

5 Bourdieu (1977: 164) explains this notion as follows: '... when there is a quasi-perfect correspondence between the objective order and the subjective principles of organisation (as in ancient societies) the natural and social world appears as self-evident. This experience we shall call *doxa*, so as to distinguish it from an orthodox or heterodox belief implying awareness and recognition of the possibility of different or antagonistic beliefs. Schemes of thought and perception can produce the objectivity that they do produce only by producing misrecognition of the limits of the cognition that they make possible, thereby founding immediate adherence, in the *doxic* mode, to the world of tradition experienced as a "natural world" and taken for granted'.

6 Bourdieu maintains that inter-personal relationships are never solely relationships between one individual and another, and that social psychology and interactionism, or ethnomethodology, reduce the objective structure of the relationship of congregated people to the conjunctural structure of their interactions in a particular situation and group (1977: 21, 81).

7 Our approach to modernity, while emphasising that fundamental transformations of social and cultural life occurred in the wake of the introduction of new economic and political institutions, does not assume that these transformations

are, as the theories of modernisation of the post-war period did (see Tipps 1973), 'progressive' or 'evolutionary'.

8 We recognise that there is a vast literature that critically reflects on questions of secularisation and disenchantment but we make no effort here to summarise this literature. We note only that our thinking is grounded in the work of Max Weber, whose *Protestant Ethic and the Spirit of Capitalism* (Weber 1958) is often said to have begun debates on these issues.

9 By far the best work in English on the reformation begun under Mongkut is Craig Reynolds's (1973) 'The Buddhist monkhood in nineteenth century Thailand'. Reynolds's (1976) seminal paper, 'Buddhist cosmography in Thai history, with special reference to nineteenth-century culture change', traces well the radical shift in the worldview of the elite that derived from Mongkut's reforms. For the creation of an establishment Buddhism under the leadership of the Thammayut order, see Keyes (1971), Kirsch (1973), Tambiah (1976), Butt (1978), and Ishii (1986).

10 On the colonial origins of modernisation in Laos, such as they were, see Gunn (1988, 1990); Stuart-Fox (1995).

11 By far the best book on Laos since 1975 is that by Evans (1998); also see Stuart-Fox (1996).

12 While 'rational choice' has probably always underlain certain human actions, it has, we think is clearly demonstrable, significantly increased with modernity. Thus, we do not choose between 'rational economy' theory, as exemplified in the argument of Popkin (1979), and 'moral economy' theory, as advanced by Scott (1976), but see the relationship between these as having shifted as a consequence of both changes in practical morality and in economic practice associated with secularisation, demystification, and the expansion of capitalism (see Keyes 1983).

13 On the economic boom in Thailand and its social consequences, see Grit Permtanjit (1982), Hewison (1985, 1989), Suntaree Komin (1989), Suehiro (1992), Muscat (1994), and Pasuk Phongpaichit and Baker (1995).

14 See the following for discussions of the opening of the Lao economy since the mid-1980s: Worner (1989), Ljunggren (1993), and Mya Than and Tan (1997).

15 Foucault's (1977a) idea of a 'technology of power' has been creatively elaborated on with reference to the development of the modern state by Cohn and Dirks (1988). Also see in this connection, the added chapters in Anderson (1991).

16 The idea of 'invention of tradition' is primarily associated with the book by this name, edited by Hobsbawm and Ranger (1983).

17 On the creation of the modern state of Thailand, see Riggs (1966), Wyatt (1969), Jacobs (1971), Tej Bunnag (1977), Keyes (1987), and Murashima (1988). For a comparison of modernisation in Thailand and Laos, see Cohen (1987).

18 On resistance movements to the creation of the modern state in Siam, see Keyes (1971, 1977), Ishii (1975), Ramsay (1979), Tej Bunnag (1981), Turton (1976, 1984), Chatthip Nartsupha (1984), Tanabe (1984), and Grabowsky (1995).

19 Vella (1978) has provided a detailed account of the monarchical-centred nationalism of King Vajiravudh. On the development of a Buddhist nationalism, see Keyes (1971), Frank Reynolds (1973), Tambiah (1976), and Reynolds and Clifford (1980), and on the creation of a national language, Diller (1991) and Smalley (1994). On the development of Thai nationalism more generally, see Likhit Dhiravegin (1985), Thongchai Winichakul (1994), Keyes (1995, 1997), and the papers in Craig Reynolds (1991) and Grabowsky (1995).

20 On the creation of the Lao state, see Stuart-Fox (1995) and Taillard (1989).
21 Anderson (1991) sees printing as the beginning of modern media. While print was very important, we agree with Giddens (1991: 25), who sees print media as playing a major role in the juxtaposing of space and time after it is linked to electronic media.
22 On the role of the mass media in shaping identities in Thailand, see Hamilton 1991, 1992, 1993a, 1993b), Ubonrat Siriyuvasak (1991), Thitinan Pongsudhirak (1997), and Van Fleet (1998).
23 On premodern conceptions of the relationship between merit and power, and on the millenarian movements that used this idea to resist the authority of the Siamese state, see Ishii (1975) and Keyes (1977).
24 In addition to these two chapters in this volume, see also Tanabe (1999a), Morris (2000), and Pattana Kitiarsa (1999).
25 As Wertsch distinguishes appropriation from mastery, the former connotes the way in which one makes texts, narratives, or rules of one's own legitimate and reasonable, as opposed to Lev Vygotsky's 'internalisation', which is concerned only with the mastery of mediational means in the form of language (Wertsch 1997: 17). Appropriation is obviously different from Bourdieu's 'practical mastery', denoting acquisition of embodied and skilled practices through mimetic actions (Bourdieu 1977: 87).
26 There are some antecedents for such modern monuments in premodern times. One example is the large standing image of the Buddha on Mandalay Hill that has been given a unique stance among such images. One arm of the Buddha is outstretched and points to the valley below where Mandalay now exists. The monument was erected at the time of the founding of Mandalay in the mid-nineteenth century, and is associated with a legend that tells of a visit of the Buddha in his life time, when he prophesied that one day a great city would be built below.
27 Although not addressed in any of the chapters in this volume, there is a significant difference in Thailand between images of the Buddha and the now numerous images of particular Buddhist monks, most of whom lived within the last century. These images point to those who have offered distinctive interpretations of the Buddhist message for those facing the new experiences associated with modernity, as distinct from the universalist message associated with the Buddha himself. Some images, such as those of Khruba Sriwichai in Northern Thailand, recall monks who have challenged the authority of a national sangha created as part of the process of making Thailand a modern nation-state.

References

Anderson, Benedict 1991 *Imagined Communities: reflections on the origin and spread of nationalism* (revised and expanded edition), London: Verso.
Baker, Chris 2000 'Thailand's assembly of the poor: background, drama, reaction', p.5–30 in *South East Asia Research* 8(1).
Bartlett, Frederick C. 1923 *Psychology and Primitive Culture*, Cambridge: Cambridge University Press.
—— 1932 *Remembering: a study of experimental and social psychology*, Cambridge: Cambridge University Press.
Bateson, Gregory 1958 *Naven* (second edition), Stanford: Stanford University Press.
Bellah, Robert N., Richard Madsen, William M. Sullivan, Ann Swilder and Steven M. Tipton 1985 *Habits of the Heart: individualism and commitment in American life*, Berkeley: University of California Press.

Bloch, Maurice 1971 *Placing The Dead: tombs, ancestral villages, and kinship organization in Madagascar*, London: Seminar Press.

—— 1998 (1992) 'Internal and external memory: different ways of being in history', p.67–84 in M. Bloch, *How We Think They Think: anthropological approaches to cognition, memory and literacy*, Boulder, Col.: Westview Press.

Bencha Yoddumnern-Attig, et al 1992 *Changing Roles and Statuses of Women in Thailand: a documentary assessment*, Nakhon Pathom: Mahidol University, Institute for Population and Social Research.

Bourdieu, Pierre 1977 *Outline of a Theory of Practice* (translated by Richard Nice), Cambridge: Cambridge University Press.

—— 1990 *The Logic of Practice* (translated by Richard Nice), Cambridge: Polity Press and Stanford: Stanford University Press.

Brummelhuis, Han ten and Gilbert Herdt (eds.) 1995 *Culture and Sexual Risk: anthropological perspectives on AIDS*, New York: Gordon and Breach.

Butt, John W. 1978 'Thai kingship and religious reform', p.34–81 in B.L. Smith (ed.), *Religion and Legitimation of Power in Thailand, Laos and Burma*, Chambersburg, Pa.: Anima Books.

Carsten, Janet 1995 'The politics of forgetting: migration, kinship and memory on the periphery of the Southeast Asian state', p.317–335 in *Journal of the Royal Anthropological Institute* 1.

Carsten, Janet and Steve Hugh-Jones 1995 'Introduction', p.1–46 in J. Carsten and S. Hugh-Jones (eds.) *About the House: Lévi-Strauss and beyond*, Cambridge: Cambridge University Press.

Certeau, Michel de 1984 *The Practice of Everyday Life* (translated and edited by Steven Rendall), Berkeley: California University Press.

Chatthip Nartsupha 1984 'The ideology of "holy men" revolts in North East Thailand', p.111–134 in A. Turton and S. Tanabe (eds.) *History and Peasant Consciousness in South East Asia*, Senri Ethnological Studies 13, Osaka: National Museum of Ethnology.

Cohen, Erik 1987 'Thailand, Burma and Laos – an outline of the comparative social dynamics of three Theravada Buddhist societies in the modern era', p.192–216 in S.N. Eisenstadt (ed.) *Patterns of Modernity, Volume II: beyond the West*, London: Frances Pinter.

Cohn, Bernard S. and Nicholas B. Dirks 1988 'Beyond the fringe: the nation state, colonialism, and the technologies of power', p.224–229 in *Journal of Historical Sociology* 12.

Connerton, Paul 1989 *How Societies Remember*, Cambridge: Cambridge University Press.

D'Andrade, Roy 1994 *The Development of Cognitive Anthropology*, Cambridge: Cambridge University Press.

Deuve, Jean 1984 *Le royaume du Laos, 1949–1965 (Histoire événementielle de l'indépdendance à la guerre américaine)*, Paris: École Française d'Extrême-Orient.

Diller, Anthony 1991 'What makes central Thai a national language', p.87–113 in C. J. Reynolds (ed.) *National Identity and Its Defenders: Thailand, 1939–1989*, Melbourne: Monash University, Monash Papers on Southeast Asia, no.25.

Douglas, Mary 1986 *How Institutions Think*, London: Routledge & Kegan Paul.

Evans, Grant 1988 *Agrarian Change in Communist Laos*, Singapore: Institute of Southeast Asian Studies, Occasional Paper no.85.

—— 1990 *Lao Peasants under Socialism*, New Haven: Yale University Press.

—— 1998 *The Politics of Ritual and Remembrance: Laos since 1975*, Chiang Mai: Silkworm Books.

Evans-Pritchard, E.E. 1940 *The Nuer: a description of the modes of livelihood and political institutions of the Nilotic people*, Oxford: Clarendon Press.

Feeley-Harnik, Gillian 1991 'Finding memories in Madagascar', p.121–140 in S. Küchler and W. Melion (eds.) *Images of Memory: on remembering and representation*, Washington and London: Smithonian Institution Press.

Fentress, James and Chris Wickham 1992 *Social Memory: new perspectives on the past*, Oxford: Blackwell.

Foucault, Michel 1977a (1975) *Discipline and Punish: the birth of the prison* (translated by Alan Sheridan), New York: Pantheon.

—— 1977b (1971) 'Nietzsche, Genealogy, History', p.139–164 in D.F. Bouchard (ed.) *Language, Counter-Memory, Practice: selected essays and interviews by Michel Foucault*, Ithaca, New York: Cornell University Press.

—— 1977c (1970) 'Theatrum philosophicum', p.165–195 in D.F. Bouchard (ed.) *Language, Counter-Memory, Practice*.

—— 1980 (1976) 'Two lectures', p.78–108 in Colin Gordon (ed.) *Power/Knowledge: Selected interviews and other writings 1972–1977*, New York: Pantheon Books.

—— 1997 (1984) 'Ethics of the concern of the self as a practice of freedom', p.281–301 in P. Labinow (ed.) *Ethics: subjectivity and truth*, New York: The New Press.

Giddens, Anthony 1990 *The Consequences of Modernity*, Stanford: Stanford University Press.

—— 1991 *Modernity and Self-identity: self and society in the late modern age*, Stanford: Stanford University Press.

Goffman, Erving 1961 *Asylums: essays on the social situation of mental patients and other inmates*, New York: Doubleday Anchor.

Grabowsky, Volker (ed.) 1995 *Regions and National Integration in Thailand, 1892–1992*, Wiesbaden: Otto Harrassowitz.

Grit Permtanjit 1982 *Political Economy of Dependent Capitalist Development: study on the limits of the capacity of the state to rationalize in Thailand*, Bangkok: Chulalongkorn University Social Research Institute.

Gunn, Geoffrey 1982 'Theravadins and commissars: the state and national identity in Laos', p.76–100 in Martin Stuart-Fox (ed.) *Contemporary Laos: studies in the politics and society of the Lao People's Democratic Republic*, New York: St. Martin's Press.

—— 1988 *Political Struggles in Laos (1930–1954): Vietnamese communist power and the Lao struggle for national independence*, Bangkok: Editions Duang Kamol.

—— 1990 *Rebellion in Laos: peasant and politics in a colonial backwater*, Boulder, Col.: Westview Press.

Habermas, Jürgen 1987 *The Philosophical Discourse of Modernity* (translated by F. Lawrence), Cambridge, Mss.: The MIT Press.

Halbwachs, Maurice 1952 (1925) *Les cadres sociaux de la mémoire*, Paris: Presses Universitaires de France.

—— 1980 (1950) *The Collective Memory* (translated by F.J. Ditter and V.Y. Ditter), New York: Harper & Row.

Hamilton, Annette 1991 'Rumours, foul calumnies and the safety of the state: mass media and national identity in Thailand', p.341–380 in C. J. Reynolds (ed.), *National Identity and Its Defenders: Thailand, 1939–1989*.

—— 1992 'Family dramas: film and modernity in Thailand', p.259–273 in *Screen* 33(3).

—— 1993a 'Video crackdown, or the sacrificial pirate: censorship and cultural consequences in Thailand', p.515–531 in *Public Culture* 5.

—— 1993b 'Cinema and nation: dilemmas of representation in Thailand', p.81–105 in *East-West Film Journal*, 7(1).

Hewison, Kevin J. 1985 'The state and capitalist development in Thailand', p.286–294 in R. Higgott and R. Robison (eds.) *Southeast Asia: essays in the political economy of structural change*, London: Routledge & Kegan Paul.

—— 1989 *Bankers and Bureaucrats: capital and the role of the state in Thailand*, New Haven: Yale University Southeast Asia Studies, Yale Center for International and Area Studies.

Hobsbawm, Eric and Terence Ranger (eds.) 1983 *The Invention of Tradition*, Cambridge: Cambridge University Press.

Ishii, Yoneo 1975 'A Note on Buddhistic millenarian revolts in Northeastern Siam', p.121–126 in *Journal of Southeast Asian Studies* 6(2).

—— 1986 *Sangha, State, and Society: Thai Buddhism in history* (translated by Peter Hawkes), Honolulu: University of Hawaii Press, Monographs of the Center for Southeast Asian Studies, Kyoto University.

Jacobs, Norman 1971 *Modernization without Development: Thailand as an Asian case study*, New York: Praeger Publishers (Praeger Special Studies in International Economics and Development).

Jackson, Peter A. 1995 *Dear Uncle Go: male homosexuality in Thailand*, Bangkok: Bua Luang.

Kapferer, Bruce 1976 'Introduction', p.1–22 in B. Kapferer (ed.) *Transaction and Meaning: directions in the anthropology of exchange and human behavior*, Philadelphia: ISHI Publications.

Kasaba, Resat 1997 'Kemalist certainties and modern ambiguities', p.15–36 in S. Bozdoòan and R. Kasaba (eds.) *Rethinking Modernity and National Identity in Turkey*, Seattle: University of Washington Press.

Keyes, Charles F. 1971 'Buddhism and national integration in Thailand', p.551–568 in *Journal of Asian Studies* 30(3).

—— 1975 'Buddhist pilgrimage centers and the twelve year cycle: Northern Thai moral orders in space and time', p.71–89 in *History of Religions* 5(1).

—— 1977 'Millennialism, Theravada Buddhism, and Thai Society', p.283–302 in *Journal of Asian Studies* 36(2).

—— 1983 'Introduction', p.753–768 in C.F. Keyes (ed.) *Peasant Strategies in Asian Societies: perspectives on moral and rational economic approaches*, *Journal of Asian Studies* 42(3).

—— 1986 'Ambiguous gender: male initiation in a Buddhist society', p.66–96 in C. Bynum, S. Harrell, and P. Richman (eds.) *New Perspectives on Religion and Gender*, Boston: Beacon Press.

—— 1987 *Thailand: Buddhist kingdom as modern nation-state*, Boulder, Col.: Westview Press.

—— 1991 'The proposed world of the school: Thai villagers entry into a bureaucratic state system', p.87–138 in C.F. Keyes (ed.) *Reshaping Local Worlds: rural education and cultural change in Southeast Asia*, New Haven: Yale University Southeast Asian Studies

—— 1995 'Who are the Tai? reflections on the invention of identities', p.136–160 in L. Romanucci-Ross and G.A. De Vos (eds.) *Ethnic Identity: creation, conflict, and accommodation* (third edition), Walnut Creek, Calif.: Alta Mira Press.

—— 1997 'Cultural diversity and national identity in Thailand', p.197–232 in M.E. Brown and S. Ganguly (eds.) *Government Policies and Ethnic Relations in Asia and the Pacific*, Cambridge, Mass.: The MIT Press.

—— 1999. 'Moral authority of the Sangha and modernity in Thailand: sexual scandals, sectarian dissent, and political resistance', p.121–147 in Sulak Sivaraksa (ed.) *Socially Engaged Buddhism for the New Millennium: essays in honor of the Ven. Phra Dhammapitaka (Bhikkhu P.A. Payutto) on his 60th birthday anniversary,* Bangkok: Sathira-Nagapradipa Foundation and Foundation for Children.

Keyes, Charles F., Helen Hardacre, and Laurel Kendall 1994 'Introduction: contested visions of community in East and Southeast Asia'. p. 1–16 in C.F. Keyes, L. Kendall, and H. Hardacre (eds.) *Asian Visions of Authority: religion and the modern states of East and Southeast Asia,* Honolulu: University of Hawaii Press.

Kirsch, A. Thomas 1973 'Modernizing implications of 19th century reforms in the Thai sangha', p.8–23 in *Contributions to Asian Studies* 8.

Küchler, Susanne and Walter Melion (eds.) 1991 *Images of Memory: on remembering and representation,* Washington and London: Smithsonian Institution Press.

Lambek, Michael 1996 'The past imperfect: remembering as moral practice', p.235–254 in P. Antze and M. Lambek (eds.) *Tense Past: cultural essays in trauma and memory,* New York: Routledge.

Likhit Dhiravegin 1985 *Nationalism and the State in Thailand,* Bangkok: Research Center, Faculty of Political Science, Thammasat University, Monograph Series, no.8.

Ljunggren, Börje 1993 'Market economies under communist regimes: reform in Vietnam, Laos, and Cambodia', p.39–122 in B. Ljunggren (ed.) *The Challenge of Reform in Indochina,* Cambridge, Mass.: Harvard University Press for Harvard Institute for International Development.

Middleton, David and Derek Edwards 1990a 'Introduction', p.1–22 in D. Middleton and D. Edwards (eds.) *Collective Remembering,* London: Sage Publications.

—— 1990b 'Conversational remembering: a social psychological approach', p.23–45 in D. Middleton and D. Edwards (eds.) 1990a *Collective Remembering.*

Miller, Daniel 1987 *Material Culture and Mass Consumption,* Oxford: Blackwell.

—— 1994 *Modernity: an ethnographic approach,* Oxford: Berg.

—— 1995 'Consumption studies as the transformation of anthropology', p.264–295 in D. Miller (ed.) *Acknowledging Consumption: a review of new studies,* London: Routledge.

Mills, Mary Beth 1995 'Attack of the widow ghosts: gender, death and modernity in Northeast Thailand', p.244–273 in A. Ong, and M.G. Peletz (eds.) *Bewitching Women, Pious Men: gender and body politics in Southeast Asia,* Berkeley: University of California Press.

—— 1997 'Contesting the margins of modernity: women, migration, and consumption in Thailand', p.37–61 in *American Ethnologist* 24(1).

Morris, Rosalind C. 1994 'Three sexes and four sexualities: redressing the discourses on gender and sexuality in contemporary Thailand', p.15–43 in *Positions* 2(1).

—— 2000 *In the Place of Origins: modernity and its mediums in Northern Thailand,* Durham, NC: Duke University Press.

Murashima, Eiji 1988 'The origin of modern official state ideology in Thailand', p.80–96 in *Journal of Southeast Asian Studies* 19(1).

Muscat, Robert J. 1994 *The Fifth Tiger: a study of Thai development policy,* Armonk, NY: M.E. Sharpe.

Mya Than and J.L.H. Tan (eds.) 1997 *Laos' Dilemmas and Options: the challenge of economic transition in the 1990s,* Singapore: Institute of Southeast Asian Studies.

Neisser, Ulric 1976 *Cognition and Reality,* New York: W.H. Freeman.

Ortner, Sherry 1984 'Theory in anthropology since the sixties', p.126–166 in *Comparative Studies in Society and History* 26(1).

Pasuk Phongpaichit and Chris Baker 1995 *Thailand's Economy and Politics,* Kuala Lumpur: Oxford University Press.

Pattana Kitiarsa 1999 "'You may not believe but never offend spirit": spirit-medium cult discourses and the postmodernization of Thai religion', unpublished PhD dissertation, University of Washington.

Peleggi, Maruzio 1997 'The making of the Siamese monarchy's modern public image', unpublished PhD dissertation, Australian National University.

Polanyi, Karl 1957 (1944) *The Great Transformation: the political and economic origins of our time*, Boston: Beacon.

Popkin, Samuel 1979 *The Rational Peasant: the political economy of rural society in Vietnam*, Berkeley: University of California Press.

Ramsay, Ansil 1979 'Modernization and reactionary rebellions in Northern Siam', p.283–298 in *Journal of Asian Studies* 38(2).

Reynolds, Craig J. 1973 'The Buddhist monkhood in nineteenth century Thailand', unpublished PhD dissertation, Cornell University.

—— 1976 'Buddhist cosmography in Thai history, with special reference to nineteenth-century culture change', p.203–220 in *Journal of Asian Studies* 35(2).

Reynolds, Craig J. (ed.) 1991 *National Identity and Its Defenders: Thailand, 1939–1989*, Melbourne: Monash University, Centre of Southeast Asian Studies, Monash Papers on Southeast Asia, no.25.

Reynolds, Frank E. 1973 'Sacral kingship and national development: the case of Thailand', p.40–50 in B.L. Smith (ed.) *Tradition and Change in Theravada Buddhism: essays on Ceylon and Thailand in the 19th and 20th centuries, Contributions to Asian Studies* 4.

Reynolds, Frank E. and Regina T. Clifford 1980 'Sangha, society, and the struggle for national integration: Burma and Thailand', p.56–91 in F.E. Reynolds and T.M. Ludwig (eds.) *Transitions and Transformations in the History of Religions: essays in honor of Joseph M. Kitagawa*, Leiden: E.J. Brill.

Ricoeur, Paul 1981 *Hermeneutics and the Human Sciences* (edited and translated by John B. Thompson), Cambridge: Cambridge University Press.

Riggs, Fred W. 1966 *Thailand: the modernization of a bureaucratic polity*, Honolulu: East-West Center Press.

Scott, James C. 1976 *The Moral Economy of the Peasant: rebellion and subsistence in South-east Asia*, New Haven: Yale University Press.

—— 1990 *Domination and the Arts of Resistance*, New Haven and London: Yale University Press.

Shotter, John 1990 'The social construction of remembering and forgetting', p.120–138 in D. Middleton and D. Edwards (eds.) *Collective Remembering*.

Simmel, Georg 1987 *Philosophy of Money* (translated by T. Bottomore and D. Frisby), London: Routledge & Kegan Paul.

Smalley, William A. 1994 *Linguistic Diversity and National Unity: language ecology in Thailand*, Chicago: University of Chicago Press.

Stoller, Paul 1995 *Embodying Colonial Memories: spirit possession, power, and the Hauka in West Africa*, New York and London: Routledge.

Stuart-Fox, Martin 1983 'Marxism and Theravada Buddhism: the legitimation of political authority in Laos', p.428–454 in *Pacific Affairs* 56(3).

—— 1986 *Laos: Politics, Economics and Society*, London: Frances Pinter and Boulder, Col.: Lynne Rinner, Marxist Regimes Series.

—— 1995 'The French in Laos, 1887–1945', p.111–140 in *Modern Asian Studies*, 29(1).

—— 1996 *Buddhist Kingdom, Marxist State: the making of modern Laos*. Bangkok: White Lotus, Studies in Asian History, no.2.

Suehiro, Akira 1992 'Capitalist development in postwar Thailand: commercial bankers, industrial elite, and agribusiness groups', p.35–64 in Ruth McVey (ed.)

Southeast Asian Capitalists, Ithaca, Conn.: Cornell University Southeast Asian Studies.

Suntaree Komin 1989 *Social Dimensions of Industrialization in Thailand*, Bangkok: National Institute of Development Administration.

Taillard, Christian 1989 *Le Laos: stratégies d'un état-tampon*, Montellier: Groupement d'Intérêt Public Reclus.

Tambiah, Stanley J. 1976 *World Conqueror and World Renouncer: a study of Buddhism and polity in Thailand against a historical background*, Cambridge: Cambridge University Press.

Tanabe, Shigeharu 1984 'Ideological practice in peasant rebellions: Siam at the turn of the twentieth century', p.75–110 in A. Turton and S. Tanabe (eds.) *History and Peasant Consciousness in South East Asia*, Senri Ethnological Studies 13, Osaka: National Museum of Ethnology.

—— 1991 'Sacrifice and the transformation of ritual: the Pu Sae Ña Sae spirit cult of Northern Thailand', unpublished paper presented at the symposium 'Spirit cults and popular knowledge in South East Asia', National Museum of Ethnology, Osaka, November.

—— 1999a 'Suffering and negotiation: spirit-mediumship and HIV/AIDS self-help groups in Northern Thailand', p.93–115 in *Thai Culture* 4(1).

—— 1999b 'Practice and self-governance: HIV/AIDS self-help groups in Northern Thailand', unpublished paper presented at the Seventh International Conference on Thai Studies, Amsterdam, 4–8 July.

—— 2000a 'Memories displaced by ritual: the Khon Müang spirit cults in Northern Thailand', p.707–726 in *Bulletin of the National Museum of Ethnology* 24(4).

—— 2000b 'Autochthony and the *Inthakhin* cult of Chiang Mai', p.294–318 in A. Turton (ed.) *Civility and Savagery: social identity in Tai states*, Surrey: Curzon.

Tej Bunnag 1977 *The Provincial Administration of Siam, 1892–1915*, Kuala Lumpur: Oxford University Press.

—— 1981 *Khabot R. S. 121* (1902 Rebellions), Bangkok: Munnithi Khrongkan Tamra Sangkhomsat lae Manutsat.

Thitinan Pongsudhirak 1997 'Thailand's media: whose watchdog?', p.217–232 in K. Hewison (ed.) *Political Change in Thailand: democracy and participation*, London and New York: Routledge.

Thirayuth Boonmi 1998 *Thammarat haeng chat* (Good Governance of Thailand), Bangkok: Samnakphim Saithan.

Thongchai Winichakul 1994 *Siam Mapped: a history of the geo-body of a nation*, Honolulu: University of Hawaii Press.

Tipps, Dean C. 1973 'Modernization theory and the study of national societies: a critical perspective', p.199–225 in *Comparative Studies in Society and History* 15(2).

Tonkin, Elizabeth 1992 *Narrating Our Past: the social construction of oral history*, Cambridge: Cambridge University Press.

Trouillot, Michel-Rolph 1995 *Silencing the Past: power and the production of history*, Boston: Beacon.

Turton, Andrew 1976 'Northern Thai peasant society: twentieth-century transformations in political and jural structure', p.267–298 in *Journal of Peasant Studies* 3(3).

—— 1978 'Architectural and political space in Thailand', p.113–132 in G.B. Milner (ed.) *Natural Symbols in South East Asia*, London: School of Oriental and African Studies.

—— 1984 'Limits of ideological domination and the formation of social consciousness', p.19–74 in A. Turton and S. Tanabe (eds.) *Historical and Peasant Consciousness in South East Asia*, Senri Ethnological Studies 13, Osaka: National Museum of Ethnology.

Ubonrat Siriyuvasak 1991 'Cultural mediation and the limits of "ideological domination": the mass media and ideological representation in Thailand', p.45–70 in *Sojourn* 6(1).

Van Fleet, Sara 1998 'Everyday dramas: television and modern Thai women', unpublished PhD dissertation, University of Washington.

Van Landingham, Mark and Nancy Grandjean 1994 'Some cultural underpinnings of male sexual behaviour patterns in Thailand', unpublished paper presented at the IUSSP Conference on 'Sexual subcultures and migration in the era of AIDS/STDs', Bangkok, 27 February–3 March.

Vella, Walter F. assisted by Dorothy Vella 1978 *Chaiyo! King Vajiravudh and the development of Thai nationalism*, Honolulu: University of Hawaii Press.

Weber, Max 1958 (1930) *The Protestant Ethic and the Spirit of Capitalism* (translated by T. Parsons), New York: Charles Scribner's Sons.

Werblowsky, R.J. Zwi 1976 *Beyond Tradition and Modernity: changing religions in a changing world*, London: Athlone Press.

Wertsch, James V. 1997 'Narrative tools of history and identity', p.5–20 in *Culture and Psychology* (Special Issue on History and National Identity) 3(1).

Winship, Michael 1986 'Early Thai printing: the beginning to 1851', p.45–61 in *Crossroads* 3(1).

Worner, William 1989 'Economic reform and structural change in Laos', p.187–208 in *Southeast Asia Affairs 1989*, Singapore: Institute of Southeast Asian Studies.

Wyatt, David K. 1969 *The Politics of Reform in Thailand: education in the reign of King Chulalongkorn*, New Haven: Yale University Press.

Young, Allan 1977 'Suffering and the origins of traumatic memory', p.245–60 in A. Kleinman, V. Das and M. Lock (eds.) *Social Suffering*, Berkeley: University of California Press.

PART I

Embodied Memories in Cultural Crisis

Spirit Possession and Ritual

CHAPTER ONE

The Person in Transformation

Body, Mind and Cultural Appropriation

Shigeharu Tanabe

> Once you had passions and called them evil. But now you have
> only your virtues: they grew out of your passions.
> You laid your highest aim in the heart of these passions: then they
> became your virtues and joys.
>
> (F. Nietzsche 1961 *Thus Spoke Zarathustra*)

Introduction

In modern Thailand, there are two viewpoints of how the person is
constituted in terms of its relations to larger social settings, and, at the
same time, to internal psychological states. The first is a sociological or
social psychological formulation, seeing the person as a moral subject; it is
seemingly of an 'individualistic' nature, but is morally and emotionally
attached to domestic relational ties and to patron-client relations to form
institutional social settings (cf. Phillips 1965). This rather stereotyped
mirror image of Euroamerican individualism has formed a discourse
dealing with the particularity of the Thai personhood, and been dominant
even in other fields of the social sciences, especially in Euroamerican
ethnographic descriptions. On the other hand, the person has also been
defined in terms of the political economy. The 'nationalist' tradition has
long expounded a dominant idea of a unified nation throughout the
modern period. According to the nationalist idea, the person is seen as a
subject of the Thai nation-state, who should serve the Nation, Buddhism
and the Monarch, and be disciplined in line with economic development,
particularly since the period of the Sarit administration of the mid-
twentieth century. Conversely, there has been a counter-formulation to
this, in which the person is to be located in 'community culture', having
rather imagined and nostalgic communal ties, along with the associated
cultural practices. This type of the imagined person is to be sought in Tai

cultural groups both in and also outside Thailand, where capitalist relations are still less intrusive (Chatthip 1991; cf. Thongchai 1995).

The social psychological formulation has often led to a rather simplistic idea of the morally constituted person in Thailand, as opposed to the Euroamerican obsession with individuated self (cf. Brummelhuis 1984). This has also a political implication, leading to the crude idea that the Thai construction of the person could be associated with obstacles to the democratic development of political institutions, and the industrialisation of the national economy. On the other hand, the nationalist and its counterpart views of the person are intrinsically a-historical, and tend to ignore ways in which the person is culturally and historically constructed in conjunction with wider institutional development, like nation-state and globalised relations. All these ideas presuppose the modernist totalising concepts of social entity, such as the state, village community, kinship etc. that are believed to define individual actions and thoughts.[1] This eventually leads to naturalising and legitimating the 'possessive individual person' within a bounded, homogeneous nation-state, and fails to account for alternative forms of knowledge and perspectives, through which the individual person could appropriate shifting contexts in the changing environment.

This chapter is an attempt to see the person in transformation, not as an unchanging entity totally moulded by an overarching framework, as typically disseminated by the above mentioned traditions. Against this background, I shall put forwards an anthropological idea that the person is culturally constructed through embodied knowledge and practices, with particular reference to spirit possession and spirit mediumship in Northern Thailand. It also addresses the point of how the person constructed as such could cope with the sense of displacement and insecurity provoked by the recent capitalist transformation and the growth of the nation-state. In so doing, this chapter intends to identify the creative potential of the appropriation of the stability of mind-body relations through permeable interactions between the self and the other in the current transformation.

Mind-body relationship

Phya Anuman Rajadhon is one of the earliest ethnographers who paid special attention to the folk category of the person among the Siamese in Central Thailand. Anuman argues that the Siamese person is constituted of the relationship between physical body and *khwan*, life essence or soul, which is affected by animistic beings, called *phi*. The *phi* penetrates the human body and causes a variety of illness whereby the *khwan* leaves the body. A number of rituals have, therefore, been developed to call back the *khwan* into the body, its proper place to reside (Anuman 1986). In a similar fashion, Sanguan Chotisukharat, another ethnographer in Chiang

Mai, frequently mentions a wide variety of ritual practices associated with the Khon Müang person vulnerable to spirits (Sanguan 1969). This earlier formulation of the person as a folk category is thus basically concerned with the associated rituals and its status within the cosmological background, with its complex configuration of Buddhism, spirit belief, and other kinds of knowledge. However, the folk conception of the person fails to account for how people with such a notion act in real situations. This is mainly because it draws only on representations appearing in the cosmological background, without any consideration of the process by which such representations are construed in the individual subject.

Thus, it would be pertinent to explore some of the cognitive aspects involved in construction of the person, which have been left unexamined in the earlier ethnographies on Northern Thailand. The folk category of the person significantly identifies the distinction between the body and *khwan*, and their unstable relationship. It should be noted that such instability of the person is totally different from the modern Euroamerican folk psychology that establishes an affirmation of dominance of the mind over the body and its distinctive nature that eventually leads to the individuated person. Conversely, the characteristic Khon Müang idea is that the individual subject consists of the body (*tua*) and *khwan*, which maintains an ever unstable equilibrium, which is exposed and susceptible to external powers. This Khon Müang person is rooted in a particular schema that organises perceptions and inferences so as to enable the individual subject to respond quickly and automatically to renewed and diverse contexts. What I shall call 'the person-spirit schema' is such an abstract organisation of experiences, particularly activated in critical moments such as fright, pain, misfortune, anxiety, affliction, and illness (Tanabe 2000).

The person-spirit schema is basically composed of the person with unstable equilibrium and its relations to external powers, often represented as spirits (*phi*). The inferences of an individual subject about affliction, misfortune, or anxiety tend to be bound to attacks by spirits through the schema, which involves direct destruction or destabilisation of the relationship between *khwan* and body. In personal episodic events, such as a traffic accident or being hit by a falling tree in the forest, one may faint, or lose consciousness, and later on the victim often explains that his *khwan* left the body due to an attack by a spirit. A similar inference is also activated when the subject has an acute pain, or goes into a violent possession trance. It is notable that in such episodic events, the schema emerges at the level of human bodily perception and movement, and constrains inferences in certain basic ways.

In Khon Müang society, the person-spirit schema is linked to a variety of rituals and healing remedies. One of the most significant rituals associated with the schema is *hòng khwan* or *hiak khwan* (calling back the *khwan*), in which a practitioner, mainly an ex-monk or a male elder, chants

Plate 1.1 Ritual of calling back the *khwan* in Chiang Mai, Northern Thailand.

spells to call back the *khwan* to the body of the patient or client. The ritual is invariably concluded by tying white cotton threads to his/her wrists (*mat mü*), which signifies tying up the *khwan* within the body. In addition, there are numerous rituals to cure illness, or affliction, and to alter destiny and misfortune, all of which are ultimately associated with stabilising the mind-body relationship. These include *song khò* (driving away bad destiny), *song thaen* (driving away bad fortune determined by the heavenly deities), *süp chata* (stretching the length of one's life), *yan* (magical formula) and *khatha* (magical spell) related to Buddhist magic; all these practices are performed by monks or ex-monks who possess well-defined, objectified knowledge, oral or textual, often associated with the Buddhist tradition. Tattooing (*sak mük*) and other forms of invulnerability magic, generically called *kham*, are more explicitly connected with the person exposed to the outer forces. They are also relevant to a technique of stabilising the mind through the body by inscribed magical formulae or patterns on the skin, or carrying magical objects (Turton 1991; cf. Tannenbaum 1987).

Thus, the Khon Müang personhood grounded in the cognitive processes activated by this schema has historically developed the embodied technologies and arts dealing with the vulnerable mind-body relationship. The disturbed equilibrium is to be stabilised through ritual actions that are embedded in the configuration of diverse knowledge and discourses,

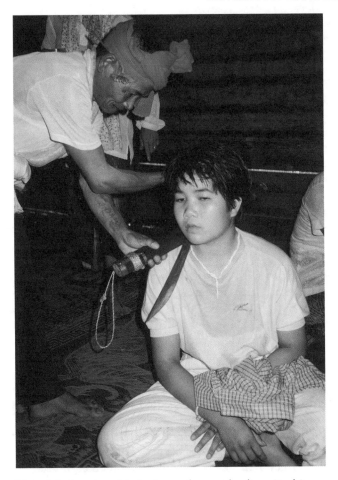

Plate 1.2 A male spirit doctor performs a healing ritual in Chiang Mai, Northern Thailand.

ranging from the ever-dominant Buddhism to spirit belief. Therefore, what I want to focus on in this chapter is spirit possession, a phenomenon widely disseminated in the contemporary life of the people in Northern Thailand.

This spirit possession is a technique to cope with affliction and illness, and with desires to attain well-being in this life, in contrast to many Buddhist rituals envisaging spiritual and material welfare in the next life. The professional spirit medium (*ma khi* or 'riding horse') has long served to respond to these needs in rural and urban settings in Northern Thailand. Some particular features associated with such spirit mediumship are part of a long-established tradition. Spirit possession as a cultural phenomenon among the Khon Müang varies from unpredictable violent possession by malevolent spirits, including a forest spirit (*phi pa*), a witch-spirit (*phi ka*) etc. to more routinised possession by tutelary spirits of professional spirit mediums. Whether violent or routinised, they are intrinsically embodied practices in which the host possessed by a spirit speaks in the manner and tone, and performs the role, of the spirit through bodily movements to communicate to the audience, clients, or witnesses who happen to be there. The practices also imply that the knowledge involved in spirit possession is fundamentally embodied; meanings are transmitted through speech and action in possession scenes; and, furthermore, the learning process involved in becoming a spirit medium, is accomplished also through the same means (cf. Lambek 1993). In short, I would say, the embodied knowledge is a fusion of action and knowing. The salient nature of this embodiment differentiates spirit possession from the more objectified knowledge in Buddhism, though its monastic disciplinary learning of chanting, meditation, etc. often involve similar processes.

Embodiment in spirit possession is related to the workings of powers of the external other, here represented as spirit. The spirit invades and occupies the body of a spirit medium; she abandons her self to be completely transformed into the spirit, or the external other, who is the source of authority in giving oracles and healing rites to the participants.[2] What should be noted here is that the spirit medium, often a woman, is transformed into a male tutelary spirit, who performs and expresses himself/herself through interactions with the clients and participants. In general terms, a spirit, often represented as an ambivalent power is, in ritual, transformed into a truly tutelary power to provide access to health and well-being for the people. It is in the medium's body itself that the transformation of external powers occurs. This indicates that the medium is able to internalise the external other within the subject (cf. Kramer 1993), having no solid boundaries around herself.

Let me, then, consider briefly a few points concerning a possible conceptualisation of the Khon Müang personhood that could be deduced from the spirit possession, though the people concerned are not always spirit mediums. This can be justified, because spirit possession is far from being an unusual phenomenon, reflecting as it does the most immediate and apprehensible manifestations of the imagined self in Khon Müang society. The Khon Müang personhood has no solid boundaries, since it accepts and internalises the external other (spirit) through embodied practices and knowledge, as opposed to the modern Euroamerican construction of the individuated person. This fusion of the other within the self is apparent in everyday situations as well, but is most profoundly observable in ritual sequences. Thus the person could be transformed through ritualised actions, from woman to man, or transvestite (*pu mia*), or even from prostitute to prince, or Buddhist monk, from human being to spirit. And in everyday situations, this transformation implies a potential for shifting relations from one to another without presupposing any overarching, totalising, wholly-encompassing entity like the nation-state. However, its very plasticity, and especially its embodied nature, make the Khon Müang person extremely susceptible to external powers, in the sense that Michel Foucault refers to the body as a target or focus of disciplinary practices in modern Europe (Foucault 1979). In Khon Müang society, therefore, the person is a locus where external powers work, sometimes destructively.

The growing nation-state and displacement

I have examined so far the particular nature of the Khon Müang construction of the person in cognitive and cultural terms. I shall here focus on some problems of how such personhood is individually experienced under the current globalised environment in Northern Thailand.

As a consequence of ongoing globalisation since the late 1980s, the Thai nation-state has undergone increasing linguistic uniformity, intensified mobility and migration of the people, greater changes than ever before in work discipline, flows of goods, dissemination of electronic devices, and intensification of consumption. Under these social and cultural processes, the nation-state has worked towards achieving far greater institutional and social control over the local populations than hitherto. It has redefined and strengthened many boundaries, not only of the state territory with neighbouring countries, but also of the internal spatial, social, and ethnic boundaries of the people, and their places of living and working. These processes involve constant patrolling and surveillance of the boundaries by the agencies of the nation-state. The earlier divisions of labour, of industries, and of centre-peripheral relations established since the 1950s, have been disrupted through industrialisation, combined with the globalised flows of capital and information, and strengthened by constantly evolving technologies. One of the most conspicuous features of such a process is discernible in the relationships between highland communities and lowland villages and cities, which have been fundamentally reorganised, creating new forms of inter-regional and even international labour migration. In Northern Thailand in particular, increased economic opportunity in major cities, huge constructions of tourist sites and locations, and expansion of agro-businesses and hi-tech/low-tech industrial firms, are prominent features in the reorganisations involved in these patterns of human migration.[3] Yet the intensified human movements always contain contradictory elements to the nation-state's homogenising projects, which are intended to fix ordered hierarchies and boundaries within the territory. This creates instability of the reorganised hierarchies

49

and boundaries, and causes a renewed tension between nationalising projects of the nation-state and re-localisation by the local subjects (Appadurai 1995: 213–216). It is this basis that provides the current conjunctural situation for the state-defined development, with its paranoiac obsessions with 'national security' and sovereignty, in opposition to the alternative NGOs and other movements concerned with environmental protection, life security, and social justice.

There is a general tendency as a result of which the local subjects are confronted by the state-defined development programmes that involve displacement of local populations, forced division of social boundaries, and so forth.[4] The people who migrate and settle down in cities, or who commute from their villages, are forced to adjust their practices to a new labour discipline and the rhythms of urban and industrial life, with which they had formerly been entirely unfamiliar. They have no control over, and little awareness of, the huge, distant and globalised institutions and mechanisms that determine most of their life circumstances.

Displacement involves a general sense of confusion experienced by a local subject who moves into a new environment, which can induce emotional disorders and psychosomatic disturbances. In modern Western settings, dislocation may be appropriated through adjusting ways of the 'presentation of self' to a variety of different encounters and contexts, as Erving Goffman plausibly formulates (Goffman 1959, 1971). However, displacement under the current rapid transformation undergone in Northern Thailand does not seem to allow the people to adopt such sensitive and skilful adjustments so easily. As opposed to the Goffman-esque modern settings, this is because embodied practices neatly constructed in the rural locality are strongly resistant to the strict control of labour process and time, and everyday interactions in working places and urban life circumstances, even though the Khon Müang personhood is potentially transformable. For the newcomers to Chiang Mai, the displacement often provokes feelings of anxiety, powerlessness and insecurity in everyday life, though they also normally recover their sense of ease with self, if not by Goffmanesque means, then through diverse kinds of cultural knowledge more readily available in cities.

At this point, it may be thought that this picture of such an anxious person in Chiang Mai is resonant with post-modernist sociological images of a human being represented as the frail and vulnerable creature seeking personal satisfaction through intimate, direct, and playful personal experiences (Bauman 1992), or even post-modernist anthropological perspectives of fragmentary or hybrid cultures (Hannerz 1990). Yet it is particularly important to note that what I am dealing with is the process of individual and cultural experiences affected by the nation-state reacting to globalised forces, not with the post-modernist perspective, which is itself a particular Euroamerican modern construction.

50

Anxiety is a generalised state of the emotions of the individual subject, as opposed to fear, a response to a specific threat (Laing 1965, Giddens 1991: 43). Nevertheless, it is culturally constructed and associated with practical ways of inference as to where it comes from. For the Khon Müang, anxiety, or *cai bò di* (*witok kangwon*) is concerned with insecurity and uncertainty, lending impetus to the unstable state of the mind-body relations. Anxiety is mainly generated by insecurity involved in making money, the political future, health, marriage, jobs, relations with bosses, and numerous aspects of the life circumstances in urban and industrial settings. It is always linked to 'chance', as Stephan Feuchtwang puts it, 'unforeseeable eventualities, including those already experienced' in the past (Feuchtwang 1989: 15).

Whether one gains a profit, enjoys good health, or gets a better job depends on fortune, even though one may think of alternative objective causal relations that bring about the outcome. A judgement made in terms of fortune or misfortune rather than relying on more objective calculation is particularly significant in coping with such insecurity and uncertainty. In Khon Müang society, interpretations and predictions of fortune or misfortune are anchored to certain kinds of cultural knowledge. In village contexts, Buddhist *karma* (*kam*), astrologically defined destiny (*chata*), misfortune (*khò*), violation of customary practices (*khüt*), and spirit beliefs among others are major sources of knowledge, through which inferences and interpretations are formulated. A variety of practitioners such as diviners (*mò müa*), spirit mediums, Buddhist monks, or ex-monks make divination and predictions based on these kinds of cultural knowledge. But for the newcomers in cities, all these local sources are not necessarily available. They then seek available technologies of stabilisation, though these may not be identical to those in the home localities, a point to which I shall return later.

While anxiety among the newcomers may be ameliorated through divination, it sometimes leads to more severe instabilities of mind-body relations and emotional disorders. Marjorie Muecke had already suggested in the mid-1970s that the 'wind illness (*rok lom*)', quite a common complaint mainly among adult women in Chiang Mai, has come increasingly to refer more generically to deterioration of body and morale that cannot be cured either by Western biomedicine or traditional healers (Muecke 1976: 292). She maintains that this wasting syndrome is associated with a malignant socio-economic pressure on the poor, and those who have lost hope in attempts at improving their life circumstances. Two decades later in Chiang Mai and surrounding areas, we more frequently come across people who have symptoms such as nightmares of dying, chronic headaches, lack of energy, etc., which eventually lead to social withdrawal and hyperviolent behaviour. What is called in psychiatric terms 'depressive syndrome' and 'anxiety' are increasingly prevalent among the newcomers in cities. But, as Muecke suggests, these symptoms are often manifested by more somaticised symptoms and physical complaints.

Thus, the consequences of the particular form of globalisation evident in the minutiae of social life in Northern Thailand are apparently experienced as a critical conjunction of capitalist development and the individual subjects, not only for the dominant Khon Müang but also for minority groups. The processes of modernity inscribed in the body and mind of the people expose them to greater risk potentials than ever experienced in their history. Nevertheless, there is no complete fragmentation and dissociation of the person. This is because if we look closely at the conjunction, it becomes clear that they are able to cope with it through a variety of possible ways of dialectical transformation. I will, therefore, examine in detail some such possibilities, focusing on the spirit mediumship currently being developed in the new environments.

Shifting contexts and the renewed techniques and practices

In urban settings, and also to a considerable degree in rural areas, traditional techniques of mind-body stabilisation are declining. The ancestor worship (*phi pu ña*) that has provided the locality-based security of the members of the Khon Müang matrilineal kin group has now become a minimal ritual practice (Irvine 1984). All such practices are increasingly inconsequential and losing their efficacy and reality in the life circumstances of the people. This is particularly so in matrilineal ancestor cults, village spirit cults, and *müang* guardian spirit cults, which represent territorial locality. The traditional representations of locality are currently being disrupted or modified, symbolically or organisationally, along with the advancement of reorganisation of spatial and social divisions by the nation-state. The human mobility and movements, expanded means of information flows, and increasing involvement in capitalist relations have made these locality-based techniques only a minor option, or even merely a nostalgic practice. The substantial separation from the matrifocality (*phi pu ña*) and the locality (*khwan, phi ban, phi müang*), however, doesn't mean that the techniques and the schematic constitution of the person are completely dissolved. Conversely, the growing alternatives, and modified or reconstructed techniques since the 1980s, prove that the stabilisation becomes more individually pursued and more directly embodied, reflecting detachment or semi-detachment from locality in the de-territorialised landscape.

Thus, a diversity of stabilising practices are developed in response to individually differentiated experiences of the people in cities, ranging from new Buddhist practices of (male and female) meditation and 'Protestant' asceticism, worship of Buddhist saints and amulets, and Bangkok style

Plate 1.3 Possession dance in a matrilineal kin group (*phi meng*) in Lampang, Northern Thailand.

astrological divination, to various kinds of spirit mediumship. Relevant to these practices is a certain distinction of tastes according to class differentiation. While, on the one hand, middle-class people are keen on cultivating a distinctive self or pursuing tranquillity and concentration through more discursive practices like meditation, the poor newcomers, on the other, are more attracted by cheaper divination and spirit cults which offer more entertaining and embodied experiences. All these practices are based on stabilising techniques, but an emphasis is increasingly laid on material prosperity and life security rather than the conventional idiom focused on bodily safety within the territorial, and social, space in village settings. This shift from locality-based security to more individually oriented prosperity and security is also consonant with the general tendency of a decline of male-power magic in favour of more Buddhist forms of ensuring security. Thus, while tattooing and other art and magic forms conferring invulnerability have become unpopular, worship of Buddhist saints (*arahant*) and their consecrated medals has become increasingly popular (cf. Tambiah 1984). It is also detectable that the worship of saints and their amulets, with its emphasis on physical and on military security, that was attached to such saints as Luang Pu Waen and others mainly derived from the Ajarn Man's tradition, are now passing away, with more explicit worship of individual prosperity, currently represented by Luang Phò Khun, becoming a more fashionable substitute.[5]

It is precisely this increasing popular concern with individual prosperity and security that has given rise to the professional spirit mediumship in the cities and neighbouring areas in Northern Thailand. Such spirit mediumship in its present form has developed since the 1960s, concomitant with the decline of locality-based technologies of stabilisation, and has become particularly prominent since the early 1980s, at least in Chiang Mai.[6] Even before this period, though, it had long been one of the major techniques concerned with divination and healing in the Khon Müang village settings. However, the current popularity of spirit mediumship cannot be solely attributable to the social conditions that determine the decline of other techniques. It would be, therefore, pertinent to look at how the spirit mediumship has taken its present form, along with the accompanying transformation of its own knowledge and techniques.

Reconstructed spirit mediumship

One of the most striking features of the Khon Müang spirit mediumship is that it is associated with the most susceptible and vulnerable form of the personhood, as I have described above. This spirit mediumship is firmly based on the socially defined idea that the Khon Müang women have a weak *khwan*, as opposed to men, who have a strong one, while the strongest may be that of a spirit doctor (*mò lai phi*). Thus, being a spirit medium means that she who has a devalued weak *khwan* becomes one who has the power and authority to provide divination and healing. The spirit mediumship thus shows a dialectical process, in which the plasticity and vulnerability of the Khon Müang woman is transformed into a source of power and authority. Even before the 1970–80s, this dialectical transformation was a general condition underlying spirit mediumship during the sporadic emergence of semi-professional mediums in village settings.

But it is still more conspicuously detectable nowadays in the transformation into mediumship, particularly in the newly developed professional cults in Chiang Mai and neighbouring areas. Those who eventually become mediums have almost invariably experienced psychosomatic disturbances, chronic afflictions, or some type of severe illness or accident. After prolonged disturbances and afflictions, a patient visits a spirit medium and is told that a tutelary spirit wants to possess her body. The spirit medium first identifies that spirit, and then has repeated sessions involving interactions with the patient, before she/he becomes able to become possessed voluntarily by the spirit. Having completed a series of rituals associated with the medium, she/he becomes a new medium who is able to form a new cult to provide services to the public. It is in the course of this long dialectical process that a new spirit medium is reproduced through the transformation from patient to healer, which eventually opens up new professional economic opportunities (Irvine 1984, Wijeyewardene 1986, Tanabe 1995).

Another salient feature characterising the newly developed spirit mediumship is its increasing adoption of magical knowledge that previously was almost always monopolised by male practitioners, like spirit doctors or even Buddhist monks, and ex-monks. In addition to the divinatory oracles that are given as a speech by the possessed tutelary spirit, mediums have acquired various magical spells (*khatha*), ranging from Buddhist ones (*khatha yen*, or cool magic) to more powerful and dangerous ones (*khatha hòn*, or hot magic), to be utilised for healing, bodily security, and sorcery. What is still more significant in connection with the male magical knowledge is the way in which a medium acquires and transmits her sources of power. The divinatory and curing power of the medium is derived from the *khu*, or *phi khu* (literally, teacher or teacher's spirit) to be worshipped by her. The *khu* is not identical with the tutelary spirit itself that possesses the medium, but is an authoritative power that makes her possession effective, and derives from the spirit of the teacher who made her a medium. The genealogy of teachers is therefore important, and spirit mediums hold a ritual, every few years, to propitiate the teacher's spirit (*yoeng khu*, or *yok khu*), inviting fellow mediums who thus form a lineage of the same original teacher's spirit. This indicates that the spirit mediumship is organised along the genealogy of the teacher's spirit, hence networks of mediums have come into being extending over a huge area. It is important to note that this kind of transmission of knowledge centred on a teacher's spirit has long been a characteristic form among male magical practitioners, both artisans and artists, such as a spirit doctor, tattooer, blacksmith, singer, musician, and so on. Thus, the recent development of professional spirit mediumship is achieved not only through adoption of male magical knowledge itself, but, moreover, through appropriation of the means of its transmission, including the associated organising principles.

In addition to the appropriation of male magical disciplines, spirit mediumship has recently been increasingly involved in Buddhist practices, as I have described elsewhere (Tanabe 1995). The emphasis laid on Buddhist morality and practices is particularly prominent among mediums in the city, and this has contributed to its rapid expansion since the 1980s. Thus, it should be noted that the present form of spirit mediumship is not a mere continuation from that of the past before the consolidation of the recent Thai nation-state's projects, but a result of the multiple processes of reconstruction, involving the female re-appropriation of the power hitherto placed under the strongly naturalised male domination of cultural capital. Conventional services of divination, healing, etc., are in the repertory of any spirit medium cults as in the past, but these techniques have become increasingly associated with a variety of fragmented sources of knowledge the spirit medium has thus historically customised.

The fragments of knowledge, like astrology, tattoos, magical spells, herbal medicine, Buddhist morality, and above all the power of the tutelary spirit, are all combined to form a new amalgam of divinatory and healing practices deployed by a spirit medium. There is a mosaic of multiple sources of knowledge from which the medium is able to quite flexibly respond to the diverse desires and demands of the clients and patients. The nature of this multiply based knowledge enables the spirit medium to attract differentiated classes of people, from poor newcomers to middle-class people, in the milieu of rapid industrialisation, particularly in urban settings.

In fact, mediums now provide a quite wide range of services, in addition to the old-established ones such as divination and healing. Findings during my survey in the city of Chiang Mai in 1985–86 show that the most popular services include, first of all, business consultancy (*prüksa tang thurakit*), followed by an attempt to avoid military service (*bò pen thahan*), love magic (*ñia sanae*), exorcism (*lai phi*), searching for lost property (*ha khòng hai*), and removing sorcery (*haksa tu*) (Tanabe 1995). Here, under the item 'business consultancy', I include most cases of consultancy about interpersonal problems occurring in the work place, as well as divinatory suggestions concerning better jobs, business transactions, and the chance of obtaining money and property, and so on. It is also interesting to note that, particularly from the late 1980s, the divination of winning numbers for the lottery draw (*bai huai*) has gained increasingly in popularity as an extra service given by mediums. Most mediums provide these services not only to well-to-do clients and business persons but also to labourers working in service industries or factories, and lower-middle-class people, such as pedlars, retail shopkeepers, mini-bus drivers, teachers, farmers selling land, and the like. However, there is a differentiation between well-to-do mediums with rich clients, who expect to pay a large reward only after their wish has been realised, and poor mediums who earn money only from the less well-rewarded services of curing and divination. Therefore, a certain distinction between rich cults and poor ones is detectable in terms of the economic status of the clients. But it should be noted that among the mediums themselves, techniques and the associated morality are less distinctive, even to the extent that they determine and naturalise the differentiated tastes between these class divergences.

Mimetic representation

While the current spirit mediumship is reconstructed through the appropriation of male-oriented knowledge and the novel adoption of different practices, it shows another particular feature in its representation of power. As I have argued before, the Khon Müang personhood is fundamentally construed as besieged by ever-threatening external powers, and this state is ritually internalised and transformed in spirit possession. The tutelary spirit possessing a spirit medium is almost invariably a powerful male deity, often derived from the past mysterious power-holders featured in Khon Müang mythologies and folktales. This was particularly the case in village settings before the 1970s. Cao Luang Kham Daeng, Cao Khò Mü Lek, and Cao Khun Sük, etc., have been quite familiar as guardian spirits of village or *müang* domains, and many mediums are reputed to be possessed by such spirits in the Chiang Mai area.

Yet this traditional pantheon of tutelary spirits has been gradually undermined by Bangkok-based deities since around the 1970s; these include Hindu gods like Siva, Narai, Phra Phrom (Cao Phò Erawan), but also historical figures from Bangkok such as King Naresvan, King Chulalongkorn, Krom Luang Cumphòn Khet Udomsak, or even King Mangrai, as a recently revived administrative symbol of Northern Thailand constructed by the nation-state. Princess Camadevi (Camthewi), a controversial figure in Northern Thailand's history, also possesses some mediums, and interestingly Buddhist nuns as well. However, the theatres of memory of spirit mediums are not necessarily confined to the figures linked to mythology and the nation-state, but more importantly also involve alien and peripheral representations. Reflecting diverse social experiences and globalised relations, these include spirits of hill-dwelling minority groups such as the Yao and Lisu, spirits of Kwan-im (Guan-yin) of Chinese Buddhism, spirits of Chinese Kungfu masters of Hong Kong films, and Saudi Arabian deities, etc. (Shalardchai 1984, Anan and Shalardchai 1987). Thus, the recent explosive proliferation of spirit mediumship generates a diversification of new representations between the dominating powerful figures derived from the metropolis and the nation-state, on the one hand, and more alien and re-localised powers rather detached from the nation-state, on the other.

The tutelary spirits are in the vast majority of cases those of powerful male figures, whether derived from local mythology, metropolitan and nationalist discourses, or alien and deviating sources. And this indicates that the Khon Müang spirit possession is not only a state of possession by external powers, but is also intrinsically associated with the acquisition and utilisation of these powers. A spirit medium is able to gain power through the embodied transformation, which enables her to provide divination, healing, and other oracular statements to the clients. What underlies this process is that the medium appropriates power by identifying herself with, or more precisely, copying or imitating, the external other, whether authoritative mythical figures, nationalist heroes, strangers, or, more fundamentally, dominant male powers. The embodied transformation grounded in the ever-threatened equilibrium is in turn directed towards power. According to Walter Benjamin, the mimetic faculty that organises human perception and expression through seeing resemblances, discovering and creating similarities, as in dance and spoken language, have historically transformed into the 'nonsensuous similarity' contained in language, which requires careful reading and decoding (Benjamin 1978: 334).[7] However, in spirit possession, the mimetic sensuous experience is fully activated to incorporate the power of the external other that generates the differentiating identity of the medium herself (cf. Kramer 1993, Boddy 1994; Stoller 1996).

The representation of powers through imitating the other is not a recent invention, but 'a rudiment of the powerful compulsion' (Benjamin 1978: 333) underlying the Khon Müang spirit possession in general. Many of the ancestor spirit cults of matrilineal kin groups, for instance, have copied sources of power from other cultural and ethnic groups that they have come into contact with. Groups sharing a particular type of ancestor spirits called *phi mot* hold periodically a collective possession dance; the *phi mot* themselves are supposed to be derived from the spirits of other cultural groups, if yet unidentified, in the Shan States of Burma or in Laos. Other groups holding *phi meng*, or the spirit of the Mon, have taken it from the Buddhist Mon in Burma; and similarly *phi lua*, is from the Lawa, the most immediate neighbours in Northern Thailand. Mimesis is in modern Western aesthetics devalued in favour of discrete creativity. But, in the Khon Müang aesthetics, mimesis is one of the most fundamental forms of representation of the other, and even a means of appropriating power from the external other. In the gender contexts, the devalued female gender re-empowers itself by means of mimesis of powerful male political figures, or the monkhood, which are acted out in most spirit possession scenes both in professional spirit mediumship and ancestor spirit cults (Tanabe 1991). It is this mimetic process that enables the medium to become, if only temporarily, an authoritative actor addressing the clients morality, through judgements of good and evil, which legitimate her oracular statements about the cause of affliction – or the winning number in the lottery – as the case may be.

On the other hand, if we put it in a social context, the mimetic representation of powers by the current spirit mediumship involves considerable ambiguity towards the existing power relations. A tutelary spirit is a representation of power, but it does not necessarily coincide with the present hegemony, along with its associated discourses. As the nation-state reproduces and disseminates selective powerful symbols through the media, education and ritual, for its continuation of paranoiac sovereignty, many spirit mediums accept them apparently at face value as their own representation of power. However, when these powerful symbols are acted out in the possession scenes, they are often done so in a playful, parodical and reshaped manner rather than being identical to what the hegemonic discourses intend to reproduce. King Chulalongkorn, Prince Mangrai, or any other powerful male figure may be represented by a medium, but the mimetic actions always produce endless proliferation of differences, which even exhibit a parody and distortion of the disseminated images. Walter Irvine describes the nationalist features of many spirit mediums in Chiang Mai in the late 1970s and early 1980s (Irvine 1982). This may be true because they responded sensitively to the conjunctural situations where anti-communist forces overwhelmingly dominated the society during that period. However, it would be rather plausible to assume that such external ideologies, nationalist or otherwise, can be easily incorporated and naturalised through the very nature of embodiment of spirit mediumship (cf. Lambek 1995: 276). Nonetheless, the mimetic representation of the medium is more likely to show political ambiguity through the repeated differentiation from the hegemonic image production, also reflecting the mediums' localised contexts and morality.

To the contrary, ambiguity is also discernible in cases where subversive elements are involved in spirit mediumship. A recent anthropological study of violent possession trance depicts overt resistance against capitalist work discipline and its violation of embodied gender distinction by female workers in a Malaysian multinational factory (Ong 1987). However, in Chiang Mai, such cultural resistance associated with spirit possession or mediumship is, instead, more implicit, also being minutely focused on more localised contexts. Thus, the medium's representation of power sometimes involves alternative moral voices and corporeal critiques of hierarchies of gender, and national or global forces threatening local security and resources. During the interlude of curing and divinatory sessions, some mediums speak of the degradation of male human beings, of environmental concerns, presumably caused by the recent establishment of a multinational industrial estate, and of parodical pictures of corrupted politicians and monks. All these critical utterances are embodied in nature, and articulated with the medium's past affliction and personal and social trauma. I would, then, argue that the ambiguous position of spirit mediumship in Chiang Mai is derived from its embodied and mimetic will to power; on the one hand, the body itself easily incorporates external existing powers, but, on the other hand, it is also linked to cultural resistance in the form of moral critiques generated from their localised episodic and more socialised memory.[8]

Permeable interaction

The activity of spirit mediumship is carried out in an imagined space and time, in which the medium's will to power and her morality are played out through actions and interactions among the participants involved. One of the salient features of the spirit possession cults is its theatrical character, which distinguishes it from many other more institutionalised rituals in the

Khon Müang society. It is a theatre of interactions rather than merely a theatre of symbols. It creates contingency, anticipation, and astonishment, arousing strong emotional, aesthetic and psychic effects in the people, alongside more stereotyped feeling involved in routinised and liturgical practices. The theatrical performance of the cult allows the participants to experience embodied interactions with the medium, or the possessing tutelary spirit. Any session of a cult always starts with the transformation of the medium into the tutelary spirit; after a few moments of agonies and dissociation on the part of the medium, the spirit begins to manifest itself through her body. Thereafter, the embodied spirit talks to the client, and divination, curing, or whatever, services are given according to his/her request. Most sessions consist of a series of neatly woven interactions between the medium and the client. Characteristic of these sessions are dialogical relations, in which, together with incoherent and chaotic utterances, gossip, jokes, parodical critiques of the gender relations, and the local and national politics, are frequently dominant. As I have earlier referred to, moral contentions and guidance to the client are often incorporated in these interactive processes, and, in recent years, a particular emphasis has been laid on the Buddhist moral precepts.

The embodied interactions in spirit mediumship are most conspicuously depicted in a condensed form in the process by which a new spirit medium is identified. To a visiting client or 'patient' who complains of sufferings and afflictions, the medium may declare that a particular spirit wants to possess the patient's body. A series of curing sessions are subsequently held with face to face interactions between the possessed medium and the patient. During this period, the patient may often experience mental and somatic disturbances, and frequently an acute violent possession. The medium persistently asks the patient which spirit is going to possess her/him, and eventually she identifies the spirit, which may be an ancestor spirit of the matrilineal kin, a village spirit, or, more likely, even a spirit with a name invented by the medium. Then, the medium insists that it should be subordinate to her own spirit. And the patient begins to respond to her spirit with relief. After such dialogical interactions, the patient begins to have a feeling of reality about a steadily possessed state in the body. The repeated interactions, then, lead to a controlled state of possession, while shedding violent possession states and chronic disturbances. A new spirit medium is thus 'born', or, in other words, transformation is accomplished of 'patient' into 'healer'. This transformation is marked by performing a ritual of conferring the teacher's tray (*khan khu*) to the new medium. During the ritual of receiving the teacher's tray (*hap khan khu*), the medium confers a tray on the new disciple, who thus pays homage to the teacher's own tutelary spirit. Through this ritual the medium establishes a master-disciple relationship with the new-born medium, who is thereafter called 'disciple' (*luk sit*).

Plate 1.4 Ritual of conferring the teacher's tray on the newly fledged medium in Chiang Mai, Northern Thailand.

Even in routinised sessions of divination and curing for clients who complain of less severe afflictions and pain, dialogical interactions are also predominant. The boundaries between the medium and the client or other participants are blurred in a direct communion, where the spirit manifests itself in an embodied form. The spirit is acted out through the medium's bodily movement and speech, to which the client is able to respond directly. These permeable and embodied interactions enable the client and participants to have new experiences of relief and liberation, which are becoming rather difficult to attain, particularly in urban and industrial settings. Among the matrilineal kin groups called *phi mot* and *phi meng*, the permeable interactions are concentrated periodically in the occasions of a collective possession dance dedicated to the ancestor spirits. However, in this case, the legitimisation of healing and relief is delimited within the boundaries of the kin group. On the contrary, the cults of spirit mediums provide relief through permeable interactions to anyone who visits the medium as a client, including middle-class businessmen, labourers and newcomers from the countryside. In both cases, the technology of stabilisation utilises permeating interactions that allow the people to negotiate with the external other to find ways of controlling their decisions, achieving emotional stabilisation, and acting out a fantasy to gain a new status and situation. In short, the current spirit mediumship, together with the collective spirit possession in more territorialised settings, renders to the people the governance of their self, in which they deal with their fortune, misfortune and fantasy through permeable interactions with the imagined other.[9]

It would be pertinent here to note how such a form of permeable and embodied interactions relates to what has been sociologically formulated as 'charismatic communion'. In the sociological tradition, such permeable interactions, as exemplified in spirit possession and other similar situations, are often explained as stemming from charismatic desire for loss of self, or for dissolution of self and other, as exemplified in the social psychology of the crowd, Fascism, or, in more 'postmodern' conditions, narcissism and consumerism (cf. Lindholm 1990). It would be obvious that the notion of charismatic communion is rather negatively constructed as opposed to the Euroamerican conception, or rather obsession, with the individuated person. The sociological theory as such eventually fails to account for the permeable interactions so prevalent in Khon Müang society, and elsewhere in South East Asia. This is because its very presumption of the delimited, individuated person is never formulated as relative to other possible forms of personhood. The embodied and permeable relations of the Khon Müang personhood are not restricted to spirit possession, but are also widely extended to everyday situations, including face-to-face interactions. For the Khon Müang, spirit possession is not an abnormal phenomenon, but a legitimate and possible state of mind-body relations derived from their basic schematic construction. What they experience in possession scenes is, therefore, not a loss of self, but a process through which the self and the other enter repeated negotiations and interactions to deal with afflictions, and to fulfil desires. The interactions between the medium and the participants are the locus where the permeable relations are cohesively experienced.

Conclusions

The persistence of the practices of spirit possession and its current version of spirit mediumship shows that they are a societal reproduction of the Khon Müang personhood. A variety of Khon Müang practices of divination, healing, and expulsion of bad spirits are techniques of dealing with the unstable equilibrium of mind-body relations. The spirit mediumship that has recently proliferated explosively in Northern Thailand is a continuation and development of these embodied ideas and practices. As I have argued earlier, however, the way in which the present form of spirit mediumship has arisen is not a simple continuation, but a complicated process of appropriation of diverse knowledge and practices hitherto almost invariably monopolised by male practitioners. In this sense, spirit mediumship can be seen as a process of societal reproduction in which the dominated try to articulate diverse and heterogeneous sources of knowledge, as in what Gramsci formulated as 'a series of negotiation' with the dominant discourse (Gramsci 1971: 273; cf. O'Hanlon 1988).

On the one hand, Khon Müang spirit mediumship responds flexibly to the insecurity and anxiety caused by recent capitalist transformation and the territorial rearrangements of the nation-state in the globalised milieu. It provides a quite wide range of services, such as divination, healing, and business transactions, and so on, for both middle-class and lower-class people. But more significantly, it renders relief and remedy to those who are suffering from emotional disorders and psychosomatic disturbances, which are implicated in the displacements experienced by a number of newcomers in urban and industrial settings. This therapeutic capacity of the spirit mediumship phenomenon attracts many newcomers, and also secures its own reproduction through recruitment of new mediums.

On the other hand, for the urban populace, including newcomers, spirit mediumship is seen as an object of modern consumption, completely different from those available in village settings, where stereotyped divination and healing focusing on kinship and other types of legitimate territoriality have been dominant. It can provide services in terms of their individual and diverse desires and afflictions, through which they try to cope with their completely changed life circumstances.[10] It is consumption of this multifaceted technology of stabilisation that enables, in part, newcomers to appropriate their displaced conditions and contexts and to recover stability of mind-body relations. Yet, as in many cases of modern consumption, appropriation through spirit mediumship involves contradictory aspirations. On the one hand, there is a strong individual desire for material prosperity and the fantasy of gaining new status and fortune. But, at the same time, they are induced to submit to subordination to the power represented by the tutelary spirit, embodied by the medium, which is clearly indicated in ritual actions within the cult organisation. Displacement is fundamentally a modern experience, which allows coexistence of contradictory values and aspirations, and, in this case, they share qualities both of emancipation and subordination (cf. Miller 1995: 288).

Finally, I would consider the way in which the embodied knowledge of Khon Müang spirit mediumship relates to other types of discourse. Permeable interaction involves aesthetic and moral contents, and enables negotiation with the other. It also blurs boundaries and creates intimate interdependency between the medium and participants, as radically opposed to more objectified, semantic-oriented discourses, which are shared in part with the Buddhist tradition, and are also particularly dominant in modern education, bureaucracy, and the administration of the nation-state. It is this embodied interaction that gives rise to the recent popularity of spirit mediumship in response to anxiety and insecurity among the newcomers and lower-class peoples. The permeability and embodiment is a way of knowing, of negotiation, and of appropriation, that leads to differentiation from dominant discourses and the possibility of contesting fields of power relations. It is on this practical ground that cultural appropriation of the mediums and displaced newcomers becomes possible, through continuing negotiation with the other and the dominant in the current transformation. As I have mentioned earlier, I would, however, emphasise again that the permeable interaction is accompanied by vulnerability to more politically active external power, because it can be easily accepted and naturalised by the very nature of the plastic and transformable body. This chapter is only an attempt to identify the way in which the people achieve cultural appropriation in the current transformation through their embodied knowledge, that is anchored on the Khon Müang personhood. How the embodied knowledge is utilised or articulated in the power relations within the contested fields of globalised environments, however, needs further consideration.

Acknowledgement

The original version of this chapter was delivered as a conference lecture at the Sixth International Conference on Thai Studies at Chiang Mai, October 1996. My gratitude goes to Rujaya Abhakorn, the Conference Secretariat, Chayan Vaddhanaphuti, the Academic Committee Chairperson, and Chatthip Nartsupha, the Theme Co-ordinator, who enabled me to participate in the conference and to think over the many issues discussed in the original paper. I am extremely grateful to Alfred Gell, Esther Goody, Charles Keyes, Marjorie Muecke, Verena Stolcke, Marilyn Strathern, and Geoffrey Walton who gave criticism on earlier draft versions.

Notes

1 Recent anthropological studies try to reformulate conceptions of person and society. For instance, Strathern speaks of the Melanesian construction in which the person is a pivot of changing configurations of social relationships, without any assumption of an overarching greater unity (Strathern 1992).
2 The process of such transformation of powers occurs not only at a symbolic level, as often argued by anthropologists, but more importantly it is grounded in the cognitive and even neurological conditions. Certain ritualised actions, such as maintenance of rigid postures and gazing at a fixed point, lead to voluntary destruction of the sense of equilibrium, which eventually induces the medium to possession-trance (Gell 1980; Tanabe 2000).
3 Let me give a brief illustration of the process. The agricultural population in the six districts immediately surrounding the city of Chiang Mai is now only 33 per cent of the total; 51 per cent of the populace is working in Chiang Mai and beyond, mainly on construction sites and in service industries, etc. (Dom 1994); some to the south are employed in high-tech/low-tech industrial firms at the Northern Industrial Estate, Lamphun and nearby; service industries, especially restaurant, hotels, and brothels in the city and major district towns are

now full of girls from the hills and neighbouring countries; and in the Night Bazaar, the biggest commercial concentration in Chiang Mai, the majority of the working population are those from the hills, and they speak a strange mixture of Kham Müang and Siamese.

4 Displacement associated with the globalised economy is linked to a new formulation of centre-periphery relationship, which eventually brings about the destruction of development among hill dwellers around the borderlands of Northern Thailand (Tapp 1991).

5 One of such Buddhist saints recently widely accepted in Northern Thailand is Luang Phò Khun, who is the abbot at Wat Ban Rai in the North East. The current flourishing worship of Luang Phò Khun, and dissemination of his amulet medals and associated goods, are obviously linked to concerns with individual success, prosperity and security (cf. Anurat et al 1996). While the growth of the Rama V cult represents a fantasy envisaging modernity among the urban middle-class people, the worship of Luang Phò Khun portrays security derived from an imagined locality. As to the cult of Rama V, see Nithi 1993.

6 While Irvine, who carried out the survey in the late 1970s, counts 250–300 mediums in the city area of Chiang Mai (Irvine 1984: 315), I estimate about 500 within the urban area in 1986, or 0.25 per cent of the total population of about 200,000 (Tanabe 1995).

7 Spirit possession is a direct, sensuous experience, as opposed to astrology, which relies on non-sensuous reading of already lost correspondences (Benjamin 1978).

8 A different possibility of cultural resistance is illustrated by Cohen when he speaks of the subversive appropriation of elite discourses in his analysis of political rhetoric used in the speeches of a peasant leader in Northern Thailand (Cohen 1987).

9 The displacement engenders new types of cultural consumption of technologies of dealing with chance. Feuchtwang sees recent growth of divination practices among Chinese in southern China as a way of dealing with chance by tradition, hence depending on traditional authority (Feuchtwang 1989: 22; cf. Feuchtwang 1993). Although this may be true in part, his emphasis on the persistence of a hegemonic discourse tends to ignore the possibilities of 'creativity' among both diviners and participants. In fact, the Khon Müang divination in general, and specifically that of spirit mediumship, shows rather opposite traits, if we look at the interactions rather than merely the symbolic representations involved. It can be said, then, that in Khon Müang divination is a way of dealing with chance through permeating and negotiating interactions, whether the outcomes may or may not be accepted.

10 The increasing importance of consumption in everyday life, not only in urban and industrial settings but also in the countryside, indicates that it is becoming embedded in the Khon Müang cultural forms, as in many parts of the world.

References

Anan Ganjanapan and Shalardchai Ramitanondh 1987 'Khrongkan süksa phithikam lae khwam chüa lanna' (Research project on Lanna rituals and beliefs), unpublished project report, Faculty of Social Sciences, Chiang Mai University.

Anuman Rajadhon, Phya 1986 (1953) 'The *phi*', p.99–126 in Phya Anuman Rajadhon, *Popular Buddhism in Siam and Other Essays on Thai Studies*, Bangkok: Thai Inter-Religious Commission for Development.

Anurat Watthanawongsawang et al 1996 'Wan ni na wat ban rai' (Today at Wat Ban Rai), p.85–115 in *Sinlapa watthanatham* (Arts and Culture) 17(6).

Appadurai, Arjun 1995 'The production of locality', p.204–225 in R. Fardon (ed.), *Counterworks: managing the diversity of knowledge*, London: Routledge.

Bauman, Zygmunt 1992 *Intimations of Postmodernity*, London: Routledge.

Benjamin, Walter 1978 'Notes on mimetic faculty', in p. 333–336 *Reflections: essays, aphorisms, autobiographical writings* (translated by E. Jephcott), New York: Harcourt Brace Jovanovich.

Boddy, Janice P. 1994 'Spirit possession revisited: beyond instrumentality', p.407–434 in *Annual Review of Anthropology* 23.

Brummelhuis, Han ten 1984 'Abundance and avoidance: an interpretation of Thai individualism', p.39–54 in Han ten Brummelhuis and J.H. Kemp (eds.) *Strategies and Structures in Thai Society*, Amsterdam: Universiteit van Amsterdam, Anthropologisch-Sociologisch Centrum.

Chatthip Nartsupha 1991 'The "community culture" school of thought', p.118–141 in Manas Chitakasem and A. Turton (eds.) *Thai Constructions of Knowledge*, London: School of Oriental and African Studies.

Cohen, Paul 1987 'From moral regeneration to confrontation: two paths to equality in the political rhetoric of a Northern Thai peasant leader', p.153–167 in *Mankind* 17(2).

Comaroff, Jean 1994 'Defying disenchantment', p.301–314 in C. F. Keyes, L. Kendall and H. Hardacre (eds.) *Asian Visions of Authority*, Honolulu: University of Hawaii Press.

Dom Sridao 1994 'Value of land used in agriculture in areas around Chiang Mai town: analysis of selling price', MA thesis (in Thai), Chiang Mai University.

Feuchtwang, Stephan 1989 'Chance and tradition: social and ethical formation in popular Chinese temple rituals', p.4–23 in *Hong Kong Anthropology Bulletin* 3(June).

—— 1993 'Historical metaphor: a study of religious representation and recognition of authority', p.35–49 in *Man* (N.S.) 28.

Foucault, Michel 1979 (1975) *Discipline and Punish: the birth of the prison* (translated by Alan Sheridan), Harmondsworth: Penguin.

Gell, Alfred 1980 'The gods at play: vertigo and possession in Muria religion', p.219–248 in *Man* (N.S.) 15.

Giddens, Anthony 1991 *Modernity and Self-identity*, Cambridge: Polity Press.

Goffman, Erving 1959 *The Presentation of Self in Everyday Life*, Harmondsworth: Penguin.

—— 1971 *Relations in Public: microstudies of the public order*, New York: Harper Torchbooks.

Gramsci, Antonio 1971 *Selections from the Prison Notebooks* (edited and translated by Q. Hoare and G.N. Smith), London: Lawrence and Wishart.

Hannerz, Ulf 1990 'Cosmopolitans and locals in world culture', p.211–225 in *Theory, Culture & Society* 7.

Irvine, Walter 1982 'The Thai-Yuan "madman", and the "modernising, developing" Thai nation, as bounded entities under threat', PhD thesis, University of London.

—— 1984 'Decline of village spirit cults and growth of urban spirit mediumship', p.325–334 in *Mankind* 14(4).

Kramer, Fritz 1993 *The Red Fez: art and spirit possession in Africa* (translated by M.R. Green), London: Verso.

Laing, Ronald D. 1965 *The Divided Self*, Harmondsworth: Penguin.

Lambek, Michael 1993 *Knowledge and Practice in Mayotte: local discourses of Islam, sorcery, and spirit possession*, Toronto: University of Toronto Press.

—— 1995 'Choking on the Quran and other consuming parables from the Western Indian Ocean front', p.258–281 in W. James (ed.) *The Pursuit of Certainty: religious and cultural formulations*, London: Routledge.

Lindholm, Charles 1990 *Charisma*, Oxford: Blackwell.

Miller, Daniel 1995 'Consumption studies as the transformation of anthropology', p.264–295 in D. Miller (ed.) *Acknowledging Consumption: a review of new studies*, London: Routledge.

Muecke, Marjorie 1979 'An explication of "wind illness" in Northern Thailand', p.267–300 in *Culture, Medicine and Psychiatry* 3.

Nithi Iawsriwongse 1993 'Latthiphithi sadet phò rò ha' (The cult of the ascending of Rama V), p.76–98 in *Sinlapa watthanatham* (Arts and Culture) 14(10).

O'Hanlon, Rosalind 1988 'Recovering the subject: subaltern studies and histories of resistance in colonial South Asia', p.189–224 in *Modern Asian Studies* 22.

Phillips, Herbert P. 1965 *Thai Peasant Personality: the patterning of interpersonal behavior in the village of Bang Chan*, Berkeley and Los Angeles: University of California Press.

Sanguan Chotisukharat 1969 *Prapheni thai phak nüa* (Northern Thai Customs), Bangkok: Odeon Store.

Shalardchai Ramitanondh 1984 *Phi cao nai* (Spirits of the Lords and Masters), Chiang Mai: Sun Nangsü Chiang Mai.

Stoller, Paul 1996 *Embodying Colonial Memories: spirit possession, power, and the Hauka in West Africa*, London: Routledge.

Strathern, Marilyn 1992 'Parts and wholes: refiguring relationships in a post-plural world', p.75–104 in A. Kuper (ed.) *Conceptualising Society*, London: Routledge.

Ong, Aihwa 1987 *Spirits of Resistance and Capitalist Discipline*, Albany, NY: State University of New York Press.

Tambiah, Stanley J. 1984 *The Buddhist Saints of the Forest and the Cults of Amulets*, Cambridge: Cambridge University Press.

Tanabe, Shigeharu 1991 'Spirits, power and discourse of female gender: the *phi meng* cult of Northern Thailand', p.183–212 in Manas Chitakasem and A. Turton (eds.) *Thai Constructions of Knowledge*, London: School of Oriental and African Studies.

—— 1995 'The person and capitalist transformation: reconstruction of spirit cults in Northern Thailand', unpublished paper presented at the Department of Social Anthropology, University of Cambridge.

—— 2000 'Memories displaced by ritual: cognitive processes in the spirit cults of Northern Thailand', p.707–726 in *Bulletin of the National Museum of Ethnology* 24(4).

Tannenbaum, Nicola 1987 'Tattoos: invulnerability and power in Shan cosmology', p.693–711 in *American Ethnologist* 14.

Tapp, Nicholas 1990 'Squatters or refugees: development and the Hmong', p. 149–172 in G. Wijeyewardene (ed.) *Ethnic Groups across National Boundaries in Mainland Southeast Asia*, Singapore: Institute of Southeast Asian Studies.

Thongchai Winichakul 1995 'The changing landscape of the past: new histories in Thailand since 1973', p.99–120 in *Journal of Southeast Asian Studies* 26(1).

Turton, Andrew 1991 'Invulnerability and local knowledge', p.155–182 in Manas Chitakasem and A. Turton (eds.) *Thai Constructions of Knowledge*, London: School of Oriental and African Studies.

Wijeyewardene, Gehan 1986 *Place and Emotion in Northern Thai Ritual Behaviour*, Bangkok: Pandora.

■ CHAPTER TWO ■

Crises of the Modern in Northern Thailand

Ritual, Tradition, and the New Value of Pastness

Rosalind C. Morris

Genealogies of tradition: plurality and the longing for origins

During the last three decades, Northern Thailand has seen an efflorescence of publication (in English and Thai) on Northern or 'Lanna' Thai custom and cultural history in both the academic and popular presses (e.g. Sommai and Doré 1991; Mani 1986a and 1986b; Sanguan 1969, 1971a and 1971b).[1] Much of this literature has taken the form and ethos of salvage ethnography, and has been imbued with a deep sense of cultural crisis. Among recent publications, Sommai Premchit's and Pierre Doré's (1991) account of Northern Thai calendrical rites, *The Lan Na Twelve Month Traditions*, is both typical and exemplary in its cataloguing of ritual method and its nostalgic effort to distinguish between traditional practice and modern accretion. Precisely because of its typicality, however, the most surprising conclusion of their text is that which admits the influence of Central Thailand on Northern Thai custom. Not that the influence or its admission is particularly unexpected. Rather, what is noteworthy is the assertion that such influence began a mere 35 years ago (Sommai and Doré 1991: 198).[2] Given that the processes by which Chiang Mai was encompassed by Bangkok and inserted into the modern Siamese state commenced more than a century ago, being formalised in the treaties of 1874 and 1883 (Ramsay 1971; Ratanaporn 1989), and given the fact that the Buddhist *sangha* reform of 1902 was deployed with especial force in the North during the early decades of this century (Keyes 1971; Saeng 1980), it is necessary to ask in what sense one can claim that Central Thai influence on Northern Thai calendrical traditions has a history of merely thirty-five years' duration.

Many observers agree, of course, that the last few decades have been especially tumultuous for Chiang Mai and the surrounding provinces. If the last century saw the first steps toward the capitalisation of industry and agriculture (Anan 1984b), and the centralisation of education (Wyatt

1994a), the last three decades have witnessed increased rates of land-lessness, underemployment and poverty, characteristics of speculative economies in which finance capital and tourism have assumed dominance. The latter forms of transnationalism have displaced the U.S. military as the main foreign presence in Northern Thailand. They have also ensured that culture (*watthanatham*), a relatively new invention in the Thai language (Sulak 1991), has become a commodity, the object of desire and the fetish of those seeking souvenirs of lost authenticity. However, as the following pages attempt to demonstrate, these new longings merely index the growing instability, which has come to afflict notions of 'Thainess' over the past three decades. They mark the decline of a period in which the forces of capital and state came together, producing and legitimating 'national identity' (*ekkalak thai*) through a series of oppositions in which 'ritualism' and 'traditionalism' were opposed and then overcome in the idea of culture.

Although I will deal with these issues more fully in the body of this essay, it is worth noting here that the destabilisation of 'Thai-ness' has been manifest in many domains, including the emergence of new and especially Sino-Thai ethnicities (Keyes 1995, personal communication 1997), the proliferation in new religiosities, and new forms of secularism. But, while the dissipation of national identity probably has its origins in the very heart of mid-century nationalism, in the impossible effort to abolish difference, its most spectacular sign is to be found in the political violence of *hok tula*, referring to 6 October 1976. On that now infamous and epoch-making occasion, proponents of a despotic alliance between the military and capital struck at those espousing a socialist alternative, murdering many and driving even more into exile (Anderson 1977; chapter 10 in this volume). Despite the centrifugal force represented by these movements and events, or perhaps because of it, they have been paralleled by a countervailing effort to recover the lost terms of unity. What is of particular interest for this chapter is that the traditionalism born of such longing has been mapped onto older geopolitical relations, in which Chiang Mai and Northern Thailand constituted the site of relative pre-modernity for Bangkok and its modernist ideologues. As antiquity has been revalued, Chiang Mai has increasingly been read as a locus of authenticity, and in a redoubling circuit, has seen the revival of many practices that had seemed on the verge of disappearance only thirty years ago (Nithi 1991). These are the practices to which Sommai and Doré devote their affectionate labours.

In actuality, the most visible shift in what Sommai and Doré call Northern Thai custom is to be seen not in the form or method of calendrical rituals (as they suggest), but in their very performance. Many rites, such as that to restore the fate of the city (the *süp chata müang*), had fallen into disuse during the early and middle twentieth century, and have been revived only since the 1960s (Sanguan 1971b: 214). Similar stories can be told of other rites, and the period is characterised by the revival and proliferation of those practices now deemed to be part of the 'local tradition', as well as the restoration of physical sites and monuments associated with them. Of these, many have been consciously nurtured by the municipality and by the formal institutions of the central government, but other more heterodox practices, such as professional spirit medium-ship, have also re-emerged, sometimes in competition with more legitimate practices. Indeed, the dramatic surge in spirit mediumship, estimated by both Irvine (1984) and Tanabe (1996) to have grown by several hundred percent in the past three or four decades, suggests that the discursive forces which have supported revivalism far exceed the formal policies of government bureaucracies, and are symptomatic of a broad, epistemic shift.

The ambivalence and the contradictions within the newly constituted field of ritual practice make ethnography difficult, of course. They forbid recourse to the notion of a singular culture, and prohibit the fiction of shared meanings or beliefs. Accordingly, we shall be concerned here with the often agonistic relationships between officially legitimated rites and heterodox practices like mediumship, as well as with the tensions and contradictions within mediumship itself. To this end, I offer as a focal point the narrative of a contest between two ritual events, the *süp chata müang* and the annual praise ceremony (*prapheni yok khru*) for the spirits of the Northeast Corner of Chiang Mai City. In the course of explicating that contest, I attempt to sketch the history in which mediumship has been discursively revalued: transformed from a practice inimitably woven into the political apparatus of pre-modern Northern Thailand, to a site of excessive ritualism associated with ideologically denigrated spirit beliefs, to the newly valuable sign of a vanishing tradition. However, as will become clear, mediumship's new value is itself ambivalent, unevenly acknowledged, and variously understood and advocated in a field of other signs whose claim upon the traditional is equally persuasive – or untenable. The point, of course, is not whether mediumship or any other ritual is descended from the past, but how its history is refigured according to the value that pastness and tradition are themselves accorded.

In order to pursue the implications of this argument, it is first necessary to clarify the terms of both 'ritualism' and 'traditionalism'. In this paper, I use 'ritualism' to refer to the valuation of ritual in and of itself, in contrast to 'ritual', which refers to those individual practices which seek to have an influence on the material world through the repetition of standardised but magical acts. It should be noted, however, that in colloquial (non-elite) conversation, the term 'ritual' is rarely used as a generic category. One hears much more often of particular practices, such as the 'calling back of the essential spirit (*kan hòng khwan*)' or 'making pledges to the spirits' (*kae bon*), than of ritual (*phithi*) in general. However, in formal and elite discourse, in writing, and even among spirit mediums, who are attempting to emulate the speech of aristocracy, the language of ritual proliferates. It is, perhaps, an inherently ethnographic term, one that has already achieved that level of conceptual abstraction and alienation which banishes the particular and is then saturated by the sense of loss. As will become clear, ritualism in Northern Thailand, as elsewhere in the world, is often associated with the perceived disappearance of a particular cultural tradition. It is for this reason that 'traditionalism' appears to subsume ritualism despite being a much broader category. Just as ritualism is to be distinguished from ritual, so traditionalism needs to be understood as a discourse, which has been elaborated around the fear of tradition's loss. 'Traditionalism' does not mean a mode of practice characterised by historical repetition, nor actual continuity. It is, rather, a paradoxical concept encompassing various kinds of practices, one whose definitive but abstract characteristic is pastness and whose theoretical *raison d'être* is the healing over, or sublimation of, radical discontinuity. Clearly, there were practices whose value accrued partly from the perception of their antiquity in pre-modern times, but these are better understood as individual practices with singular histories than as part of a generic conceptual category. And, insofar, as such a contrast is possible, it seems likely that the value of such pre-modern pastness assumed continuity with antiquity rather than a rupture. 'Traditionalism' on the other hand, is the inherently belated effect of modernity, and not its displaced antecedent.

In this context, it is important to note that 'traditionalism' is often perceived by its modernist proponents as a means of returning to origins through processes of purification, and these frequently include a ban on ritual. Under such circumstances, ideological contests then emerge around the assignation of the term 'ritual' to practices, which are deemed to be more or less essential. Thus, while traditionalism can breed ritualism, it often understands itself to be denuding a system of gratuitous ritual elements. It is hardly surprising, then, that events which are thought, by some, to have their origins in antiquity and, by others, to represent pastness, are the sites of ideological contest. On such occasions, the historical tensions between scripturally based traditionalism, and the ritualism, which it produced through abjection, are manifested. The possible relationships that one can have with the past are also made present, variously upheld, and attacked by adherents and sceptics. To explore these issues I want to focus on the events of June 11, 1992, a day on which the *süp chata müang* (rite of extending the fate of the city) and the annual praise ceremony for the spirits of the *san lak müang* came together in the same place. On that day, members of the Chiang Mai municipality (*thetsaban*) and the *sangha* faced off with spirit mediums in a competition over space, authenticity, and the claim to antiquity. In their mutual accusations, and in their attempts to find legitimacy in the rhetoric of tradition, we learn much about the contested terrain that is modernity in Northern Thailand.

Urban renewal and the return to origins

And so: June 11, 1992. Under a sober grey sky and on the cusp of the monsoon, Chiang Mai's annual rite of renewal and extension, the *phithi süp chata müang*, was performed 'According to tradition'.[3] Like many public rites performed in Chiang Mai, a city renowned equally among Bangkok's culture brokers and tourist promoters for its devotion to custom, the *süp chata müang* is organised and staged by the municipality as an assertion of Thainess (albeit a Northern Thainess) in the context of the modern nation state. Although it marks the specific history and future of a particular northern city, it also announces the insertion of Chiang Mai into a hierarchy of religious and political institutions centred in the monarchical capital of Bangkok. It does so by having the appointees of the central government undertake the procedures, which will sustain the locality. Official participants at the *süp chata müang* include soldiers and Buddhist monks, teachers and civil servants, all of whom are understood to be members of the national body politic with the Chakri King as head. Their role, beyond that of simply displaying the human face of a bureaucratic state apparatus, is to provide a point through which the illuminating powers of Buddha's teachings texts can enter again into the quotidian world of sensuous activity. In other words, their role is that of the collective ear. But this ear is not simply the point or symbol of auditory reception; it is also the locus for a transformation, in which the spatial and temporal dimensions of the spiritual landscape are fused in the moment of hearing. In actuality, individuals become the points of intersection for a literal and metaphorical web of transmitting lines. These lines bind subjects together, make mediums of all people, and knit a weave of meaning that transcends the present in the directions of both past and future.

The manual for the *süp chata müang* is now maintained by the municipality, and although the rite now takes the form of an annual *tradition*, it originated during the reign of Phra Müang Kaeo (1485–1515) as a contingent procedure to restore the city's fate in moments of disaster, or to bring about general prosperity (Mani 1986b: 94–95). Apart from its intended function, however, the *süp chata müang* is a rite of cartographic narrative. Linking together a series of points at which events of historical importance occurred, the extension rite maps and re-maps a spatio-temporal narrative of the city's coming into being, while imbuing it with the life or fate-renewing powers contained in the Buddha's words. These points in the landscape, which are elaborated in local story and myth (and often in more formal chronicles, or *tamnan*), have been described to me as resembling batteries in their capacity to hold a charge, and to give off energy that is at once invisible and irresistible.[4] The words also possess an energising capacity and partake of electricity's idiom. Believed to be eternally present in the Pali suttas of Theravada Buddhism, these traces of transformative potential are rendered as speech via public broadcasts during the rite, and disseminated through an elaborate network of unspun cotton, which is entwined with the cables of amplifying systems. Quite literally, the cotton – medium of dhammic energies and instrument of a cosmic *parole* – is stretched from the distant town of Chiang Dao (Chiang Mai's mythic point of origin) to the modern city, encompassing the latter's four corners and five gates, and touching upon its major *wat*s, including Wat Sadoe Müang (Navel of the City), and Wat Cedi Luang, where the vihara (*wihan*) of the city pillar stands. The putative effectiveness of the rite – its capacity to renew the city in times of crisis – is said to depend upon the temporally proportional reception of the *dhamma*. Each year, the city's age is matched by the number of attendants present to receive the *dhamma*, and thus the rite expands annually, even as it promises to extend the city's fate into the future.

The touristic representations that accompanied the *süp chata müang* in 1992, as in other recent years, suggested that it was performed then as it had been performed in every other year in the City's history. And this is what passers-by and formal participants said. In fact, the rite has been regularly performed only in the last couple of decades, having been revived under the auspices of the municipality at the same time that the city began to receive its preservationist face-lift, with the ruins of old city walls, gates, and the sites of princely power being restored – as more picturesque ruins – during the late seventies and early eighties. The backward projection, or 'retrojection', of recent history to form a seamless trajectory from Phra Müang Kaeo's reign to the present suggests the rapidity with which new practices can heal back into a presumptive tradition. But, even without this assumption of pure repetition, 1992 could not be deemed a year like any other. It was a year of crisis, a year of bloody political tumult, a year in which the repressed traumas of the late 1970s came back to haunt a newly bourgeois democratic movement. It was also a year of local catastrophes, in which a plane crash claimed the lives of eleven of Chiang Mai's most prominent residents, and the rift between development and environmentalist forces assumed agonistic dimensions. On a longer-term scale, 1992 was a year unlike that of the century before, or even the half-century before. At the end of the city's septecentenary, the terms of cultural discourse had shifted dramatically, and the elaborate staging of a rite *as the sign of tradition* took place as an ironic reclamation of tradition from ritualism.

Between past and future: instances of contest

If the grey dawn of June 1992 revealed a city festooned with cotton threads, a city adorned by flags and small mountains of sand, whose dissipation by the wind signified the spread of *dhamma* to the world – a city in thrall to the signs of its ritual renewal – it also revealed a space of conflict. At the Northeast corner of the city, the most charged point in the directional topography of Chiang Mai's cityscape, a feast had been prepared. The shrine of the *san lak müang* (which houses a generic category of founding spirits) had been transformed overnight into an altar, on the long tables of which were heaped the tributary offerings appropriate to princely power: beautifully wrapped fruits of all kinds, several chickens, carefully constructed *suai*,[5] flowers, whisky.[6] The simultaneous occupation of the city's Northeast corner by forces deemed, by most people, to be antithetical – the one expressing official state power (which is always a fusion of religious and political power) and the other expressing a marginal group's aspirations to extraordinary power – came as something of a surprise to many of the participants at both events. However, the day selected (through astrological methods) by the *thetsaban* for the city's extension rite had coincided with the day on which the spirit of the Northeast corner was to receive the honours of an annual praise rite termed the *prapheni yok khru*. In fact, the spirit of this place has been without a vehicle for some years, his medium having died. But other mediums, who are woven into loose but hierarchically structured communities based on the recognition of each other's spirits, tend the *san lak müang* with other knowledgeable lay-people, and give praise on an annual basis, marking the absence of the medium in a manner that testifies, ironically, to the presence of the spirit.[7]

In fact, there is some tension between the mediums and the ageing Sino-Thai man who generally cares for the shrine. A former monk, locally renowned for his profound knowledge of Buddhist esoterica and the mythic traditions of the North, he is visible at most of the city's calendrical rites, especially those associated with fertility and patriarchal authority – such as the parade of the 'Buddha of one hundred thousand rains' which opens the week-long festivities associated with the City Pillar. At his home, in a small enclave outside and north of the old city, the impresario of the rites at the *san lak müang* told me (in a tone more of dismissal than contempt) that he was sceptical of the decrepit old women who would dance in possession at the Northeast Corner. Yet, he freely recognised that such practices are also ancient (*boran*), and he expressed no desire to keep them away. He did, however, maintain the Theravada Buddhist prohibition against women's bodies on the actual sites of spiritual significance, and he was adamant that no female medium be permitted to enter the shrine itself (a small elevated building just inside the walls' corner).[8] In this insistence on the contaminating potency of a woman's body, the old man revealed his commitment to patriarchal orthodoxy. And, in general, his training in Buddhism and in astrological method, gave him claim to a knowledge that had much greater legitimacy than that of the mediums, even if his own affection for merit-making rites was deemed excessive by the standards of a more restrained reform Buddhism. Indeed, although tensions between mediums and the impresario of the *san lak müang* revealed a gendered division in the conceptualisation of ritual propriety, they did not evidence the enormous opposition between a commitment to locality and a logic of national de-centring, as did the relationship between the officiants of the city's fate-extending rite and those who tended to the shrine at the Northeast Corner. That opposition was evident in the outright contempt and ridicule which solders and monks expressed about the mediums assembled there.

This is not the place to detail the practice of mediumship, nor the procedural aspects of such events (but see Shalardchai 1984; Cohen and Wijeyewardene 1984; Wijeyewardene 1986; and Morris 2000). Suffice to say, there exists in Chiang Mai, and in many other parts of Northern Thailand, an elaborate custom of possession by spirits, which may or may not be tutelary, and which were once associated with particular places, but are now more likely to be located in the time-space of a generalised (because commodified) antiquity. Most scholars agree that the practices associated with the veneration of such spirits are the residue of a pre-Buddhist past, which was largely displaced with the advent of Theravada Buddhism in Thailand, but whose traces are nonetheless still present in the popular forms of Buddhism, which both accommodated and integrated spirit belief despite orthodox prohibitions against it (Tambiah 1970; Kirsch 1977; Davis 1984; Keyes 1987). In the opaque eras of pre-Buddhist history, it is said, place itself had a power so potent that even after Buddhism had overlain it with the universalising mappings of a peripatetic religion, the powers of locality and local spirits remained to haunt religion (*satsana*) (Mus 1975). Their spectral presence remains encrypted from the perspective of a text-based religion, and especially that form of textualist religion which has dominated since the reforms of King Rama IV (1851–1868) were put into effect, but mediums claim, implicitly, to have – or indeed to *be* – the means to decipher the secret of that residue. Mediums, in effect, are the instruments of what Derrida would call an 'orgiastic recurrence': the return of an ecstatic principle in which the possibility of automatic magic was still available. Through them, history gives back what it has buried but not completely effaced, namely a pure and temporally unmediated relationship to corporeal power (Derrida 1995: 21).

In mediumship, the spirits of that buried past which continues to recur are thought to be those of warrior princes, Buddhist heroes or saints who have, for reasons of an excessive worldliness during their life-times (usually in the form of militarily-legitimated bloodshed), been forced into a nether-realm where they remain dependent on sensuous form to make sufficient merit for a forward movement in the cycle of rebirths.[9] Heterodox in this regard, because they assume the material existence of the spirit (*winyan*) after death, spirit mediums provide the instruments of that temporary incarnation which is necessary for yet another heterodox practice, namely merit-making. Mainly women (but with the number of men – and not only transgender (*kathoei*) men – increasing), such mediums believe themselves to have been chosen for a task which is at once onerous and honour-producing, but never desirable. Often experiencing their first possession as mere disorientation during a time of crisis, mediums accommodate themselves with the help of acolytes called *luk liang* (literally, step-children, or the children of feeding), and other mediums, to a process which, after several years, may entail daily possession by several different spirits of various status. At least in its ideal form, this possession is experienced as a complete alienation of bodily subjectivity, a severance of memory, and an absolute forgetting of the possession by the medium. During the period of the spirit's visitation, the possessed medium/spirit provides therapeutic and/or divinatory services to clients, who pay minimally for consultations that may address everything from health issues to lottery probabilities.[10] What we might call 'private' mediumship, in the doubled sense of domestic location and economic interest, is competitive, and although clients may visit more than one medium, the latter request unmitigated loyalty, and often accuse other vehicles of being charlatans. However, during the months immediately preceding the monsoon (and this period is lengthening as the number of mediums in Chiang Mai continues to grow), mediums enter into collective rites of mutual acknowledgement and subordination, through which they form loose lineages under a tutelary figure.

On 11 June, it appeared as though the praise rites for the *san lak müang* would take place as at any other such rite. A musical ensemble, an electronic gamelan, was seated next to the tarpaulin-covered space in which tributary dances (*fòn phi*)[11] would be performed, and mediums sat around the periphery, not yet attired in the brilliantly coloured imitation-silks, which mediums believe to have been worn in the courts of pre-modern Lanna Thai. The enormous bodhi tree that provides shade at the corner, with its branches supported by braces, was surrounded by small incense sticks, whose sweet smoke ostensibly disseminates verbal offerings across the realms of existence. As the morning progressed, more than thirty mediums arrived and departed, were possessed and dispossessed, and, during those moments when the spirit descended (*long ma*), danced themselves into beauty and offered it to the spirits of this place.

Some hundred metres away, uniformed soldiers and a few monks gathered to sit on the tin chairs laid out for them, and received the broadcast of the *dhamma* by which the city would be renewed. Passers-by paced between the two ritual spaces, as did some of the soldiers and mediums, the former snapping photographs as curious mementoes. In their comments to me, the soldiers and monks both made it clear that they saw the spectacle of mediumship as a grotesquerie, a ridiculous display of antiquated ritualism without the benefit of doctrine. According to the mediums, the presence of the soldiers was pathetically inadequate to the task before them, namely the restoration of a city, which, for reasons already discussed, was in desperate need of spiritual realignment.

My own shuttling back and forth between sites prompted more than one medium to scold me for doubled, and perhaps ambiguous, loyalties. The terms of that scolding are instructive because they included claims to both realness and antiquity, the former being read precisely as a function of the latter. Indeed, these two came together in an extremely potent combination. One medium in particular chided me: 'We know you've been here for a while. Don't go over there (gesturing to the tin chairs). Why do you want to go over there? They're nothing but soldiers and pretenders. Soldiers want nothing but money and power. Remember Bangkok? They come here only to get money and power. This is the ancient rite. This rite started before that one. This is the real thing, the Northern thing'.

What is the difference between being antiquated and being real because ancient? Answering this question ultimately demands that one understand the forms of historical consciousness now operating in Northern Thailand. In the process, we can begin to understand the experience of cultural crisis that now grips the late capitalist world of Chiang Mai. Unfortunately, there is no single answer to the question because, as has already been suggested, the episteme, which now inhabits Northern Thailand, is not singular. For the mediums, possession is indeed a form of return, a return of the past to the present. It is pure magicality, and it is innocent of the contamination of representation. Yet, the medium who reprimanded me was also inhabited by a logic and a rhetoric in which the efficacy of mediumship has been displaced by its signifying capacity. Hence, the only terms within which she could assert her primacy where those of a generic pastness. She might have said, mediumship survives because it works, is real, and it is valuable because it is ancient.

In essence, the medium's claim to magicality could only be made through a claim to the representational function of mediumship. She defended herself in the language of her opponents. But many people who no longer accord the practices of mediums any magical potency none-theless share some sense that the mediums do *represent* an authentic Northern Thai reality, which is now under threat by the forces of speculative capital and its attendant consumerism. I stress the verb, represent, because what is at issue for them is not the actual power of mediumship as an instrument of material transformation, divinatory insight, or even curative processes. What is at issue is the capacity of mediumship to signify authenticity. In this respect, the spectacle of mediumship reveals the degree to which Northern Thailand has entered into that episteme of representation which Foucault identifies in *The Order of Things* (1973b): a space in which signs have lifted off from the particular world and become autonomous, interchangeable entities in a vast universe of exchangeability. This is why mediums tend to emphasise their spirits' claim upon a generic pastness (*khwam boran*) rather than the relationships between those spirits and particular sites in the narrated landscape. It is also why the sphere of spirits now includes not merely the figures of local chronicles but of global history (spirits now come from Egypt, India and Iraq, and not only Chiang Saen or Chiang Dao). Authenticity no longer requires locality. Yet, if mediumship has been overtaken by the logics of generalised exchange, it still derives its value for believers from an apparent and temporalised exteriority to the market place. Hence, the scrutiny to which mediumship is subjected – in venues as diverse as local *wats* and national newspaper stories. Hence also the alacrity with which it is condemned when mediums accept money, exhibit wealth, or show themselves to be engaged in the worldly pleasures of commodity consumption.

Ritualism or traditionalism: histories of reform

How then does one read the contest between mediums and monks, between the *süp chata müang* and the *yok khru*? How does one understand its agonistic structure and, at the same time, come to terms with its encompassment by the commensurating power of the general commodity, with the fact that patrons of either event accuse each other in the same language, and claim the same virtues? To answer this question requires a consideration of two historical junctures: the first occurring in the nineteenth century, when the reforms of the Buddhist *sangha* produced a discourse of anti-ritualism, the second coming a century later in the development of nationalist ideology and a concept of Thai culture, for which a newly redeemed ritual can stand as metonym. The latter is made possible by the former, but does not become inevitable until newness emerges as a fetish and history assumes the commodity form (Buck-Morss 1989: 82). Let me consider first the history of Reform Buddhism.

Anthropological studies of the Thai State have, of course, been overwhelmingly dominated by the study of Buddhism. But they have also been confronted by the fact of 'two Buddhisms'. On the one hand, there exists an official, textually-biased tradition, which eschews spirit belief, and those practices, which seek an immediate, and personally economistic relationship between deed and consequence. On the other hand, there exists a populist tradition, the hallmarks of which are those of orality and bodily repetition, rather than the book and its sober hermeneutics of the rule. Here, one finds the propitiation of spirits and the love of merit-making ceremony that orthodoxy so condemns. That such a bifurcation of the religious world is itself an ideological fiction is evidenced by the repeated efforts to purge the institutions of state religion of the excesses which have seeped across the boundary of legitimacy.[12] Nor is this merely a feature of Rama IV's reformist zeal. Accusations of decadence within the *sangha* continue to be a staple of the national news media, and they provide the spectacle within which the line between orthodoxy and populism can constantly be redrawn. However, the supernaturalism of popular Buddhism, which stands as the alterity against which the state religion addresses itself, is also temporalised. Rendered in the idiom of 'ritualism', the belief in spirits and the practices associated with it (generally referred to as 'animism'), have continually been represented in the dominant discourse as the excess which both *antedates* and *haunts* Buddhist modernity in Thailand. Because a belief in the existence of spirits is imagined to be a historical substratum, which is nonetheless present in contemporary Buddhism, the revival of mediumship can be understood as that 'orgiastic recurrence', in which the pastness of spirit is theatricalised in an act of presencing. And this is why spirit mediumship is among the most reviled of ritualisms among conservatives of the Thammayut patriarchy. In essence, it threatens the rationalist regime's claims to have achieved modernity through the sublimation of such beliefs, and the magicality associated with them.

Political power in the modern state seems to be founded upon the spectacular but ironic displacement of 'ritual' practices into a space, with the marked temporal and spatial alterity of this securing the claim of the political to be authentically generative – foundational and effective – rather than 'citational' or merely 'theatrical'. This is not to say that there are no political rituals in modern societies (what else is a *kathin* ceremony if not a ritual?), merely that such rituals work precisely by denying themselves as *mere* (which is to say empty or impotent) rituals through reference to a field that is explicitly and even monstrously ritualistic. It is therefore the discursive production of this field – of ritualist ritual – which marks the modern, as much as the disappearance or atrophy of actual practices believed to be traditional or pre-modern.

Nowhere is this process more visible than in the history of spirit mediumship. This does not mean that mediumship is a uniquely representative or ideal venue for the analysis of history. It is marginal and other, abject and, though increasingly popular, rather ridiculed by religious orthodoxy. However, it is precisely in the genealogy of that marginality that one discovers the history of ritual's coming into being.

Let us consider, then, the moment in which mediumship emerges as an object of discourse, and indeed as a problem demanding commentary. Although there are occasional descriptions of what appears to be mediumship in traveller's accounts of the sixteenth century and later, spirit mediumship really bursts onto the documentary horizon in the late nineteenth century – in the accounts of *both* Siamese and English origin. It appears there as a site of contention, an obstacle equally to British efforts at market rationalisation and Siamese attempts at politico-economic encompassment of the area. Indeed, in the 1880s, when both Siam and the British were attempting to secure treaty rights in Chiang Mai – either in the form of taxes or access to markets – spirit mediums provided a site of local resistance and the vehicle for self-othering on the part of the Siamese. Thus, Krom Mün Phichit, the designated Siamese representative in Chiang Mai, wrote the following account in frustration at Northern resentment toward the newly invasive Siamese bureaucracy. 'Propitiating spirits and having mediums throughout the entire city, the spirit of Chaofa Chaikaeo (Kawila's father) came to reside in Chao Mahawong. He called on the Chao Nakhon Chiang Mai [*chao luang*] to force abolishment of the wine tax and spirits tax. The *prachao* Chiang Mai consented. [When] that spirit demanded that or wanted this, [he] complied. Finally a rumour surfaced that this was because the southerners were doing that and this' (Cited in Ratanaporn 1989: 272).

At about the same time, Carl Bock, a British observer of the area, described the case of Cao Ubon, a 'sister of the chief's wife', who was 'called upon to question the spirits when any difficulty occurred either in private or public affairs'. On one occasion, when her sister was stricken with illness, the medium was possessed and the spirit issued forth the following exclamation: 'The spirit forbids the whiskey monopoly (Bock 1986: 340)'.

Commentary is always belated, of course: the after-effect of alienation.[13] The fact that mediumship had emerged as a problem in need of commentary, at least for the outsiders who would soon dominate the area, suggests that it already appeared as something extrinsic to both everydayness and the operations of state. Indeed, this is so, and spirit belief in general was assuming an increasingly pejorative connotation in the representations of dominant (Buddhist) institutions in the North.[14] But it had not always been the case. What emerges as the thorny intransigence of mediumship in accounts like these is the fact that it had once been (and perhaps still was at century's end) a crucial element in the political apparatus of Chiang Mai. The princess-medium, Ubon, was herself a major economic player in the North, owning several thousands of slaves and controlling several commodity monopolies. Documents are unfortunately scanty, however, and it is therefore impossible to know whether the performance of her (or other's) possession at the time entailed the same degree of flamboyant cross-dressing, or the same kind of deferral to past authority, that marks mediumship today. What is clear is that mediumship did not constitute a mode of compensatory power, was not a response to deprivation. If mediumship was at all mimetic, its mimesis was the instrument of (legitimate) power's own citational claims to originary authority.[15] Mediumship in this early period was not derivatively imitative of, and hence resistant to, political power; it was a source of political authority. Yet, not long after this dramatic appearance on the stage of archival history, both mediums and princely power in the North are overwhelmed by the reforms instigated by Rama IV. Subsequently, they are shucked off, and cast into the realm of antiquated, pre-modern, and even feudal status, from the perspective of Central Thailand, and there they remained, for several decades, saturated with the aura of a primitive supernaturalist and ritualist illegitimacy.

Rama IV's reforms were, of course, intended to purify Thai Buddhism of its ritualist elements and to do so in a systematic fashion. In this regard, they reiterated Rama I's (1782–1809) own efforts to purge the *sangha* of sin through the codification and revision of ecclesiastical laws in 1782. However, if Rama I's interventions commenced what David Wyatt has termed a 'subtle revolution' (Wyatt 1994b: 145–154), Rama IV's efforts were buttressed by a broad social movement, which was itself propelled by the forces of transnational modernism. It is, of course, unfair to attribute to single men the forces of social history, and I do not to mean to render Rama IV as the heroic author of modernity. Nonetheless, the pressures of space in this chapter demand that the events of particular eras be linked, in shorthand, to the men who dominated them. And I therefore hope to be forgiven for a kind of monarchist historiography while attempting a genealogy of epistemes.

It is often remarked that Rama IV's reforms achieved a degree of stringency comparable to that of Calvinism and early Protestantism. Emphasising meditation and the eight precepts, they famously rejected excessive merit-making and they took Rama I's earlier subordination of spirit belief to Buddhism to new levels by denying outright the ontological existence of spirits in the world of humans. In their denigration of much Brahmanic ritual, they 'freed the Thai institutional order of at least some of its magical underpinnings' (Kirsch 1978: 60). The liberation was inevitably partial, however, and 'scripturalism produce[d] its own kind of ritualism' (Tambiah 1976: 212).[16] In particular, state and monarchical ceremony, including coronation and tonsure rites, received additional elaboration (Wales 1931; Gerini 1976). This development may have been stimulated by the perceived need to maintain appearances in a newly international visual field, and Rama IV began the practice of having photographs of himself in royal regalia sent to the monarch of other states as part of his diplomatic missions (Anake 1987: 56). Both the rationalism and the ironic ritualism of Rama IV's endeavour would be furthered by his successors, and especially by Rama V (1868–1910). In equal measure, they would also define the process by which the expansionist integration of Siam's dependent states, and especially Northern Thailand, would take place. Not incidentally, the second stage of Siamese modernism would find its chief ideologue and most eloquent spokesman in the person of Prince Damrong Rajanubhab, the man who would serve as Minister of the North during the crucial years of transition between 1892 and 1915. It was undoubtedly his experience in facilitating the integration of Northern Thailand that led Damrong to identify 'assimilation' as a singular attribute of Thailand's national character (Reynolds 1991: 13).

But Siamese attempts to secure an encompassing nationhood had begun in earnest at the beginning of the eighteenth century, following its successful joint effort with Chiang Mai to expel the Burmese after almost two hundred years of occupation in Northern Thailand. However, it was largely in response to the threat of British and French colonialism, tentatively deferred through the Bowring Treaty (which granted Britain exclusive and largely unfettered access to Siamese markets in 1855) that Chiang Mai's tributary subordination to Bangkok was converted into a relationship of provincial membership in an expanded Siamese state (Ratanaporn 1989). The need to mediate treaty disputes with the British led to the establishment of what has been called the beginnings of a modern judiciary (Engel 1978: 11). An international court was established on the basis of an entirely new rule of law, one separated from the personal authority of the ruling *cao* and immune to the caprice of his particular judgement. Variously supported by the Siamese, the British, and the still tenuously ensconced Presbyterian missionaries living on Chiang Mai's outskirts, the court was but one institution of many that displaced the Northern *cao*'s personal influence. Aware of the degree to which local ceremonies authorised the *cao*'s power, the Siamese attempted to re-map the urban landscape and impose a newly nationalised spatial logic. The well from which lustral waters were drawn for tributary oaths was sealed over (it was restored and re-marked with a sign in 1986). The old palace was remade as a prison, and Wat Cedi Luang was converted from a Mahanikai to a Thammayut-nikai *wat*. Although the City Pillar remained in Wat Cedi Luang's compound, it continued to be the site of rituals which were otherwise eschewed by Reform Buddhism. At the same time, Wat Suan Dòk, which was situated outside and to the south of the old city, assumed new significance as the centre of the Mahanikai order in Chiang Mai. It was at Wat Suan Dòk, under the revered monk Phra Khruba Sriwichai, that localist resistance to national centralisation assumed its most virulent and threatening form (Swearer and Sommai 1978; Keyes 1971). Though Phra Khruba Sriwichai was ultimately unable to balk the forces that were overtaking Chiang Mai, he became the centre of a significant cult and the icon of Northern autonomy. To this day, his name incites awe in many Northerners and he is remembered as the champion of a people's religiosity.

The tension between the scripturalist emphasis of Rama IV's Thammayut order and the older practices of Northern Thailand's (Mahanikai) Buddhism did not, however, dissipate with the quelling of Phra Khruba Sriwichai's resistance. They persist in the quieter competitions between *wats*, and the monks who tend them, and in the accusations of ritualism that are so regularly levelled at mediums, wayward monks, and even the remaining adherents of Mahanikai Buddhism. When, for example, I asked the abbot of Wat Phra Sing about the annual rites of renewal associated with the *lak müang*, he rebuked me with a contemptuous disavowal of any such ritualism, claiming ignorance of local custom (*prapheni*), and suggested that I speak instead with the monks of the small Mahanikai *wat* where one finds the fertility icon that is paraded through the streets at the beginning of the rites associated with the pillar.

The second time is farce? recuperating ritual

How then, has the Bangkok-appointed municipal government come to be the patron of rituals, which were once deemed the antithesis of Reform Buddhism's doctrinal propriety? What forces account for the revival of both the *süp chata müang* and mediumship in the last three decades? The crucial moment in this history of seeming inversion, wherein ritual moves from abjection to symbolic investment, can be traced to the nationalism of the thirties, forties, and fifties, the period of Phibun Songkhram and Luang Wichit Watthakan. It is most apparent in the state's assumption of an explicitly ritualist function in its effort to claim traditional authority. Much has been written on the nationalism of Phibun Songkhram, and I do not intend to rehearse it all here. I do, however, want to remark on a few points of relevance for the present discussion. As Chai-anan Samudavanija (1991: 69) has so eloquently summarised it, 'The state was given a specifically *Thai* character in Pibun's period as a result of a combination of factors ranging from the desire to claim jurisdiction over other Tai races beyond the existing territory of Siam to the suppression of emergent ethnic Chinese influences in politics and society'. The form of nation-building or, to use Chai-anan's (1991) term 'state-identity creation', which emerged in response to these anxieties was one in which culture was first reified and then bureaucratised. Beginning with Prince Wan's development of a notion of culture, *watthanatham* (Sulak 1991), and continuing with the emergence, in the 1950s of a concept of Thai identity (*ekkalak thai*) (Reynolds 1991), there came into being a vast apparatus centred in a racialised vision of nationhood, which was retroprojected onto a space that pre-dated Sukhothai and encompassed much of Lao, southern China, and parts of Burma (Chai-anan 1991: 72). Its institutional supports took the form of The National Cultural Maintenance Act of 1940 and the National Culture Acts of 1942 and 1943, and it was manifest in the numerous publications on national culture that emerged from the ideological partnership of Phibun and Luang Wichit. As Chai-anan remarks, it was Luang Wichit's singular accomplishment to bridge the gap between official and public culture, and he did so through the writing of plays, songs, novels and essays, through which the ideology of the newly cohering nation could become a point of identification and pleasurable consumption. These productions were largely the stuff of bourgeois entertainment, but they had enormous appeal in urban areas where working class audiences soon internalised bourgeois taste in their longing for the cultural capital that attended that class position (Chai-anan 1991: 71; Barmé 1989). In retrospect, one of the most striking features of this period is the impact it had on the previously reigning conceptions of tradition and ritual. In addition to the infamous demand for ritualised and gendered everyday performances (such as kissing and the doffing of caps), particular kinds of dress, and such things as *ramwong* dancing at the soirées of bureaucrats in the 1940s and 50s, the new cultural policy generated a proliferation of local rituals but placed them under the authority of the Bangkok government and its local representatives. Some of these appeared immediately, while others, like the *süp chata müang*, emerged after some delay, but their lineage is clear and derives from the ideas of national culture developed at mid-century. Still abject in the official ideologies of Thammayut Buddhism, rituals of culture nonetheless began to return as the uncanny other, and the seeming origin of the modern polity. Because they represented that past from which modernity claimed to emerge, and to which it opposed itself in the process of self-definition, they also constituted an ironic source of its legitimacy.[17]

Mediumship, of course, was not included in that polite repertoire of national custom encouraged by the various cultural mandates of the Phibun administration, and the ministerial offices that it spawned. Nor was it included in the local rituals for which municipal bureaucracies were to take responsibility under the co-ordinating efforts of the National Culture Commission, which was established in 1979 as part of a security programme aimed at the elimination of communist and un-Thai activities (Reynolds 1991: 13–16). However, mediumship did take on a vehemently nationalist tone during this period, reflecting the insertion of Bangkok's cultural imaginary into the most intimate domains of Northern practice and consciousness (Irvine 1984; Sanguan 1971b). The pantheons of possessing personae began to be populated by figures associated with visibly Thai rather than Lanna history, with individuals such as Kings Ramkhamhaeng and Chulalongkorn (Rama V, r.1868–1910) entering a community, in which those like Queen Camadevi (Camthewi) and Cao Luang Kham Daeng had held sway as the images of spectacular power. Photographs of Chakri monarchs began to appear in the shrines of mediums, and national flags became part of the decor. And, as Walter

Irvine (1984) has argued, border penetration became a metaphor for possession.

Yet, if mediumship seemed allied with the new nationalism of post-World War II Thailand, something else was also beginning to happen. Neither the government's patronage of aestheticised local practices, nor the more aggressive tactics of military counterinsurgency and populist recruitment[18] under the post-Phibun dictatorship of Sarit-Thanom-Praphat, could mitigate the growing disaffection that was afflicting the rural population and the gradual dissipation of that phantasmal unity which had been Luang Wichit's dream.[19] Nationalism reached its apotheosis in the violent clash between students and the military on October 6, 1976 (Anderson 1977). After the spectacle of soldiers murdering civilians was etched into the consciousness of a traumatised nation via the mass media (see chapter 10 in this volume), the distinct and unprecedented fragmentation of Thai society could never again be denied.[20] It was a process that could only be accelerated by the forces of tourism, transnationalised mass media and transnational finance capital. Not even the repetition of military brutality against democracy protestors in 1992, nor the perfidious invocations of 'national stability' by which it was justified, would convince the Thai population that a return to unity was possible again.[21] The newly culturalised space of ritual practice partook of the same pluralisation.

As representation, the ritual that had been transposed from religion to culture opens onto vast new universes of possible meaning. This turn to representation both introduced a new ambivalence into the social field and invoked its opposite. Along with the secularism that inevitably attends such transformations, there has emerged in Thailand a multiplicity of fervent religiosities. Sects like Santi Asoke and Dhammakaya draw thousands, while the sale of amulets has never been so brisk. Mediums would perhaps have anticipated this, would have been the repositories of a knowledge that the past cannot be summoned without bringing the risk of that multiplicity from which all inheritance must be chosen (Derrida 1994: 16). To reproduce the magic of a prior moment, even in the nullified form of spectacle, is to entertain the possibility that magic itself will return – or at least that it will be embraced again. Indeed, this is precisely what has happened. The fetishism of the past, which cultural nationalism generated, ultimately converged upon the theatricalised re-presencing of possession. For mediumship does not understand itself to be a mere sign of pastness, nor a theatre of supplementary representation. It claims instead to be haunted by that pre-Buddhist logic, in which it is the instrument of the past's actual return to the present. Nor is it alone in its promise of immediate power, and it now inhabits a broad field in which increasingly popular astrologers and powerful monks (*phra saksit*), amulet salesmen and renegade Buddhisms all offer the magicality of the pre-modern as a means to survive the modern. Vying for legitimacy within this extraordinarily fecund space, mediums nonetheless partake of orthodox ideology. They make extravagant gifts to Buddhist *wats* and, much like their reform critics, advocate meditation in an ironic bid to compensate for the supernaturalism which is their *raison d'être*.

One may conclude that the new popularity of mediumship, evidenced in its growth, derives simultaneously from its claim on magic, its appeals to Buddhist orthodoxy, and its new, abstract representational power. It now has value for both secularists and believers, and finds vocal critics only among the most doctrinaire. For this reason, the gendering of mediumship has also changed. Although I have not attended specifically to questions of sexual difference in this chapter, it is significant that the history of nationalism is one in which tradition itself, or rather the sign of tradition, has become increasingly masculinised. So, an increasing number of men are entering the field,[22] and monks who might once have eschewed ritualism in general, and mediumship in particular, are not infrequent guests at the annual tributary rites of prominent mediums.

Conclusions: after farce, the return of a dialectic

In the world of orgiastic consumerism, where display value has come to supersede exchange value, the poles which once separated tradition and supernatural ritual collapse into each other. Traditionalism, by which a racialised nation sustains itself, generates an aura for the past, rendering it an object of longing and covetous desire: making it a commodity on route to fetishisation. Thus, rituals which can lay claim to being of the past, are transformed into symbols *of pastness*, and in that moment, traditionalism generates a love of ritualism. For its part, ritualism promises to bridge that aching chasm opened up by modernity in the moment that it insists – as it must – on its distance from origins, its progress through history (even though that progress is made possible by the immanent force of those very origins). In this context, however, the chastening efforts to privilege hermeneutics over experience, rationality over affect, are often unable to contain the force of desire, as also the love of excess that they also prohibit in the interest of traditional values. This is precisely why the contemporary era has seen so many charismatic cults and so many ascetic movements, to say nothing of mediumship's efflorescence. Recently, Chiang Mai has also witnessed the arrival of new kinds of ecstatic mediumship, in which practices like fire-walking and self-mutilation are displacing the milder manifestations of sickness and trembling which conventional possession entails. Common in South and Central Thailand, such dramatic practices have been rare in the North.

Proliferation is itself a symptom of ambivalence (Bhabha 1994). Thus, it is not only the facilitation of a recurrence, by which originary power would return to the present across the space of rupture, that makes mediumship attractive to tourists, soldiers, and academicians alike. Rather, it is the additional (and in some ways contradictory) capacity of mediumship to signify pastness that accounts for its extraordinary new popularity and growth. Not only is it the vehicle of a continuity with the past, but is also the symbol of its hypostatisation. The defenders of official state religion deny this, of course, and they do so through vociferous protests against the legitimacy, or the realness, of mediumship's traditions. But, as we have seen, these kinds of insults can be – and are – cast both ways. Perhaps, in the end, it will be in opposition to the new and more extreme kinds of possession that the mediums and the monks will finally acknowledge their mutual encompassment by commodity logics, and what Marilyn Ivy (1995) calls the 'discourses of the vanishing'. For, unlike the rampant nostalgia that now possesses Chiang Mai, these newly radical kinds of ritual ecstasy portend something unprecedented in this area: a return to the memory of forgetting, a return to absolute possession, and that kind of possession which is not a symbol but a mode of being – other.

Foucault would perhaps have called this kind of practice 'ritual libertinage', and seen in it the end of ritual's capacity to represent. For the power of the new medium accrues from his (supposedly spiritually-induced) capacity to transgress the laws of the human world, and like the libertine's, his value is forged in risk. But commodity logics have an extraordinarily plastic and capacious quality. Their ability to re-encompass what has been lost, or what claims to have slipped out from their net, is virtually limitless. And thus, the medium who promises real magic may turn out to be as imbricated in national politics as any of his more familiar contemporaries. He may be patronised by generals and disparage democracy activists, while disavowing consumerism and promulgating the impossible economy of speculative real estate. Such is the case of one medium who lives on the outskirts of Chiang Mai, and who has become the centre of a cult featuring fire-walking and extreme forms of asceticism. His fabulously adorned shrine, which includes flashing bulbs, a wall of statues and photographs, and a neon sun, also includes a room full of videotapes. These feature the medium presiding over various rituals and reveal a careful directorial eye, one informed by both Hollywood and ethnographic film aesthetics. They are professionally edited, over-dubbed with Indian film music, and titled in a format that would make them eligible for commercial distribution. They are also carefully archived. As the medium himself says, he has become his own movie star, the source of his own cinematic fame. Glowing in the light of an aura for which cinema is as much a metaphor as an origin, he is an enigmatic figure: at once beyond the realm of the more conventional mediumship patronised by sentimentally nostalgic bourgeois clients, and closer to the truly magical mediumship of the pre-modern which contemporary representations extol as their origin.

This raises the question of whether the episteme of representation, which is also, as Foucault says, the episteme of exchanging, can ever accommodate truly libertine practice. Certainly, the 'ritual' that occupies this small empire of signs is antithetical to libertinage in its transgressive forms. In the end, there are perhaps only two possible exits from the discursive circle in which 'ritual' begets magic and magic is neutralised in 'ritualism'. One of these is the refusal to be ritualised, as in the case of the Javanese spirit described by John Pemberton. That spirit brought to an end the annual rites associated with his remembrance with an abrupt command that articulated local resistance to the national phantasmagoria of the 'Mini Indonesia' theme park (1994: 267). The other is the abandonment of the magic associated with State power for that of finance capital's entrepreneurial economy. In this case, claims to disclosure may permit the production of a new occult, and the rebirth of magic in another form. Silence might serve to remark the power of the spirit who will be observed even in the apparent cessation of observation, as Pemberton suggests. Recanting can also perform power, if only to assign it to one's opponent.

Such departures ultimately threaten the tenuous dialectic between orthodoxy and the alterity it produces and requires. And it is for this reason that mediums and monks can converge in their opposition to the ritual libertine. The most pointed and dramatic instance of this convergence of which I am aware occurred in November 1997, when a Chantaburi medium named Chuchad, nationally renowned for his spectacular acts of self mutilation and miraculous possession by Phra Indra, made a nationally televised confession of fakery. Admitting to a charade that had lasted twenty-six years, the medium joined forces with Phra Phrom of Wat Suan Kaeo and not only revealed the secrets of his long deceit but called on other mediums to recant and give up their spectacular rites and spirit belief in favour of a more rational Thammayut Buddhism. Trading the profession of spirits for that of Amway, the medium enacted the most public conversion in recent memory, and provided dramatic force to the criticisms of mediumship, which had emphasised the unreality of its possessions. In three hours of confession, Chuchad insisted that he had performed his tricks with the aid of science (*witthayasat*) rather than magic (*saiyasat*). But such statements could only effect the re-entrenchment of magic as that power which lies beyond the boundary of the rational, the other of science and of the modern. Apparently projected elsewhere, magic can then be smuggled back into the economy, where speculation produces the magic of apparent wealth and the dangers of absolute loss. Not surprisingly, Chuchad's effort to subsume all mediums within his own gesture, and to attribute to them (and especially those of Northern Thailand), the subterfuge that he had performed fell flat. Not only the protesting mediums at the news conference but audience members, and some of his own former clients, rejected the confession. In so doing, they testified to the ironies of modernity, and what Weber understood so well – that rationality breeds irrationality, and that auratic power is never completely destroyed, even in the moment of its representation. It comes back as a trace, a haunting, and in that manner, it possesses us all.

Acknowledgements

This chapter is based on field research carried out over seventeen months, between 1991 and 1993. I wish to thank Dr. Anan Ganjanapan for assisting me during my stay in Thailand, and for sharing invaluable data. I am also indebted to him for extending the invitation to write this paper, and to the Conference Secretariat of the Sixth International Thai Studies Conference for making it possible to accept that invitation. Finally, I wish to acknowledge Rujaya Abhakorn and Kruamas Woodtikarn for their encouragement and to thank Charles Keyes and Shigeharu Tanabe for their insights, examples, and editorial assistance.

Notes

1 The paradigm for this kind of work is Phya Anuman Rajadhon's (1962, 1986) series of writings on culture and tradition in Siam. For a handsome bibliography of additional works on custom, religion, and ritual in both English and Thai, see Tanabe (1991b), esp. p.68–101.
2 The thirty-five year estimation is simply an up-dated version of Sommai's and Doré's 1991 claim that the influence can be traced back thirty years.
3 Most of the people whom I interviewed around the time of the *süp chata müang* in 1992 were emphatic about the traditional nature of the event, its historical precedent, and its exact reproduction of similar events in previous years.
4 My own research suggests that place remains a powerful force in the mythopoeia of Northern Thailand, but that it has become more abstract and generalised – in a word, less local, under the influence of nationalist discourse and transnational economic forces. The rhetoric of place in this modern sense is woven into other forms of power attribution, forming a secreted but often effective logic of spirit, which can be discerned in new forms of localist practice. For example, during the *phithi sap caeng* of 1992 – which occurred as part of the public protest against the military's oppression of democracy protests – the spirits of the mountains and of the North were called upon to wreak vengeful havoc. No longer the spirits of the City Pillar or even of Dòi Suthep, these spirits were called back from a realm of rather vague location and, perhaps for this reason, the rite was easily transposed to Bangkok, where it was performed again with equally menacing invocations of a spiritual power whose primary attribute is antiquity. See also Tanabe (1996: 8; p.57 in this volume).
5 *Suai* are tree-like flower arrangements which mimic the gold and silver trees once demanded as tribute by senior *caos*.
6 In Chiang Mai, the founding spirits include Luang Kham Daeng, the warrior-hero from Chiang Dao, as well as those of Dòi Kham in Mae Hia – namely, Pu Sae and Ña Sae (Tanabe 1991a). However, there is considerable difference of opinion among both lay people and academics as to which spirits occupy the *san*

lak müang at the Northeast Corner as opposed to the vihara (*wihan*) of the City Pillar, and what their significance might be. On this issue see Wijeyewardene (1986: 3–4); Davis (1984: 274).

7 It is interesting to consider the possibility that, in this way, mediumship might be performing some of the 'work of culture' that mortuary ritual would accomplish in other contexts and via other means: it extends that period during which the essence of a person – even a mythified person – can be sustained in the world as a locus of merit. See Keyes (1987: 199).

8 A similar prohibition attaches to the City Pillar, the shrine of which is situated in the compound of Wat Cedi Luang. No woman may enter that space, nor look upon the pillar, and to this day myths abound about women who were rendered mad after attempting to do so. I interviewed several elderly women at the *wat* during the City Pillar festivities of 1992 and found them earnest in their belief. Many also felt that the city itself would be wounded – by earthquakes or plagues – if a woman transgressed this most basic of regulations. Younger women who expressed frustration with the rule nonetheless did not venture inside.

9 Derrida remarks that the demonic or orgiastic impulse, which is repressed but also recurrent in Christianity, is intimately linked with the forces of sexual desire, these being both manifestations and expressions of the will to a transcendent non-self in fusion (Derrida 1991: 3). It is interesting to note in this context, that a hallmark of possessing spirits is their sexual appetite, an appetite which is often polymorphous (in the Freudian sense) and, not incidentally, completely antithetical to the forms of comportment demanded by the Buddhism which mediums invariably claim to observe. On the question of mediumship and sexuality, see Wijeyewardene (1986).

10 In this regard, my research further substantiates the claims of Shigeharu Tanabe (1996). See especially his discussion of pages 11–12 (also p.56 in this volume).

11 *Fòn phi* is a style of dancing which borrows elements of spirit dancing associated with the *phi meng* and *phi mot* cults of Northern Thailand, as well as the *ramwong* made popular in the fifties. On the *phi meng* and *phi mot*, see Tanabe (1991a).

12 The recent debates over the status of Phra Phothirak embody precisely these issues. Phothirak's own claims to authority stem from the fact that he has used orthodox Buddhism's own disavowal of ritual against it, and accused the *sangha* of moral laxity and corrupt worldliness. The Sangha's Supreme Council has returned the accusation by suggesting that Phothirak has not observed the forms demanded by the texts, arguing that his capacity to ordain others is not only suspect but that he sinned in his claims to having reached a level of enlightenment beyond his actual achievements.

13 On the belatedness of commentary, see Foucault (1973a: xvi–xvii).

14 Anan Ganjanapan's essay, 'The idiom of "*phii ka*": peasant conception of class differentiation in Northern Thailand' (1984a) remains the finest treatment of the process by which spirit belief was transformed into a technology of discipline and a vehicle of mutual antagonism in the period during which class relations were transformed on the basis of monetisation.

15 Here, I am using the term 'citational' after Judith Butler, who elaborates upon the linguistic theory of performativity first offered by John L. Austin, and inserts it in a Foucaultian logic (of subjectification) to develop a theory of the process by which authority refers to an original performance as the source of its legitimacy. See her *Bodies that Matter* (1993).

16 For a fine overview of this history, see Charles F. Keyes, *Thailand: Buddhist kingdom as modern nation-state* (1987b); The ideological and institutional

reforms of Rama IV were entwined and enacted at several levels, including those of the Buddhist *sangha*, the state apparatus and the cartographic imagination. In regard to the latter, Thongchai Winichakul has provided a brilliant account of the processes by which Siam mapped itself as a nation-state. See his *Siam Mapped* (1994).

17 On the relationship between the uncanny and the nostalgic impulse in ethnographic nationalism, see Marilyn Ivy's masterful account of Japanese folklore studies in her *Discourses of the Vanishing* (1995).

18 Among the most powerful of these other movements was the Village Scout organisation, which brought villagers into a cell-based community that both mirrored and opposed that of the communists. For an excellent account of this movement, see Bowie (1997).

19 Benedict Anderson's classic essay on the 'intellectual revolution' of 1973 and the coup of 1976, remains the most informative account of this period. I would therefore like to note that while I rely on Anderson's reading of the seventies as a period in which the hegemony of the ruling classes began to collapse, I have not adopted his terminological distinction between the 'traditionalism' of the previous era and the military ideology of 'Nation-Religion-King' (1977: 14). This is not because I do not share his sense of radical departure in the post-Phibun era but because I am interested here in the ways in which the category of 'tradition' was mobilised by the new movement, even in contest with the claims of other groups.

20 The fragmentariness of this period needs to be distinguished from that which characterised the 'nation' in the pre-modern period, when distinct linguistic groups and small, politically autonomous units coexisted or paid tribute to each other in a looser structure. The fragmentation of which I write in the 1970s appears only in the aftermath of unification.

21 I am grateful to Charles Keyes (personal communication) for a stimulating and ultimately persuasive discussion on this issue.

22 The predominance of women and *kathoei* in mediumship is gradually giving way. I know of several heterosexual men who now practise as mediums, and at least two husband-wife couples in which both the man and woman are mediums. I also know of a few partnerships in which the woman is a medium but her husband serves as a kind of impresario of possession. In one case, the husband actually claims to have negotiated with spirits to have his wife taken instead of himself, but he attends all possession performances and acts as the virtual patriarch of a large lineage of mediums.

References

Anake Nawigamune 1987 *Thai rup müang thai nai samai raek* (Early photography in Thailand), Bangkok: Saengdaeng.

Anan Ganjanapan 1984a 'The idiom of *"phii ka"*: peasant conception of class differentiation in Northern Thailand', p.325–329 in *Mankind* 14(4).

—— 1984b 'The partial commercialization of rice production in Northern Thailand, 1890–1981', unpublished PhD dissertation, Cornell University.

Anderson, Benedict 1977 'Withdrawal symptoms: social and cultural aspects of the October 6 Coup', p.13–30 in *Bulletin of Concerned Asian Scholars* 9(3).

Anuman Rajadhon, Phya 1962 *Kan süksa rüang prapheni thai* (The Study of Thai Customs), Bangkok: Royal Academy.

—— 1986 *Popular Buddhism in Siam and Other Essays on Thai Studies*, Bangkok: Thai Inter-Religious Commission for Development.

Appadurai, Arjun 1996 'Genealogies of the present: Asian modernity in the era of globalization', unpublished paper presented at the symposium, 'Fast Forward: The Contemporary Art Scene in Asia', New York, The Asia Society, 4 October.

Barmé, Scot 1989 'Luang Wichit Wathakan: official nationalism and political legitimacy prior to World War II', unpublished MA thesis, Australian National University.

Bhabha, Homi 1994 'The other question: stereotype, discrimination and the discourse of colonialism', p.66–85 in Homi Bhabha *The Location of Culture*, New York: Routledge.

Bock, Carl 1885 (1986) *Temples and Elephants: the narrative of a journey of exploration through Upper Siam and Lao*, London: Low, Marsten, Searle and Rivington (Reprint, Singapore: Oxford University Press).

Bowie, Katherine H. 1997 *Rituals of National Loyalty: an anthropology of the state and the Village Scout movement in Thailand*, New York: Columbia University Press.

Bourdieu, Pierre 1977 *Outline of a Theory of Practice* (translated by Richard Nice), Cambridge: Cambridge University Press.

Buck-Morss Susan 1989 *The Dialectics of Seeing: Walter Benjamin and the Arcades Project*, Cambridge, Mass.: MIT Press.

Bunnag, Jane 1973 *Buddhist Monk, Buddhist Layman*, Cambridge: Cambridge University Press.

Butler, Judith 1993 *Bodies that Matter: on the discursive limits of 'sex'*, New York: Routledge.

Chai-anan Samudavanija 1991 'State-identity creation, state-building and civil society', p.59–86 in Craig J. Reynolds (ed.) *National Identity and its Defenders*, Chiang Mai: Silkworm.

Cohen, Paul T. and Gehan Wijeyewardene (eds.) 1984 *Spirit Cults and the Position of Women in Northern Thailand* (Special Issue), *Mankind* 14(4).

Davis, Richard 1984 *Muang Metaphysics*, Bangkok: Pandora.

Derrida, Jacques 1991 *Given Time: I. Counterfeit Money* (translated by Peggy Kamuf), Chicago: University of Chicago Press.

—— 1994 *Spectres of Marx: the state of the debt, the work of mourning, and the New International* (translated by Peggy Kamuf), New York: Routledge.

—— 1995 *The Gift of Death* (translated by David Willis), Chicago: University of Chicago Press.

Engel, David 1978 *Code and Custom in a Thai Provincial Court*, Tucson, Az.: University of Arizona Press.

Foucault, Michel 1973a (1963) *The Birth of the Clinic* (translated by A.M. Sheridan Smith), New York: Vintage.

—— 1973b (1966) *The Order of Things: an archaeology of the human sciences*, New York: Vintage.

Gerini, G.E. 1976 (1893) *Chulalantamangala or the Tonsure Ceremonies as Performed in Siam*, Bangkok: The Siam Society.

Irvine, Walter 1984 'Decline of village spirit cults and growth of urban spirit mediumship', p.325–334 in *Mankind* 14(4).

Ivy, Marilyn 1995 *Discourses of the Vanishing*, Chicago: University of Chicago Press.

Keyes, Charles F 1971 'Buddhism and national integration in Thailand', p.551–568 in *Journal of Asian Studies* 30(3).

—— 1983 'Merit-transference in the karmic theory of popular Theravada Buddhism', p.261–286 in C. Keyes and E. Valentine Daniel (eds.) *Karma: an anthropological inquiry*, Berkeley: University of California Press.

—— 1987a 'From death to birth: ritual process and Buddhist meanings in Northern Thailand', p.181–206 in *Folk* 29.

—— 1987b *Thailand: Buddhist kingdom as modern nation-state*, Boulder, Col.: Westview Press.

—— 1995 'Who are the Tai? reflections on the invention of identities', p.136–160 in Lola Romanucci-Ross and George A. De Vos (eds.) *Ethnic Identity: creation, conflict and accommodation* (third edition), Walnut Creek, Ca.: Alta Mira Press.

Kirsch, A. Thomas 1977 'Complexity in the Thai religious system: an interpretation', p.241–266 in *Journal of Asian Studies* 36(2).

Mani Phayomyong 1986a *Prapheni sipsòng düan lanna thai* (The Twelve Month Traditions of Lanna Thai), Chiang Mai: Sopkan Phim.

—— 1986b *Phithikam lanna thai* (Ceremonies of Lanna Thai), Chiang Mai: Sopkan Phim.

Moerman, Michael 1968 'Ban Ping's temple: the center of a "loosely structured society"', p.137–174 in M. Nash (ed.) *Theravada Buddhism in Southeast Asia*, New Haven: Yale University Press.

Morris, Rosalind C. 2000 *In the Place of Origins: modernity and its mediums in Northern Thailand*, Durham: Duke University Press.

Mus, Paul 1975 (1933) *India Seen from the East: Indian and indigenous cults in Champa* (translated by I. Mabbert), Melbourne: Monash Papers on South East Asia, no.3.

Nithi Aeusriwongse 1991 'Sao khrua fa: fan thi pen cing' (Madame Butterfly: the dream has become reality), p.180–185 in *Sinlapa watthanatham* (Arts and Culture) 12(6).

Pemberton, John 1994 *On the Subject of 'Java'*, Ithaca: Cornell University Press.

Plaek Sonthirak 1971 *Phithikam lae prapheni* (Ceremonies and Customs), Bangkok: Thai Watthana Phanit.

Ramsey, James Ansil 1971 'The development of a bureaucratic polity: the case of Northern Siam', unpublished PhD dissertation, Cornell University.

Ratanaporn Sethakul 1989 'Political, social, and economic changes in the northern states of Thailand resulting from the Chiang Mai Treaties of 1874 and 1883', unpublished PhD dissertation, University of Illinois.

Reynolds, Craig J. (ed.) 1991 'Introduction', p.1–39 in C. J. Ryenolds (ed.) *National Identity and Its Defenders*, Chiang Mai: Silkworm.

Saeng Chandragam and Narujohn Iddhichiracharas (eds.) *Buddhism in Northern Thailand*, Chiang Mai: Tippanetr Publishing Co.

Sanguan Chotisukharat 1969 *Prapheni thai phak nüa* (Northern Thai Customs), 2 volumes, Bangkok: Odeon Store..

—— 1971a *Prapheni lanna thai lae phithikam tang tang* (Lanna Thai Traditions and Rituals), Chiang Mai: Prathüang Witthaya.

—— 1971b 'Supernatural beliefs and practices in Chiang Mai' (translated by Gehan Wijeyewardene), p.211–231 in *Journal of the Siam Society* 59(1).

Shalardchai Ramitanondh 1984 *Phi cao nai* (Spirits of the Lords and Masters), Chiang Mai: Chiang Mai University.

Sommai Premchit and Pierre Doré 1991 *The Lan Na Twelve Month Traditions: an ethno-historic and comparative approach*, Chiang Mai: Faculty of Social Sciences, Chiang Mai University and C.N.R.S, France.

Sulak Sivaraksa 1991 'The crisis of Siamese identity', p.41–58 in C. J. Reynolds (ed.) *National Identity and Its Defenders*.

Swearer, Donald K. and Sommai Premchit 1978 'The relation between the religions and political orders in Northern Thailand (14th to 16th centuries)', p.20–33 in Bardwell L. Smith (ed.) *Religion and Legitimation of Power in Thailand, Laos, and Burma*, Chambersburg, Pa.: Anima Books.

Tambiah, Stanley J. 1970 *Buddhism and the Spirit Cults in North-east Thailand*, Cambridge: Cambridge University Press.

—— 1976 *World Conqueror and World Renouncer: a study of Buddhism and polity in Thailand against a historical background*, Cambridge: Cambridge University Press.

—— 1984 *The Buddhist Saints of the Forest and the Cult of Amulets*, Cambridge: Cambridge University Press.

Tanabe, Shigeharu 1991a 'Spirits, power and the discourse of female gender: the *phi meng* cult of Northern Thailand', p.183–212 in Manas Chitakasem and Andrew Turton (eds.) *Thai Constructions of Knowledge*, London: School of Oriental and African Studies.

—— 1991b *Religious Traditions among Tai Ethnic Groups: a selected bibliography*, Ayutthaya: Ayutthaya Historical Study Centre.

—— 1996 'The person in transformation: body, mind and cultural appropriation', conference lecture, Sixth International Conference on Thai Studies, Chiang Mai, 15 October (also chapter 1 in this volume).

Thongchai Winichakul 1994 *Siam Mapped: a history of the geo-body of the nation*, Honolulu: University of Hawaii Press.

Wales, H.G. Quaritch 1931 *Siamese State Ceremonies: their history and function*, London: Bernard Quaritch.

Wijeyewardene, Gehan 1986 *Place and Emotion in Northern Thai Ritual Behaviour*, Bangkok: Pandora.

Wyatt, David K. 1994a (1975) 'Education and the modernization of Thai society', p.219–244 in D. K. Wyatt *Studies in Thai History*, Chiang Mai: Silkworm.

—— 1994b (1982) 'The "subtle revolution" of Rama I', p.131–172 in *Studies in Thai History*, Chiang Mai: Silkworm.

CHAPTER THREE

Hmong Confucian Ethics and Constructions of the Past[1]

Nicholas Tapp

'I conceive', said Mr. Foster, 'that men are virtuous in proportion as they are enlightened; and that, as every generation increases in knowledge, it increases in virtue'.

'I wish it were so', said Mr. Escot, 'but to me the very reverse appears true ... '

(Thomas Love Peacock 1816 *Headlong Hall*)

I

Distinctions have been drawn between a type of morality which reflectively applies moral criteria, involving self-consciousness, and a type of morality which is a 'habit of affection and behaviour', acquired in the same way that we acquire language, without the formulation of conscious rules (Oakeshott 1962 in Connerton 1989: 29). Despite Winch's well-known critique (1958), Connerton sides with Oakeshott and in fact his notion of a habitual social memory incorporated in culturally specific bodily practices and commemorative rituals is largely a development of Oakeshott's habitual morality in the light of phenomenological theories of perception (especially Merleau-Ponty 1962).

Connerton's weakness, like that of Giddens, lies in a too-sharp distinction of traditional from modern societies, the oral from the literate tradition, the incorporated from the inscribed (particularly in relation to those traditional societies which have enjoyed a long historical relationship with literate civilisations). His concern to emphasise the physical aspects of social memory (which after all may as well be inscribed as incorporated), leads him to a separation of 'social memory' from other processes of 'historical reconstruction' (Connerton 1989: 13) which is quite unjustified, as a number of commentators have noted, referring to the selectivity of 'history' itself. As Carr (1961: 129) puts it, 'History begins when men begin to think of a passage of time not in terms of natural processes ... but of a series of specific events in which they are consciously involved, which they can consciously influence ...' and 'It is only through the ever-widening horizons of the future that an approach can be made to "ultimate objectivity" in historical studies' (Carr 1961: 117). Historical reconstruction is actually not limited to the work of historians, as Connerton supposes; whole societies may reconstruct their past, as Fentress and Wickham (1992) show, and indeed, history itself may be seen as a process of 'organised forgetting', although Connerton sees this as characteristic only of state apparatuses depriving citizens of their proper memories.[2]

Surely it is the question of how the past is *forgotten* which should concern us; indeed, in bodily social memory, it is precisely the processes which have been forgotten and have become unconscious which are important. While the distinction between rule-governed and habitual behaviour should stand, this too is ultimately a matter of consciousness; habitual behaviour is automatic and involuntary, as Connerton himself says (Connerton 1989: 94); that is, it is unconscious of itself. If we are to follow Halbwachs (as both Connerton and Fentress and Wickham do), in seeing personal and social memories as inextricably interconnected, then all social customs and morals must be seen too as a kind of organised forgetting (including those commemorative rituals Connerton sees as examples of remembrance), which derive their constraining power, their 'impulsion', from this very involuntariness; a kind of pathological inability to come to terms with the realities of a present and ever-changing reality. Then, I do not murder only because of (socially) ingrained habit, rather than because of some moral maxim; like Elias' table-manners, morals too 'are "forgotten" as maxims only when they have been well remembered as habits' (Connerton 1989: 83).

I would not, therefore, follow Connerton in his separation of social memory from other kinds of historical reconstruction. In fact, Connerton opens a space for the consideration of legend and folklore (surely classic forms of 'historical reconstruction') in terms of social memory, but fails to develop this theme, taken much further forward by Fentress and Wickham (1992). I would prefer to emphasise instead (as do Fentress and Wickham) that social memory is to be found just as much in legends and folk tales, idioms and verbal expressions, and some writings as in the rituals and physical embodiments Connerton stresses. However, recent work with the urban Hmong of Chiang Mai pointed indeed to a change from a *habitual* kind of morality to a morality which had become *self-reflective*, conscious and contested between different groups. This change had taken place in the context of a larger shift of spatial contexts from the local to the global which had implied the *universalisation* of a morality which had hitherto been socially relative. Moreover, these changes accompanied a massive transformation of the view of both personal and a social past, a conscious *reconstructuring of historical consciousness* through the use of sharp contrasts between the morality of rural life and the decadence of urban existence to repaint the recent historical past as a nostalgic idyll. Social memory is, then, not necessarily embodied in physical practices, and does not always preserve the 'true' memories of the dispossessed against the literate accounts of stronger peoples, but like those accounts is also constantly reinventing the past in ways which may fit the present situation and utopian future; it is, therefore, precisely a kind of historical reconstruction.

So 'social memory' is here seen to entail a kind of organised forgetting of the past which may indeed be its most important aspect. Indeed, as Fentress and Wickham put it (1992: xi), 'Social memory is ... often selective, distorted, and inaccurate'.

My original work on the Hmong was concerned with what they saw as the most important aspects of their culture – their *kevcai*; a term which may be translated as 'customs' or 'traditions' but which literally refers to 'ways' in the sense of roads/paths (with a plausible connection to *caiv*, things prohibited or taboo, that are forbidden). It was the Hmong *kevcai*, classified predominantly as those of marriage and death, but also including those of the New Year celebrations, and more widely birth, subsistence, litigation and dispute, which formed the site of conscious modern struggles over what should now be preserved and what rejected, particularly in the context of recent secularisation and the appeal of Buddhist or Christian moralities to certain sectors of the Hmong.

But once we start to inquire into social ethics and the role of memory among the Hmong in formulating these, it is obvious that the generalisations, which have been made about the relative morality of lineage societies (Sahlins 1968), should also apply to the Hmong. That is, the kind of traditional morality we might expect to find among the Hmong, should not be of an ethicised, universalistic/absolute kind; there should be no generalised, decontextualised, semantic or purely cognitive conception of absolute standards of good or evil, for example, which would be separable from the social structure of the Hmong, but that ethical standards among the Hmong would traditionally be relative to the social structure, and vary according to social distance. For example, only the killing of a close lineage relative would traditionally be seen as 'murder'; the severity of punishment for a crime varied according to the social proximity. Only the adultery of married *women* was heinous, since men were permitted to take second wives, and a measure of pre-marital sex was normal. Again, the horror of incest applied not only to one's blood sisters, but to all women with the same surname as oneself.

One might draw a diagram of this relative kind of social morality, following Sahlins, as follows:

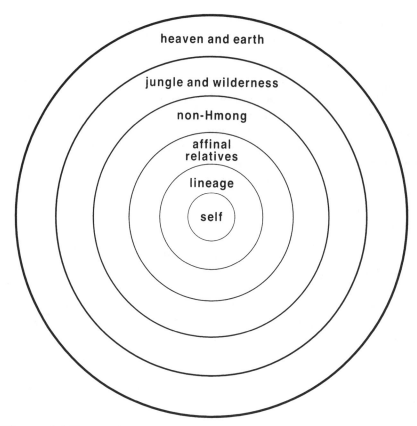

Diagram 3.1 The moral universe.

One informant suggested these terms when I questioned him along these lines, and it was most significant that he added 'Heaven and Earth' at the outermost concentric circle, as this reached back to an older, and somewhat overlooked influence on the Hmong, that of Confucianism.

II

Ua dab ua qhuas, pe niam txiv

Although I had been aware of the importance of everyday social etiquette and habitual behaviour among the Hmong, as well as the more spectacular ritual occasions which have formed the object of much research, I had not however realised how much the everyday ethos of the Hmong was permeated by what we may call a Confucian ethic until when, in 1994,[3] a primary informant revealed to me what, in his opinion, were the most important things about being a good person, which a father could teach his children, and which he hoped the Hmong would now be able to preserve in their new lives in the cities and overseas. What he saw as the most crucial aspect of customary Hmong morality to maintain was 'filial piety' (*pe niam txiv*) – or, more fully, to respect and pay obeisance to one's mother and father; in full, *ua dab ua qhuas* (to perform the ancestral and household sacrifices and rituals), for *niam txiv* and *pog yawg* (mother and father, paternal grandfather and grandmother), to respect (*pe*) and love (*hlub*) them, to *laig niam txiv* (propitiate their spirits), so they will protect (*povhwm*) one.[4]

He went on to tell me about a Hmong family he had heard about near the Burmese border who were famous for the *civility* of the children towards their parents; the children would salute their parents each morning on rising and each evening before going to sleep, and often solicitously inquired after their health.

He then recounted a tale about Confucius himself (Khoo Meej in Hmong, a star). Once there was a man who had farmed a field next to a field belonging to Khoo Meej, he said, and the gourds Khoo Meej had planted in his field came and sprouted in his own field, so after harvesting them he took a portion of the harvest to offer to Khoo Meej as a tribute/thanks-offering. But Khoo Meej refused the gift, saying it was not to him that the harvest was due, but to the man's own mother and father, since it was they who had succoured him as a child and taught him everything he knew, including how to farm.[5]

Ua neeg tsim txiaj

It was not such a simple matter to frame the subsequent inquiry into social morality among urbanised Hmong in Chiang Mai in such a way that Western notions of 'ethics' or 'absolute morality' were adequately represented; one can talk somewhat glibly about *ua neeg zoo* or being a good person, *ua qhov zoo* as opposed to *ua qhov phem* (doing good as opposed to doing evil), and one could talk of *siab dawb siab zoo*, being white and good hearted, or 'being straight' (*ua neeg ncaj ncees*), but there is no abstract set of cognitive principles, divorced from specific social occasions, which can be pulled out in such a way that they correspond to this formulation; the concept which most often emerged in the focus group discussions we organised among the urbanised Hmong of Chiang Mai, however, was that of *ua neeg tsim txiaj*, or being a *worthy man*, with something of the same resonance which a 'worthy man' has in English – a *man of substance*, implying some kind of social stature or status, and some degree of wealth (see discussions of 'bobility', Gellner 1970).

It was easier for informants, even urban residents, to describe *traditional* notions of the 'worthy man' than it was for them to conceive of how it might be possible to be a 'worthy man' in the modern, urban world; there seemed to be no clear guidelines, which clearly reflects the material difficulties the Hmong in Thailand still have in gaining wealth or social status in Thai society. However, the position of the 'worthy man' could quite easily be described in terms of a respected traditional village elder, who would help and maintain good relations with others without excessively favouring his own family (for example in bridewealth disputes), and by dint of hard work and careful judgement had gradually attained a position of esteem and trust in his own local community. The notion of the 'worthy man' was also associated with ideas of leadership, and the Thai term *phu nam* was frequently used together with, or in association with, the Hmong term for the 'man of worth', which was seen as not unallied to being cultured or having an education (*paub ntawv*).

Traditionally, then, Hmong morality has indeed been a socially embedded ethic, in that it has been closely connected to their lives as subsistence farmers in village communities, organised through a patrilineal lineage structure; a relative, 'tribal' ethic of behaviour and social relations not radically different to that of other lineage-based peoples described in the literature, but nevertheless an ethic permeated throughout by Confucian notions of etiquette and civil behaviour, in which the importance of *filial piety*[6] and the traditional notion of the *worthy man* stand out as central, organising, guiding principles. Etiquette and ritual are here intricately connected with ideas of moral worth, leadership, and ancestral worship in a way which does well illustrate the notion of an embodied social knowledge (Connerton 1989).

III

Returning to our original model of a *relative* tribal morality, it would seem reasonable to conclude that what will have occurred under the impact of urbanisation, is a kind of gigantic stretching of the traditional boundaries of the Hmong moral universe, in which the boundaries between self, community, and the world have been ex-ploded, and the relative basis of traditional Hmong morality therefore having largely collapsed.

Tos txais qhua

The *contested* nature of modern morality was most often described by informants in terms of simple contrasts between a previous, remembered life in the villages, and the difficulties and changes brought about by urban life (which had also changed modern village life). Begging in Dòi Pui to the west of Chiang Mai was often cited as paradigmatic of the kind of changes which have taken place. It was said that before, the Hmong had always greeted each other when they met as friends; and the strangeness of now not doing so, or possibly passing other Hmong in the town and not knowing that they were Hmong, was much discussed. In the past, it was said, the Hmong would always invite others to eat with them, but away from the village community this was no longer done. In the past there had been no stealing in the villages, now there was a lot. Clearly what was referred to and discussed here is a *general breakdown of the traditional social order*, encompassing areas of everyday etiquette, politeness and the structuring of social relations as much as what is conventionally seen as 'moral' behaviour; not locking doors or stealing, eating together, greeting passers-by, are interconnected aspects of everyday behaviour. Hospitality and the treatment of guests, politeness and courtesy, stood out as characteristics of a 'worthy man' as much as of 'being Hmong'; the importance of knowing how to *tos txais qhua*, how to treat guests and offer them food, to know enough about genealogical networks and family structures to inquire after relatives or friends in common in different parts of Thailand, to know how to introduce a stranger, all this was a vital part of being able to function adequately in a Hmong society, and was one of the most important things the parents interviewed did *not* wish their children to lose.

This was sharply contrasted with the recent changes in Hmong society which were seen to have occurred. Cases of brothers killing brothers, and whole families breaking up over land inheritance disputes were complained of – unthinkable in the past, when land was rarely inherited. One wealthy Hmong had refused to help his own brother in need, but instead had referred him to a welfare agency.

Particularly revealing in these, very common kinds of complaint, were the remarks on passing other Hmong in towns without greeting, or even necessarily recognising them, as these point to a general collapse in the traditional social boundaries I have outlined, which determined the structure of a *relative* morality. In this respect, some of the criticisms of returning overseas refugee Hmong which were voiced (by young girls as well as more mature researchers) were particularly illuminating; male visitors were criticised for returning, particularly at the Hmong New Year, and misleading young village Hmong girls with promises of future grandeur, riches and marriage, which they had no intentions of fulfilling. While overseas Hmong may be accused of 'un-Hmong' behaviour in these cases, at the same time the Hmong returning from overseas find it difficult to fulfil traditional cultural expectations of their behaviour. One of the returning refugees spoke of his genuine discomfort in visiting a Hmong village, where he was expected to give a speech; he felt that his paternal cousin and others living in the village *saw* him as a stranger – 'like a Chinese, or a Thai', he said – and had begged him to take his tie off for the occasion, but that he had felt he should wear a suit and tie to mark the formality of the occasion!

It is in this sense that the traditional, kinship-related boundaries structuring a relative Hmong morality have broken down, and a new, 'decontextualised' (Bloch 1996) sense of a universal morality has emerged; some Hmong (like the returning overseas settlers, or perhaps the educated businessmen in Chiang Mai) have become 'as' strangers to those Hmong who have led a more continuously 'Hmong' existence, while at the same time there is the awareness that the Hmong community is now wider than it has ever been – and globalised, including Hmong communities not only in neighbouring countries but also overseas, in the US, France, Canada, and Australia. Young Hmong living in Chiang Mai may feel they have more in common with young Thai or Chinese there than with their own village elders; important relationships have obtained in the hills between the Hmong villagers and the members of other minorities which may at times be more substantial than relations with Hmong who have visited from overseas. The feeling is either that some other Hmong have become like foreigners, *or* there is a general (and new) recognition that all people are the same despite their ethnic differences, a diminished sense of the value of Hmong ethnicity; so that there has been a kind of universalisation, or democratisation, of the types of *immoral* behaviour previously equated with a large degree of social distance. Behaviour formerly appropriate to those furthest from oneself, in the sense that a Chinese/Thai/American may be, is now also appropriate to fellow villagers, if all human beings are the same: social distance has immeasurably widened (ex-ploded); the distance between people has increased, and therefore behaviour previously appropriate to those *furthest* from oneself is now appropriate to those (relatively) close to one.

IV

I have dealt so far with simple contrasts of the type most easily elicited to describe changes in customary Hmong morality. Another simple contrast which emerged, but which pointed however towards more fundamental features of the Hmong moral system, was the contrast between the simple farming existence of the past, and the current success of some Hmong traders, which was seen as linked to trickery and deception.

Siab ntshiab

The most widespread opposition in terms of which most contrasts between a previous, more idyllic, and a present more decadent state, were phrased was a wide-reaching opposition between *innocence* and *deception*, in which the profits accrued through trading, were opposed to the innocence or 'clear-heartedness' (*siab ntshiab*) of the idyll of a natural morality of reciprocity practised in traditional society. Hmong tended to emphasise how their ignorance of the 'wider world' and its ways allowed them to be easily exploited and taken advantage of by external agencies (like ravaged virgins, or the children whose souls are endangered by malevolent spirits, and must be rescued through shamanic rites). This is why the stories of the refugee Hmong exploiting young Hmong girls are so particularly telling; since they seem to refer to the exploitation of the Hmong by Hmong themselves – or can they really be seen as Hmong? Hence the current crisis of identity, the ex-ploding (ex-ploring?) of social distance, and the universalisation of a previously relative immorality. Hence, too, the strong conscious emphasis on the need for education by nearly all informants, which is now something more than the traditional respect for and desire for culture (Tapp 1989).

For this is now allied with a new fear that the Hmong are 'backward' (*poob qab*, have fallen behind); many of the young people in our discussion groups talked openly of the difficulties of being recognised as 'Hmong' in town; they said they were *txaj muag* (shame-faced) to be seen as Hmong, since the Hmong were backward, and that this was why they wore urban clothes in town and tried to talk Thai with other Hmong, or to disguise their Hmong accents when speaking Thai, so that the Thais would not recognise them and discriminate against them. A number of cases were recounted of typical job discrimination against those recognised as Hmong at work in Chiang Mai.

Koob meej

The growing rates of heroin addiction (and gambling) among Hmong both in villages and in the towns (a direct result of the inept suppression of opium production) was a major topic of concern, often cited as a threat to the very survival of Hmong society and culture. As my co-researcher pointed out, traditionally the families of opium or heroin addicts have been looked down on in the villages; opium and heroin addiction was not seen moreover as an individual affair, but as something which affected the whole *koob meej* of the family, so that any member of the family, whether young or female, would have had the right to scold or cajole the addict.

What is of interest here is how individual moral behaviour is not seen as only individual, but immediately reflects on and involves the wider social grouping, and particularly the immediate family and lineage segment; the notion of *koob meej* is thus importantly related to the notion of *ua tsim txiaj neeg* or the 'man of worth' who, as we saw, helps others as well as his own family, and importantly assures his position through the performance of appropriate ritual, etiquette, and courtesy to strangers and visitors. With the breakdown of traditional distinctions between self/family/clan/other clans/strangers/enemy, however, it has become increasingly impossible to become a 'worthy man' or to remain 'clear-hearted' in this sense.

The movement to trading and away from farming is therefore reflected in a breakdown of the traditional, and very Confucian, morality connected with notions of clear-heartedness, worth and moral reputation, and there is a consequent *loss of the sense of worth* (cf. Hutheesing 1990), of value, rectitude, probity, of virtue and fresh-heartedness, of face, self-esteem, reputation, and consequently dignity, which is widespread – and, most importantly, not one that is limited to urban life but one which importantly affects the new rural life, as urban-rural trading relations and emergent wealth differentials become instituted.

Yet, that it should be such values which are causing so much overt concern and alarm shows their very strength and continuing importance, and also the extent to which a customary, habituated type of social morality has now become a morality which is *conscious* of the maxims which need to be formulated, in order to understand these behaviours and explain them to others. Among concerned Hmong, traditional morality has indeed become a matter of cognitive reflection rather than unthinking or habitual adoption, and this has led to a conscious concern with the need for education, and the importance of inculcating traditional moral values in the younger generation. One Hmong businessman was particularly aware of the problems in, as he saw it, the loss of traditional Hmong culture, and while resident in Chiang Mai, and having taken every opportunity to provide his children with a Thai education, which means they are now thoroughly at home with Thai friends and have a bright future in Thai society, has still made efforts every year to bring his children for one to two months back to his home village to visit his wife's parents, so that they will never forget the traditional Hmong village life he himself grew up in (an apt example of how 'we conserve our recollections by referring them to the material milieu that surrounds us', as Connerton (1989: 37) puts it in commenting on the work of Halbwachs (1925, 1930)). What he saw as the most important aspects of Hmong culture for the younger generation not to lose hold of were the traditional cultural specialisation that young men attempt to excel in, to build a position for themselves in the village, which is not wholly dependent on economic status or family support, but to do with excellence in, for example, shamanism or the songs of death, the marriage rituals, the reed pipes or courtship songs, as well as *tos txais qhua*, or the correct treatment of guests and visitors. It is in these particular skills and capabilities, these technical excellences and habituated social responses reflecting Confucian values, that the excellence ('virtue') characteristic of the 'worthy man' is achieved.

V

Particularly important changes in gender relations have occurred, though this is not the place to go into them; while the female prostitution, which some other minorities have been forced into, has been largely resisted by the Hmong, gender relations were the aspect of traditional society which came in for the most frequent criticism.

Paub cai

One Christian girl, for example, said that she thought it good that her father had taught her, before she left the village, not to steal or talk ill of other people, to be polite, to be worthy, not to quarrel or fight (*sib ntaus*), to be patient (*ua siab ntsev*) and diligent (*ua tis neeg gua*), but nevertheless she said she thought her father had been wrong to say that since she was a *girl*, who would eventually get married, she wouldn't need an education. It is still quite unusual to hear young people criticising their elders, and particularly a young girl her father. Other women in Chiang Mai, however, were still more outspoken in their criticisms of Hmong parents not allowing their daughters to study past MS3, the junior high school level (*mò sò* 3 in the Thai system). While they did not favour any radical change in elder/junior relations, since as they said the elders *paub cai* (know the customs)[7] and could teach the youth, at the same time they complained that women had no rights of legal representation (*tsis muaj cai hais plaub*). There have even been efforts to establish a Hmong Women's Association in Chiang Mai. It is clear that male-female relations are and have been changing dramatically, as the movement away from a traditional subsistence economy continues, and generally in the direction towards more equality for women. One of the commonest contrasting statements encountered referred to the changes in sexual relations between young people which take place in the towns; in the village a boy would not dare address his girlfriend if her parents were present, or in her own house, but in the absence of parental controls among groups of youths studying in Chiang Mai, boys and girls have moved in with each other with no regard to the opinions of parents, saying 'their bodies are their own'. Yet this is not necessarily true of those brought up by families in the city, where, as I have said, stricter parental controls still tend to be maintained.

Muaj hlob, tsis paub txaj muag

I mentioned that the relation of trickery and deception (to fraud and profit) was a particularly important aspect of a fundamental Hmong moral system, as opposed to notions of innocence concerned with notions of moral worth intrinsically connected to clear-heartedness; I find this particularly important because of the emphasis which emerged throughout informant's statements and discussions, on notions of modesty linked with speech. The moral feature most stressed in informants' accounts of parental advice and instruction was that *one should not boast*, since this was likely to provoke envy and jealousy among one's friends and group, leading to attempts to *trick* and deceive one (a good example of the utilitarian argument for morality, that such deeds are recognised to be harmful, and therefore should be avoided). A very high value was placed on the importance of not *khav theeb* (showing off/boasting), since this would be to be proud (*muaj hlob*), and both city and overseas Hmong were criticised by other Hmong for this. One who is not proud (*tsis muaj hlob*) is said to 'know shame' (*paub txaj muag*), which importantly implicates both the notions of reputation (*koob meej*) and worth (*txiaj neej*) referred to. It is particularly noteworthy that both these two fundamental moral values – not boasting, and not lying (*dag*) or speaking falsely (*hais lus cuav*) – are concerned with *speech*, like other negatively valued types of behaviour which formed an aspect of parental advice such as not *sib cag sib cem*, cursing and quarrelling, and point again to the traditional Confucian emphasis on correct conduct, behaviour, and etiquette (cf. Connerton's ceremonies, proprieties, and techniques, of the body).

Hais lus cuav

Gossip (*hais xaiv lus*) was almost equally disapproved of. At the same time, to be proud (*muaj hlob*) is to 'look down on others' (*saib tsis tau luag*), contrasting with the soft-spoken man of worth in the traditional village community, who helped others as he helped his own family. What is referred to here is a traditional moral economy, in which an egalitarian social structure called for the restriction of expressions of inequality or distinction that is characteristic of peasant societies. Lying and deception – characteristics of speech, like gossip and boasting, all expressions of social inequality – are seen as intrinsically linked with making a profit, as *ua luam ua lag* (trading) replaces *ua teb* (farming).

The indigenous notion of profit is that, somehow, the perfect correspondence or equivalence of words with facts has been disturbed, and profit corresponds to this new-found inequivalence between words and facts. I must be cheating you if I sell you something for more than I got it, as one Hmong trader said. In Chiang Mai one must lie a bit, and *hloov yoog yuav txuj*, imitate others. The natural system of poetic equivalences and correspondences, the natural equality characteristic of innocence, has been disturbed, so that things are no longer equal; people occupy different statuses, and something you buy for 100 baht you may sell for 120 baht, which is as the Hmong have traditionally seen it a kind of deception. In this disjuncture of words and events, brought about by the emergence of social differentiation, gossip, slander, boasting, pride, cheating, lying, deception, trickery, become possible and necessary, leading inevitably to further jealousy and competition. The competition between different social statuses, brought about by the existence of profit and interest, leads to the breakdown of all the traditional sanctions against social inequality, such as gossip and boasting. The very high value placed on these two was intrinsically linked with a social system which is rapidly transforming, collapsing, and unfolding as social distance widens and deepens.

While, therefore, there is no traditional sense of a universalised morality among the Hmong (no codified system of values abstracted from the social system), behaviour which was traditionally seen as only appropriate to those beyond the pale of the social system has now been universalised, and it is this kind of behaviour we would consider as immoral. Yet the essential bases of a natural Hmong morality, linked with a set of verbal propriety practices concerned with the transformation of the self, importantly linked with Confucian notions of filial piety and humility, remain linguistically intact, and will continue to structure Hmong responses to what are seen as attacks on (the innocence of) Hmong culture and the inroads of the market economy. The importance of maintaining Hmong customs in the city continues to be upheld; in other words, the importance of knowing what to say, and when to say it ('how to speak and what to say'). Indeed, the importance of this should be paid particular attention to in theories which seek to distinguish the cognitive from the sensory or experiential, and the incorporated from the inscribed, too rigidly.

VI

Sharp contrasting binary oppositions are not only characteristic of structuralist anthropology but are also well reflected in many highly developed traditional systems of thought (which is why, of course, structuralist analyses of these made so much sense). In his comical 1816 novel *Headlong Hall*, Thomas Love Peacock mimicked the current philosophical debate between adherents of historical pessimism and optimism. Mr. Escot, the 'deteriorationist' (like Rousseau), looked back to a Golden Age in which perfect equality, liberty and fraternity had reigned, and deplored the moral degradation of modernity, which was seen as surely and inexorably leading to ultimate cataclysm. For Mr. Foster, the 'perfectibilian', on the other hand, history had been a progressive freeing of human dependence from material constraint, through science and technology, leading directly to the more enlightened society represented by the eighteenth century in Europe (Robinson 1970).

It is not so easy to distinguish social memory from other forms of historical reconstruction, as Connerton maintained (1989). In fact the 'organised oblivion' which Connerton rightly criticises in the case of Czech history may be a characteristic of historical consciousness in general, and it may not be what is remembered which is inscribed in cultural practice, so much as what has been forgotten. In this sense the sharp contrasts, which the Chiang Mai Hmong more and more tend to use to describe the degradation of their present social situation in relation to a more idyllic past, serve an important purpose in instilling in a new generation a sense of the importance of a Hmong cultural identity and reaffirming traditional moral values; but more has been forgotten here than is remembered; the poverty and isolation, the exploitation and mortality, the hardship and suffering. Indeed, a kind of 'principled forgetting', followed by a 'rhetoric of pastiche', may be a part of the 'core experience of modernity' (de Man 1970 in Connerton 1989: 61).

Paradoxically, in socialist accounts of the recent past, this relation would be reversed; as the collection of oral histories among Hmong in Vietnam, Laos and China, has showed, they are used to formulating their thoughts about the recent past in terms of a historically optimistic framework, emphasising the hardships, wars and injustices of the past in relation to the peace and comparative prosperity of the present. These are not exactly only overt or superficial views, although it is true that only further inquiry reveals the facts of past fortune (like silver and freedom from state interference) and the continuing inequities of the present; but they are larger overall historical paradigms, in which people have become used to expressing their views. And they square well with a theoretical viewpoint which would emphasise the moral degradation of emergent capitalism in relation to the communal solidarity of pre-capitalist, even peasant, societies, or the social benefits brought about by socialist reform in relation to the decadence and moral anarchy of, say, Shanghai in the 30s, Saigon in the 60s. Yet ultimately these are caricatures, as much as Peacock's characters are, of complex and protracted developments which cannot be reduced to sharp disjunctures of the kind favoured by old-fashioned historiography, or by societies seeking to refashion their past in situations of social crisis. As Fentress and Wickham have well put it, 'We preserve the past at the cost of decontextualising it, and partially blocking it out' (1992: 201).[8]

Notes

1 The research on which this paper is based was conducted as part of a three-year programme of inquiries into changing social ethics sponsored by the National Museum of Ethnology in Osaka. A preliminary version of the paper was presented at the Sixth International Conference on Thai Studies, Chiang Mai, 14–17 October 1996.

2 On the nature of history as an arbitrary process of selection, see also Croce (1941), Collingwood (1946), Berlin (1954).

3 I am grateful to Dr. Chayan Vaddhanaphuti and Prasit Leepreecha of the Social Research Institute, Ching Mai University, and to our research assistant Apisit Seksantikul, who participated in the Thai aspects of this research on a joint basis. The work included interviews with Hmong specialists, Hmong living in Chiang Mai, and in three village sites outside Chiang Mai which serve as catchment areas for Hmong coming to live in town, and focus discussion groups

among Hmong entrepreneurs, students, monks and women. Thanks are due to a number of people, including Dr. Leo Alting von Gesau, Dr. Chupinit Kesmanee, and Mr. Lis Npis.

4 To *ua dab ua qhuas* (to perform the rituals of ancestral and domestic worship), in the way required to establish the filial piety stressed by the Master Shaman who was my primary informant here, signifies the importance of *kwvtij* or the lineage networks of which it is necessary to be aware in order to be able to *tos txais qhua*, or treat guests and visitors correctly.

5 This legal case is a classic one in Asia, and is also found in the Indic Laws of Manu, in which Manu first decreed that the cucumber with roots in one man's garden and roots in that of another belonged to the one in whose garden the fruits were, but had to reverse his decision in favour of the one who had the roots of the cucumber because of popular disapproval. See G. Houtman, 'Manu's *samadhi*: Burmanization as Brahmanization', paper presented at the Colloquium on Burma Studies, 25–27 October 1996, Center for Burma Studies, Northern Illinois University; Richardson, D. 1896 *The Dhamathat or the Laws of Menoo*, Rangoon: Hanthawaddy Press (Fourth edition). It is conceivable, and paradigmatically South East Asian, and characteristic of the operations of social memory in finding new contexts, that my informant should have lent an Indic Buddhist story a Confucian gloss for Hmong transmission.

6 On filial piety, also see Fortes (1961) and Worsley (1956).

7 There is a sense in which someone who *tsis* (negative) *paub cai* is immoral by definition.

8 For Hmong terms, the Barney-Smalley Romanised Phonetic Alphabet has been used, in which final nasalisation is indicated by doubling the vowels, and final consonants are not pronounced, but indicate tone values.

References

Berlin, Isaiah 1954 *Historical Inevitability*, London: Oxford University Press.

Bloch, Maurice 1996 'Memory', p.361–363 in Alan Barnard and Jonathan Spencer (eds.) *Encyclopaedia of Social and Cultural Anthropology*, London and New York: Routledge.

Carr, E. H. 1961 *What Is History?* London: Macmillan.

Collingwood, R.G. 1946 *The Idea of History*, Oxford: Clarendon Press.

Connerton, Paul 1989 *How Societies Remember*, Cambridge, New York, and Melbourne: Cambridge University Press.

Croce, B. 1941 *History as the Story of Liberty*, London: Allen and Unwin.

de Man, Paul 1970 'Literary history and literary modernity', p.384–404 in *Daedalus* 99.

Elias, Norbert 1978 *The Civilizing Process* (translated by E. Jephcott), Oxford: Basil Blackwell.

Fentress, James and Chris Wickham 1992 *Social Memory*, Oxford and Cambridge (USA): Basil Blackwell.

Fortes, Meyer 1961 'Pietas in ancestor worship' (The Henry Myers Lecture 1960), p.166–191 in *Journal of the Royal Anthropological Institute* 91.

Gellner, Ernest 1970 'Concepts and society' in Brian Wilson (ed.) *Rationality*, Oxford: Basil Blackwell.

Giddens, Anthony 1991 *Modernity and Self-identity: self and society in the late modern age*, Cambridge: Polity Press.

Halbwachs, Maurice 1925 *Les cadres sociaux de la mémoire*, Paris.

—— 1930 *La mémoire collective*, Paris.

Hutheesing, Othome Klein 1990 *Emerging Sexual Inequality among the Lisu of Northern Thailand: the waning of dog and elephant repute*, Leiden and New York: E.J. Brill.

Merleau-Ponty, Maurice 1962 *Phenomenology of Perception* (translated by C. Smith), London: Routledge & Kegan Paul.

Oakeshott, Michael 1962 *Rationalism in Politics*, London: Methuen.

Peacock, Thomas Love 1816 (1987) *Headlong Hall*, Oxford: Oxford University Press.

Robinson, Joan 1970 *Freedom and Necessity: an introduction to the study of society*, London: Allen & Unwin.

Sahlins, Marshall 1968 *Tribesmen*, New Jersey: Prentice-Hall.

Tapp, Nicholas 1989 *Sovereignty and Rebellion: the White Hmong of Northern Thailand*, Singapore, Oxford, and New York: Oxford University Press.

Winch, Peter 1958 *The Idea of a Social Science*, London: Routledge & Kegan Paul.

Worsley, Peter 1956 'The kinship system of the Tallensi: a revaluation' (Carl Bequest Prize Essay 1955), p.37–77 in *Journal of the Royal Anthropological Institute* 86.

PART II

Nationalist Monuments

Competing Social Memories

CHAPTER FOUR

National Heroine or Local Spirit?

The Struggle over Memory in the Case
of Thao Suranari of Nakhon Ratchasima

Charles F. Keyes

A Monument, a revisionist history, and a dramatic protest

In late February 1996, flyers were circulated in and around the city of Nakhon Ratchasima (Khorat) in Northeastern Thailand that called people to redeem the prestige and honour of the memory of Thao Suranari, more affectionately known as grandmother Mo (*ya mo*).[1] A prominent monument to Thao Suranari in the centre of the city of Khorat honours this woman for her 'heroism' in 1827 in helping to defeat the troops of Cao Anuwong, the king of Vientiane, who had launched an attack on Siam. The call to defend the honour of grandmother Mo had been prompted by the appearance of the book, *Kanmüang nai anusawari thao Suranari* (The Politics of the Monument of Thao Suranari), by Saipin Kaew-ngarmprasert, a local teacher who had first written the work as an MA thesis at Thammasat University.[2] I quote the flyer in its totality:[3]

> **Communiqué Concerning the Insult to Grandmother Mo**
> This concerns the appearance and circulation of the publication by Matichon Press of 'The Politics of the Monument of Thao Suranari' by Saipin Kaew-ngarmprasert. The contents of this publication have created confusion and doubts in the general populace. The origins of the heroism of Thao Suranari [are said] in this book to be only stories and legends known to the people of Khorat and spread about afterwards. At the time of the Boworadet rebellion in 1934,[4] officials and people in Nakhon Ratchasima came together to build the shrine to Thao Suranari in order to erase the image of rebelliousness of the Khorat people. In short, [this publication] says that the origin of the heroism and of Thao Suranari [herself] is the result of repeated efforts to serve politics and the state during [both] the periods of absolute monarchy and democracy. Even today the characteristics and practices associated

113

with Grandmother Mo [are said to] place her in the status of a 'spirit' (*phi*) or 'deity' (*thepharak*) and not in the status of a heroine.

The descendants (*luk lan*) of the people of Khorat, those who retain pride in the past heroism of the Khorat people and the virtues of grandmother Mo are greatly upset over this insult to all the people of Khorat occasioned by the printing of this shameful publication. For another thing, when one studies the work in detail, it can be clearly seen that the author intends to attempt to extol the actions of Cao Anuwong of Vientiane, making him out as the saviour of [his] nation. [The author] thus goes beyond what any Thai should do. Consider the danger if the younger generation and subsequent generations understand [the story of Grandmother Mo] in accord with the intent of this book. It will cause a great transformation in the history of the nation (*ca koet kanplianplaeng prawattisat khòng chat yang yai luang*). Thus, let us denounce the actions of the groups who joined to create this publication. [Let us] demand that officials of Nakhon Ratchasima province and the Fine Arts Department, those who can authorise the history (*phu rapròng prawattisat*) concerning Thao Suranari, affirm clearly the heroism of Thao Suranari and the heroism of [those who fought with Thao Suranari at] Thung Samrit[5] so that the descendants of the Khorat people and all Thai may with sure heart in the future pay homage to the virtues of Thao Suranari.

Thus, this communiqué is sent to invite our Khorat kinsmen to join forces to redeem the prestige (*kiattikhun*) and honour (*saksi*) of grandmother Mo, heroine of the flesh and blood of the people of Nakhon Ratchasima, and to preserve [her memory] as the soul (*khwan*) and splendour (*si*) for the Thai nation forever.
[Signed] Group of Descendants of grandmother Mo and the People of Khorat
27 February 1996

The flyer then ends with the following: '[On] 4 March 1996 at 3 p.m. please join with your Khorat kinsmen in support of a plebiscite (*prachamati*) to redeem the honour of grandmother Mo on the platform of the Thao Suranari monument'.[6]

On 4 March, some 20,000–25,000 local people, officials and military officers joined in response to this call to protest this 'insult' to the memory of grandmother Mo.[7] I draw here on a very detailed account of the event, clearly told from the point of view of one sympathetic to the protest, that appeared on 6 March in the Thai newspaper, *Naeona* (The Front Line).

Plate 4.1 The monument of Thao Suranari, in Nakhon Ratchasima (Khorat), Northeastern Thailand.

Some of the protestors came wearing headbands with such inscriptions as 'My grandmother was a warrior'. Others carried banners such as one that read: 'I (*ku*) will not permit any lowly being (*man*) to show disrespect to my grandmother. If you insult me, it does not matter; but don't insult my grandmother. You lowly one (*man*) will be dragged by the neck to beg forgiveness of grandmother Mo in front of the city of brave women'. Straw effigies were brought along of Saipin, Sujit Wongthet, the editor of *Sinlapa watthanatham* (Arts and Culture), under whose auspices the book had been published, Mr. Khanchai Bunpan, the publisher of *Sinlapa watthanatham* as well as the newspaper *Matichon*, and the rector of Thammasat university.

These props were used to incite the crowd whose mood was described as furious. The effigies were burnt 'with rage' and chilli peppers and salt were burnt 'in a rite to curse those involved with the making of the thesis'. Mr. Bunthüng Phonphanit, 'chair of the group of descendants of grandmother Mo', held up a copy of the book that he said should be destroyed, but the cover should be kept because it had a picture of the statue. As the atmosphere became very heated, a number of people sought to persuade the crowd to remain peaceful.

Several political leaders addressed the protestors. Mr. Suwat Lipataphanlop, secretary of the Chat Phatthana (National Development) Party, one of the leading parties in the country, and M.P. for Nakhon

Ratchasima, expressed not only his own support of the event but also told the crowd that General Chatichai Choonhavan, a former prime minister and then head of the Chat Phatthana Party, asked that they be told that he considered himself to be 'a son of grandmother Mo'. General Chatichai had long seen Khorat as one of the main sources of support for his party.[8] The governor of the province, Mr. Suphon Suphason, accepted a petition presented on behalf of the protestors by Mr. Rakkiat Suppharatanaphong, head of the Northeast Journalists' Association. He promised that he would work to ensure that the demands in the petition were met.

The petition asked that provincial authorities investigate to see whether those involved in writing, approving, and publishing Saipin's thesis had committed *lèse majesté*. Those in the Fine Arts Department 'who authorise history (*phu rapròng prawattisat*)' were asked to confirm that Thao Suranari had been a real person who had acted heroically, 'in order to dispel the confusion of Khorat people'. It was demanded that the Bureau of University Affairs carries out an investigation of the ethics (*canyaban*) of Saipin and her academic advisors, and that Thammasat University consider revoking Saipin's MA degree. Not only should *Matichon* press give all copies of the books to the province to be destroyed, but a boycott of all publications of this press should be undertaken. Saipin herself, together with representatives of the press, should come to the monument within fifteen days to beg forgiveness in front of the statue of Thao Suranari. Their apology should also be publicised by press, radio, and TV. Saipin herself should be made *persona non grata* by the province. The petition concluded by asking provincial authorities 'to organise a seminar for scholars and local leaders in the province in order to find ways together to fight and oppose those evil ones who try to damage the character of Thao Suranari and the dignity and reputation of the people of Khorat'.

Given the threatening tenor of the protest, Saipin had real cause to fear for her life. She left the school in Wangnam Khiao district of Khorat where she taught and went into hiding (see *Daily News* [in Thai], 7 March 1996). Subsequently, it was learned she had moved to Bangkok and had been posted to a job in the Ministry of Education.[9]

The controversy over the memory of Thao Suranari/Grandmother Mo represents the same type of struggle over 'memory' that Matsuda (1996: 25) has said characterised the conflict in 1871 over the monument to Napoleon in the Place Vendôme in Paris. Fortunately, the Thao Suranari controversy did not spawn the violence that happened in the French case. But as in that other instance, the Thao Suranari case shows that 'the past is not a truth upon which to build, but a truth sought, a re-memorializing over which to struggle' (Matsuda 1996: 15). Memory here does not mean the personal memory of any individual who actually knew Thao Suranari first hand; rather it is social memory, that is, the recalling of the past through images or narratives expressed through collective commemorative practices (see Connerton 1989; Fentress and Wickham 1992). As Trouillot (1995: 25), writing about 'power and production of history' in Haiti, has said: 'For what history is changes with time and place or, better said, history reveals itself only through the production of specific narratives. What matters most are the process and conditions of production of such narratives'.

The protest in Khorat in February 1996 entailed the contestation over the memory of Thao Suranari between three quite distinct groups, not between two as accounts at the time suggested. Those who organised the protest were proponents of a dominant nationalist narrative in which the story of Thao Suranari had been subsumed, one that clearly distinguished between 'Thai' and 'Lao', and that made Thao Suranari a female embodiment of a militant nationalism. Saipin, following her scholarly mentors, sought to show through meticulous historical research how the dominant narrative had been shaped by political agendas. Through her study of primary documents, she uncovered a political history that had been suppressed and, at the same time, raised critical questions about the politics of the past that had shaped the social memory of Thao Suranari. It was these questions that so infuriated those who organised the protest. Thai nationalists and politically engaged historians were not, however, the only contenders over the memory of Thao Suranari. For many, not only in Khorat but also elsewhere in the country, grandmother Mo is not a personage of the past, but a potent spirit who acts in the present. In the end, as I will argue, it is the remembering of grandmother Mo as a powerful local spirit rather than national heroine that is far more threatening to the proponents of a Bangkok-centred nationalism than an erudite and meticulously researched scholarly work that few will ever read.

The politicisation of the story of Thao Suranari

The story of Thao Suranari as told in narratives that have 'official' standing in Thailand – that is, as told in texts associated with the monument, in school texts, and in guides to Nakhon Ratchasima province – focuses on the role she played in resisting an invasion of forces from Vientiane. The most succinct version of the story is contained in an inscription placed near the monument, presumably in 1967 when the present statue was erected.

> In 1826 Cao Anuwong of Vientiane rebelled against Bangkok. He brought his army and seized Nakhon Ratchasima. Then he [ordered] that the population of Nakhon Ratchasima be moved [to Vientiane]. [When] they reached Thung Samrit, Lady (*than phuying*) Mo, with the backing of the [captive] women and men [of Khorat], fought in hand-to-hand combat with the Vientiane troops

117

and annihilated them. Cao Anuwong withdrew his forces. Subsequently, a Thai army was mobilised, suppressed [the rebellion], and captured Cao Anuwong.

The noble and courageous lady [Mo] was the heroine (*wirasatri*) who saved Nakhon Ratchasima by her skill. [Her action] was of the greatest benefit for the nation (*prathetchat*). King Rama III was pleased to bestow on Lady Mo [the title and rank] of 'Thao Suranari' and also raised her husband, Phraya Palat Müang Nakhon Ratchasima (Thòngkham) to [the title and rank of] Cao Phraya Mahitsarathibodi. [This royal honour] appears in the royal chronicles and [is remembered] to this day. (My translation)

This account, along with other official ones,[10] focuses on the heroism of Thao Suranari. Her heroism, however, is not very marked in what was probably the first modern version of the story. In 1926, Prince Damrong Rajanubhab, who created the foundations on which the dominant national historical narrative was constructed, published a collection of documents relating to the 1827 conflict between Vientiane under Cao Anu and Bangkok (*Cotmaihet rang prap khabot wiangcan* [Documents concerning the suppression of the Vientiane Revolt] 1926; hereafter *CRPKW*). Prince Damrong himself wrote a narrative history of the 'suppression of the Vientiane revolt' as the introduction to the collection.[11]

After describing the capture of Nakhon Ratchasima by the Vientiane forces and the order that the people of the city move to Vientiane, Prince Damrong introduces Lady Mo:

It happened that Lady (*khunying*) Mo, wife of the deputy governor of Nakhon Ratchasima was swept up to be sent as well. Lady Mo was clever and was able to plead for a delay while the families were gathered at Thung Samrit. When [those gathered] were sufficiently strong in number, both men and women were able to seize the arms of the Vientiane soldiers. [They then] attacked the soldiers, killed many of them, and forced the others to flee. Then the families co-operated in establishing a military encampment at Thung Samrit (*CRPKW* 1926: ix–x). (My translation)

In recognition of her role in the 'suppression' of the Vientiane revolt, Prince Damrong says, King Rama III vested Lady Mo with the title of Thao Suranari (*CRPKW* 1926: xi).

While Lady Mo is said to be 'clever', Prince Damrong's account hardly makes her out to be the great heroine that she is subsequently acclaimed as being. It is a puzzle – one that set Saipin on her quest – why a person with such an apparently small role in history should be recognised in 1934 by the erection of a public monument in Nakhon Ratchasima. In the second inscription found at the site of the present monument, the genealogy of the monument is given. From Thao Suranari's death in 1852 until 1934, the only memorials to her are said to have been reliquaries containing ashes. In 1934, however, a new memorial was erected:

> ... Phraya Kamthòn Phayaphit (Dit Intharasolot), governor of Nakhon Ratchasima, Colonel Phra Roengruk Patcamit (Thòng Raksangop), commander of the 5th army, together with the officials and people of Nakhon Ratchasima, unanimously decided to erect a bronze statue as a monument to Thao Suranari. Her ashes were brought and enshrined in the base [of the statue]. The monument was completed and installed at the Chumphon gate [in the old wall] on 15 January, B.E. 2477 [AD 1934]. (My translation)

This inscription points to, but also obscures, politics that were manifest in the combination of military and civilian officials joining in erecting the monument in 1934.

Saipin (1995: 120) begins to recover the history of that politics by focusing on the fact that the Suranari memorial was the first public monument erected after the 1932 revolution that resulted in King Prajadhipok accepting the imposition of a constitution, and the shifting of suzerainty from the monarchy to the 'people'. She links the erection of the monument to the suppression not of an invasion by an alien power but of a rebellion of Thai against Thai. In 1933, Prince Boworadet, with troops based in Nakhon Ratchasima, staged a nearly successful counter-coup against the government that had forced a constitution on King Prajadhipok. Although Prince Boworadet was defeated by forces from Bangkok, the support he had received in Nakhon Ratchasima made the province suspect. The erection of the monument, Saipin argues, provided the people of Khorat with a palpable and emotive image of loyalty to Bangkok. Those who had the monument built would have been aware of the local legends about Lady Mo's deeds. Once situated within a political framework, the story of Thao Suranari lent itself to yet other political purposes.[12]

Saipin shows, again in a well documented and well argued way, how over the years the political uses of the story have contributed to its acquiring additional meanings – militant patriotism, regional loyalty, and even gender equality – that were, at best, only vaguely foreshadowed in the original telling, such as that found in Prince Damrong's account. Her work is an excellent example of the point made by Trouillot (1995: 28), another historian writing about a very different place – Haiti – that 'power is constitutive of the story'. Saipin, like Trouillot, has tracked power through various 'moments', thereby emphasizing 'the fundamentally processual character of historical production'.

In her work, Saipin followed the historiographic models of such contemporary Thai historians as Charnvit Kasetsiri, Nithi Iawsriwongse, and Thongchai Winichakul, who have contributed to a deconstruction of the dominant national narrative as first envisioned by Prince Damrong. While she intended to write primarily for an academic audience, her study was recognised by several intellectuals as being of more than academic interest. The publication of Saipin's book became, although such was most certainly not her intent, another 'moment' in the politics of the past associated with the monument. That there should be such a strong reaction to her book in 1996 stems in part, I believe, from the recent intensification of an ideological debate over the 'Lao' in Thai and Lao history.

Thai and Lao debates about the Cao Anu War

Saipin was accused of 'insulting' the patriotism of Suranari by siding with the Lao in the war of 1827. In the call to the protest, it is asserted that 'when one studies [Saipin's] work in detail, it can be clearly seen that the author intends to attempt to extol the actions of Cao Anuwong of Vientiane, making him out as the saviour of [his] nation. [The author] thus goes beyond what any Thai should do. Consider the danger if the younger generation and subsequent generations understand [the story of Grandmother Mo] in accord with the intent of this book. It will cause a great transformation in the history of the nation'. This accusation of treason (framed in terms of *lèse majesté*) makes sense if Cao Anu and Thao Suranari are remembered as embodiments of different nations – the former 'Lao' and the latter 'Thai'. The situating of both in national narratives is, however, quite recent – a product of modern nationalisms.[13]

Until the end of the nineteenth century, the term 'Lao' was used by the rulers, and even ordinary people in Bangkok, in a rather vague way to refer to peoples living to the North and Northeast of what had constituted the core of old Siam (Ayudhya), who followed cultural traditions and spoke languages related to but clearly different from those of Siam. Under this rubric came not only peoples living in the principalities of Vientiane, Luang Prabang, and Champasak that would later be included within French-controlled Laos, but also those in the principalities of Chiang Mai, Nan, and others that would subsequently constitute Northern Thailand. In addition, most people living on the Khorat plateau in what is today Northeastern Thailand were also considered Lao, although in the southern part of the region there were substantial numbers of peoples who were recognised as being related to the Khmer. Others in the southwestern part of the region, centring on the town of Nakhon Ratchasima, that had been an outpost of the Ayutthayan kingdom since the sixteenth century, were more closely related to the peoples of Siam proper. Even today, these people are referred to as Thai Khorat, that is the 'Thai' of Nakhon Ratchasima (Khorat).

In the early nineteenth century, statecraft took little account of cultural identities. What was significant to the rulers in Bangkok about Vientiane was that it was a vassal state, only one of several that were considered 'Lao'. Nakhon Ratchasima was a Siamese province, one that extended the authority of the Siamese empire over a population that would also have been considered predominantly 'Lao'. It should be noted that there is no information on the origins of Thao Suranari herself; although married to the presumably 'Thai' deputy governor of the province, she could well have been from the local Thai Khorat community, or could even have been a 'Lao'.[14]

Cao Anu, for his part, did not launch a war against the 'Thai', but against an overlord whom he considered to be vulnerable because of changing geopolitical circumstances. In particular, he assumed Bangkok to be threatened by the British, having seen the latter seize territory from the Burmese empire. He also anticipated the backing of another overlord, the emperor of a now powerful Vietnam. While Cao Anu had the support of Champasak – King Rama II of Bangkok had been persuaded to place Anu's own son on the throne of this small principality – he did not have the support of Luang Prabang, the other 'Lao' state that would later be included in Laos.[15] The defeat of Anu – that resulted in Vientiane being razed to the ground and with Cao Anu and his family being captured and sent to Bangkok, where they were first publicly humiliated and then either died or were executed – was not a defeat of the 'Lao', since many 'Lao' states were peripheral to the war.

Although there is some nineteenth century historical writing about the war,[16] it only became the subject of historical reflection when narratives defining the heritages of the 'Thai' and 'Lao' nations began to be written. In the late 1880s, King Chulalongkorn, together with some of his close associates, became aware that the French might use the cultural and linguistic differences between 'Lao' and 'Thai' as a justification for expanding their colonial control over Indochina (Streckfuss 1993: 134). In 1893, this fear became a reality when the French forced the Siamese to cede control over the 'Lao' domains to the east of the Mekong. The creation of French Laos, that ended in 1907 when Siam made additional territorial concessions on the right bank of the Mekong, impelled the rulers of Siam to define clearly who was 'Thai' and who was 'Lao'.

The man who had by far the greatest influence in this undertaking was Prince Damrong Rajanubhab (1862–1943). As Minister of the Interior in the last two decades of the reign of King Chulalongkorn, he played a pre-eminent role in the construction of the modern Thai state. In addition, he laid the foundations for the writing of national history (Charnvit 1979: 164–166).

Despite the fact that well over half of the population of Siam, the boundaries of which were fixed during the colonial period, had previously been called 'Lao' by the Siamese, Prince Damrong literally wrote the Lao out of Thai history. In a memoir on his role in the construction of the Thai nation, Prince Damrong Rajanubhab wrote: 'People in Bangkok have long called [the peoples of Northern Siam] Lao. Today, however, we know they are Thai, not Lao' (Damrong Rajanubhab 1971 [1935]: 318).

When Prince Damrong took up the materials relating to the war with Vientiane in 1826, he does not portray Cao Anu as a 'Lao'; rather, he is depicted as an insurgent vassal who attempts to take advantage of Siam's preoccupation with a British threat by invading. It is not until Lao national history comes to be written that Anu's war is interpreted as one of Lao against Thai.

The first telling of the story of the 1827 war from the Lao point of view appears in a book published in 1931 that was actually written by a Frenchman, Paul Le Boulanger. Le Boulanger drew, however, on sources in Lao and, in his introduction to *Histoire du Laos Français* (Le Boulanger 1931: vii–vii), he acknowledges his debt to Prince Pethsarath, who played a somewhat comparable role in Laos to that played in Siam by Prince Damrong. Le Boulanger's work is the first to subsume the histories of Vientiane, Luang Prabang, and Champasak as part of the national heritage of Laos.

In Le Boulanger's account of Cao Anu's war on Bangkok, the Vientiane king holds centre stage. He is credited with reigning over a 'brilliant court' (Le Boulanger 1931: 161). But his reign that begins so auspiciously ends with the 'total and final destruction of his domain' (1931: 159). He takes offence at the 'categorical refusal' of King Rama III to allow Lao captives from an earlier war to return to Vientiane – captives who 'have never become Siamese' (1931: 166). Having 'thrown away his mask' of compliant vassalage, he declares war on Siam. In this account, there is no mention of Lady Mo. Rather, Anu is said to have suffered a defeat at Thung Samrit because a detachment of Vientiane troops escorting captives from Nakhon Ratchasima 'were taken by surprise, encircled, and destroyed by a small Siamese force' (1931: 168).

Although Le Boulanger's history was that of a French colony rather than a nation, it laid down the foundations for what would become the dominant narrative of a Lao nation. In the 1930s, this history was re-presented in the first Lao language text books, and in the 1940s a vision of distinct Lao nation was articulated in the first Lao language newspaper (see Ivarsson 1999). Also in the 1940s, Maha Sila Viravong, a learned ex-monk and an active proponent of Lao nationalism, wrote a history that would become the most widely known history of Laos until the communist-led revolution of 1975.[17] It remains to this day the basis for all national histories of Laos and has been translated into Thai several times as well as into English.

In his *History of Laos*, Maha Sila devotes extended attention to the reign of Cao Anu (Sila Viravong 1964: 111–135). He praises Cao Anu for his 'bravery and experience in warfare', and his effectiveness as a ruler of

Vientiane. He also sees Anu's war with Bangkok as being impelled by his desire to regain his kingdom's independence (Sila Viravong 1964: 114). In his story of the war, he mentions Lady Mo, but credits her husband with devising the plan that would lead to the defeat of the Vientiane forces at Thung Samrit (1964: 117–118). Her role is obviously of far less significance to Maha Sila than that of the Vientiane commander, whose defeat at Thung Samrit marks the beginning of the end of Cao Anu's campaign.

The turmoil in Laos between 1954 and 1975 left little possibility for any Lao to press their interpretation of the Cao Anu narrative against that which was known in Thailand. But an independent Laos was seen a potential threat to Thailand should the peoples of Northeastern Thailand, who shared the same language and cultural traditions as the dominant people of Laos, see themselves as having a common cause in promoting Lao nationalism. Saipin shows in her book that the new attention to the monument of Thao Suranari, culminating in the erection of a new monument in 1967, was prompted in part by the concern of governments of the time that the people of Northeastern Thailand should see themselves as Thai rather than Lao.[18]

Following the founding of the Lao Peoples Democratic Republic in 1975, the story of Cao Anu was incorporated into the national history taught in Lao schools. In a text that has been in use at least since the early 1980s, and that remains the standard text for the first grade of secondary school (Lao People's Democratic Republic, Kasuang süksa lae kila [Ministry of Education and Sports]. n.d.), two chapters (11 and 12) are devoted to a discussion of Siamese 'aggression' and Lao 'resistance' in the eighteenth century, while the next two (chapters 13 and 14) tell of the efforts of Cao Anu to lead 'the Lao people to rise up to fight to recover [their] nation'.

The Lao version of the 1827 war, that sees Cao Anu as a Lao national hero rather than a vassal in rebellion against his king in Bangkok, has in recent years been argued in a highly sophisticated way by two Lao historians, who have written in Thai and English as well as Lao. In 1988, Mayoury Ngaosyvathn and Pheuiphanh Ngaosyvathn published in Bangkok in *Sinlapa watthanatham* (Arts and Culture) an article entitled 'Cao Anu: old story, new meaning'.[19] The article was intruded into on-going intellectual and political debates – in which the journal, *Sinlapa watthanatham*, was taking a leading role – concerning certain facets of the dominant Thai national history, and also about Thai relations with Laos. The writings of Mayoury and Pheuiphanh followed on the publication of two revisionist interpretations of the 1827 war from the perspective of Northeastern Thai, who recognised the strong ties between people in their region and the Lao (Prateep Chumpol 1982 and Thawat Poonnotok 1983). Given that *Sinlapa watthanatham* (through Matichon Press) is also the publisher of Saipin's book, it is hardly surprising that the book should be seen as a contribution to the 'Lao' challenge to 'Thai' national identity.

It is fortunate that the charge of treason against Saipin was advanced in an open society rather than one like Iran that still seeks the death of Salman Rushdie. An editorialist, Niran Yaowaka, for *Phucatkan raiwan* (The Manager Daily) (6 March 1996) commenting on the Saipin affair observed: 'At a time when the political atmosphere is open and historians are more able to follow their duty, disputes about many important issues arise'.[20]

Perspectives on the relationship between Thai and Lao identities that depart from officially sanctioned ones are not limited to the ranks of historians. In 1990, Princess Sirindhorn, the highly esteemed daughter of King Bhumipol Adulyadej, made a state visit to the Lao Peoples Democratic Republic, despite the strong protests of former Prime Minister Kukrit Pramote. Her visit contributed to a much more positive view of the Lao than many in the Thai ruling elite had previously held (Keyes 2000). In such a context, the politicians who organised or associated themselves with the Khorat protest were unable to look to the authority of the state to impose sanctions against someone who had challenged the dominant national narrative.

It may well have been, however, that Saipin was only a surrogate for a much more threatening challenge, namely one posed by the adherents to the cult of grandmother Mo.

The cult of Grandmother Mo

Niran Yaowaka, in the same editorial mentioned above, notes that a major cause for the emotions expressed at the protest against Saipin lies in the popularity of the cult of grandmother Mo. Saipin has successfully documented the emergence of this cult and argued that the spirit (*thepharak*) of grandmother Mo has replaced the cult of the pillar of the city (*lak müang*) as the pre-eminent local cult. Despite the insistence at the demonstration that the people of Khorat revere Thao Suranari as an historical personage rather than as a spirit, the fact remains that contemporary interest in her stems primarily from the belief that at the sites commemorating her, or through spirit mediums, it is possible to seek a positive intervention of her spirit. Even a brief visit to Khorat makes one aware that the cult of grandmother Mo has become very significant. As I observed on a trip to the city in July 1996, the cultural landscape of Khorat city is now organised to a remarkable degree around the cult of grandmother Mo.[21]

The monument to Thao Suranari dominates the centre part of the city. Early on the July Sunday morning when I visited the monument, there were already dozens of people making offerings. While I was there, a bus-load of army officers and their family members from the southern army headquarters in Nakhon Sithammarat also drove up to the monument, where most disembarked to make offerings at the monument. The activity around the new monument stands in sharp contrast to that which existed in 1963 when I first saw the older one, then located on the reconstructed wall of the city. At that time, the monument was scarcely noticed by most who passed in front of it. Today, in an area behind a Chinese shrine across from the new monument – the oldest Chinese shrine in Northeastern Thailand and once a far more important cult centre than the monument itself – there are stages on which performances are given of *phlaeng Khorat* or *lae Khorat* – a distinctive form of dancing and singing using the Thai Khorat language. These performances are paid for by men and women who had vowed to make offerings (*kaebon*) to the spirit of grandmother Mo in return for the spirit assisting them in achieving some goal (better health, success in business or in love, and so on).

The shrine of the pillar of the city (*lak müang*) has also become strongly linked to the memory of grandmother Mo. This shrine has its origins in the cult of Siva that was established at a time when what is today Northeastern Thailand was under the control of the Angkorean empire. Since at least the late nineteenth century, the shrine has also assumed a strongly Chinese character as immigrant Chinese thought of it as the site in which the local god of place resided. The shrine today still houses a pillar that represents a Siva lingam – a phallic symbol of potency – but it is surrounded by signs in Chinese. A few years ago, the provincial government sponsored the creation of a very large ceramic mural depicting the story of Thao Suranari to be placed on a wall behind the *lak müang* shrine. One might think it odd that the very male power of Siva, and of a Chinese god, should now be linked to a female spirit, but the story of Thao Suranari is one of heroism in battle, a characteristic more typically associated in Thai thought with males.[22]

The third major complex associated with the cult of grandmother Mo in Khorat is at the Sala Lòi temple, located in the eastern suburbs of the city. Although the temple complex (*wat*) is well known to some for its ultra-modernistic congregation hall built in 1967, it is clearly of interest primarily because of its association with the cult of grandmother Mo. The wat is said to have been built by Thao Suranari herself following her return to the city after the battle with the troops from Vientiane. At the entrance to the old ordination hall are statues of Thao Suranari, her husband, and Miss Bunlüang, one of her relatives, who according to local legend was her chief aide in defeating the Vientiane troops.[23] There is also a reliquary that is believed to contain the ashes of Thao Suranari. Near the reliquary is a stage on which *phlaeng Khorat* performances, paid for by those seeking the aid of the spirit of grandmother Mo, are given. The first thing one sees as one enters the *wat* is a large billboard encouraging people to contribute so that a larger reliquary shrine can be built.

The last major spatial component of the cult of grandmother Mo in Khorat lies some 50 kilometres north of the city at Thung Samrit, located

Plate 4.2 Statue of Thao Suranari, in Nakhon Ratchasima (Khorat), Northeastern Thailand.

in Phimai district. Thung Samrit, the place where Thao Suranari is said to have organised an attack on the Vientiane troops holding a large number of people from Khorat as prisoners of war, has only become marked in any significant way since the late 1980s.[24] In 1988, local villagers contributed money to build a shrine to the spirit of Miss Bunlüang 'and the other heroes of Thung Samrit', and in the 1990s the support of followers of the cult made possible the building of open-sided pavilions used for ritual purposes. When we visited the site, we met Mrs. Sa-atrak Dupakphi, a woman from Chanthaburi who is a medium for the spirit of grandmother Mo. She had come to the site, along with others from Chanthaburi, a city of considerable wealth derived from the gem industry, to participate in an annual ritual event that would include offering alms to local monks as well as a séance.

In Khorat city, another medium, Mrs. Wanthani Surakkhaka, has gained a reputation for being the vehicle through whom the spirit of grandmother Mo speaks. On 14 July 1996, I was taken to meet Mrs. Wanthani and interviewed her about her role; she then went into trance and spoke to us as the spirit of grandmother Mo.[25]

Mrs. Wanthani, like Mrs. Sa-atrak, is not a native of Khorat, nor is she of Thai Khorat origin. Mrs. Wanthani, who is originally from Bangkok, told us she had been a medium for seven years. When we asked why she became a medium, she was somewhat vague, but indicated that there were

Plate 4.3 A medium in Nakhon Ratchasima (Khorat) while possessed by the spirit of Thao Suranari.

troubles, and that becoming a medium had made it possible for her to know herself. It would appear that she became a medium about the time her husband, an army officer, retired from the military (he subsequently died). After the spirit of grandmother Mo informed her that she had been chosen as her medium, she moved to Khorat. She told us that she is sought out by people with a variety of problems.

The room in which Mrs. Wanthani receives her clients is dominated by a large altar complex. In addition to a number of images of Thao Suranari, there are also images of Guan-yin (Thai, Kwan-im), the Jade Emperor, other Chinese figures, the Hindu god Brahma among others, and pictures of King Chulalongkorn and several monks. An image of the Buddha is placed at the highest point in the complex. In other words, the iconography indicates a fusion of supernatural powers drawn from Chinese, Indian, Buddhist and Thai national traditions, a linking of these with the power of grandmother Mo, and subordination of all these to the ultimate authority of the Buddha.

Mrs. Wanthani asked if we wished to meet 'Her' (*than*), referring to the spirit of grandmother Mo. We agreed and made a donation through Mrs. Wanthani's son, who was called in to assist. The son then prepared betel nut while Mrs. Wanthani changed into a white costume in the style of a nineteenth century upper-class lady. After she had lit incense and chewed

127

betel for a few moments, the spirit manifested herself through Mrs. Wanthani. The spirit then asked me what I wanted. While the question was presumably meant to elicit some problem for which a client would seek supernatural help, I asked her, instead, about her history. Her response, with a few embellishments, was similar to what one would read in one of the official accounts. I then asked about the controversy over the book by Saipin. She was very disdainful, saying that Saipin had tried to say that the stories about Grandmother Mo were not true. 'She has an MA, but she does not know history. She had to move within 24 hours or she would have been executed'. The spirit (and/or Mrs. Wanthani?) admitted, however, she had not read the book. She said that Saipin never came to talk with her. I asked her about her attitudes toward the Lao. She answered that 'Vientiane Lao are cheaters' (*Lao Wiangcan khiko*). We took our leave before she had returned to being Mrs. Wanthani.[26]

The cult of grandmother Mo is but one of a number of new cults that have emerged in Thailand in recent years as a response to the destabilising influences of rapid economic growth and, more generally, of the Thai pursuit of modernisation.[27] In the Khorat area, while there are mediums for a variety of spirits, there is little question but that of Grandmother Mo holds by far the most prominent place.

The rapid growth of the cult of grandmother Mo provided, I believe is evident, a major impetus for the organisation of the demonstration. Both in the flyer that was circulated to encourage people to join the demonstration and in the denunciations of the Saipin's book at the demonstration, the point was strongly emphasised that Thao Suranari should be revered as a historical person, not a spirit. Such a challenge notwithstanding, those who seek the help of the spirit of grandmother Mo are far less likely to be interested in the actual historical facts about the actions of Thao Suranari in 1827 than they are in whether or not a vow made to her spirit at the monument, at another of the shrines to her, or at a séance with a medium, can produce the desired results. This was apparent in my 'meeting' with the spirit through her medium, Mrs. Wanthani. While my questions about her story were answered, it was clear that what was really expected of me was to ask for some supernatural intervention to handle a problem I faced. That Thao Suranari should be remembered as a powerful local spirit rather than a national heroine is very threatening to those who would have the past recalled only in the service of national unity. What was most disturbing to some about Saipin's book, it would appear, was that she emphasised the remembering of grandmother Mo as a spirit.

The demonstration can also be understood as being as much an attempt by the state to wrest control of the memory of Thao Suranari from local people as it was an attack on outsiders who have 'insulted' her memory. The reverence accorded to the memory of grandmother Thao Suranari reflects an effort, mainly unconscious, of Khorat people to assert a claim to a distinctive local heritage.[28] The heritage of Thao Suranari manifest in the monument and shrines in the city and province has local significance rather than representing – as do government offices, military camps, and state-sponsored institutions like schools and colleges – the presence of the state. Such efforts to reclaim local worlds, in response to the heavy-handed centralisation policies of Thai governments over the past century, have been emerging in several different parts of the kingdom. For those in the ruling elite who maintain that all Thai share a unitary heritage in common, the phantasm of grandmother Mo manifest in the cult surrounding her memory is threatening. The fragmentation of cultural worlds, that was supposed to have been eliminated through the modernisation and national integration projects of the state, appears to be re-emerging.

A monument to whose past?

I have attempted in this paper to show how a dramatic and disturbing protest about a rather erudite history book is indicative of deep debates in Thailand today about national identity and about the consequences of modernity, a theme also explored in the introductory essay to this volume. The building of the modern state of Thailand has been closely associated with the construction of a history of the 'Thai' nation. This history posits an unbroken continuity from certain pre-modern states, the most proximate being the Siam that made Bangkok its capital in 1782, but not from others, notably those that were considered by the Siamese to be populated by 'Lao'. In the modern national history, some conflicts between polities in the past have been re-construed as conflicts between nations; that of 1827 is seen not as a rebellion of a vassal but as one between 'Thai' and 'Lao'. Local historical memories have been suppressed, as has been the case in Northern Thailand, or subsumed within a national narrative, as in the case of Thao Suranari in Khorat.

The dominant narrative of the Thai nation was first shaped in the early part of the twentieth century, and then became hegemonic with the spread of compulsory schooling instituted by governments from the 1920s on. In the late 1960s and early 1970s, this hegemonic domination began to be questioned. By the mid-1970s, this questioning had become so intense among a younger generation of urban Thai that the self-appointed guardians of the nation, the military, sought to re-impose domination through the use of coercive force. The violent suppression of the student movement in 1976 had, however, quite the opposite effect to that intended, at least by those who staged the coup of 6 October 1976. The memory of '6 October' (hok tula), even though publicly silenced (see chapter 10 in this volume) has proven a goad to critical reflection on national identity. Since the early 1980s, the questioning of the dominant national narrative has

129

only grown stronger, and has spread to many sectors of society. As the events in Khorat in 1996 demonstrate, such questioning pits not only scholars against those who still seek to legitimate their power by aligning themselves with icons of an older nationalism, but also many others who find local rather than national potency in such icons.

Behind all versions of the stories about Thao Suranari are events that took place in 1827. The recording of these events – the remembering of them in either oral or written form – entails a decision that something about the events is significant, and the attachment of significance to any historical events must needs evoke some authority. That social memory is subject to 'revision' is a function not only of the discovery of new historical facts, but also of changes in either the powers that 'authorise' history, or in the perspectives as to what constitutes significance.

The story of Thao Suranari/grandmother Mo is today an inextricable part of Thai history, but what the story means depends on which authority one turns in order to make sense of it. The struggle for meaning about this story today is carried out self-consciously by some members of the ruling elite, who seek to maintain a unitary and hegemonic narrative about the history of the Thai nation, and academics who challenge – using the methods of contemporary historiography – this narrative. Also contending, but in a much less selfconscious way, are the adherents to the cult of grandmother Mo, who take their authority neither from the state nor from academia but from the power they believe to be immanent in the physical, spatial, and spiritual reminders of her. This power is very compelling because it is expressed in emotive voices – notably, those of a spirit who speaks through mediums – that are felt to speak to the emotional problems of those who face the exigencies of choice – about sexual or marriage partners, about education, about occupational futures, about investments, and even about winning elections – that are so characteristic of modern Thailand.

The social memory indexed by the monument to an early nineteenth century woman in the provincial capital of Khorat in Northeastern Thailand can be understood, I argue, only by exploring the field of power within which the monument has been and is situated. As an inquiry into the controversy over the politics of the past associated with the monument has led us to see, such a field can be one of contesting voices and authorities. As Prasenjit Duara (1995: 10) has written in his critique of the linear history of a nation, 'in place of the harmonised, monologic voice of the Nation, we find a polyphony of voices, contradictory and ambiguous, opposing, affirming, and negotiating their views of the nation', and, I would add, their views of the past. In the end, the voice speaking about the memory of Thao Suranari that seems to be the strongest is neither that of an elite, who would use the monument to further a 'Thai' versus 'Lao' nationalism, nor that of academic historians, who would deconstruct the dominant nationalist narrative, but that of the spirit of grandmother Mo herself, who makes the past directly effective in the present. In October 1996, on the eve of an national election, candidates for a parliamentary seat representing Khorat from at least two competing political parties sought the aid of the spirit in the belief 'that those who please the spirit of Thao Suranaree succeed' (*Bangkok Post*, 24 October 1996). While the candidate for the New Aspiration Party, a party then very much on the rise, laid out only a vegetarian offering made up of fruits and flowers worth 5,000 baht, General Chatichai Choonhavan, a former prime minister and long-time Khorat MP, who was the candidate for the weaker Chat Patthana Party, offered her pork, duck, chicken, and liquor, as well as fruit and flowers. His offerings cost 10,000 baht. General Chatichai was once again returned as Member of Parliament for Khorat.

Notes

1 'Suranari' is also found in many English-language works as 'Suranaree'. *Thao* is an old title indicating membership in the class of nobility; it is usually considered to be a 'Lao' term.

2 The book was published in Bangkok in 1995 by Matichon for the magazine *Sinlapa watthanatham* (Arts and Culture).

3 I am indebted to a friend living in Khorat for obtaining a copy of this flyer for me. The translation of this and other texts in Thai in this paper are my own.

4 In 1934, Prince Boworadet, a former Minister of War, staged a rebellion against the government formed by the People's Party that in 1932 had succeeded in compelling King Pradhipok to accept the monarchy's subordination to a constitution. Prince Boworadet used troops based in Khorat in a failed effort to restore the absolute monarchy. The significance of the relationship between the Thao Suranari monument and the rebellion is discussed later in the paper.

5 A plain (*thung*) located 50 km. north of Khorat. *Samrit* can mean a metal alloy that includes gold; it also means 'success' or 'accomplishment'.

6 The following appears at the very bottom of the flyer: 'Mr. Nopphadon Phithakwanit sponsored this printing'.

7 The Thai newspaper, *Naeona* (The Front Line), 6 March, placed the number of protestors at 50,000, but other papers, such as *The Bangkok Post* on 5 March, and local sources estimated the number to be between 20,000 and 25,000.

8 General Chatichai died in 1998.

9 There was considerable concern expressed among Thai scholars, mainly outside of Thailand, carried out through discussions on the internet, about the danger in which she was in. There is some indication from this discussion that she had been advised to remain silent about the controversy and she has, in fact, given (at least through 2000) no public comment about the controversy.

10 One of the first modern guides to Khorat, published in 1959, provides an account very similar to the one found in the inscription. Although this account includes more details, some phrases are exactly the same as in the inscription (see Manit Vallibhotama 1959: 38-44; English translation in Manit Vallibhotama 1962: 25–27). I recall seeing a very brief version of the story in a primary school history in use in the early 1960s. A more recent and more elaborate 'school' narrative is the biography of Thao Suranari written for young people by Manit Lophinit (1993).

11 In his *Siam under Rama III*, Walter Vella (1957: 80, n.3) asserts unequivocally that Prince Damrong wrote the introduction.

12 I am indebted to Dr. Ratana Boonmathaya for providing a summary of Saipin's book. I used this summary in my own reading of the book.

13 As Thongchai Winichakul (1994) and David Streckfuss (1993) demonstrate, the understanding of Siam/Thailand as a 'nation' populated by 'Thai' began only in the late nineteenth century as a consequence of the influence of Western 'racial' thought and the imposition of colonial power, especially by the French. Also see my paper, 'Who Are the Tai? reflections on the invention of identities' (Keyes 1995).

14 Two women who serve as her mediums whom I interviewed (see below) presumed her to have different origins. One when serving as her medium spoke in what appears to be the dialect of Thai Khorat. The other said that when the spirit first came to her, it spoke Lao.

15 The war with Bangkok begun by Cao Anu has been the subject, as we shall see, of an extraordinary amount of scholarly and often partisan attention, especially in recent years. Accounts in English that include most of the facts that everyone agrees on can be found in Vella (1957) and Wyatt (1963).

16 Saipin (1995: ch. 4) reviews the contemporary historical sources on the war and finds almost no reference to Thao Suranari in any source prior to the 1930s.

17 Maha Sila's history of Laos would become widely known only after the independence of the country in 1954. Although Maha Sila was born in Roi-et province in Northeastern Thailand, he had travelled to French Laos while a monk. There he left the monkhood, married a woman of French-Lao origins, and became secretary to Prince Petsarath. The latter clearly had a strong influence on his ideas about Lao nationalism. For an extended discussion of the role of Maha Sila, see Sisana Sisane, et al (1990).

18 The monument was, however, only a minor instrument in the effort to promote identification of the people of Northeastern Thailand with the Thai state and nation. As I have argued elsewhere (Keyes 1991), compulsory education, in which all subjects, including history, were taught in the national language, was by far the most effective instrument.

19 This article (Mayoury Ngaosyvathn and Pheuiphanh Ngaosyvathn 1988a) is a summary of their longer book (Mayoury Ngaosyvathn and Pheuiphanh Ngaosyvathn 1988b) in Lao. Some of their argument, with the supporting evidence, also appears in English (see Mayoury Ngaosyvathn and Pheuiphanh Ngaosyvathn 1988c and 1989). See also Vickery (1990) for an extended review of this work. The longer book has also been published in an English version (Mayoury Ngaosyvathn and Pheuiphanh Ngaosyvathn 1998).

20 He goes on to cite the still-running debate about the origins of the 'Thai', the controversy about what is known as 'inscription one', that is, the first inscription in the Thai language, and the questioning of the historicity of the battles between forces of Siam and Burma that are commemorated in a monument in Suphanburi province. He then concludes: 'Debates like this are commonplace in the circle of historians'.

21 On July 14 1996, I was able to visit all of the major sites associated with the cult of grandmother Mo. I am very grateful to Professor (Ajarn) Suriya Smutkupt of Suranaree University for organising this field trip. Also accompanying us on this trip was Dr. Pattana Kitiarsa, then a PhD student in anthropology at the University of Washington who is also affiliated with Suranaree University and was engaged at the time in joint researches with Ajarn Suriya on the role of spirit cults in contemporary Thailand. They subsequently published two studies in Thai (see Suriya Smutkupt, Pattana Kitiarsa, Silpakit Tikhantikul, and

Chanthana Suraphinit 1996 and 1997), and Pattana has written a dissertation based on this work (Pattana Kitiarsa 1999). Because so much prior fieldwork had preceded my visit, I was able to gain far more information about the cult of Grandmother Mo than I could have on my own in such a short visit.

22 I have not attempted in this chapter to examine in any depth the gender meanings associated with the Thao Suranari controversy. I would note that Thao Suranari stands almost alone in the dominant national narrative as a woman recognised for heroism. Whereas the officials responsible for promoting the national interpretation of her story are almost entirely men, the mediums that dominate the cult are women.

23 Miss Bunlüang figures in no official story of Thao Suranari, and Saipin (1995: 197–203) devotes a section of her book to the question, 'was Miss Bunlüang a real person?' In local legend, she is said to be a young relative of Lady Mo who sacrificed her virginity to the commander of the Vientiane troops while her compatriots took arms away from the drunken troops. She is believed to have been killed in the ensuing battle. Her spirit also manifests itself through mediums.

24 Information on Thung Samrit is taken from a brochure obtained at the site in July 1996.

25 Ajarn Suriya Smutkupt and Pattana Kitiarsa (see above), who arranged the visit to the medium, had previously interviewed Mrs. Wanthani and introduced me to her as their 'teacher' (Ajarn). I am grateful to Suriya and Pattana for having previously established sufficient rapport with Mrs. Wanthani that the fact we were from academic institutions, and presumptively therefore associated in some way with the stance taken by Saipin, did not deter Mrs. Wanthani from answering our questions, or from going into trance so we could speak with the spirit of grandmother Mo. Although I had no difficulty understanding Mrs. Wanthani before she went into trance, I found it quite difficult to understand her when she spoke as grandmother Mo. This was, in part, a function of the fact that she chewed betel nut throughout the séance; but it was more a function of the fact that the dialect she spoke was very difficult for me to follow. I assume she was speaking in Thai Khorat dialect of the nineteenth century. Fortunately, Ajarn Suriya Smutkupt, who had interviewed her previously, was able to translate for me when I did not understand.

26 Pattana Kittiarsa (1999), in his dissertation on spirit cults in Thailand, discusses the complex question of what stance an ethnographer might adopt in relating an encounter with a spirit medium who has entered a trance and is accepted by many as being a vehicle for a spirit. My own strong impression during the interview with Mrs. Wanthani as the medium for the spirit of Grandmother Mo was that she was engaged in a performance. Nonetheless, as Lévi-Strauss showed long ago (1963a and 1963b), even when a medium or sorcerer or shaman is quite aware of staging a performance, she or he can still truly believe that one has unique abilities to serve as a vehicle for supernatural beings.

27 The religious and cultic ferment found in Thailand today is characteristic, as my associates and I have shown in *Asian Visions of Authority* (Keyes, Kendall and Hardacre 1995), of a more general response to modernity.

28 Some in the Northeast outside of the Khorat area also see themselves as sharing in the local heritage represented by grandmother Mo. In 1993, I noticed on the dashboard of a taxi I had taken in Bangkok an image of Thao Suranari. I asked the driver, whom I had already learned came from Roi-et, a Northeastern province where the people are culturally and linguistically closely related to the dominant people of Laos, about the image. He replied: 'She is a symbol of Northeastern Thailand' (*pen sanyalak isan*).

References

Charnvit Kasetsiri 1979 'Thai historiography from ancient times to the modern period', p. 156-170 in A. Reid and D. Marr (eds.) *Perceptions of the Past in Southeast Asia*, Singapore: Heinemann Educational Books (Asian Studies Assoc. of Australia, Southeast Asia Publications Series, 4).

Damrong Rajanubhab, Prince 1971 (1935). *Nithan borankhadi* (Historical Anecdotes), Bangkok: Phrae Phitthaya.

Ivarsson, Søren 1999 'Bringing Laos into existence: Laos between Indochina and Siam, 1860–1945', unpublished PhD thesis, University of Copenhagen.

Keyes, Charles F. 1991 'The proposed world of the school: Thai villagers entry into a bureaucratic state system', p.87–138 in Charles F. Keyes (ed.) *Reshaping Local Worlds: rural education and cultural change in Southeast Asia*, New Haven: Yale University Southeast Asian Studies.

—— 1995 'Who are the Tai? reflections on the invention of identities', p.136–160 in Lola Romanucci-Ross and George A. De Vos (eds.) *Ethnic Identity: creation, conflict, and accommodation* (third edition), Walnut Creek, California: Alta Mira Press.

—— 2000 'A Thai princess in a Peoples' Republic: a new phase in the construction of the Lao Nation', p.206–226, in Andrew Turton (ed.) *Civility and Savagery*, Surrey: Curzon.

Keyes, Charles F., Helen Hardacre and Laurel Kendall 1994 'Contested visions of community in East and Southeast Asia', p.1–16 in Charles F. Keyes, Helen Hardacre and Laurel Kendall (eds.) *Asian Visions of Authority: religion and the modern states of East and Southeast Asia*, Honolulu: University of Hawaii Press.

Lafont, Pierre-Bernard 1964 *Bibliographie du Laos*, Paris: École Française d'Extrême-Orient.

Lao People's Democratic Republic, Kasuang süksa lae kila (Ministry of Education and Sports) n.d. *Pawatsat lao san matthañom pithi 1* (History: middle school grade 1), Vientiane.

Lévi-Strauss, Claude 1963a (1949) 'The sorcerer and his magic', p.161–180 in Claude Lévi-Strauss *Structural Anthropology* (translated by Claire Jacobson and Brooke Grundfest Schoepf), New York: Basic Books.

—— 1963b (1949) 'The effectiveness of symbols', p.181–201 in Claude Lévi-Strauss *Structural Anthropology* (translated by Claire Jacobson and Brooke Grundfest Schoepf, New York: Basic Books.

Manit Lophinit 1993 *Thao Suranari* (Thao Suranari), Bangkok: Aksaraphiphat, (Series on) Prawattisat bukkhon samkhan khòng Thai phròm phap prakòp (Illustrated biographies of important people in Thai [history]).

Manit Vallibhotama 1959 *Namthiao Phimai lae boransathan nai cangwat Nakhòn Ratchasima* (Guide to Phimai and the Antiquities of Nakhon Ratchasima), Bangkok: The Fine Arts Department.

—— 1962 *Guide to Phimai and the Antiquities of Nakhon Ratchasima (Khorat)* (translated in abridged form by M.C. Subhadradis Diskul), Bangkok: The Fine Arts Department.

Matsuda, Matt K. 1996 *The Memory of the Modern*, New York and Oxford: Oxford University Press.

Mayoury Ngaosyvathn and Pheuiphanh Ngaosyvathn 1988a 'Cao Anu: rüang kao panha mai' (Cao Anu: Old Story, New Meaning), p.58–74 in *Sinlapa watthanatham* (Arts and Culture) 9(11).

—— 1988b *Cao Anu, 1767–1829: pasason Lao lae asia-akhane (lüang kao, panha mai)* (Cao Anu, 1767–1829: the Lao people and Southeast Asia [old story, new meaning]), Vientiane: Samnakphim camnai S. P. P. Lao.

—— 1988c 'World super power and regional conflicts: the triangular game of Great Britain with Bangkok and the Lao during the Embassies of John Crawfurd (1821-1822) and of Henry Burney (1825-1826)', p.121–133 in *Journal of the Siam Society* 76.

—— 1989 'Lao historiography and historians: case study of the war between Bangkok and the Lao in 1827', p.55–69 in *Journal of Southeast Asian Studies* 20(1).

—— 1998 *Paths to Conflagration: fifty years of diplomacy and warfare in Laos, Vietnam, and Vietnam 1778–1828*, Ithaca, NY: Cornell University, Southeast Asian Studies Program, SOSEA, no.24.

Pattana Kitiarsa 1999 '"You may not believe, but never offend spirits": spirit-medium discourses and the postmodernization of Thai religion', unpublished PhD dissertation, University of Washington.

Prasenjit Duara 1995 *Rescuing History from the Nation: questioning narratives of modern China*, Chicago: University of Chicago Press.

Prateep Chumpol 1982 *Phün wiang: wannakam haeng kankotkhi* (*Phün Wiang*: Literature of the Suppression), Bangkok: Adit Press.

Saipin Kaew-ngarmprasert 1995 *Kanmüang nai anusawari Thao Suranari* (The Politics of the Monument of Thao Suranari), Bangkok: Matichon, Sinlapa watthanatham chabap phiset.

Sila Viravong, Maha 1964 *History of Laos*, New York: Paragon Book Reprint Corp.

—— 1989 *Phongsawadan Lao* (Lao Chronicles) (translated from Lao to Thai by Sommai Premcit), Chiang Mai, Thailand.

Sisana Sisane, et al 1990 *Maha Sila Wilawong: siwit lae phonngan* (Maha Sila Viravong: life and work), Vientiane: Khanakammakan Witthayasat Sangkhom (Committee for Social Sciences).

Streckfuss, David 1993 'The mixed colonial legacy in Siam: origins of Thai racialist thought', p.123–153 in Laurie J. Sears (ed.) *Autonomous Histories, Particular Truths: essays in honor of John R.W. Smail*, Madison: University of Wisconsin, Center for Southeast Asian Studies, Monograph, no.11.

Suriya Smutkupt, Pattana Kitiarsa, Silpakit Tikhantikul, and Chanthana Suraphinit 1996 *Songcao khaophi: watthakam khòng latthiphithi lae wikrittakan khòng khwamthansamai nai sangkhom Thai* (Spirit-Medium Cult Discourses and Crises of Modernity in Thailand), Nakhon Ratchasima: Suranaree University of Technology, Center for Research on Social Technology, Research Monograph of the Thai Studies Display Room.

—— 1997. *Raingan kanwicai rüang withikhit khòng Thai: phithikam 'khuang phifòn' khòng 'laochao cao' cangwat Nakhon Ratchasima* (Cultural Constructs of Local Knowledge: ethnic Thai-Lao spirit-medium cults in Khorat villages), Nakhon Ratchasima: Suranaree University of Technology, Center for Research on Social Technology, Research Monograph of the Thai Studies Display Room.

Thawat Poonnotok 1983 *Phün wiang: kansüksa prawattisat lae wannakam isan* (*Phün Wiang*: a study of Isan history and literature), Bangkok: Thammasat University Press.

Thongchai Winichakul 1994 *Siam Mapped: a history of the geo-body of a nation*, Honolulu: University of Hawaii Press.

Thongsüp Suphamak 1985 *Phongsawadan Lao* (History of Laos), Bangkok: Khurusapha.

Trouillot, Michel-Rolph 1995 *Silencing the Past: power and the production of history*, Boston: Beacon.

Vella, Walter F. 1957 *Siam under Rama III, 1824-1851*, Locust Valley, NY: J.J. Augustin (Association for Asian Studies Monographs, IV).

CHARLES F. KEYES

Vickery, Michael 1990 'Review of *Chou Anou 1767 pasason Lao lae asia-akhane* (Chao Anou, 1767–1829, the Lao People and Southeast Asia), by Mayoury and Pheuiphanh Ngaosyvathn', p.441–445 in *Journal of Southeast Asian Studies* 21(2).
Wyatt, David 1963 'Siam and Laos, 1767–1827', p.13–47 in *Journal of Southeast Asian History* 4(2).

CHAPTER FIVE

Monuments and Memory

Phaya Sihanatraja and the Founding of Maehongson

Nicola Tannenbaum

Statues and monuments, like other material objects, require interpretation (Thomas 1991). Who or what is being commemorated, by whom and when, and what meaning, if any, does the location of the monument have? None of these questions have straightforward, absolute answers (Thomas 1991; Jeffrey 1980; Anderson 1990; Reynolds 1992). The meaning of the monument or statue is an arena of contestation from the beginning when it is first planned and until after it is torn down (Jeffrey 1980; Trouillot 1995). While it stands, different people may perceive and interact with it in diverse ways. A statue may both be a memorial to a particular historical figure and an object filled with spiritual power, as is the case of statues to King Chulalongkorn in Bangkok and Thao Ying Suranari in Khorat (see chapters 4 and 6 in this volume; Apinan 1992: 8; Cummings 1995: 199).

Monuments may be erected to commemorate events such as national liberations, historical figures, great battles, and national leaders. Thailand, like other nation-states, has its share of monuments – to democracy, to victory – and statues of Kings and, more recently, to important local and regional figures in Chiang Mai and other provincial capitals (see Apinan 1992 for a history of such monuments).

These monuments do not always evoke the unity that they might at first suggest. A statue to a heroine in the Northeast, Thao Suranari, locally known as grandmother Mo (*ya mo*), has been the focus of controversy that began with questions about her historical existence (chapter 4 in this volume). One of the reasons for the strong reaction was that grandmother Mo had become a locally important and powerful spirit. Another potential monument – to those killed in the October 1976 uprising in Thailand – is creating controversy, albeit for different political historical reasons (chapter 10 in this volume). Whether it is grandmother Mo or the students killed in 1976, monuments and statues are arguments about history, and how the past should be remembered and commemorated, if at all.

In this chapter, I explore the implications of the creation in 1990 of the monument to Phaya Sihanatraja,[1] the 'founder' of Maehongson. His life was much more modest than that of grandmother Mo, who is remembered as a heroine who helped defeat the Lao, and much less contentious than the monument to those who died in 1976. The very modesty of his life raises questions as to why a statue of Phaya Sihanatraja was even erected. To answer this question, I explore the role Phaya Sihanatraja played in founding Maehongson, and speculate as to why Maehongson needed a 'founder' statue in 1990 and not before. I first discuss sources of information about Phaya Sihanatraja and provide a synopsis of his story. In order to understand why the statue was erected when it was, I consider heroes and statues in the broader Thai context and then return to a discussion of Phaya Sihanatraja and his statue. I conclude with a discussion of the nature of founder statues and founder cults.

Phaya Sihanatraja

Phaya Sihanatraja is of interest to a Thai audience; people who would have access to, and an interest in, popular histories. While local Shan might have an interest in provincial histories, these texts are not available in Maehongson. Most of the writings about Phaya Sihanatraja are in Thai (but see Wilson 1985). Guidebooks written in English (Cummings 1995; Averbuck 1994; Gray and Ridout 1992; Levy and McCarthy 1992; Richardson 1993), even relatively recent ones, do not mention Phaya Sihanatraja or suggest that monument is a sight worth seeing. In contrast, Thai guidebooks recount the history of the province, and often locate the Phaya Sihanatraja monument on the map (see Sarakhadi 1993: 136 for a Thai map with the monument prominently displayed).

The information I have about Phaya Sihanatraja comes from a variety of texts. These include an elementary school textbook (Ministry of Education 1983), assorted guides to Maehongson for Thai (Samai 1996; Sarakadi 1993; Warangkhana 1992), and Tourist Authority of Thailand (TAT) brochures (1996). An additional source of information is the plaque on the monument itself. The version on the plaque differs from other accounts (see note 2; for a discussion of these texts and their variations see Tannenbaum 1996).

The accounts of the history of Maehongson, and Phaya Sihanatraja's role in it, are all in the realm of popular, not academic, history. The textbook and the TAT brochures have added authority because they are government publications. The history of Maehongson that they report is straightforward: the events occurred in the sequence as told and there are no other possible interpretations or alternative accounts. Popular, as opposed to academic, histories have different standards for authority and authenticity, which suggests that each type of history plays a different role in constructing arguments about the past (Appadurai 1981; Reynolds 1992). Popular histories are related to the construction of national identity and the emerging awareness of a 'national' past. As the national past is more secure, it becomes possible to turn to local histories and the ways the regional is related to the national.

Phaya Sihanatraja's story is embedded in a larger account of the history of Maehongson, one which opens when the Chiang Mai court begins to take an interest in the area. Before they tell the history of Phaya Sihanatraja, these accounts begin with the story of Cao Kaeomüngma who was sent from Chiang Mai to capture elephants in 1831 in the area that would become Maehongson. While the plaque[2] on the monument is the only exception to this, even here Chiang Mai rulers still play an important role in establishing Maehongson.

Cao Kaeomüngma creates the political landscape by collecting people living in scattered settlements and establishing villages. He founded Pang Mu, considered to be the oldest village in Maehongson, and appointed Phaka Mòng to be its leader. Phaka Mòng was appointed as *haeng*, a Shan term which refers to 'an official that has jurisdiction over a district' (Cushing 1914: 637). *Haeng* is translated into Thai as *kamnan*, which has the modern meaning of sub-district officer and implies an administrative hierarchy that was not in place when these historical events occurred. Cao Kaeomüngma also created the first settlement of Maehongson, and appointed Saen Kom, Phaka Mòng's son-in-law, to be its leader. Saen Kom was appointed *kang* (Shan, 'chief of a village', see Cushing 1914: 6) or village headman (*phu yai ban*), suggesting that Saen Kom was subordinate to Phaka Mòng.

With the story of Cao Kaeomüngma as background, the authors begin the tale of Phaya Sihanatraja. Before he became Phaya Sihanatraja, he was Chan Kale, a refugee from Möng Mòk Mai in what is now the Shan State in Burma. Chan Kale's arrival was part of a larger movement of Shan. Around 1865, Tsao Kolan, the ruler of Mòk Mai, went into exile because of disputes with his Burmese overlord (for a sympathetic account of Tsao Kolan see Mangrai 1965: 227–228; for a less sympathetic Thai view see Wilson 1985: 34–35).

Chan Kale came into what was to become the Maehongson area and went to live in Pang Mu. There he took refuge with the headman, Phaka Mòng, who came to love him as a son and gave him his daughter, Nang Sai, as his wife. Chan Kale then went to Khun Yuam, where his good character was recognised and the people of Khun Yuam appointed him their first ruler. After his first wife died, Tsao Kolan gave him his niece, Nang Mia, to be his second wife. His virtue and value were recognised and, in 1874, Cao Inthawichayanon of Chiang Mai gave him the title and name of Phaya Sihanatraja and made him the first ruler of Maehongson. He reigned for ten years and died in 1883.

The initial incident of Cao Kaeomüngma's elephant hunting expedition seems irrelevant to the story of Phaya Sihanatraja. By the time Chan Kale came to found Möng Maehongson, the original settlement had disappeared. Yet Cao Kaeomüngma's role is central to these popular accounts – he establishes and names villages and appoints leaders, in essence civilising the area and creating connections with Chiang Mai. It is Chiang Mai and Chiang Mai officials whose authority establishes Maehongson, and Chiang Mai's authority is confirmed in the eventual appointment of Chan Kale as Phaya Sihanatraja, the first ruler of Möng Maehongson.

There are two related questions: why build a statue to Phaya Sihanatraja at all and why do it in 1990? The answers to these questions require a shift in focus from the texts to what else was going on in Thailand and Maehongson when Phaya Sihanatraja founded Maehongson, and when the statue was erected.

Maehongson and Thailand

Maehongson does not often appear in Thai administrative writing, although this may simply be because historians have not yet systematically explored what is available in the National Library. Wilson (1985) found and translated a Thai surveyor's report of 1890, which included a visit to Maehongson and an account of its recent history.[3] What is of interest here is not the account of the history but the context which led to the surveyor making the report.

The survey was made in 1890 during the project of delimiting the Thai-Burma border, something which concerned the British in Burma more than the Thai (Thongchai 1994). Wilson (1985: 30) speculates that the surveyor, Nai Banchaphumasathan, was trained at the Royal Thai Survey Department, created by McCarthy, the British surveyor who established the Royal Thai Survey Department[4] (see also Thongchai 1994: 119). The establishment of the western border and the continuing reorganisation of the administrative system placed Maehongson firmly in what would become Thailand (Thongchai 1994).

Once situated in Thailand, Maehongson became marginal to the developing Thai nation-state. Its population is ambiguously 'Thai'. The majority call themselves 'Tai', and are called 'Thai Yai' in the national language and 'Shan' in English. Shan differ from the Central Thai in language, alphabet, and Theravada Buddhist practice. Similar linguistic and religious differences between Bangkok and Northern Thailand led to the suppression of Northern Thai practices (Ishii 1986; Kamala 1997; Keyes 1971). However, this did not occur in Maehongson because it was so isolated and its variant forms of language and religion were seen as irrelevant as rallying points for opposition to the increasing centralisation from Bangkok.

In 1900, Maehongson and the communities of Mae Sariang, Khun Yuam, and Pai were incorporated into Western Chiang Mai. The ruling prince was pensioned off and replaced with regular Thai officials (Anusansasanakorn 1977; Durrenberger 1977). Maehongson became a province in 1907 (Samai 1996: 10).

Maehongson never was a popular place for government officials to serve, being so distant from the centre. It had been characterised as the Siberia of Thailand, where officials got posted if they had offended their superiors (Hudson 1987: 43; Knopf Guide 1993: 287; Parkes 1992: 331; Pramote 1975: 8). There was some doubt as to how 'Thai' this area really was – it was certainly remote, rural, and lacking in many amenities (Pramote 1975: 8–9).

When I first arrived in Maehongson in 1977, there was little apparent Thai presence. On the streets, in the market, and in the shops, all one heard was Shan. While street and most store signs were in Thai, there were occasional store signs in Shan or Burmese. There was little question that this was a Shan area, even if most Shan in the area were Thai citizens (see Keyes 1989: 1–3 for a description of Maehongson in 1968).

During the early 1980s, the only symbolic markers of Maehongson's place in Thailand were the buildings associated with provincial and district government, and the schools. These building plans are standard and a district office or school in Maehongson looks no different from those in any other provincial town. The architecture replicates the administrative structure, which made Maehongson formally part of Thailand

Maehongson remained off the beaten track. While Pramote's (1975) book *Maehongson,* in Thai, urged people to visit Maehongson before it changed, I had little sense that many Thai took Pramote's advice. The first tourist agency in Maehongson did open in 1977 and served primarily a Thai and Chinese clientele. However, serving tourists was only a small part of their business. There were few tourists in the area and no accommodation specifically for Western tourists until 1984 (Tannenbaum 1994).

Around 1984, Maehongson began receiving international attention when a French fashion magazine used Long Neck Karen women in one of their features. These are exotic looking women who have a number of heavy brass rings on their necks. The weight of the rings causes the shoulder bones to bend and gives them the appearance of having 'long necks'. Pictures of Long Neck Karen now appear on postcards, and in Tourist Authority of Thailand brochures, and the odd anthropology text. A number of these women were brought to the Karen Army camp near the Thai border. Western tourists and fashion photographers were charged fees to see and photograph them. The then Governor of Maehongson wanted them moved into Maehongson proper, and eventually two 'Long Neck' villages were established. Recently, a number of these women were moved to Chiang Mai, sparking a human rights controversy about their treatment (AFP 1997).

The presence of the Long Neck women helped create the tourist boom in Maehongson, as did the sense that other, older tourist areas such as Chiang Mai or Chiang Rai were 'too developed'. Perhaps it was the presence of the Long Neck women that made Maehongson, rather than Nan or other mountainous areas, the new location for tourist development. The Tourist Authority of Thailand began to actively promote Maehongson as a place for Western tourists.

Along with this influx of outsiders into the tourist trade came other business people seeing Maehongson as a good place to expand. There has been a real increase in businesses in Maehongson – there are now car dealerships, housing developments, restaurants, and 'department' stores where, in the recent past, there was only the market which closed in the afternoon. Most of these businesses are owned by Northern or Central Thai (Tannenbaum 1994). One Northern Thai businessman who was involved in the opening of the first resort in the area said that in 1989, with the filming of the movie Air America[5] in the area, businesses in Maehongson 'boomed'.

Shan villagers talking about changes in Maehongson town say that the central downtown area is becoming less and less Shan as outsiders buy property and Shan move to the edge of town. It is true that now you can use Central Thai, the national language, in almost all the shops downtown, and you can hear it on the street.

Against this background of increased commerce and increasingly easy access to Maehongson – Thai Airways makes up to four roundtrips from Chiang Mai a day in 1996 compared to the three trips per week in 1977 – Maehongson had become attractive to Thai tourists. This is partly due to the scenery, especially the bua tòng[6] flowers that bloom in November, and the presence of the Long Neck Karen. But it is also attractive culturally: because of its remoteness, Shan are seen as remaining relatively untouched by Western influences and have preserved their 'traditional' way of life remaining more Buddhist, and, perhaps, more 'Thai' than those in urban areas (Emmons 1994; Pramote 1975; Suthon 1989).

In the past, rural Thai were seen as backwards and uncivilised, but now they are more and more seen as repositories of Thai-ness. This construction of rural people as 'Thai' collapses a range of ethnic diversity into a single national identity as citizens and people of Thailand. Advocates of the rural source of Thai identity actively seek 'villagers' wisdom' as the way to solve current problems of industrialisation, modernisation, alienation and the loss of Thai cultural values (Proceedings of the Conference on Villagers' Wisdom 1990; see also Catholic Council of Thailand for Development 1990; Seri 1986, 1988; Seri with K. Hewison 1990; Seri and Bennoun 1988). This concern for Thai identity appears in Thai academia with the development of Thai studies and the urge to discover and record local histories and Thai traditions, which include Tai varieties such as Tai Lue, Tai Long (Shan, Thai Yai), the Black Thai in Vietnam, and so on.

This is part of the discussion about the nature of Thai-ness, modernity and progress (see the volume on Thai identity edited by Reynolds 1991b; see also Apinan 1992; Mills 1997; Vella 1978). This discourse is built around two opposing but interconnected perspectives: urban areas are modern and progressive while villagers and village life are backwards and uncivilised or, alternatively, villagers and village life are the true repositories of Thai values which are threatened by the corruption and decay inherent in urban industrial lifestyles (Ekavid 1990; *Proceedings of the Conference on Villagers' Wisdom* 1990; Sanitsuda 1990; Seri 1986, 1988; Sulak 1985, 1992; see O'Connor 1989 for an analysis of how rural romanticism is linked to 'modernity'). Each view implies a commitment to different political and ideological agendas (Jackson 1993). While the opposition of rural virtue to urban decadence is neither new nor unique to Thailand (Williams 1973), rural areas as a domain of virtue is new in Thai discourse. In the recent past, village life was seldom seen as idyllic or attractive (see O'Connor 1989 for a discussion as to why 'rural' meant backwards; see also Reid 1988, 1993; Tambiah 1976).

Heroes, histories, and monuments

In addition to the romantic view of the countryside, there is the current interest in local histories and statues to local heroes. While these two movements may not be related, they are both indicative, in their different ways, of a changing relationship with the past (Jeffrey 1980). Rural areas now are seen as being reservoirs of an idyllic Thai past, while statues of local heroes embody that past in the present. Both raise the question of what kind of past is being presented for inspiration in the present and the future (Anderson 1990).

The tradition of realistic statues commemorating historic figures is relatively recent in Thailand, beginning in the early twentieth century during the reign of King Chulalongkorn (Apinan 1992). This tradition that began under kings continued, after the coup in 1932, under both parliamentary and military governments. Monuments included Democracy Monument erected in 1939–40 and Victory Monument in 1940–41 and, in 1934, the statue of Thao Suranari. Sponsoring and constructing these statues and monuments were acts, primarily, of the national government, with statues being erected in Khorat, Songkhla, Chiang Mai, Lopburi, Sukhothai, Chonburi, Ayutthaya, and Phitsanulok (Apinan 1992: 47–48).

Thailand as a bounded nation-state creates the problem of the contents contained within its boundaries (Thongchai 1994), and a parallel need to defend its boundaries against perceived threats (Irvine 1982). The initial concern was with the maintenance of boundaries against outside enemies. Early monuments and statues commemorate heroic acts of defending the nation, for example the Monument to the Villagers of Bang Racan in Singburi Province, who were all killed fighting against the Burmese (Apinan 1992: 48). Similarly, Thao Suranari is a national hero who helped defeat the Lao in 1826. What made these local heroes fit subjects for statues were their roles in defending the nation. These are 'Thai' heroes, like the monument to the Thai hero erected in Nakhon Si Thammarat in 1946. The hero:

> ... is a symbol of bravery and masculinity. The officer stoops with his bayonet-pointed rifle as if to defy the invisible enemy (the Japanese invaders), confirming that he who serves the government will protect those who live far away in the southern provinces (Apinan 1992: 48).

While the defence of boundaries was being celebrated in statues to heroes, there was a parallel concern with what was contained within these protected boundaries. Regional identification such as Northeastern Thai, or ethnic names such as Thai Yai, were replaced by the broad cover term, 'Thai' (Vella 1978).

Lowland Thailand was seen as ethnically homogenous, at least until the recent past. Vella suggests that this was a self-conscious government practice begun during Chulalongkorn's reign.

> The Lao of the Northeast and the Thaiyai of the North could have been regarded as separate from the Thai of the Chaophraya Plain on historical and, to some extent, cultural grounds ... [i]n any event and for obvious reasons the Siamese government, even before Vajiravudh's time, had decided on a policy of treating all these peoples as Thai and using the term 'Thai' for all of them (Vella 1978: 199).

Reynolds (1991a: 21–24) extends this argument into the Phibun era. Ethnic minorities, particularly the Chinese, were seen as improper contents for the container (Vella 1978: 188–195).

Boundary maintenance concerns persisted through the 1970s, with the Indochinese wars and the expansion of the Vietnamese in areas previously controlled by the French (Irvine 1982). At the same time, Thailand's internal integrity was threatened by the unruliness of improperly Thai populations – communists, uplanders, and Malay separatists (Reynolds 1991a; Thongchai 1996). One consequence of this improper contents perception is that villages with unruly populations were renamed with blatantly patriotic names – Ban Rak Thai, the village which loves Thailand, formerly Mae Ao, a Kuomintang village in Maehongson province. The name 'Mae Ao' is still used because of its association with the Kuomintang, and as such it has become a tourist attraction.

As the borders have become less threatened, and there is less internal unrest, the idea of the proper contents of the Thai container has shifted. While uplanders as non-Thai are seen as increasingly inappropriate contents of this Thai container (Jonsson 1996), and a monument to the students killed in 1976 is still contentious, it is now acceptable, in fact encouraged, to celebrate local traditions. One of the consequences of the creation of Thailand, with its assumption of a 'geo-body' that has persisted through time, is the creation of 'regional Thai' groups defined and identified in terms of their geographic relationship to the centre, defined as Bangkok. This is a relatively recent usage, something which stresses the national Thai character of what were previously ethnic groups.

Regions and provinces are now seen as sub-units with histories that reflect their places within Thailand. These parts cannot threaten the Thai nation as they are constituted as parts of Thailand, defined in terms of it – Northern Thailand, Northeastern Thailand, Southern Thailand – and only exist so long as Thailand does. This regionalism defined in reference to the Thai nation-state is also reflected in the names of the Thai dialects – Northern Thai, Central Thai. It now becomes possible to develop markers of difference which highlight the cultural diversity and creativity contained within the nation, as long as it is on a provincial and not ethnic level.

This expanded sense of appropriate contents and the interest in local histories (Reynolds 1992) provide the context for a new wave of statues and local monuments. Chiang Mai has been refurbishing its past, rebuilding the walls around the inner city, and holding ceremonies at the city pillar (Renard 1996). Statues to local figures such as Cao Müang Sot in Mae Sot, Phaya Sihanatraja, and others are relatively recent, being built in the late 1980s and early 1990s. These are different sorts of local heroes, ones who played only minor roles in defending Thailand from its enemies, yet they did play an important role from a certain perspective in sustaining the modern nation-state.

The Phaya Sihanatraja statue

One way of making sense of the Phaya Sihanatraja statue is to look at the actors involved in creating it. The inspiration for the statue and the prime mover in its construction was the provincial abbot, Cao Khana Cangwat Thao Khun Samon, locally known as Tu[7] Mahalak. Tu Mahalak was travelling in Mae Sot and saw the people there erecting a statue to Cao Müang Sot. He thought that Phaya Sihanatraja would be good for a statue because he wanted to 'honour (*yok yòng*) the good person who established the country (*sang ban müang*) and made it prosper (*yu li mi suk*)'. He added that Chiang Rai had the statue of Mengrai, Chiang Mai had one of

145

Kawilorot, Lamphun had that of Camadevi (Camthewi), and it would be good if Maehongson had a similar image (interview with Tu Mahalak, 20 June 1996). Tu Mahalak is Northern Thai and his interest in the monument is provincial rather than ethnic.

Because of his position in the monastic hierarchy, Tu Mahalak was able to interest the governor in this project. The governor appointed the assistant governor to head the statue committee. The committee included Tu Mahalak, Ajarn Surasak, the director of the local cultural centre located at the high school, and a number of business leaders. Ajarn Surasak is a Shan born in Maehongson Town, who graduated from Chiang Mai Teacher's College and taught art at the local high school. He is the head of the local cultural centre and actively promotes Shan culture, being the author of a number of locally produced pamphlets on Shan culture, including one on tattoos and tattooers. The business leaders on the committee included Mr. Thawachai, who managed the Maehongson resort when it first opened, and who now owns his own resort and a restaurant that offers traditional Shan foods. He actively encourages government officials and others to build offices that incorporate Shan architectural details.

Ajarn Surasak provided the drawing for the statue. He searched old photographs, talked to the descendants of Phaya Sihanatraja, and interviewed old people for details, so that Phaya Sihanatraja would be dressed in a style appropriate to a prince. He also used the information gathered from interviewing old people to write the text for the plaque on the monument. The story on the plaque states that Phaya Sihanatraja founded Khun Yuam, which later become Maehongson, something which is not confirmed in the other texts. This suggests that the committee was less concerned with history *per se* and more concerned with erecting the monument (see note 2).

The impetus for the statue of Phaya Sihanatraja came from outside the local Shan community. Rather than memorialising Shan culture and a Shan cultural hero, the statue represents provincial, not 'Shan', interests. This is clear from Tu Mahalak's statements that he wanted Maehongson to be like other provinces, so that Maehongson would have respect and esteem (*mi ta mi na*). The referent is not Shan, or the place of Shan in Maehongson and Thailand, but rather Maehongson as a province within Thailand.

The motivation for erecting the Phaya Sihanatraja statue differs from erecting statues elsewhere in South East Asia. There statues were erected because ethnic leaders wish to commemorate their ethnic group's role in nation building (Cunningham 1989; Hoskins 1987). The issue is not one of authenticity but rather a different awareness of history and different abilities to create historical markers. Local Shan seem only marginally interested in such historical or cultural activities, and Ajarn Surasak, as an educated Shan with an interest in such concerns, is the exception, not the rule.

The celebration of local cultures also emphasises traditional songs, dance, and costumes – folklorisation (see Salemink 1997) – which provide a quick stereotypical portrayal of the community, and suggest a unity of shared experience. Shan dances are similar to other Thai dances, and can be understood as a kind of Thai folk dance. The label Shan adds an awareness of minor variations within the larger corpus of Thai folk dances. Errington (1984), writing about a festival of nations celebration in Montana, argues that celebrations of ethnic festivals present 'ethnic differences as acceptable and indeed laudable variations on common themes' (1984: 657). Participation in this collective recognition requires that the people share a general understanding of what is comparable and acceptable. The festival in Montana excluded Native Americans and African Americans (Errington 1984: 657–658), while similar provincial festivities in Thailand often include uplanders as exotic attractions. Provincial festivals in Maehongson begin with parades that include Long Neck Karen women, and Shan, Karen, and Hmong women dressed in traditional clothes

Provincial level festivals are for both internal and external consumption, celebrating 'Thai' history and culture for Thai and Western tourists. As part of the King's sixtieth birthday celebration, each province was directed to hold a traditional festival. These festivals helped reify provinces as culture and history bearing units while at the same time they provided colourful ceremonies for tourists. Suddenly it is possible to buy books about local history (Samai 1996), guidebooks (Sarakhadi 1993; Warang-khana 1992), and books on assorted festivals and ceremonies (Chalern 1993; Nithi 1993). While local cultural traditions are being celebrated, local is defined with reference to its place in the Thai geo-body. This shifts attention to regional histories and away from the centre, especially Bangkok, as the locus of all history and culture. However, centres still play an important role in initiating events (Tannenbaum 1996).

Not all local cultural creations are equally acceptable (see Salemink 1997 for a discussion of Vietnamese state approved minority cultural creations). The statue in Maehongson is to Phaya Sihanatraja and not his wife Nang Mia or her uncle Tsao Kolan. Nang Mia is Phaya Sihanatraja's second wife and the niece of Tsao Kolan (Wilson 1989; Mengrai 1969). From the evidence in the surveyor's report, Nang Mia played a more active role than Phaya Sihanatraja in actually founding the town (Wilson 1989), but this is not acknowledged in the Thai sources, although she is recognised as the second ruler of Maehongson (Suan Watthanatham 1994).

From a provincial Thai perspective, Phaya Sihanatraja was a good candidate for a monument since his history is one of a reliance and dependence on leaders appointed by Chiang Mai. He is placed firmly within Chiang Mai's domain and, by extension in popular historiography, Bangkok's. Phaya Sihanatraja was active at a point in time when Thailand

147

was being created out of 'Siam' (Thongchai 1994); he marks Maehong-son's place as a province within Thailand. Given this increasing interest in the contents of the Thai container, founder statues such as that of Phaya Sihanatraja begin to make sense. They highlight connections with a national Thai history, and project a 'Thailand' identical to the modern nation-state back in time.

Founder cults reconsidered

Phaya Sihanatraja does not look like a classic 'founder'. Although he came with a number of other refugees from Mòk Mai, Maehongson, which he ostensibly 'founded', actually already existed, having been established by Cao Kaeomüngma, who appointed Saen Kom as its leader. Nor did Phaya Sihanatraja's authority to rule in Maehongson come from relationships with the local cadastral spirits; instead he was appointed by Chiang Mai. If Maehongson already existed, and people were already living in the area, how can Phaya Sihanatraja be seen as the 'founder'? Phaya Sihanatraja did not found Maehongson, but what he did do was to establish Maehongson's relationship to Chiang Mai and, by extension, to the rest of Thailand.

If, as Lehman (1997) argues, founder cults served to localise a population and facilitate rule, then Phaya Sihanatraja does fit the bill. However, his founder role did not become important until there was a concern with what was contained within Thai boundaries and until Tai ethnic variation became non-threatening and identified as 'provincial', and Thai, rather than 'ethnic' and separatist.

What is happening in the lowlands now with founders' cults and statues suggests a different political dynamic than in earlier state formations or in upland communities. Phaya Sihanatraja and other similar founders, Cao Müang Sot, Mengrai, Camadevi, etc. do not mark relationships between cadastral spirits and rulers. But they serve a parallel function of highlighting the connection between regions and centres.

In other areas of South East Asia, there is a parallel concern for founders and the creation of founders' statues. However, the context and meaning of such statues are somewhat different. In Indonesia, with its war for independence, ethnic groups erect statues of their war heroes to place themselves and their group firmly within modern Indonesian history (Cunningham 1989; Hoskins 1987). These heroes and their statues are more similar to Thao Suranari and the Monument to the Thai Hero (Apinan 1992: 48) that appeared earlier in Thailand. Like those heroes, the ones celebrated in Indonesia are people who helped create and/or defend the nation. The actions for which they are celebrated relate directly to the creation or defence of the modern nation-state. War heroes, who as actors might be local, are celebrated for their national, not local, role.

Founding a province is less dramatic than helping to establish a nation. Phaya Sihanatraja and other provincial 'founders' celebrate local concerns, and help to place the local within the national. While founder statues relate the local to the national, it is the local that is given prominence. Statues to local heroes such as provincial 'founders' suggest a historical concern that takes the larger container – the nation-state – for granted, while statues to Thao Suranari, or those heroes celebrated in Indonesia, reflect the concern for the container.

Notes

1 This chapter draws on research I've done about the Phaya Sihanatraja statue off and on since the summer of 1990, when I saw the statue emplaced. My research has been supported by a Franz Fellowship from Lehigh University and a Fulbright Senior Research Fellowship.

2 Plaque on Phaya Sihanatraja Monument: 'Phaya Sihanatraja, whose original name was Chan Kale, was a Thai Yai who came to stay with Phaka Mòng in Pang Mu in B.E. 2399 (1856). Chan Kale [three words illegible]. Phaka Mòng loved him because of this and gave him his daughter Nang Sai to be his wife. When she died, Caopha Kolan, the Cao Müang of Mòk Mai, gave [Chan Kale] his young niece, Nang Mia, to be his wife. Chan Kale collected people to form the settlement of Khun Yuam. Phra Cao Inthawichayanon, the Cao who ruled Chiang Mai, saw that Chan Kale was industrious and strong and capable of doing good work so he gave him Khun Yuam to rule and appointed him Phaya Sihanat in B.E. 2408 (1865). Müang Khun Yuam's name was changed to Müang Maehongson. Phra Cao Inthawichayanon saw that the population had increased and so he made Phaya Sihanat the first *caopha* and gave him the title Phaya Sihanatraja. Phaya Sihanatraja built up the country and the fields so that the country was prosperous and orderly and the people could make a living easily. He supported the Buddhist religion and the temples; he established the small *cedi* on Dòi Kòng Mu. He also looked after the people so they would increase in goodness and virtue forever and were able to stay in coolness and happiness until B.E. 2429 (1886) when he passed away'. The account on the plaque is abbreviated and does not include the elephant hunt led by Cao Kaeomüangma. The dates also differ from those in other accounts, although there is some variation in the published accounts (see Tannenbaum 1996). The plaque differs from other accounts in that it suggests that Chan Kale founded Khun Yuam, which then became Maehongson, and that he first received the title of Phaya Sihanat and then Phaya Sihanatraja, which is not confirmed in any other account.

3 This report tells a different story about who Phaya Sihanatraja was, where he was from, and his role in founding Maehongson. This history, which appears in the realm of Western academic writing, is not reflected in the popular Thai histories (see Tannenbaum 1996).

4 For an account of his work, see Tips' (1994) introduction to the reissue of McCarthy.

5 Air America was filmed in Maehongson in 1990. It is loosely based on Robbins (1987, 1989) accounts of United States involvement in insurgency and drug running in Laos during the Vietnam War Era. The movie brought an influx of foreigners, which stimulated the opening of guesthouses and other tourist related activities.

6 *Bua tòng* flowers are often identified as sunflowers, but they appear to be some kind of daisy.

7 *Tu* is a Northern Thai address term for monks, Shan also use it; the Central Thai term is *phra*.

References

AFP (Agence France Press) 1997 'Thailand Will Not Use Long Neck Karens in Tourism Drive', posted on web-cite: soc.culture.burma, no.118700, 18 December.

Anderson, Benedict 1990 *Language and Power*, Ithaca, NY: Cornell University Press.

Anusansasanakorn, Phra Khruu 1977 *Maehongson and Phrathart Doi Kong Moo Temple* (translated by P. Curwen), Bangkok.

Appadurai, Arjun 1981 'The past as a scarce resource', p.201–219 in *Man* (N.S.)16.

Apinan Poshyananda 1992 *Modern Art in Thailand: nineteenth and twentieth centuries*, Singapore: Oxford University Press.

Averbuck, Alexis (ed.) 1994 *Let's Go: Thailand: the budget guide*, New York: St. Martin's Press.

Catholic Council of Thailand for Development 1990 *Rice from Our Field*, Bangkok: The Catholic Council of Thailand for Development.

Chalern Tanmahaphran 1992 *30 Phithikam phitsadan* (30 Extraordinary Ceremonies), vol.1, Bangkok: Saengdaet.

Cummings, Joe with Richard Nebesky 1995 *Thailand: a lonely planet travel survival kit*, (sixth edition), Sydney: Lonely Planet.

Cunningham, Clark 1989 'Celebrating a Toba Batak national hero: an Indonesian rite of identity', p.167–200 in Susan D. Russell and Clark E. Cunningham (eds.) *Changing Lives, Changing Rites: ritual and racial dynamics in Philippines and Indonesian uplands*, Ann Arbor, MI: University of Michigan, Michigan Studies in South and Southeast Asia, no.1.

Cushing, J. N.1914 (1971) *A Shan English Dictionary*, Rangoon: American Baptist Mission Press (Reprinted by Gregg International Publishers, Limited).

Durrenberger, E. Paul 1977 *A Socio-Economic Study of a Shan Village in Maehongson Province*, Chiang Mai: Tribal Research Centre.

Emmons, Ron 1994 'Three days off the ground', p.26, Leisure section, *Bangkok Post*, 3 April.

Ekavid Nathalang 1990 'The wisdom of Thai farmers: contemporary efforts for cultural reproduction', p.97–124 in *Phumi panya chao ban* (Villagers' Wisdom), Bangkok: Thai National Culture Commission.

Errington, Frederick 1987 'Reflexivity deflected: the festival of nations as an American cultural performance', p.654–667 in *American Ethnologist* 14(4).

Gray, Paul and Lucy Ridout 1992 *Thailand: the rough guide*, London: Rough Guides.

Hoskins, Janet 1987 'The headhunter as hero: local traditions and their reinterpretation as national history', p.605–622 in *American Ethnologist* 14(4).

Hudson, Roy 1987 *Hudson's Guide to Maehongson*, Chiang Mai: Dararat.

Irvine, Walter 1982 'The Thai-Yuan "madman" and the "modernising, developing Thai nation" as bounded entities under threat: a study in the reflection of a single image', unpublished PhD thesis, University of London.

Ishii, Yoneo 1986 *Sangha, State, and Society: Thai Buddhism in history* (translated by Peter Hawkes), Kyoto: Kyoto University, Monographs of the Center for Southeast Asian Studies.

Jackson, Peter A. 1993 'Reinterpreting the *Traiphuum Phra Ruang*: political functions of Buddhist symbolism in contemporary Thailand', p.64–100 in Trevor Ling (ed.) *Buddhist Trends in Southeast Asia*, Singapore: Institute of Southeast Asian Studies.

Jeffrey, Robin 1980 'What statues tell', p.484–502 in *Pacific Affairs* 53(3).

Jonsson, Hjorliefur Rafn 1996 'Shifting social landscape: Mien (Yao) communities and histories in state-client settings', unpublished PhD dissertation, Cornell University.

Kamala Tiyavanich 1997 *Forest Recollections: wandering monks in twentieth-century Thailand*, Honolulu: University of Hawaii Press.

Keyes, Charles F. 1971 'Buddhism and national integration in Thailand', p.551–568 in *Journal of Asian Studies* 30(3).

—— 1989 *Thailand: Buddhist kingdom as modern nation-state*, Boulder, Col.: Westview Press.

—— 1996 'National heroine or local spirit? the struggle over memory in the case of Thao Suranari of Nakhon Ratchasima', paper presented at the Sixth International Conference on Thai Studies, Chiang Mai, October (chapter 4 in this volume).

Knopf Guides 1993 *Thailand*, New York: Alfred Knopf.

Lehman, F. K. 1997 'The relevance of the founders' cult for understanding the political systems of the peoples of northern Southeast Asia and its Chinese borderlands', unpublished paper presented at the Association for Asian Studies meeting, Chicago, March.

Levy, John and Kyle McCarthy 1992 *Frommer's Comprehensive Travel Guide: Thailand '92–'93*, New York: Prentice Hall Travel.

Mengrai, Sao Saimong 1969 *The Shan States and the British Annexation*, Ithaca, NY: Cornell University, Southeast Asia Program, Data Paper, no.57.

Mills, Mary Beth 1997 'Contesting the margins of modernity: women, migration, and consumption in Thailand', p.37–61 in *American Ethnologist* 24(1).

Ministry of Education 1983 *Müang sam mòk* (The Country of the Three Mists), Bangkok: Ministry of Education.

Nithi Iawsriwongse 1993 *Thòng thiao bun bang fai nai isan* (Visiting Rocket Festivals in Isan), Bangkok: Sinlapa Watthanatham.

O'Connor, Richard 1989 'From 'fertility' to 'order', paternalism to profits: the Thai city's impact on the culture-environment interface', p.393–414 in *Culture and Environment: a symposium of the Siam Society*, Bangkok: The Siam Society.

Pramote Tatsanasuwan 1975 *Maehongson* (in Thai), Bangkok: Odeon Press.

Proceedings of the Conference on Villagers' Wisdom 1990 *Phumi panya chao ban* (Villagers' Wisdom), Bangkok: Thai National Culture Commission.

Reid, Anthony 1988 *Southeast Asia in the Age of Commerce 1450–1680: the lands below the wind*, New Haven: Yale University Press.

—— 1993 *Southeast Asia in the Age of Commerce 1450–1680: expansion and crisis*, New Haven: Yale University Press.

Renard, Ronald D. 1996 'Blessing and Northern Thai historiography', p.159–180 in Cornelia Ann Kammerer and Nicola Tannenbaum (eds.) *Merit and Blessing in Mainland Southeast Asia in Comparative Perspective*, New Haven: Yale Univesrity, Yale Southeast Asia Studies Monograph, no.45.

Reynolds, Craig 1991a 'Introduction: national identity and its defenders', p.1–40 in C. Reynolds, (ed.) *National Identity and Its Defenders: Thailand, 1939–1989*, Chiang Mai: Silkworm Books.

—— 1992 'The plot of Thai history: theory and practice', p.313–322 in Gehan Wijeyewardene and E. C. Chapman (eds.) *Patterns and Illusions: Thai history and thought*, Singapore: Institute of Southeast Asian Studies.

Reynolds, Craig (ed.) 1991b *National Identity and Its Defenders: Thailand, 1939–1989*, Chiang Mai: Silkworm Books.

Richardson, Derk 1992 *2–22 Days in Thailand: the itinerary planner*, Santa Fe, NM: John Muir Publications.

Robbins, Christopher 1987 *The Ravens: the men who flew in America's secret war in Laos*, New York: Crown Books.

—— 1988 (1979) *Air America*, Guernsey: Corgi Books.

Salemink, Oscar 1997 'The dying god revisited: the king of fire and Vietnamese ethnic policy in the Central Highlands', unpublished paper presented at the Association for Asian Studies, Chicago, March.

Samai Suthitham 1988 *Pòi sang lòng* (Ordination Festival), Bangkok: Surusopha.

—— 1996 *Maehongson* (in Thai), Bangkok: Odeon Books.

Sanitsuda Ekachai 1990 *Behind the Smile: voices of Thailand*, Bangkok: Thai Development Support Committee.

Sarakhadi 1993 *Maehongson* (in Thai), Bangkok: Sarakhadi.

Seri Phongphit 1988 *Religion in a Changing Society*, Hong Kong: Arena Press.

—— with Kevin Hewison 1990 *Thai Village Life: culture and transition in the Northeast*, Bangkok: Thai Institute for Rural Development, Mooban Press.

Seri Phongphit (ed.) 1986 *Back to the Roots: village and self-reliance in a Thai context*, Culture and Development Series, no.1, Bangkok: Rural Development Documentation Centre.

Seri Phongphit and Robert Bennoun (eds.) 1988 *Turning Point of Thai Farmers*, Culture and Development Series, no.2, Bangkok: Rural Development Documentation Centre.

Suan Watthanatham Maehongson 1994 *Prawattisat Maehongson lae bukkhon khòng Maehongson* (The History of Maehongson and the Important People of Maehongson), Maehongson.

Sulak Sivaraksa 1985 *Siamese Resurgence: a Thai Buddhist voice on Asia and a world of change*, Bangkok: Asian Cultural Forum on Development.

—— 1992 *Seeds of Peace: a Buddhist vision for renewing society*, Berkeley: Parallax Press.

Suthon Sukpisit 1989 'The most colorful festival in Mae Hong Son', p.1, Outlook section, *Bangkok Post*, 18 April.

Tambiah, Stanley J. 1976 *World Conqueror and World Renouncer*, Cambridge: Cambridge University Press.

Tannenbaum, Nicola 1994 'History of tourism related businesses in Maehongson', unpublished report to the Thai National Research Council and the Fulbright Association.

—— 1996 'Phaya Sihanatraja and the history of Maehongson' p.355–362 in *Proceedings of the Sixth International Conference on Thai Studies, Theme II: Cultural Crisis and the Thai Capitalist Transformation*, Chiang Mai: Silkworm Books.

Thomas, Nicholas 1991 *Entangled Objects*, Cambridge, Mass.: Harvard University Press.

Thongchai Winichakul 1994 *Siam Mapped: a history of the geo-body of a nation*, Honolulu: University of Hawaii Press.

—— 1996 'Remembering/silencing the traumatic past: the ambivalent narratives of the October 1976 massacre in Bangkok', paper presented at the Sixth International Conference on Thai Studies, Chiang Mai, October (chapter 10 in this volume).

Tips, Walter E. J. 1994 'Introduction', p.v–x in James McCarthy *Surveying and Exploring in Siam*, Bangkok: White Lotus.

Tourist Authority of Thailand 1996 *Cangwat Maehongson* (in Thai), Bangkok.

Trouillot, Michel-Rolph 1995 *Silencing the Past: power and the production of history*, Boston: Beacon Press.

Vella, Walter 1978 *Chaiyo! King Vajiravudh and the development of Thai nationalism*, Honolulu: University of Hawaii Press.

Warangkhana Sumetwan (ed.) 1992 *Phak nüa* (The North), D. K. Thai Tour Guides, Bangkok: D. K. Books.

Wilson, Constance 1985 'A Thai government survey of the Middle Salween, 1890', p.29–62 in C. Wilson and Lucien Hanks (eds.) *The Burma-Thailand Frontier over Sixteen Decades: three descriptive documents*, Athens, OH: Ohio University, Monographs in International Studies, Southeast Asia Series, no.70.

■ CHAPTER SIX ■

Immobile Memories

Statues in Thailand and Laos

Grant Evans

Public statues in Thailand and Laos are a source of social, cultural and political memory. Indeed, that is why they were erected. Statues of human beings in public places in Asia are a feature of the modern world. Therefore they tell us something about the *mentalité* of this world. Prior to this period, one only found statues of deities. Of course, statues of guardian soldiers may have been made for the tombs of emperors in places like Vietnam or China, but they were considered part of the emperor and they were not public.

Central to this modern *mentalité* is nationalism, and one author has argued that statue building in Europe in the nineteenth century 'both constructed and reflected the birth of what may be referred to as "national time"' (Lerner 1993: 177). That is the cultural production of the 'eternal nation'. Associated with the rise of nationalism in Europe was, of course, capitalism and urbanism and they too influenced statue making.

Primarily sponsored by states, statues and monuments are intended to convey the hegemonic view of the nation. Yet, as we know, uniform hegemony is a chimera, and dominant views are often contested or contorted to serve other political or cultural purposes.

Statues in urban space

Writing of the 'statuemania' which swept across France in the nineteenth century, Maurice Agulhon (1978: 145) remarks 'that statuemania belongs entirely to the history of the *decor urbain*. It is in effect the expanding and enlarged city, its opening out in the nineteenth century which multiplied the places, the boulevards, the perspectives and the promenades, and which called on monuments to fill up these spaces'.

Not surprisingly, when we turn to the history of Thailand, or more specifically Bangkok, it is in the context of the transformation of the city that we see the construction of the first statue. Following his visits to Europe in the late nineteenth and the early twentieth centuries, King Chulalongkorn began his transformation of Bangkok into a modern city, as part of his more general programme of modernisation. He opened it out by ordering the construction of large avenues and streets lined with trees, such as Rajdamnoen, Yaowaraj, Unagun, Burapa, Din Sor, Suriwong, and so on. The five-kilometre long Rajdamnoen Avenue from the Grand Palace to the Ananta Samagom Throne Hall was designed after the Mall in London, the Champs Elysée in Paris, and the Unter den Linden in Berlin. The Throne Hall itself was in high nineteenth century European imperial style, and spreading out before it was a Royal Plaza. The centre-piece of this new plaza was Thailand's first statue, the equestrian monument of King Chulalong-korn himself, unveiled in 1908 on the 40th anniversary of his reign. The inspiration for this statue came directly from similar equestrian statues seen in Europe, and indeed the statue was designed by a French sculptor, George Ernest Saulo, and made at the Susse Frére moulding factory in France.

Since that time, statues have proliferated in Thailand as in no other mainland South East Asian country. I do not know exactly how many public statues have been built in Thailand to date, but possibly they run into hundreds.[1] By contrast, in neighbouring countries, and until recently in Laos, the number of statues could be counted on the fingers of one or two hands.

In his attempt at the absolutist modernisation of the Thai polity and society, Rama V consciously copied powerful European states, as did his successor Rama VI.[2] They evolved a potent form of what Anderson (1991), borrowing from Seton-Watson, refers to as 'official nationalism', that is an especially conservative version of nationalism initiated by pre-modern rulers – 'willed merger of nation and dynastic empire' (1991: 86).

Nationalism and secularism

One of the important changes that begins to occur during the reign of Chulalongkorn is an attenuation of the distance between the monarch and his subjects. One of the foundation 'myths'[3] of Rama V's reign is his first statement on being crowned when he announced that henceforth prostration in the Royal presence was forbidden – which supposedly 'shocked' the court. Another 'mythology' of his reign, repeated in school textbooks and newspapers, is that 'the keynote of his reign was the abolition of slavery'. Leaving aside the details relating to these specific questions (which is precisely what 'mythologising' demands), we can however see here the first attempts of a monarch symbolically to step closer to the people, a crucial nationalistic manoeuvre. This relates directly to statue building in a number of ways. The equestrian statue itself brings an image of the king outside the palace and into the permanent gaze of the public for the first time.

This changing concept of distance also relates to the issue of growing secularisation of the society and of the monarchy. Robin Jeffrey has broached this issue in an interesting article on the broader cultural and historical significance of statue building in India. These effigies, he suggests, are somehow mid-points between deities and men, and signify not only the changing cosmology of modern polities, but also their changing scale and the changing relations between deities and men – the lessening of the distance between them. Jeffrey comments:

> ... when religious and familial authority weakens, when the power and responsibilities of a state broaden, and when, therefore, it becomes necessary to win acceptance of the state from numbers far beyond the face-to-face kin and clan – then statues seem to flourish. Their appearance indicates that politics are becoming more secular and competitive. Yet because the statue is of the same genre as supernatural idols, the aims of statue-raising and idol-making are perhaps the same: to deify certain qualities and make men and women behave with awe (1980: 501).

He further points out that before the coming of the British to India there were no statues of mortals: 'the notion of making an effigy of a leader who had no claim to supernatural powers was a foreign one' (1980: 485). Theravadin kings in Laos and Thailand historically were *saksit* (i.e. thought to possess supernatural powers), but there is a degree of ambiguity about the exact nature of a king's divine status. To cite Vella on the Thai:

> At his coronation the king was invested as a reincarnated Brahmanic god ... It was not necessary for a king to rely on the belief that he was divine; it is doubtful whether this belief was ever widespread ... In the popular religion, Buddhism, the king was looked upon as a Cakravartin, or universal emperor, and – at least after his death – as a Boddhisattva, or Buddhist saint (1955: 319).

Thus the making of effigies of kings in the modern context seems to partake of a double movement – a permanent public demonstration of their deification, as well as being a secular symbol of the nation.

During the reign of King Rama VI, the programme of nationalist modernisation begun by Rama V continued, and during this time the arts in particular were heavily patronised. In 1922 an Italian sculptor, Corrado Feroci (alias Silpa Bhirasri after 1944), was appointed by the king to direct fine arts in Thailand. Thai artists were sent to Europe, and on their return they 'helped to satisfy the demand for new secular forms of expression (portraits, historical paintings, monuments, statues, public architecture, etc.) which had not existed in the traditional art context in Thailand' (Michaelson 1993: 62).[4]

The second public statue of a king in Thailand was of Rama I, which stands at the base of the Memorial Bridge, and was unveiled on 6 April 1932, some two months before the fall of the absolute monarchy.

After the coup d'état of June 1932, the establishment of a constitutional monarchy 'meant that the state and not the king was now the main formal commissioner' of monuments (Michaelson 1993: 63). During this period, the Thai monarchy went into decline, helped along by the alleged antipathy of Thai strongman, Phibun Songkhram to it. During the late 1930s and early 1940s the government of the latter was strongly influenced by the 'fascist' axis powers. The populist and 'democratic' element of their ideology was represented in the first major monuments commissioned by Phibun's government – the Democracy Monument (completed in 1940), and the Victory Monument (completed in 1941). These public monuments contain the first public representations of the 'common man' in reliefs representing the close connection between the military and civilians, and the realistic statues of armed forces members at the base of the Victory Monument obelisk. As Helen Michaelson (1993: 69) comments: 'The main aim of the new rulers was to build a modern nation. The creation of a modern and, in military terms, strong nation was meant to be visualised by such artistic presentations for foreign countries as well as for the Thai public'.

Yet it would be unwise to overstress Phibun's hostility to the monarchy.[5] As Vella (1978) points out, much of Phibun's nationalism drew directly on themes already established by Rama VI. And indeed, it was Phibun's government which in 1940 commissioned the next statue of a Thai king, that of Rama VI, which now stands outside the Lumpini Park in central Bangkok. Opening his campaign for funds, Phibun sang the praises of the former monarch:

> The most important and highly beneficial kindness handed down to the Thai country and nation, however, lies in the fact that King Vajiravudh was responsible in rousing the Thai nation as a whole from its lethargy to realize the importance of carrying out patriotic and other goods acts for the betterment and glory of the nation (cited in Vella 1978: 272).

Indeed, the next major public statue erected in Bangkok, and the only other equestrian monument, was commissioned by a later Phibun government and unveiled in April 1954, that of King Taksin – a somewhat controversial choice.[6]

The precise history of statue building in the next twenty years is unclear to me. The pattern, however, remained of statues of kings, now added to by lesser nobility, some key military-political figures, and some folk-heroes. Based on my survey of the *Bangkok Post*, we can take up the story again in the late 1960s with the commissioning of a statue of Ramkhamhaeng 'the Great, the inventor of the Thai alphabet' (*BKP* 9/9/

68) in 1968, which was finished in 1974 and installed at Sukhothai. Other monuments were also being built around the country to, for example, King Naresuan 'the Great, the hero of the elephant wars' against the Burmese (*BKP* 11/11/68), of Rama V for Prathum Thani (*BKP* 31/12/69), of King U-thong at Ayutthaya (*BKP* 2/1/70), of Rama VI for a boy scout camp in Chonburi (*BKP* 21/8/71), of King Ananda, installed in Wat Suthat Thep Wararam (*BKP* 28/2/73),[7] in 1975 a statue of King Pin Klao was placed outside the National Theatre (*BKP* 8/1/75), in 1980 a statue of Rama VII was placed outside the Parliament (*BKP* 10/12/80), in 1986 a statue of Rama V was installed at the Ministry of Science (*BKP* 5/4/86), in 1990 of King Rama III on Rajdamnoen Klang Road in Bangkok (*BKP* 22/7/90), of Rama IV in the compound of the Police Department on Rama I Road in 1992 (*BKP* 17/1/92), and a marble statue of Rama V was installed at the National Memorial Centre at Don Müang in 1994 (*BKP* 20/6/94).

Paralleling these monuments of kings, we have statues of members of the aristocracy being installed outside various ministries: Prince Chantha-buri Nareunart, the first Minister of Economics outside the Economic Affairs Ministry in 1972 (*BKP* 1/8/72), in 1980 a statue of Somdej Chao Phraya Borom Maha Sri Suriyawongse outside a teachers college bearing his name in Thonburi (*BKP* 11/4/80), of Prince Devawongvaroprakan, founder of the Ministry of Foreign Affairs outside the Ministry also in 1980 (*BKP* 19/8/80), and in 1988 of Prince Krom Phra Kamphaeng Phet Akara Yotin at the Signals Department of the Royal Army which he founded (*BKP* 1/3/88).

In July 1982, a statue of Field Marshal Phibun Songkhram was inaugurated at the Army Artillery centre in Lopburi (*BKP* 17/7/82), and in January 1982 plans were announced for the building of a statue of Field Marshal Sarit Thanarat in Khon Kaen (*BKP* 20/1/82), but I do not know if it was built. In 1990, another statue of Phibun was unveiled in Saraburi province (*BKP* 9/9/90), but this attempt to place these military dictators back on the public stage stalled here.

Various other monuments were unveiled over this time, such as the Heroes Monument at Singburi province in 1974 to commemorate resistance to the Burmese '200 years ago' (*BKP* 1/2/74), or the Border Patrol Monument at Mae Sai to commemorate resistance to communists and other enemies of the nation (*BKP* 20/10/86).

The catalogue, *Statues and Monuments in Thailand* (Thailand 1996) provides further examples, and what is perhaps of most interest here is that out of the 76 statues contained in this volume only 20 were constructed before 1980. 'Statuemania' in Thailand, therefore, appears to be a phenomenon of the latter part of the twentieth century. And clearly, they were mostly part of a nationalist project, which identified the monarchy in particular with the nation, and physically marked out the monarchy's place in the nation.

Plate 6.1 A statue of Auguste Pavie, now in the grounds of the French Embassy, Vientiane, Laos.

Statues in Laos[8]

The first public statue of a king to be erected in Laos was that of Settathirat, who now sits jauntily in front of his creation, the That Luang. This statue was erected in 1957, and it was to commemorate the 2500th year of Buddhism.[9] In fact, the first statue of a mortal was created by the French, who carried their statuemania into their Indochinese colonies.[10] The statue was of the famous French explorer Auguste Pavie being offered flowers by a young Lao male and female, and was first situated in front of the Ho Phra Keo. Then the statue of Pavie himself was transferred to the Pavie square in 1947, and later moved to its present site inside the French embassy when the Lane Xang Hotel was built on the square in 1961.[11]

159

Plate 6.2 Statue of King Sisavang Vong at Vat That Luang Dai, formerly in Vientiane, Laos, that went 'missing' in 1994.

The most imposing statue in Vientiane is that of King Sisavang Vong (r.1904–1959) standing in front of Vat Si Muang, which houses the city pillar (*lak muang*). This statue of the King granting the Constitution to the people, written on traditional *bay lan* (palm leaves), was donated by the Soviet Union following King Sisavang Vatthana's visit to the USSR in 1972. It was erected in 1974. In communist revolutions (or revolutions against communism), statues of old regime figures have often been torn down, symbolising as they do, the old regime. In what must count as one of the nicer ironies of Lao history, the statue of King Sisavang Vong could not be torn down, because it had been donated by the 'fraternal' Soviets. Indeed, a second identical statue, was made for Luang Prabang and was installed inside the old palace grounds in 1977! The only other extant large statue of King Sisavang Vong was one made in the years just prior to 1975, by a metallurgist who specialised in making Buddhas, in Vat That Luang Dai in Vientiane. He made a large statue of the King in ceremonial military garb out of war materiel. It was, however, never erected because King Sisavang Vatthana thought it was a poor likeness of his father. Thus this statue lay on its back under a tin roof inside the grounds of the temple for the next twenty years. Suddenly, in 1994, officials from the Ministry of Information and Culture from the Vientiane Municipality came to the temple and carried the statue away. Where to remains a mystery. But what is significant is that this statue was removed at a time when there was a clampdown on royal references within the LPDR (See Evans 1988a). According to one informant, there was talk at the same time of removing the statue in front of Vat Si Muang, but it was not carried out because it would have caused a popular outcry.

Other statues erected during the old regime were dismantled. The statue of the former King of Bassac, Kham Souk (r.1863–1900), was erected in Champassak by Boun Oum at the same time as the statue of Settathirath in Vientiane. After the revolution, Pathet Lao soldiers tore it off its pedestal and smashed the explanatory plaque. They were intent on throwing it in the Mekong River, but the townspeople pleaded to be able to place it in the town's main temple, Vat Thong, where it now stands forlornly in a corner beside the main altar for the Buddha. It does not take much imagination to realise that when the people pay their respects to the Buddha, they are also making them to the former king. The other statue pulled down in the south was a large one of Katay Don Sasorith (1904–1959), which stood in a garden opposite Vat Luang, out of which his tall stupa still looms. The statue of this implacable opponent of the Pathet Lao was erected in 1969, and came down immediately after the revolution. Many people in Pakse believe it was then thrown in the Sedone River, but the Chau Muang of Pakse assured me that it had been stored away. Relatives of Katay visiting from France were allowed to see it in 1994, and this was confirmed to me by one of the relatives.

In Savannakhet, however, and to my surprise, I found one other statue which had been recently erected, in 1995 – that of Kou Voravong (1914–1954). He was Minister of Defence in Prince Souvanna Phouma's first government in 1954 and favoured negotiations with the Pathet Lao. His assassination in September led to the collapse of Souvanna Phouma's government and of the negotiations under the government now led by Katay. In the early 1960s, Kou's two younger brothers, along with his brother-in-law, the notorious rightwing general Phoumi Nosavan (a relative of Thai Prime Minister, Sarit), sponsored the casting of a statue of Kou in Thailand. In the mid-1960s, however, Phoumi was forced to flee to Thailand and so the statue was never erected. Confident in the changing

Plate 6.3 A bust of Kaysone Phomvihane in the headquarters of Vientiane City Administration.

line of the state in 1989 the Voravong family petitioned the LPRP leadership for permission to erect the statue, citing Kou's resistance to the Japanese in WW2 (but no doubt leaving out his resistance to the formation of the Issara government), and his conciliatory line towards the Pathet Lao in 1954. In 1994, they finally received permission from the party and in 1995 the statue was brought across from Thailand to be ceremoniously erected on a plot of private land (which happens to be just opposite Kaysone's natal home). The erection of this dainty, well crafted little statue of Kou dressed in a traditional gentleman's *sampot* is extremely significant in the midst of the Kaysone statue building mania which I shall come to shortly. It is the first step back onto the historical stage of a non-Pathet Lao figure from the past, and registers, I think, part of a play by major families in Laos to have their roles in history recognised, too. Kou's relatives, who live opposite the statue's square, said that they had heard a rumour that Katay's statue may be erected again. Although this seems far-fetched in the present climate, a few days later, a monk in Pakse also intimated that Katay's statue would be restored 'when the time is right'.

Since the death of Lao President Kaysone Phomvihane in 1992, there has been a concerted attempt by the Lao Peoples Revolutionary Party (LPRP) to build up a cult around its former leader (See Evans 1988a). A major activity associated with the cult has been the erection of memorial busts of Kaysone throughout the country. All 150 of these statues were, not surprisingly, produced by North Korea. Some were officially donated by the North Korean ambassador on behalf of Kim Jong Il, the new 'great leader', on the day of Kaysone's anniversary (*Vientiane mai* 15/12/95). The completion and the cost of these memorials was regularly recounted in the press.

The spatial locations of these busts, however, demonstrate that they are part of a state cult rather than being open to popular pilgrims. The main statue in Vientiane municipality, inscribed with the words 'Kaysone Phomvihane is in our thoughts whenever we carry out our duty', for example, is set deep within the main municipal office grounds, past a guard on the gate. Indeed, only high party officials were at its unveiling on 20 November 1995. They sat in the open air, while, in the distance, the rest of Vientiane rode past the front gate oblivious to the ceremony. Furthermore, the spatial locations of these statues across the country is revealing. Larger busts of Kaysone (1.2m) are installed at the provincial level, while the smaller (0.75m) busts are installed at the district level. One can see in this layout shades of the older *muang* structure, with smaller units being subordinate to and incorporated within larger and more central units, culminating at last in the main statues in Vientiane – in the National Assembly and in the Museum. In August 1996, three full-size statues made in China were erected: one in Houaphan province (the old revolutionary base area), one in Savannakhet (his birthplace), and one at the Kaysone Museum in Vientiane. The placement of all of these statues is an undisguised attempt to symbolise national unity by the new regime.

There are only several conventionally 'socialist realist' statues of 'the people' in Laos. One of 'the people' in arms stands outside the Military Museum in Vientiane at the far end of the That Luang parade ground. It is not open to the public. A similar statue can be found on the outskirts of Luang Prabang. In July 1997, these were joined by a statue in Xieng Khouang province celebrating the 'United Struggle of Laos-Vietnam' for 'Liberation'.[12]

The iconography of the statues

Let me turn briefly to the iconography contained in these various statues. The original equestrian statue of Chulalongkorn has him dressed in modern military uniform, a style derived from Europe of the nineteenth century, which suggests his modernising legacy, while his place on a horse suggests his strength, and his outward orientation. But it is not a militaristic monument, and in this way it contrasts with the Taksin equestrian monument built by the military dictatorship of Phibun during the Cold War of the 1950s. Here Taksin is dressed in the uniform of a traditional soldier, and is brandishing his sword, 'defending the country'.

The statue of Vajiravudh outside Lumpini Park also has him dressed as a moderniser in modern military uniform, as does the statue of King Ananda at Wat Suthat, and most of the statues of the lesser aristocracy (i.e. founders of government ministries) also take this 'modernising' form.

Of course, the very early kings can only be clothed traditionally, but in some instances there have been conscious attempts to clothe a modern king in traditional garb, most notably the statue of Rama VII outside the parliament house, which was installed there on Constitution Day in December 1980, no doubt in order to underline the continuity between the traditional monarchy and the constitution rather than any discontinuity.

The statues of Phibun Songkhram, of course, show him in the military uniform of the 1950s standing boldly on marble pedestals.

Just as Thailand's statue building has been influenced by styles it derived directly from Europe, so in Laos this influence was mediated by Thailand during the former regime, and then by North Korea and China under the communist regime.

The statue of Settathirat is very much in the style of the representations of traditional monarchs in Thailand. The statue of Sisavang Vong presenting the constitution to the Lao people also reminds one of the later statue of Rama VII outside the Parliament House in Thailand. Like the latter, it stresses continuity between the idea of a constitution and the monarchy, rather than discontinuity. The statue of Kou Voravong is in the style of the lesser Thai aristocracy. The statue of Katay, however, is the only one to strike an off-key note. Portraying him in military uniform, it no doubt is designed to stress his role in the Lao Issara and his resistance to communism, but it stands at odds with the real historical person, who was a non-militaristic intellectual. But then, by this time his image had been captured by the rightwing in Laos in the turbulent days of the early 1960s.

Kaysone's statues are indistinguishable from those associated with a socialist realist style – those of Lenin, Stalin, Mao or Kim Il Sung. Dressed in the suit of a modern secular politician, and gestureless, he epitomises the modern bureaucratic politician.

Statues and states

In both Thailand and Laos, it is invariably state institutions, which commission public statues, and it is the state which grants permission for the erection of them. In Thailand, it has been the state sponsored Fine Arts Department, which has over the years designed and made most of the public statues. The majority of public statues in Thailand are of kings, and of royal figures, all of which serve to underline the prevailing equation of Monarch and Nation-State.

This, however, has not been an invariable equation. We have seen that just after the overthrow of the absolute monarchy there was a temporary shift towards more populist styles of statuary. And it has been suggested that even the building of the Taksin equestrian monument was an attempt by the Phibun government in the early 1950s to undermine the authority of the reigning Chakri Dynasty, who in fact overthrew and disposed of Taksin.[13] But even if this was Phibun's original intention, the Taksin monument has now been well-incorporated into the annual round of homage at the monuments of former kings by the Chakri Royal House. Indeed, in October 1981, the Thai government decided to upgrade Taksin's formal title to King Taksin Maharaj – the Great – thus firmly enshrining him in the grand lineage of Thai kings.[14]

As has been well-documented by historians, it was after the rise of the military dictatorship of Sarit Thanarat in 1957 that the palace began to regain its power within the Thai social order. By the late 1960s, this starts to be reflected in statue building, which gains a momentum that continues into the 1990s. Through this massive expansion in statues of the monarchy, in particular of kings and lesser nobles associated with the Chakri Dynasty, the royal house has physically staked out its pre-eminence throughout Thailand, and statues have been a key means for physically embodying the state ideology of nation and monarchy.

In many cases, the statues have been explicitly associated with the state in the sense that they have been placed in only semi-public places – that is within the precincts of a government ministry, a military base, or a school, and outside the main provincial offices – while others are more clearly in the public arena and more accessible to pilgrims. But even statues within semi-public spaces are open to private offerings, at least by the employees of these institutions.

In Laos, the few statues constructed during the old regime were all in openly accessible public spaces. The statue of Settathirath in front of That Luang did not have a fence around it until the early 1990s, when the LPDR adopted That Luang as a national symbol.[15] The statues of Boun Kong in Champassak and of Katay in Pakse were in public spaces, and the statue of King Sisavang Vong erected in the early seventies is in a public park, while the one erected in Luang Prabang is in a semi-public garden at the old

Plate 6.4 Statue of King Sisavang Vong in front of Vat Si Muang, Vientiane, Laos.

palace, which is now a museum. Interestingly, none of the statues of Kaysone Phomvihane are in openly accessible public spaces. They are all in fenced-off areas, either ones specially constructed for the statue, as in, for example, Luang Prabang or Pakse, or within the semi-public boundaries of state offices. The control of these statues by the state and their association with the state is total. This is also true for the socialist realist statues referred to earlier. As we have seen, the placement of these more than 150 statues of Kaysone throughout Laos in an orgy of state statuemania is designed to clearly mark out the territory controlled by the LPRP.

Plate 6.5 Students paying homage to the statue of King Chulalongkorn at the Royal Plaza in Bangkok, Thailand.

The statue of Kou Voravong in Savannakhet occupies what can only be described as liminal space. It sits in a fenced-off open plot of private land, and therefore is considered to be a private monument by the state. But it is placed within open public view, and is clearly making a play for more general recognition. This is likely to be less true of Katay's statue if it is ever allowed to be re-erected. His daughter, who owns a private hotel on the northern boundary of Vientiane, may be given permission to re-erect the statue within the gardens of the hotel.

Statues in Thailand are also gathering points for large state-sponsored occasions, such as National Day and Chulalongkorn Day, when thousands of students are gathered at the Royal Plaza to kneel and humbly *wai* the king's statue. And once a year on Chakri Day, the Phra Dep Pidorn Palace in the compound of the Emerald Buddha is thrown open to the public, so that they can gaze on the statues of the kings of the reigning dynasty which are enshrined there. In Laos, the only comparable occasion is the gathering of state officials at Kaysone memorials throughout the country on his anniversary to lay wreaths and give speeches, which are then reported in the press.

Up until the 1970s, statue building in Thailand was an outgrowth of official nationalism, but from that time on a more popular, 'democratic'

167

expression of statuemania, such as Agulhon and others noted for Europe, could be observed. Indeed by 1978, the government felt the need to issue regulations on the building of statues and monuments in order to monitor the upsurge in statue building.[16] As explained in the introduction to *Monuments and Statues in Thailand* (Thailand 1996):

> The building of monuments multiplied bringing with it problems and misunderstandings of history. For example, the building of various local heroes' monuments brought forth academic problems concerning symbolism, and when built they perhaps can give rise to misunderstandings and spread misinformation. In some instances characters have been taken out of traditional dramas as if they are real persons, and in some instances they are figures resulting from contacts with superior natural powers but which have no basis in historical fact. If in these various instances monuments are built, then they may give rise to an incorrect knowledge of history (no pagination).

If this was allowed to continue, the introduction argues, then it would devalue other monuments. Thus the state felt compelled to issue regulations in order to rein in popular heterodoxy.

Statues viewed from below

As we have seen, the Thai state uses the Chulalongkorn equestrian statue as the focus of a grand state occasion. Since 1992, however, the monument has become the popular focus of a quite different event. Every Tuesday, crowds gather at the Royal Plaza to worship the statue because many people believe that it can work miracles concerning their problems in everyday life, and especially in business matters. Some believe that on Tuesdays, the day of the King's birth, his spirit descends to earth at the Plaza, and so they gather there to receive his blessings. This activity is all part of the booming Chulalongkorn cult in Thailand today, which has also spread across the border into Laos. And the cult has grown well beyond the confines of state-promoted activities. The non-state nature of the worship is underlined by the privacy of the rituals conducted by the various groups (usually families) and individuals present. In contrast to the state-style wreath laying ceremonies, the worshippers incorporate the cult into a more traditional religious frame through their use of incense, flowers and various offerings.

Nithi Iawsriwongse argues that it is 'the first cult that truly belongs to the masses' (Sanitsuda 1993). The gatherings on Tuesdays, however, are a direct outcome of the aspirations of new social groups created by Thailand's industrialisation. 'King Chulalongkorn stands for modernity, progress, and prosperity. In short, he is the symbol of an ideal state that people want, but which does not exist in reality. A state that is efficient, accessible, accountable, and compassionate. The kind that uses wisdom instead of force ... What followers want is to have access to the state. So they want a symbol that can answer this need' (Sanitsuda 1993). But clearly the symbol also answers many needs besides these. Some are unabashedly commercial, while others are more diffuse. One worshipper, accompanied by his wife, said: 'We've been coming here regularly since about six months ago. We are not expecting anything in return. It's for the sake of feeling *sabai cai* (sense of well-being). Besides, we cannot rush luck. These things take time' (Sanitsuda 1993).

At Chulalongkorn University, two statues were erected, one of Rama V and one of Rama VI, and initially the university forbade worship and the placing of offerings before these statues, because they were 'not a shrine'. (One can see here the university making an effort to uphold its reputation as a place where modern rationality reigns). But to no avail, as offerings piled up before the images – especially before exam time (Saowarop 1992).

Yet although such popular elaborations on the cult are not orchestrated by the state, they are clearly compatible with the state promoted cult, and arguably help reinforce it. Indeed, it seems perfectly plausible to argue that there has been a strong popular feedback into Chulalongkorn statuemania. Of the forty statues of Chulalongkorn catalogued in the *Monuments and Statues in Thailand* (Thailand 1996), only seven of them were built before 1980, whereas 33 of them have been built since then. A large number of these stand in front of main provincial offices. It would seem that the emergence of the popular cult spurred local officials and notables into petitioning the state for permission to erect their own statue of the revered king.

The equestrian statue of Taksin has also become the focus of a minor popular cult with its own spirit medium. Beside the state celebrations associated with this statue, it is also clearly a ritual focal point for the Chinese and Sino-Thai population of Bangkok, which thereby draws attention to this King's Chinese ancestry rather than his 'Thainess', which is the emphasis of the official ritual. Thus on King Taksin Day the statue is feted with a dragon dance. Many of the people of Thonburi, on the opposite side of the Chao Phaya river from central Bangkok, make offerings to this statue in the belief that it can grant their wishes and believe it is a protector spirit. One resident said: 'A lot of people heard the horse neigh and its hooves clatter on the ground when there were bloody incidents in Bangkok like May 1992 and October 1973' (*BKP* 15/6/96). A controversy blew up around the statue in mid-1996 when Bangkok's deputy governor Yarndej Thongsima suggested that the statue be relocated to ease traffic congestion. The popular storm, which erupted quickly, led to his temporary suspension. No doubt part of the popular resistance to relocation is related, perhaps even only tangentially, to Chinese ideas of *feng shui*, that is the propitious location of objects within a landscape in order to channel spiritual power, as well as indigenous ideas of the inviolability of sacred ground and sacred objects. Yarndej countered his critics ineffectually in their own terms: 'I've known the king well ... I even made a wish to him to help me win the (Bangkok governor) election. I think the king would want his statue to be moved to a better place. I wish he would come into my dream tonight and say I want to move ...' (*BKP* 15/6/96).

Finally, I would like to briefly refer to the Democracy Monument in Bangkok, originally built by the Fascist inclined Phibun regime in 1940 to celebrate Thailand's brief war with French colonialism to regain 'lost' Lao and Cambodian. After the fall of the military dictatorship in Thailand in 1973, the democracy movement at the time focused on the name of the monument, and for a time, up until they were crushed by the military in 1976, it became one of their emblems of this movement (Reynolds 1992: 319–322). Such is the potential semantic lability of certain state constructed monuments.

In Laos, the only public statues which receive private offerings are the statues of Settathirath, and Sisavang Vong outside Vat Si Muang. The former receives much more attention than the latter because of its association with the revered That Luang stupa, which also makes offerings to it more legitimate within the current political context, compared with Sisavang Vong. But recall the surreptitious worship of Boun Kong who stands to the side of the altar of Vat Thong in Champassak.

The semiology of statues

Among the Thai and Lao in the past, i.e. prior to the rise of nationalism, the only statues that were built were those of deities – of Buddhas and Thevadas – not of mortal men, not even of semi-divine kings.[17] In fact, Buddhas were stylised so as not to look like mortals. Of course, Buddhas can also be statues if they have not been consecrated, and these form an important part of tourist trade paraphernalia in Thailand today. But again this secular treatment of Buddha images is a modern phenomenon. Nevertheless, a sacral ambiguity adheres to these images for Buddhist practitioners.

The making of modern statues appears to involve a double movement: the elevation of mortals in the direction of deities, and a certain secularisation of the deities. In Thailand and Laos, kings were *saksit* and it was only natural in the context of official nationalism that they would become the first images represented by statues. The interesting question is, why weren't they represented in this form before the modern period? Within Buddhist cosmology, the king only achieved the status of a deity – a Boddhisatva or Buddhist saint – after his death. The one king who sought to claim immanent Buddahood – Taksin – brought about his own downfall.

Thus, prior to the modern period, it did not make sense to represent a dead king as himself because he had already been transformed into a Buddha who, of course, does not look like a mere mortal.

The creation of a statue of a king in the modern period, therefore, does involve his elevation towards the deities, in the sense that the only other category of images is Buddhas and Thevadas, but it also involves a shift in the direction of secularisation, in the sense that the image is designed to be an exact likeness (if known) of the king. The ambiguity is made explicit in the design, for example, of the statue of King Ramkhamhaeng for Sukhothai when, it was said, 'because there are no pictures of the king available, the face will be modelled on the style of the Buddhist images of the Sukhothai period' (*BKP* 9/9/96).[18] The preservation of Boun Kong's statue along side that of the Buddhas in Vat Thong is a similar expression of this ambiguity.

The creation of the equestrian statue of Rama V represents an important historical shift in cultural consciousness in Thailand because here we have an image of a king acting in this world, not unlike a Mahayanist Boddhisatva. The interesting thing about the Chulalongkorn equestrian statue, therefore, is not only that it is the first realistic public image of a king but also that it was made and erected while the king was still alive.[19] Symbolically at least, it was the closest step towards a claim to imminent divine status by a king since Taksin – a fact which makes one wonder about the cultural elective affinity between the two equestrian statues.

Statues in Thailand and Laos are clearly part of the symbolic apparatus of nation-state building, and these statues of humans partake of a more general category of national monuments spread through the country and its capital. As statues, they are indexical signs (Leach 1976) of the nation, of the monarchy, and of particular ideas or concepts. For example, the statue of Rama VII outside the Parliament building in Bangkok, or the two statues of King Sisavang Vong in Laos, both carry a message about the compatibility of kingship with a constitution, or constitutional monarchy. Other statues outside of ministries connect these institutions to the wider national structure, and so on. The statues of Kaysone spread throughout Laos are designed to represent the nation and the party, and in particular their homology or identity.

Yet, as we have seen, some of these statues are moved beyond this state programme and become cultural symbols in their own right. What are the cultural dynamics of this?

At its most general level it is obviously a consequence of what Roy Ellen has argued is a 'festishistic' cultural tendency in human societies: 'There is a generalised propensity in all human classifying behaviour, to reify through concretisation, to treat the most complex of abstractions as things' (1988: 221). For example, the compression of meanings into a single object, such as a saint's dried viscera, or in our case, a statue. Thus, through metonymy, a part, or a single object, can stand for a whole. Then there is the tendency 'to attribute inanimate objects with the properties of living things' (1978: 223), and by extension images are subjected to rites of passage usually reserved for humans. He further argues 'that you cannot define the products of fetishisation in terms of their semantic or mystical content; what is diagnostic is the ambiguity between content and form, between signifier and signified' (Ellen 1978: 227; see also Leach 1976: 22). Therefore an object can become active in its own right, in relative autonomy from its original role as a signifier. Finally, he suggests that the power of any fetish is volatile, swinging between being manipulator and manipulated.

In the context of Thailand and Laos, these general tendencies are manifested or mediated through the dominant religious complex of Buddhism/Animism. We have already seen that the only images made before the modern period were associated with this system of beliefs. It could be argued that the new statues that were created could not be assimilated to this prior set because they were secular creations. But we have seen that this boundary has been especially ambiguous in a Thai-Lao context. Not only are the images of kings in some senses those of a deity, they are also subject to rites of passage during their inauguration at which lustral water is sprinkled, usually by the present King or a member of his family, such as Princess Sirindhorn, and monks are on hand to chant their blessings, which in some respects deify the image. Even when further smaller images are cast, as with those of Taksin, with this event presided over by the then Army Commander-in-Chief, General Chavalit Yong-chaiyuhd, monks are present to lend their blessings (*BKP* 9/12/87). When the statue of Kou Voravong was finally installed in Savannakhet, it was preceded by a ceremony at the *vat* where both the statue and the Voravong family were blessed. Despite this, the statues, as far as I understand, are not fully activated in the same way that Buddhist images are by the chanting of monks and the transference of potency from one image to another, nor are their eyes opened as with images of the Buddha (Tambiah 1984: 255–257), though the practice of *unveiling* a statue is certainly analogous. But given these analogies with the consecration of Buddhas, it is only a short step to attributing to such statues powers similar to Buddha images and amulets (Tambiah 1984: 203–204). Indeed, this is what I believe has happened with the Chulalongkorn statue and the Taksin statue, and to a lesser degree with others in Thailand, and with Settathirath and Sisavang Vong in Laos.

This ambiguity is most dramatically and regularly enacted by the spirit mediums who have attached themselves to these various statues. Indeed, we have a vivid description of the role of such a medium, and the ever-present spiritual forces surrounding the images of *saksit* individuals, during the creation and erection of the Settathirath statue in Laos in 1959. The casting of the statue had continual problems, especially the casting of the head – the mould broke three times. A spirit calling ceremony, attended by monks, was therefore held to seek permission from King Settathirath to cast the statue, whereupon the casting proceeded without problems. In November 1959, just preceding the That Luang festival in Vientiane, the statue was 'invited' to leave the military camp at Phon Xai, where it had been cast, and to proceed to the That Luang. The statue was placed inside a *ho phasat* and put on the back of a truck whereupon it was to be led to its place in front of the That Luang by eighty monks, and by soldiers from the palace dressed in their green and red traditional uniforms, and other notables. In other words, it was to be conducted to the That Luang more or less in the same way as the King at the time would be. But just before the procession began, the Chao Khouang (province head) of Vientiane came roaring into the compound in his car to announce a strange occurrence: 'Right now Chao Saysetta has descended into Ban That Luang and is causing a commotion, dancing around with a red face singing loudly and brandishing an ancient sword. He yelled at me as if he was going to eat me, but I didn't reply. He yelled at me: 'You are my go-between, don't you know it? Now you are about to parade my image to That Luang. Why didn't you inform me? I must join in your procession of my image. You go and tell them now!' So I quickly hurried here to you [Tham who was in charge of the ceremony], so what is your response? Please help me!' To which Tham replied immediately: 'Superb! Our parade will now have life and spirit and is given greater meaning! Hurry and bring him to join our procession for it is close to the time when the procession will begin'. Twenty minutes later, the province chief was back 'with [the medium] Nang Khao Song, red faced and dressed smartly. After exchanging pleasantries, she was invited to mount the back tray of the truck and sit in front of the commemorative image of Prachao Saysetta'. When they reached That Luang and began the installation of the image, another transformation of the Nang Tiam [Nang Khao Song] took place, whereupon she quickly changed her clothing and announced: 'I am a sacred Buddha, a son of Chao Saysettathirath and I have joined this ritual now to give blessings to the person in charge of the making of the statue of my father Chao Saysettathirath'. Tham continues: 'When speaking his voice had changed and was not the same as before. Then he blessed us all by sprinkling water on us and the statue' (Tham 1959).[20]

There is a further question I would like to briefly explore and that is the relationship of statues with death. Statues are usually life-like depictions of someone who is dead. Indeed their life-likeness, but immobility, draws our attention either consciously or unconsciously to the fact of death. Kenneth Gross has attempted to argue that statues attempt to conceal 'the dying, entropic, and violable human body' (1992: 21), and thus are attempts to 'transcend time, survive history and physical contingency' (1992: 31). The statue, he says, 'presents a body or pose arrested in time, arresting time itself' (1992: 15). Thus, as Lerner has suggested, they are appropriate vehicles for embodying an eternal 'national time'. Anderson, in fact, begins his discussion of nationalism by pointing out that it has dealt with the central human fatality of death by aligning it with the destiny of the nation: 'It is the magic of nationalism to turn chance into destiny' (1991: 12). For this reason, he sees the cultural roots of nationalism aligned with religion rather than with political ideologies. Thus we can begin to see the attractions of statue building for nationalism, wherein statues of mortal men transact between life and death/destiny. And in a cultural universe, where the mortals being represented are already aligned with religion and are *saksit*, then this transaction becomes potentially super-charged. This is further enhanced by the immobility of these life-like forms which, as Gross argues, commonly leads to fantasies of animation, of moving statues, statues with life. Indeed, in Thailand we have already been given one example when the people in Thonburi claim to have heard the hooves of Taksin's horse. And this should be set against a long history of 'animated' Buddha images. For example, in Laos I have been told that the Buddhas in the township of Xieng Khouang burst out in sweat in 1959 as a portent of coming conflict on the Plain of Jars, while another claims that the Intha Buddha in Vat Inpheng perspired in 1960 prior to the Kong Le coup in Vientiane. In this cultural context, there is little wonder in the fact that statues attract mediums to them to facilitate their continued efficacy in the world. The symbolic power of national statues in Thailand and Laos, therefore, derives from not only their potential to point to the nation and the transcendence of individual lives through their connection to the nation's destiny, but also through their continued ability to act in this world.

Statues in Thailand and Laos exist within a cultural universe in which the material remains of the body are secondary, and what is transcendent is not an individual physical form, but a *vinyan* (*winyan*), a spiritual essence. Furthermore, as several writers have pointed out (Keyes 1987; Tambiah 1970), immediate ancestors are venerated and cared for, but cults of ancestors such as one finds in Sinitic civilisations, for example, are absent. The erection of statues of Kaysone in Laos is part of a state-promoted cult, and an attempt at his deification. Indeed, his effigies are housed in small temple-like structures on top of which are the seven-tiered umbrellas usually found above kings and Buddhas. But for various reasons which I have discussed elsewhere (Evans 1998b), this cult does not have the same cultural resonance as a Mao, a Ho Chi Minh or a Kim Il Sung cult, partly because he is not assimilable to a cult of ancestors cultural complex in the way that they can be, and nor does he partake of the potential *saksit* qualities of royalty. The difference between the two areas can be dramatised by the fact that the idea of a mausoleum, such as Mao's in Beijing or Ho's in Hanoi, would be anathema in Laos or Thailand.

Statuemania in Thailand and Laos

The statuemania we have considered in this chapter has primarily focused on its relationship to nationalism, and we have observed that its form has been dominated by 'official nationalism' in Thailand, and also in Laos to some extent under the Royal Lao Government. Communist nationalism produces its own orthodoxy in statuemania, and one which in some senses is driven by the opposite impulse to official nationalism. While the latter tries to establish symbolic connections between an *ancien regime* and the nation, communism attempts, almost hysterically, to deny such a connection through a steadfast focus on the leader of the revolution, and a claim that the nation has only found its historical fulfilment through the revolution and its leader. Statues in the former relate to a genealogy of other statues, which in turn metonymically refer to the nation's historical genealogy, while for the latter, the proliferation of statues of the 'great leader' attempt to mark a transcendent moment of the nation through the statue's 'will to eternity, its attempt to signify, in marble or bronze, the immortality of the body politic' (Lerner 1993: 177). This seems to have worked best in East Asian communist societies, where such figures could ultimately be assimilated to a cultural idea of founding ancestors.

The Kaysone statues represent the most intensive episode of statue building ever in Lao history. Their proliferation is connected directly to the LPRP's inheritance of a particular type of communist iconography, combined with the need of the party to implant signs of its legitimacy and control of Lao territory by using icons of its main political figure. It is also part of a more general attempt to construct a nationalist iconography. Unlike Thailand, the spread of Kaysone statues is not related to dramatic changes in the *decor urbain,* and it is not related to a spread of democratic sentiment, although the subject is an ordinary man. Nor is there any suggestion that Kaysone is *saksit,* and in this regard the statues have no organic relationship to Lao culture or society, in contrast to the statues of kings. They are, consequently, what one might call a weak symbol, which has a restricted range of reference and resonance. So, lacking an ability to image a transcendent moment in the nation's history, other discourses of the nation's genealogy embodied in the statues of kings of former times inevitably re-assert themselves. Indeed, this no doubt explains why several statues never left their pedestals and why others threaten to return to them.

In Thailand, statuemania proper only really began after the re-surgence of the monarchy in the 1960s. The spread of statues during this time, as earlier, was also related to the changing urban decor of Bangkok, as the centre of gravity of the city moved eastwards away from the royal compound in the 1960s (Askew 1994). Statues followed and filled out this rapidly expanding new urban landscape with royal figures, and then proliferated in the provinces. Anderson (1977) has argued the new social

175

forces, which had emerged in Thailand in the 1960s, were not yet clamouring for democracy, although they were rejecting certain forms of traditionalism. 'In response to this, there was an enormous increase in the self-conscious propagation and indoctrination of a militant ideology of Nation-Religion-King – as opposed to the *bien-passant* 'traditionalism' that reigned before' (1977: 14). Out of this atmosphere grew the creation of the National Culture Commission in 1979, responsible for co-ordinating the various units of the cultural bureaucracy, and a year later the National Identity Board (Reynolds 1991), and 1982 saw the re-conceptualisation and re-organisation of city space which came with the Rattanakosin Bicentennial celebrations. This historical context of heightened concern with notions of Thai identity intensified nationalist-royalist statuemania.

Yet by this stage, important social and political changes had begun to take place, and a more democratically conscious middle-class had emerged that was slowly changing the face of Thai politics and culture. Agulhon argued that 'the ideology implicit in statuemania was liberal humanism, of which, later, democracy was its natural extension' (1978: 147), and perhaps we can see this in Thailand, too. Indeed, I have already suggested in relation to the Chulalongkorn cult that the complex relationship of the culture to its statues ensured a popular feedback into official statuemania. Statues in Thailand have begun to diversify thematically to reflect the 'common man', and local heroes. Indeed, the regulations issued in 1979 were intended precisely to rein in heterodox popular themes. One of the most controversial battles over a monument in Thailand today concerns a proposed monument to 'the martyrs of the October 14 student uprising in 1973'.[21] A small statue sits at the Kok Wua intersection on Rajadamnoen Avenue in Bangkok,[22] and, in April 1997, a dispute over whether this should be the site for a permanent monument, or whether such a monument should ever be built, erupted once again in Thai politics, with the ill-fated Prime Minister Chavalit promising he would build one. On 14 October 1999, construction finally began on the memorial.

But our focus so far perhaps misses one of the most widespread manifestations of popular statuemania in Thailand, and that is the building of images of popular monks. It is now common for a life-like statue to be built of a famous monk and placed in his monastery after his death. By now there are hundreds of these. I am unsure when this activity began, but I am of the impression that it reached manic levels only in recent decades – and it has only just begun in Laos.[23] This phenomenon, I believe, is assimilable to the cult of images and amulets, and is part of an intensified process of fetishisation (discussed by Tambiah 1984), as people search for sources of metaphysical power in conditions of rapid social, cultural and economic change, let alone political change. Interestingly, Tambiah also ties the cult of amulets to a sense of Thai national identity:

We can thus visualize the people of Thailand physically located in different parts and following different pursuits carrying on their body or holding in possession amulets that embody the associations and 'vital energy' of the past and present (historical heritage) and of diverse persons and places within the kingdom (geographical spread). The amulets are an example of how many contemporary Thai of diverse social and regional origins carry on their persons material signs and mental images of national identity and history (Tambiah 1984: 199).

Statues of monks partake of this iconography, but are more tied to place and perhaps in this sense reflect the democratic sentiments of statuemania. Indeed, Keyes (personal communication) has suggested that such statues can become vehicles for locally or regionally based discourses, which somehow contest the dominant national discourse such as with the statue of Khruba Sriwichai at the base of Dòi Suthep in Chiang Mai (he proposes a similar interpretation of the Thao Suranari statue in this volume). But, we should be aware that they do not contest the basic nationalist premises of the discourse.

The growing acceptability of life-like statues of monks would also appear to reflect secularising and individualising tendencies within the culture and religion generally.[24] Hence it is also increasingly common in Thailand for statues to be made of living monks. Indeed, even in Luang Prabang, Laos, I came across the surprising instance of a life-like statue of the still living senior monk in Vat Saen (built in 1994). But in the latter case there would also appear to be localised concerns at work. People in Luang Prabang see this particular monk as a source of living memory of their city's royalist past, displaying as he does in his quarters, all sorts of royal memorabilia.

What then is the future of representation in Thailand and Laos? The uneven and combined development of the world of modern nationalism has seen the borrowing of cultural elements from an emerging nationalistic and democratic Europe by autocratic Asian states, demonstrated so clearly by the study of statue building. And, like in Europe, statue building gradually democratised. But today, in this era of increasingly rapid cultural borrowing, sometimes referred to as 'globalisation', has representation in Thailand now joined the crisis of representation seen in Europe? This is described by Agulhon as 'a crisis of portrait sculpture (crisis of art?); a crisis of Liberalism, and a crisis of the city' (1978: 165). Statues in Europe have been among the victims of this triple crisis, or perhaps one should say realist statues have been. Some statues are still being built there, such as the one of Jean-Paul Sartre in Paris, which is a non-realist statue that attempts to represent, almost playfully, not only some of this philosopher's idiosyncrasies but also his 'progressiveness' and controversialness (his statue is leaning into the wind). Modern art and representation in Thailand and South East Asia have also begun to bypass realism and are exploring many other avenues of representation, and no doubt this will eventually find expression in statue making.[25] Indeed, the statue which stands as a memorial to the students of 1973 is in an abstract style. Realism may live on in the state-sponsored Department of Fine Arts in Thailand, and it remains most certainly the prevailing form of state-centred representation in Laos. But realist statues seem to be an increasingly ineffective form of representation, and so statuemania as a form of nationalist iconography may have had its day. In the temples, however, where there are no obvious limits to image-making, statuemania lives on.

Acknowledgement

I would like to thank the editors for their comments on the initial version of this paper.

Notes

1 In late1996, the Fine Arts, Culture and History Departments of the government in Bangkok produced its first catalogue of *Monuments and Statues in Thailand* (Thailand 1996). This is a catalogue of not quite eighty statues and monuments and a second volume is promised. However, going by the first volume, these books will by no means be comprehensive.

2 Call this 'Westernisation' if you like – but implicit in such a description is often the assumption that there was a so-called 'Eastern' way. In fact, all modernisations have been a combination of historically evolved indigenous traits and ones borrowed (sometimes imposed) from abroad. In the context of state-building at the turn of the century, it was natural that the Thai monarchs would borrow from contemporary successful modern states. The Japanese were doing the same thing at the time. So nothing should be more obvious than the fact that modernisation in the 'East' compared with the 'West' had its own distinctive momentum and traits.

3 Here I have in mind Roland Barthes' (1972) idea of myth as the naturalisation of historical acts: 'In passing from history to nature, myth acts economically: it abolishes the complexity of human acts, it gives them the simplicity of essences, it does away with all dialectics, with any going back beyond what is immediately visible, it organises a world without contradictions because it is without depth, a world wide open and wallowing in the evident, it establishes a blissful clarity . . . its clarity is euphoric' (1972: 143).

4 The statues referred to here I believe are busts commissioned by the aristocracy to be placed in their private quarters. This aristocratic fashion spread to Laos a little later. It is perhaps of interest to note the reference to a modern statue in Anna Leonowens account of the Thai court in the nineteenth century: On either side of the eastern entrance [to the Emerald Buddha – called *Patoo* [*pratu*] *Ngam*, 'The Beautiful Gate'] stands a modern statue; one of Saint Peter, with flowing mantle and sandalled feet, in an attitude of sorrow, as when 'he turned his face and wept'; the other of Ceres, scattering flowers. . . . At a later period,

178

visiting this temple in company with the king and his family, I called his majesty's attention to the statue at the Beautiful Gate, as that of a Christian saint ... Turning quickly to his children, and addressing them gently, he bade them salute it reverently. 'It is Mam's Phra', ... (1870: 52).

5 For a recent discussion of Phibun's relationship to the monarchy, see Kobkua (1995: 67–81).

6 The stress here is on Bangkok. In fact there is another equestrian style statue of Taksin in Chantaburi Province (erected in 1982), just as there is an imitation of the original equestrian statue of Chulalongkorn in Loei Province (erected in 1979).

7 There is also a statue of King Ananda at the Chulalongkorn Hospital in Bangkok, but I do not know yet when it was constructed.

8 For the transliteration of Lao names in the following section, I have followed conventional spellings where they are available, e.g. *vat* instead of *wat*, etc. Besides these, there is no accepted convention for spelling Lao words, and so there is an element of inevitable idiosyncrasy. Luckily, however, modern computer systems allow us to easily insert the original spelling where necessary.

9 In fact initially it was a concrete statue and only in 1959 was the present metal statue cast (more on this below). A tourist booklet, *Guide to Vientiane Municipality* (1995), produced by a mixed state-private enterprise company, Inter-Lao Tourism, lists the date as 1962. This appears to be a case of simple incompetence rather than any tampering with the historical record.

10 Statues of colonial officials were erected in France during the height of statuemania, such as one at Toulouse to a colonial explorer killed in Africa. But despite the fact that statues were intended to install in all Frenchmen a sense of national pride, the inauguration at Toulouse saw the statue's meaning interpreted in different ways by conservatives and radicals. See Cohen (1989: 507).

11 The two young Lao were at some time moved to Vat Sisaket and placed in front of a Buddha there, their flower offerings were then re-interpreted as offerings to the Buddha. Some time later (I do not know when) they returned to the front of the Ho Phra Keo, and their flower offerings continued to be interpreted as offerings to the Buddha. Folklore holds that the statue was thrown in the Mekong during the Lao Issara period, but I have been unable to confirm this (amid numerous stories of statues being thrown in rivers). Arthur Dommen has a reference to a Pavie statue in Luang Prabang: 'the chief delegate in Luang Prabang of the Lao Issara government, who ostentatiously knocked over the statue of Pavie, [when] they marched on the Royal palace' (Dommen 1971: 329). But I have no knowledge of what happened to this statue.

12 The *Vientiane Times* (26–29/7/97) reported that a parallel monument had been built by the Vietnamese in Quang Tri province 'for the soldiers who had sacrificed their lives along the road number 9 route, and to pray for their spirits'.

13 This is an argument made by Maurizio Peleggi in his PhD in progress at the ANU, 'The making of Siam's modern public image'. It has plausibility inasmuch as Phibun was closely associated with the ultra-nationalist Luang Wichit, who in the 1930s revived Taksin and downplayed the Chakri, and indeed it was he who first mooted the idea of a statue for Taksin in 1937 in an effort to promote relations with the Chinese community (something he soon abandoned) by celebrating this Sino-Thai warrior king (Barme 1993: 129).

14 A *sala* in his honour was erected in Wat Dòi Khao Kaeo, Tak Province, with a seated statue of Taksin in 1972. Another southern temple, Wat Khao Khun

Phanom, where legend has it he was sent after becoming mentally deranged, has a statue of him as a monk (*BKP* 6/6/89), but the date of this is unclear. Since 1981 two public statues of Taksin have been constructed in Bangkok, and two others, one in Thonburi and the other in Chantaburi.

15 Access, however, is not restricted. One simply has to wait for the woman with the key, and the right to sell offerings there, to open up the gate.

16 A copy of these regulations can be found in the opening pages of *Monuments and Statues in Thailand* (Thailand 1996).

17 With the possible exception of the images of the Buddha-king at Angkor Thom in modern Cambodia, which are thought to be modelled on Jayavarman VII. During his reign, the Khmer empire spread over most of modern Thailand.

18 The Lao were confronted by the same problem when fashioning the statue of Settathirath: 'But the maker announced that although we did not have a picture we had evidence from various *phongsavadan* (chronicles) which spoke of the likeness of the king – that he was well-formed, tall, strong, proud, and in these things he was like Khmer and Thai royalty. Therefore this enabled us to solve this difficult problem. As for the various details in order to make it glorious and handsome – this creation was the role of the statue maker and the people in charge who would advise and make suggestions' (Tham 1959).

19 The problematic nature of this step is referred to in the introduction to *Monuments and Statues in Thailand* (Thailand 1996). Subsequently, it has become less anomalous culturally.

20 This information is taken from a manuscript written by Tham Sayasitsena, who was in charge of the erection of the statue at the time. This manuscript (which is dated as B.E. 2501, i.e. AD 1959) was submitted to the Ministry of Culture of the LPDR for publication, but was rejected no doubt because it contains accounts of 'superstition'. As far as I can tell, it was in fact written recently, after 1975 during Tham's retirement, but perhaps based on earlier notes.

21 For a concise history of the dispute, see 'In memory of a memorial' (*BKP* 6/4/ 97).

22 This monument is maintained by a group of lottery ticket vendors who work in its precincts. Significantly, they have 'animated' this statue: 'the vendors offerings have nothing to do with paying homage to those who lost their lives for the sake of democracy. 'I pay respect to the monument every day. Everybody here believes in their holy spirits. When we lose things, we ask the spirits to help us, and finally the things are always found' Anjira Assavananda, 'wish for monument coming true', (*BKP* 7/4/97).

23 This simply indicates the different degrees of cultural modernity in the two countries. Statues of dead monks are beginning to be made in Laos, such as for example the former abbot of Vat Phon Phao in Luang Prabang. A statue has been made of the Lao Phra Sangkalat, who fled to Thailand in 1977 and died there in 1984. It now stands in Vat Phone Phanao in Nong Khai.

24 Photographs have been incorporated into the stupas erected to dead family members, and, with progress in technology, these can now be etched into stone. These developments too can be considered as signs of secularisation.

25 See the essays by Apinan in Turner (1993), as well as the introductory essay by Turner in the same book.

References

Newspapers

Bangkok Post (abbreviated to *BKP*) 9 September, 11 November 1968; 31 December 1969; 2 January 1970; 21 August 1971; 1 August 1972; 28 February 1973; 1 February 1974; 8 January 1975; 11 April, 19 August, 10 December 1980; 20 January, 17 July 1982; 5 April, 20 October 1986; 9 December 1987; 1 March 1988; 6 June 1989; 22 July, 9 September 1990; 17 January 1992; 20 June 1994; 15 June, 9 September 1996; 6 April, 7 April 1997.
Vientiane Mai 15 December 1995.
Vientiane Times 26–29 July 1997.

Books and Articles

Agulhon, Maurice 1978 'La 'statuomanie' et l'histoire', p.145–172 in *Ethnologie Francaise*.
Anderson, Benedict 1977 'Withdrawal symptoms: social and cultural aspects of the October 6 Coup', p.13–30 in *Bulletin of Concerned Asian Scholars* 9 (3).
—— 1991 Imagined Communities: reflections on the origin and spread of nationalism, London: Verso.
Askew, Marc 1994 'Bangkok: transformation of the Thai city', in Marc Askew and William S. Logan (eds.) *Cultural Identity and Urban Change in Southeast Asia: interpretative essays*, Victoria, Australia: Deakin University Press.
Barme, Scot 1993 *Luang Wichit Wathakan and the Creation of a Thai Identity*, Singapore: Institute of Southeast Asian Studies.
Barthes, Roland 1972 *Mythologies* (translated by Annette Lavers), New York: Hill and Wang.
Cohen, William 1989 'Symbols of power: statues in nineteenth-century provincial France', p.491–513 in *Comparative Studies in Society and History*.
Dommen, Arthur J. 1971 *Conflict in Laos: the politics of neutralization*, (revised edition), New York: Praeger Publishers.
Ellen, Roy 1988 'Fetishism', *Man* (N.S.) 23(2).
Evans, Grant 1998a *The Politics of Ritual and Remembrance: Laos since 1975*, Chiang Mai: Silkworm Books.
—— 1998b 'Political cults in Southeast Asia and East Asia' in L. Summers and Ing-Britt Trankell (eds.) *Facets of Power and Its Limitations: political culture in Southeast Asia*, Uppsala, Sweden: Uppsala Studies in Cultural Anthropology, 24.
Jeffrey, Robin 1980 'What the statues tell: the politics of choosing symbols in Trivandrum', *Pacific Affairs* 53(3).
Gross, Kenneth 1992 *The Dream of the Moving Statue*, Ithaca, NY and London: Cornell University Press.
Keyes, Charles F. 1987 'From death to birth: ritual process and Buddhist meanings in Northern Thailand', p.181–206 in *Folk* 29.
Kobkua Suwannathat-Pian 1995 *Thailand's Durable Premier: Phibun through three decades, 1932–1957*, Singapore: Oxford University Press.
Leach, Edmund 1976 *Culture and Communication: the logic by which symbols are connected*, Cambridge: Cambridge University Press.
Leonowens, Anna Harriette 1870 *The English Governess at the Siamese Court*, London: Turner & Co.

Lerner, Adam J. 1993 'The nineteenth-century monument and the embodiment of national time', in Marjorie Ringrose and Adam J. Lerner (eds.) *Reimagining the Nation*, Philadelphia: Open University Press.

Michaelson, Helen 1993 'State building and Thai painting and sculpture in the 1930s and 1940s', in John Clark (ed.) *Modernity in Asian Art*, Sydney: Wild Peony Press.

Reynolds, Craig 1991 'Introduction: national identity and its defenders', p.1–40 in C.J. Reynolds (ed.) *National Identity and Its Defenders: Thailand 1939–1989*, Melbourne: Monash University, Monash papers on Southeast Asia, no.25.

—— 1992 'The plot of Thai history: theory and practice', p.313–322 in Gehan Wijeyewardene and E.C. Chapman (eds.) *Patterns and Illusions: Thai history and thought*, Singapore: Institute of Southeast Asian Studies.

Sanitsuda Ekachai 1993 'Sadej Pho: what lies behind a cult of worship', *Bangkok Post*, 18 August.

Saowarop Panyacheewin 1992 'Chulalongkorn as a divine being', *Bangkok Post*, 23 October.

Tãem Sayasithsena 1993 *Inpheng Temple*, Vientiane.

Tambiah, Stanley J. 1970 *Buddhism and the Spirit Cults in North-east Thailand*, Cambridge: Cambridge University Press.

—— 1984 *The Buddhist Saints of the Forest and the Cult of Amulets*, Cambridge: Cambridge University Press.

Thailand, Fine Arts Department, Literature and History Section 1996 (B.E. 2539) *Anusawari nai prathet Thai* (Monuments and Statues in Thailand), vol.1, Bangkok.

Tham Sayasitsena 1959 (B.E. 2501) 'Kan sang anusavali Phabat Somdet Phachao Saysethamaharat, thi Ban Inpeng, wanthi 28 Phachik 1959, PS 2501' (The Building of the Monument to Phabat Somdet Phachao Saysetthamaharat), Vientiane (Manuscript in Lao).

Turner, Caroline (ed.) 1993 *Tradition and Change: contemporary art of Asia and the Pacific*, St Lucia: University of Queensland Press.

Vella, Walter F. 1954 *The Impact of the West on Government in Thailand*, Berkeley and Los Angeles: University of California Press.

—— 1978 *Chaiyo! King Vajiravudh and the development of Thai nationalism*, Honolulu: The University of Hawaii Press.

PART III

Commoditisation and Consumer Identities

CHAPTER SEVEN

Exhibition of Power

Factory Women's Use of the Housewarming
Ceremony in a Northern Thai Village

Kyonosuke Hirai

Introduction[1]

One of the popular questions in recent anthropology is how the memory of
groups is conveyed, or how a tradition is invented. Ceremonies, especially
commemorative ones, are often mentioned as typical examples of
apparatuses which groups use to remember particular events in changing
social circumstances. What people commemorate in such ceremonies are
not only great revolutions or dramatic historical events but also personal
achievements or the presentation of self-images. In addition, the emphasis
is not always on the same ideology set by the social structure or asserted by
a dominant group. Being on the one hand an apparatus that a particular
group utilises so that people remember their version of statements, on the
other the ceremony is also an opportunity where ordinary people
remember other experiences, sometimes by modifying it within certain
constraints in order to create meanings or images in support of their own
interests. I argue in this chapter that the ceremony can create multivocal
social memories.

We set the argument in the context of recent changes in housewarming
ceremonies (*ngan khün hüan mai*) in a Northern Thai village, where I
conducted fieldwork. In this village, many young women have been
working in factories since the establishment of the Northern Region
Industrial Estate in the late 1980s. Many of them have invested a large
portion of their incomes from the factory in costly celebrations of the
housewarming ceremony.[2] In Northern Thailand, the main objective of the
housewarming ceremony is claimed to be the blessing of a newly built
house. In the course of the ceremony, the householding couple ask the
spirits to bring luck into the house, make merit in the Buddhist sense, and
also commemorate the completion of the new house with kin, neighbours
and friends. Factory women add other meanings to that ceremony. They
tactically exhibit their new power and, what is more, experience feelings of

liberation in the housewarming ceremony. This paper attempts to show, by demonstrating this change, the great flexibility of ritual performances.

First, we consider the socio-economic situations surrounding factory women, and their investments in the home. In order to explain their investments, we deal with the relation between house and women, and between housework and women. Then, we concentrate the investigation on factory women's experience of housewarming ceremonies. If we consider the ceremony simply as a reiteration of the tradition or the past event, we would overlook what people feel and remember about it, apart from the dominant ideology, and the process of its changes. Its significance changes, as the social relationships within which an agent places his or her experience change.

Factory women

The Northern Region Industrial Estate is located at the southern end of the Chiang Mai-Lamphun plains. It is a 30 minutes' drive from the city of Chiang Mai. The estate was completed in 1985 on 1780 rai^3 of land. In 1994, there were 86 labour-intensive factories operating in the estate. Sixteen thousand young women aged from eighteen to thirty worked there in 1994, and 85% of these were from local villages.[4] The majority of the large factories operate 24 hours a day in two shifts from Monday to Saturday.

In the estate, the workers were predominantly young women of fairly low academic levels of attainment. Women comprised 73.8% of the labour force, which was mainly engaged in assembly line work. While 31.2% of the employees were less than 20 years of age, employees aged between 21 and 30 amounted to 63.3%. Women with only primary school education made up 29.6% of the employees, while 58.5% had studied at junior or senior high school levels, and only 11.6% had any higher educational experience. In recruitment of assembly workers, the factories employ primary or junior high school female school-leavers aged 16 to 25. In short, requirements for application only concern sex and age. Unlike many industrial parks in Asia, married women are not excluded from jobs in this estate. Any female who has undergone six years of compulsory education in a state school is eligible.

In the village where I conducted fieldwork, before employment in the factory young women stayed at home all day, or at least in the village. Not only customary village morality but also socio-economic circumstances restricted women's daily round to within the village. Wage labour available for young women was limited to agricultural work around the village, or assisting with the work of their male family in nearby villages, and what is more, such work was available only on occasions. While the rhythm of their lives reflected changes in the agricultural seasons, their main role was always considered to consist of properly fulfilling household tasks, village communal activities, and seasonal agricultural work in accordance with their elder kin's instructions.

The rhythm of young women's lives significantly changed upon their gaining employment in a factory. After starting such work, a woman, especially one from a household where she was the only female, had very little free time because of the combined pressure of both housework and factory work. Operating six days a week, factories in the estate either run twenty-four hours in two shifts or nine hours in one shift. In the former, the day shift starts at 7 or 8 a.m., and the night one at 7 or 8 p.m. The workers change shifts every one or two weeks. The latter factories operate from 8 a.m. to 5 p.m. Any worker who wants to take time off, or a day's leave, needs special permission from the factory each time. Despite the nine or twelve hours at the workplace, the duties of factory women remain the same when they return home. Before they leave, they finish cooking, cleaning the house, washing the clothes, and feeding livestock, and on their return, they wash up, take care of children, sew, and prepare for ceremonies. Their Sundays are also occupied in shopping for food and household requisites, visiting kin, and other duties at home. Women's burdens are never lightened by working in the factory.

The high income, which a young woman brings into the home from factory work, has a significant impact on the life of her family. According to my census in Village N,[5] the average monthly income for 114 villagers, including factory workers, was 2,974 baht. Among them, fifteen large-income earners, bringing in over five thousand baht a month,[6] were mostly males, such as civil servants, skilled construction workers, truck drivers, and factory workers, with the exceptions being two female company workers and four retailers. On the contrary, 54.0% of the females earned less than two thousand baht per month. For the latter, some temporary agricultural work, construction work, or making hats out of straw was their only opportunities for paid work. Factory workers earned at least 102 baht a day; the minimum daily wage set by the government. Besides, many of them got allowances for overtime work, night shift, commuting, lunch, and regular attendance. As a whole, the average assembly workers putting in nine hours a day got about four thousand baht monthly, while those putting in twelve hours a day earned a total of five to seven thousand baht monthly, depending upon the factory. The former was roughly equivalent to the beginning salary for university-graduate civil servants in the area. It was observed in many families that a factory woman's income exceeded that of her husband's, father's or brothers'.

Factory women's investment

Factory women invested most of their relatively high incomes in their own houses. Although they bought personal items such as cosmetics, clothes and a dressing table, the amount they spent on personal possessions was quite limited. The major part of their wages was invested in their family house, furniture and appliances. For those who did not have their own house, the income was used for the building of their new house. The traditional type of the Northern Thai house is a wooden building with its floor set some one and a half to three metres above the ground on pilings, but the now commonly favoured types are built with concrete pillars and plastered brick walls, with their floor set on the ground. Factory women say that their appearance is more beautiful and it is cooler inside them. For those who already had their own house, the income was spent on luxury household goods, such as manufactured beds, wooden couches, chairs and tables, a kitchen range, a TV set, a refrigerator, and a stereo set. They generally bought these expensive goods on hire-purchase. Their stable income, which they had never had before, now enabled them to do so.

Factory women's investment in their own homes does not end with the building of the new house and the purchasing of expensive household goods. They also spend a great amount of money on the housewarming ceremony, sometimes equivalent to a third of the cost of the new house. In the traditional Northern Thai housewarming ceremony, after the rite[7] of blessing for the house and the householders, all participants, after the monks have eaten, share a meal together around noon. This is the end of the ceremony. In the case of factory women's ceremonies, a big night party is nowadays held in addition to the traditional rite. According to the villagers, such a party was first added to the housewarming rite of a factory wife in 1990. In 1993, I observed in Village N a more lavish party, during which hired professional singers gave performances for the first time. The hostess of that party was also a factory wife.

At this housewarming ceremony, a stage about five metres long and three metres wide was set up especially for the performance in the compound of the new house. The stage was equipped with stand microphones, two huge speakers, and musical instruments. There were tables and chairs provided for about two hundred guests in front of the stage. During the party, guests first enjoyed a meal and drinks served by the all female kin, neighbours and close friends of the host couple. After the guests had then further chatted for a while, a band of six girls from a nearby town, all costumed in colourful miniskirts, started singing and dancing on the stage, giving a performance that lasted several hours. During the course of this, important guests, such as ex-school teachers, the village headman, and factory managers, took turns in giving speeches honouring and blessing the host and hostess from the stage. As the party proceeded, the guests got drunk and more drunk, and few remained sitting at the tables. Some jumped up on the stage, and sang through microphones. Others were dancing together to the accompaniment of the band in front of or on the stage. All of this continued until midnight.

The high cost prevents an owner from holding such a housewarming ceremony just after the completion of their house. Many married couples postpone holding the ceremony until they have saved up enough money to for it. For example, the ceremony described above cost 60 thousand baht, ten times the couple's total monthly income, although they did, in fact, receive 40 thousand baht from guests as gifts at the ceremony. To hold the big party, they put it off till six months after the building's completion, borrowed from the wife's mother and sisters, and in addition sold a rice field. This was not exceptional. Couples often borrow money from kin, friends or banks, or sell properties in order to hold grand housewarming ceremonies.

During my stay in Village N, most of the houses completed were those of factory women.[8] In one case, I observed the housewarming ceremony of a non-factory hostess. She was a housewife. Her husband was the only villager working in a foreign country. Their new house was a big western-style house, with white plastered walls and a red tiled roof, which most factory women dream of. They had only a big housewarming rite, which means that they invited nine monks to the rite.[9] The wife explained the reason for the lack of a party by saying, 'I do not work in the estate'.

Here, questions arise. Why do the factory women invest their incomes so extensively in houses and the high-priced household goods? Why are they keen on holding grand housewarming parties? To answer these questions, we should inquire into the relation between the woman and the house, and the meanings of the housewarming ceremony in the Northern Thai village.

House and family

In Northern Thailand, the household, which today generally consists of a married couple and their unmarried children, constitutes the basic socio-economic unit of the village life. Children are expected to obey parents' instructions and to provide financial support for the household until their marriage. A newly-married couple starts their new life in the wife's parents' house. Before one of the wife's sisters gets married, the couple should move to their new house, which is often built in the parents' compound. After all elder sisters have married, the youngest daughter inherits the parents' house and looks after the parents in their old age, although this is not invariably the case, since it depends upon individual circumstances. The parents' wealth is in principle equally inherited by the siblings. After such an inheritance, the siblings' economic activities run independently by the household. Even if siblings live in individual houses next to each other in the parents' compound, their family budgets are strictly independent, and they never share housework or even meals, except in special ceremonies.

The structure of the Northern Thai house symbolises the family relations. The Northern Thai house is aligned to the cardinal directions of the compass, and all the posts and the walls are laid out on a grid pattern. According to the ritual elder (*pu can*) of Village N, the north is an auspicious direction, and indicates a high position (*tang sung*), so the house always faces the north. The basic composition of many houses is one couple's sleeping space and the outer space. The Northern Thai word for the sleeping room is *nai hüan*, which means 'inside the house'. Sometimes, the villagers simply call this *hüan*, 'house'. This room is supported by a pair of thick posts. The eastern post, which is often the thickest and the most distinctive post in the house, is called *sao khwan* or *sao ek*, which means 'auspicious post' or 'first post'. The name for the western post, the second thickest, is *sao nang*, which means 'lady post'. The outer space is called *nòk toen*. This is the large space inside the front entrance. The family use this as the living and dining area where they spend most of their time and welcome visitors. Tambiah (1969: 430) points out in his study of North-eastern Thai houses that all the floors of the named divisions are on different levels, reflecting symbolic values assigned to the divisions of the house. I found few such houses in Village N, although the *nai hüan* is on a higher level than the others, and the *chan* (veranda) lower in some Village N houses.

Bourdieu's (1973) demonstration that the spatial arrangement of the house among the North African Kabyle both reflects and contributes to the creation of social relationships between inhabitants can also be seen in the Northern Thai case. In the house, parents sleep in the highest room, *nai hüan*, and children sleep in the western part of that room, or in the *nòk toen*. When both parents and a married daughter and son-in-law share a house, the former occupy the eastern room whereas the latter sleep in the western one. So, the relation between junior and senior generations corresponds to the spatial order. Moreover, the husband sleeps to the right, or the north, and the wife sleeps to the left, or the south, both turning their heads toward the east. This is also identical with the symbolic relation between men and women. The kitchen, mainly a female place, and the toilet, a dirty place, are situated at the southern side. The people allowed to enter the *nai hüan* are only the family and closest kin. Kin and neighbours can freely enter the *nòk toen* if a family is present in the house. Non-kin has to wait at the foot of the stairs until he or she is invited to ascend. Outsiders are not allowed to enter even the compound without permission. Given these correspondences, we may point out in Northern Thailand, as Tambiah (1964) in fact does, the direct association between the house categories and the human categories.

In Northern Thailand, rites associated with house building well describe the relations between the house and the family. The Northern Thai hold the rite called *khün thao thang si* at the beginning of the building. The purpose of this is to ask *thao catu lok* to permit construction of, and thereafter to protect, the building. *Thao catu lok* are believed to be the guardian spirits of the human world and the heavens, which in particular govern the four directions. When the two main posts are first raised for the new house, the owner holds the rite called *su sao khwan sao nang*. In this rite, the husband's used garments are tied to the *sao khwan*, along with sugar cane, banana and coconuts, all attached by white sacred strings called *sai sin*. Similarly, the wife's garments are tied to *sao nang* with the same items. The two main posts supporting the *nai hüan*, the innermost part of the house, are identified with the husband and the wife. According to the Village N ritual elder, the *sao khwan* and the *sao nang* are also called *süa pò* (father's cloth) and *süa mae* (mother's cloth). The sacred water called *nam som pòi* is poured by a former monk on the *sao khwan* and the *sao nang*. The materials of the posts used to be the trunks of trees from the jungle, so the spirits may have inhabited them. The aim of this rite is said to be to expel the spirits and any bad luck, which may have occupied the trunks. People in Village N say that the garments represent the owners or their protectors. Sugar cane, banana and coconuts are believed to symbolise good fortune and prosperity because they grow rapidly and bear fruit in profusion. Thus, the rite represents the couple's appropriation of the posts and their being united with the house, while good luck and prosperity is also brought into the house and the family.

The Northern Thai housewarming ceremony is held traditionally just before or after the owners move into the new house. For the ceremony, the couple invite an auspicious number, an odd number, of monks, along with their own kin, neighbours and friends. The traditional housewarming ceremony consists of two parts; *fang tham hüan mai* and *süb chata khon*. In the *fang tham hüan mai*, monks recite sutras for the householders, while the latter make merit by offering food and other necessities to the former. In the *süb chata khon*, a sacred white cord is tied around the perimeter of the house, and this is also linked to the Buddha image, the *mai kam*, and the heads of the couple. The *mai kam* consists of three poles to which several necessities of life are attached. The villagers say that the three poles represent the Buddha, his teachings, and the monks. The things attached to the *mai kam* include a water jar, a mat, a pillow, a mosquito net, sugar cane, banana, coconuts, and white flags. The number of the white flags is equivalent to the combined total of the couple's ages in the following year. The villagers say that the flags represent the couple's lives. During the rite of *süb chata khon*, all the monks hold the white cotton cord, and recite sutras. According to the villagers, the *süb chata khon* symbolises that the couple will accrue these necessities of life in the new house, and will be blessed with long life and prosperity. In the course of the chanting, each participant pours water from a small bottle into a cup. This, the villagers say, also represents the wish that they will be provided with sufficient water, which is the most essential sustenance for human life. After the conclusion of the rite shortly before noon, the monks are served with food. Then, the lay participants join in a communal meal for several hours in the house or at tables in the compound.

According to the ritual elder, there are two grounds for the housewarming ceremony. The first is to bless the occupants with longer lives and also to bring good luck into the house. Several stages of the house building rites signify bringing good fortune, gold, and other necessities of life into the house. As for the sacred white cord that not only surrounds the house and links the couple to it, it also symbolises their future prosperity in terms of the water, food, and other necessities by equally including them in the sacred enclosure. The housewarming ceremony reveals the couple's request to the spirits for their own well-being in the home in the future. The second purpose, according to the ritual elder, is to make merit in the Buddhist context. Not only the *fang tham hüan mai* but also the *süb chata khon* are considered to stand for the participants' respect for the compassion of the Buddha and that they will never forget his loving kindness. Since merit-making is believed to lead to the future well-being of the donor, we could recognise that the second purpose of this ceremony is similar to the first.

As Kingshill (1991: 203) pointed out, it may be said that the Northern Thai housewarming ceremony is a rite of passage in the sense that the ceremony proclaims the couple having become mature enough to build their own house. The building of the couple's own house is an important event in their lives. They can build a temporary house made of bamboo at the beginning, but the desire for a wooden house remains strong in their minds. It is rare that the couple wait to build a permanent house until they have saved up enough money for it. With their initial savings, they start building the house. Thereafter, they gradually buy the necessary materials for the unfinished house. It often happens in Village N that it takes several years before a couple can complete the building of a new house. So, houses under construction are often seen in Village N. One of my informants still had not completed their house after twenty years, until their daughter brought in a sufficient sum of money from factory work. The Northern Thai never hold the housewarming ceremony for a temporary house. In this sense, the ritual symbolises the fact that the owner couple have succeeded well enough to construct their own permanent house. The growth of a house signifies that of its owner couple.

Women and housework

I agree with the thesis in the literature on Northern Thai houses (Turton 1978; Davis 1984; Rhum 1994) asserting that the house is structured around women. The main reason commonly given is that the house is closely connected with 'the circumscription of female sexuality' (Rhum 1994: 122). This means that, symbolising the parents, the house is conceptualised as the space where the parents circumscribe and protect their daughters' sexuality. *Phi pu ña*, tutelary spirits of matrilineal descent groups, are said to be primarily concerned with the regulation of female sexuality. Davis (1984: 59–60) says that in his research village, the house spirit is a fragmented ancestral spirit, while the identities of these two spirits are fused in the same spiritual being. In Village N, although people reject the idea that the house spirits are matrilineally inherited, they say that women whose ancestral spirits are different cannot live in the same house together for the fear of conflicts between their spirits. I never observed a woman whose spirit lineage differed from the householder's own enter the *nai hüan* except on ritual occasions. The house, especially the *nai hüan*, is inscribed with the matrilineally inherited sexual morality, which is symbolised as *phi pu ña*.

Along with the symbolic centrality of Northern Thai women, their dominant roles in housework further confirm the close association between the house and the wife and mother. According to people in Village N, until quite recently women, except elderly ones, rarely journeyed beyond the village. While they remained in the village, their central role was primarily defined by their housework (*ngan hüan* or *kan hüan*). The concept of housework in Village N is wider than what is generally assumed in English by the term. For example, while it naturally includes cooking, sweeping, sewing, washing, bringing up children, and keeping the family healthy, it also includes holding various household rites, taking part in village communal work, and attending the various rites of kin, neighbours, and friends. I observed in Village N that the ties between kinswomen, basically sustained by uxorilocality and its associated residential patterns, serve to maintain community activities, including various ceremonies. Furthermore, the villagers insist that the housework includes doing paid work in support of the household economy. A village woman said, 'The housework means *pò hüan*, to look after the home, and *caroen hüan*, to make the home prosper. The housework is to take responsibility (*hap phit chòp*) for all matters concerning the home. If one is a woman, she knows everything in herself about what to do in the housework without being advised'. Another village woman said, 'Doing housework is the women's job. Unless we do housework, nobody would do it for us, and it would never be finished. We are responsible for completing our housework'. Thus, the wife and mother are regarded as being solely responsible for looking after the home in every sense.

In Village N, people refer to the virtuous housewife as *mae si hüan*, the woman taking care of household affairs very well. Girls start learning housework, instructed by mothers and kinswomen, at the age of around ten. The girls are expected to master these skills by the age of fifteen because a reasonable competency is required before getting married. Women emphasise that if a girl fails to show a satisfactory ability at the housework, her prospective spouse's mother would not permit their marriage. Moreover, people widely share the view that the worth of a woman is largely to be judged by her ability at housework. Some villagers insist that a woman having reached a certain skilled level of attainment in cooking can never do morally unacceptable deeds. In Village N, people criticise a woman who neglects her duty of housework as a lazy (*khi khan*) or a bad woman (*mae ñing bò di*). Kinswomen and neighbours stand always ready to accuse such a woman. For example, a woman who daily serves her family dishes which she has bought at markets, not having cooked them herself, is contemptuously labelled a 'plastic housewife' (*mae ban phlasatik*).[10] The village women are ever-willing to criticise others on this issue, asserting that whenever there is a problem with a house or its family, the woman is considered to be responsible for it. Housewifery skills construct the identity of women.

This stress on the central role of a woman as that of a housewife brings into play another association between the woman and the house. The wife's duties in housework have traditionally included, and still include, keeping the house tidy and attractive. This means that the condition of the home, or more specifically, the appearance of the house, affects the honour of the wife. Her duties also include helping out with the household economy by doing paid work if necessary, and saving money for future necessities. This means that the wife should contrive to get along by making shift on a small income, and if what she has is not enough to support the family, she should go foraging in the forest or the river and, if possible, hire out for day labour. So, if a family appears to be reduced to poverty, people blame this on the wife's incapability at housework as previously defined. On the whole, people believe that the housework, the input of labour by the wife, defines the totality of the home.

Now, the income from factory work enables a woman to build a house or to decorate her house with expensive household goods within a few years. To gain honour as diligent housewives, factory women invest a large part of their incomes in the house, the furnishings, and also electrical appliances. All the furniture and the electrical goods are placed in the *nòk toen* within the house, so that they immediately attract visitors' attention. In Village N, I actually observed that members of female peer groups compete with each other over possessing a modern house equipped with costly household goods. They fear that friends or neighbours may look down upon them if they see few such goods in their house. A factory woman who had just built a fine house said:

> A woman has to own a TV or refrigerator. If a house does not have such goods, only the wife is criticised. People say, 'This woman is worthless. She is not able to save money.' Saving money and looking after the home is women's duty. The goods don't matter so

much to me personally, but I must have them. For the wife, looking after the house is the same as caring about the body. It is our etiquette. If someone visits a house and there are no goods in the house, the wife feels ashamed of it and loses face. If the visitor finds a certain amount of household goods in the house, she gains face.

What expensive household goods a family has in their house has become not only a barometer of their wealth but also an index of the wife's diligence. Thus, while factory women compete with each other to show their diligence by enhancing their homes (*top taeng hüan*), the lack of such durable goods prompts the village peers of factory women to apply for jobs in factories.

Here, an abstract idea of women's diligence or morality is set forth in their material possessions. The association of woman's worth and her house's appearance makes the invisible visible, or the equivocal quantifiable, so that one can visually compare women's worth in Village N. It became clearly evident that village women are aware of what household goods are possessed by all houses in the same hamlet and can estimate approximately how much they cost. Most women are able to say when another family bought a TV, how many inches the screen is, and whether it was bought at a shop in a nearby city or through an agent, and for cash or on credit. It is not going too far to say that both the family's prosperity and corresponding presuppositions about the wife's diligence are made on the criteria of the commodities, their brands, sizes, prices, and means of acquisition. With their relatively high incomes, factory women present their morality as embodied in the appearance of the houses.

The housewarming party

Finally, we consider why factory women enthusiastically invest in the housewarming ceremony, and how they use that ceremony. Besides the symbolic manifestations, the housewarming ceremony has provided its participants with an occasion for the exhibition of a new house. All the prohibitions about stepping into inner areas of the house are set aside only during this ceremony, so that visitors are permitted to go deeply into the *nai hüan* or look around any room. While doing so, the visitors, predominantly female, praise or criticise the wife for the house, and recently, the household goods, with or without her presence. They ask the wife or her neighbours, sometimes quite openly, the cost of the house and the household goods. The wife is very conscious of this. Factory women did not explain this to me of their own accord but admitted, in replying to my questions, that the presentation of a tidy, beautiful house in the course of the ceremony increases the wife's honour among kin, neighbours, and

195

friends. The housewarming ceremony as an exhibition of the house is one of the few crucial occasions for manifesting the wife's morality.

We found in Village N that the most significant change in recent housewarming ceremonies is that lavish parties have been added to the traditional housewarming rites by factory women. Despite remarkable changes in the houses' appearances, the rite's procedure and symbols remain unchanged. For example, even though tree trunks had not been used for posts in many houses, the two main concrete posts are still called *sao khwan* and *sao nang*, and treated as such. When the metal framework for the concrete posts are first erected, sugar cane, banana and coconuts are bound to the iron reinforcing frame of the *sao khwan* and the *sao nang*, and the rite of *su sao khwan sao nang* is conducted. Given this stability of the rite, what has changed in factory women's housewarming ceremonies is just the addition of the party. Nevertheless, we should not overlook the importance and the meanings of the party for them. According to anthropological traditions, the party may not be categorised as a rite in the strict sense, and yet it can be considered neither as an insignificant ornament nor a whim of factory women for anyone who wants to understand the changing social relations in the village.

Why did the first couple hold such a housewarming party in Village N? According to people in Village N, this kind of party was first held for wedding ceremonies, then was brought into housewarming ceremonies. Before this, the villagers state, there had been no such party in Village N, except for communal ones in the ceremony called *pòi luang*. The first lavish housewarming party accompanied by special performances was held in 1993. The wife is working as a factory supervisor. I asked her the reason for holding such a party in the housewarming ceremony. She replied, 'Just for fun'. This answer seems to be not so far from the fact, and here, the crucial question is whom she wanted to entertain. The answer seems to be not only herself but also her factory friends. If so, besides the villagers' explanation about the first housewarming party, I could say that the wife brought this form of the housewarming ceremony from the factory society.

For factory women, one prime motive for holding the housewarming party seems to be the opportunity to invite factory workmates. In the factory society, colleagues compete with each other to gain honour by possessing a modern house and luxury household goods, as in the village society. So, factory women are keen on inviting colleagues to the housewarming party to showcase their success. For a Buddhist reason, the housewarming rite must be held in the morning, that is so that monks can partake of the food offered in the rite. So, factory women who work in the daytime cannot attend the rite, even if they want to. Housewarming parties generally start at about six o'clock in the evening, which is one hour later than the closing hour of factories, for the benefit of the workers. The participants in past housewarming ceremonies were, and even at present morning housewarming rites still are, largely limited to kin and villagers. Since the addition of the party, there has been a remarkable increase in the number of those attending, most of whom are factory workmates of the owner wife.

In Northern Thai society, the mutual attendance of each others' rites is an important means of fostering the ties of friendship. Where previously all of her acquaintances were neighbouring villagers, a newly employed woman gets acquainted in the factory with many peer group members drawn from a wide catchment area, including Lamphun city, Chiang Mai city, and many remote villages. The budding friendships among workmates offer new opportunities for sustaining and strengthening the ties. Moreover, the help given during the ceremony, sometimes entailing a few days' leave of absence from the factory, rapidly increases the owner's trust in her helpers. For factory women, the housewarming party is an opportunity for deepening such ties.

In addition to this, a hostess feels that at a housewarming ceremony she should entertain workmates in a way, which appeals to them. In the factory society, one is often expected on a celebratory occasion to entertain friends by providing snacks or holding a small party. The housewarming ceremony is one of such occasions. Entertaining workmates up to, or beyond, their expectations in a ceremony brings impressive honours to a hostess. On the other hand, disappointing colleagues through a lacklustre ceremony causes her to lose face. The employment of singers in a housewarming party reflects the hostess' intention of providing an opportunity for the entertainment of her workmates through drinking and dancing, which is actually very much to their taste, although it embarrasses more conservative village women.

In practice, the more successful a housewarming party was, the better factory women remembered it and approved of the hostess. They often made comparisons between workmates' housewarming parties. The parties they remembered most vividly were the ones at which participants greatly enjoyed themselves in drinking, singing, and dancing. The greatest praise, which the hostess is given for such a party, is for her generosity. The success of the housewarming party symbolises the hostess' morals.

Furthermore, it can be said that the housewarming party displays the empowerment which young women derive from factory work. This seems to explain the contrast between the owner wife's clothes and behaviour in the housewarming rite and those at the party. In the housewarming rite, the couple dress neatly and quietly so that they may look subservient. Typical clothes worn on such occasions are a white T-shirt and blue jeans[11] for the husband, and a white T-shirt and a sarong of dark colour for the wife. The couple's elderly kin manage the rite's preparation and procedures. The couple follow their directions. I observed in housewarming rites that elderly kin brought along the couple only when the former needed the latter in the course of the proceedings. I was quite struck by the fact that the role of the young household couple in the rites was somewhat like figureheads. The housewarming rite is in a sense dominated by the elderly kin. On the contrary, the party is entirely managed by the young couple themselves, mainly the wife, with the help of other young women, both village peers and factory workmates. Wearing fashionable brightly coloured clothes, the wife takes the initiative in preparing the party, in serving guests with food and drink, and in talking, singing and dancing to entertain them. As the party mounts toward a noisy climax of enthusiasm, while a few elderly villagers still remain to observe the spectacle, most elderly villagers, after finishing dinner, gradually slip away from the party. This is the time for factory women. The owner wife enjoys her newly gained autonomy. The new house and its housewarming party assert that she can change her world by her labour. In this sense, her motive in giving the housewarming party is to signify her own capability. In doing so, she can, at least temporarily, feel liberated from the double burdens of the home and the factory, and confirm her solidarity with her workmates by enjoying themselves together.

Conclusion

We have seen in Village N how factory women make use of the housewarming ceremony in their own way. Without changing the symbolism, they impart new meanings to the ceremony. We saw them not as a form of symbols or utterances in the rite but as symbols or signs inscribed on the bodily actions at the additional party.

The housewarming ceremony forms a part of the world wherein, or process whereby, contiguous activities intermingle with each other so that we cannot discuss it apart from the whole. Socio-economic shifts alone did not give us a satisfactory explanation for changes in the housewarming ceremony. To understand them, we had to start from the examination of the link between the spatial order of house and family relations, following Bourdieu's for the Kabyle house. In so doing, we found in the Northern Thai village a close affinity between the wife and the house, and the former's morality is judged by the latter's appearance. The housewarming ceremony is an opportunity for the owner couple to exhibit their economic success, and additionally for the wife to display her diligence in housework. This is the reason why she invests income from the factory almost exclusively in the house and the housewarming ceremony. When a factory woman holds a grand housewarming ceremony, she attempts to assert her prestige in an already established manner.

However, this analysis did not fully explain meanings of the party that follows the housewarming rite. De Certeau criticises Bourdieu's theory of habitus as follows. 'It is indeed the dwelling, as a silent and determining memory, which is hidden in the theory under the metaphor of the habitus, and which, moreover, gives the supposition a certain referentiality, an appearance of reality' (1984: 58). From Bourdieu's approach, we could hardly understand what agents feel and remember in a particular interaction. What such an analysis lacks is an examination of the agents' experiences in each ceremony. We must carefully observe that factory women enthusiastically join together in singing, drinking, and dancing at the party, and these activities are suggestive of a newly-won independence from their elders. This oblique challenge to the previously prevailing status quo can thus be seen as a form of political change – even perhaps having a subversive flavour. They gain a sense of autonomy and liberation through these performances, and recall these to help produce their own self-image of solidarity and identity as empowered women. Surely, the housewarming party is directly linked with their factory interactions, which we could not adequately discuss in this chapter.

We can say that, for their own interests, factory women tactically use the ceremony where they originally took a minor part and which tended to legitimate their subordinate position to the traditional authority. The traditional housewarming ceremony dominated by the male elder conveys statements in which young women are subordinate, diligent, and chaste, to be protected and directed by men. By spending their income largely on the house, factory women show their diligence in their socially recognised roles and show respect to the social order. They neither challenge the elders' authority in the rite, nor change anything in the ceremony's symbols or procedures. Instead, they add the party to the rite, by which they dramatically demonstrate their successes in being good homebuilders. In so doing, factory women also create different meanings through their performance at the party. The party legitimates behaviour, notably drinking and dancing, that would have been condemned as immoral in most other contexts, that are associated with the assertion of new female identities. Their enjoyment of liberated behaviour at the party is a crucial experience, which they recall in constructing their solidarity and self-images as factory women.

Thus, plural modes of meanings can arise from the ceremony. It can prompt people to consider equivocal meanings. While the housewarming ceremony as a whole still continues to affirm a traditional habitus relating to gender and kinship, the housewarming party claims a new notion of female autonomy. It can be said that this reflects cultural crisis in the society. The modification of housewarming ceremonies in Village N reflects the tension between the constraints which the traditional order imposed on young women in the home, and the growing autonomy to which they feel entitled by the economic power gained from the factory. In other words, the newly intensified tension between the sexes and between the generations in social life is discussed through changes in Northern Thai housewarming ceremonies. What a specific ceremony conveys is not predetermined knowledge but something resulting from ceremonial interactions. In the grand housewarming ceremony, young factory women create, on the one hand, a social memory of their diligence and prosperity, and, on the other, that of their freedom and liberation.

Notes

1 This chapter is a revised version of a chapter that was originally prepared for my doctoral thesis. Fieldwork was conducted from June 1993 to December 1994. It was supported by a grant from the Toyota Foundation and a grant from the Matsushita International Foundation. I would like to thank the editors, Shigeharu Tanabe and Charles F. Keyes, for their helpful comments and suggestions on the final drafts of the chapter.

2 This chapter focuses on an investigation of the behaviour of married factory women. Single factory women invest similarly in their family house and in household goods but for different reasons. Moreover, their investment tends to be concentrated on the wedding ceremony rather than the housewarming ceremony.

3 1 *rai* = approximately 0.16 ha.

4 See the Bangkok newspaper, *Phucatkan raiwan* (Manager Daily), 24 February 1994; 7 April 1994.

5 Village N is a rural village located to the southeast of Lamphun city. In the village, there were 161 households, and more than 40 young women working in the factory. From October to November 1994, I conducted a household survey in Village N. I interviewed 73 males and 77 females in 50 households as samples.

6 In 1994, one baht was roughly US$ 0.04.

7 In this chapter, I use three terms for the housewarming ceremony; the rite, the party and the ceremony. By the rite, I mean the traditional Northern Thai housewarming rite conducted with monks in the morning. By the party, I mean just the party held at night, which factory women add to the rite. Then, I use the ceremony as the more general term, when we need not differentiate the rite from the party.

8 In Village N, most non-factory women cannot afford to build a new house or to hold a grand housewarming ceremony. A few elite females, such as civil servants, try to set themselves apart from the other village women, rather than attempting to emulate them.

9 It is common in Village N for villagers to invite three or five, or in very rare cases seven, monks for their auspicious rites. The more monks one invites to a rite, the more one must spend on the merit-making.

10 The reason is that, in Thailand, when one buys already cooked dishes at a shop or stall, they are always put into small plastic carrying bags.

11 In Northern Thai villages, blue jeans are not casual wear. On various ritual occasions, young people wear blue jeans with the traditional Northern Thai jacket. Blue jeans are actually an excellent replacement for the traditional Northern Thai indigo trousers.

References

Bourdieu, Pierre 1973 'The Berber house', p.98–110 in Mary Douglas (ed.) *Rules and Meanings: the anthropology of everyday knowledge*, Harmondsworth: Penguin.

Certeau, Michel de 1984 *The Practice of Everyday Life*, Berkeley: University of California Press.

Davis, Richard B. 1984 *Muang Metaphysics*, Bangkok: Pandora.

Kingshill, Konrad 1991 (1965) *Ku Daeng, the Red Tomb*, Dekalb, Ill.: Northern Illinois University, Center for Southeast Asian Studies.

Rhum, Michael R. 1994 *The Ancestral Lords*, Dekalb, Ill.: Northern Illinois University, Center for Southeast Asian Studies.

Tambiah, Stanley J. 1969 'Animals are good to think and good to prohibit', p.423–459 in *Ethnology* 8.

Turton, Andrew 1978 'Architectural and Political Space in Thailand', p.113–132 in G. Milner (ed.) *Natural Symbols in South East Asia*, London: School of Oriental and African Studies.

CHAPTER EIGHT

The Postmodernisation of Thainess[1]

Kasian Tejapira

Consumerism versus nationalism

On Wednesday the 28th April 1993, a best-selling Thai-language business daily in Thailand carried a full-page advertisement on page 22 of *Samakhom sathapanik Sayam nai phrabörommarachupatham*, or the Association of Siamese Architects under Royal Patronage (ASA), announcing its annual seminar for that year on the theme of '*Süptò winyan süpsan wela*' (or 'Tradition and Trend' in the Association's own English rendering, although a more literal translation would be 'Carry on the Spirit, Move on with the Times') to be held in the Plenary Hall at Queen Sirikit National Convention Centre from 30 April to 3 May. The advertisement itself featured a photograph of an attractive young Thai lady elegantly dressed in a business suit. Reclining at ease in an armchair and looking intently, even invitingly, at her supposed viewers, she was surrounded on all sides by graphic pointers with English captions revealing the un-Thai identity of various parts of her bodywear: namely, a hairstyle with a 'Parisian Touch', 'Italian Import(ed)' ear-rings, 'American Fragrance', a suit of 'English Wool', a 'Swiss Made' watch, and 'Japanese Silk' stockings. A big caption near the top right of the photograph asks straightforwardly in Thai: '*Bòk dai mai khun pen thai thi trong nai?*' (Can you tell which part of you makes you Thai?).

But actually who was the 'you' being questioned? And whose image of consumption of un-Thai commodities was being looked at for that matter? Was it the image of the lady in the photograph or that of her viewers? Through her reflective gaze, the viewers were enticed to look with unexpected and growing unease at her image as evidence of their own possible un-Thainess, their imagined communion with her being grounded on the common challengeability of their Thai identity. For once, the voyeurs themselves were subjected to ethnic self-voyeurism.

But not for long. The lengthy caption beneath the photograph rushed to relieve the viewers of the troubling, incipient self-doubt about their own national identity with a quick-fix soothing message in Thai:

It's not strange if we are used to bread and coffee more than rice with curry ... There's nothing wrong with the fact that we are dressed in the Western style. It's not unusual that we drive Japanese cars. Because *Thai-Thai feelings* still remain in our spirit ... That's why ARCHITECT'93 summons up the meaning of the *Thai style of living* again by presenting contemporary architectural ideas that are consonant with the *Thai way of life* in an attempt to stimulate ties between modern living and *Thai identity* under the theme 'Carry on the Spirit, Move on with the Times' (Tradition & Trend) in order to preserve *Thainess*.[2] (My translation, emphases added)

Without pausing to elaborate on what 'Thai-Thai feelings', 'Thai style of living', 'Thai way of life', 'Thai identity' and 'Thainess' were, the ad hurried along to invite architects and the public from all over the country to the seminar to learn and exchange ideas so as to formulate 'the concept of a unique contemporary Thai architecture'. Ironically, the highlight of this mission in search of contemporary Thai architectural identity turned out to be an introductory speech on 'present day new concepts' (sic) by a 'world renowned *Japanese* architect, Mr. Fumihiko Maki' (emphasis added). The ad then ended on a reassuring note: 'And we who are called 'Thais' ... will not be 'Thai' by name only'.[3]

The presumption that Thainess and the consumption of un-Thai commodities could coexist without qualms or dissonance, the fact that Thai architects these days could begin to discuss contemporary Thai architecture only after hearing words of wisdom from their Japanese counterpart, and so on, these stand in stark contrast to the Thainess of yesteryear when the burgeoning nationalist, democratic university student movement launched an effective and influential boycott campaign against Japanese goods in the early 1970s. Being then in high school, I was shown by one of my classmates (whose name, by the way, happened to be *Ekkaraj,* meaning Independence) a newspaper clipping of a contemporary Thai poem which ingeniously contained many familiar and popular brand names of Japanese consumer products in the Thai market, wittily rhymed them with Thai words, and hilariously poked fun at the way Thai people unceasingly and unthinkingly pursued the consumption of these Japanese goods in their daily lives. The poem left such a profound impression on me that, twenty years afterwards, having been through one massacre in Thammasat University, one failed guerrilla warfare in the forests of Northeast Thailand and Cambodia, one doctoral thesis at Cornell, and another recent mass uprising in the middle of Bangkok, and having completely forgotten all the details of its reference save for a vague idea of its cultural-political whereabouts, I could still recite its first and final rhyming couplets without fail.

Needless to say, it was the lady with un-Thai bodywear in the above-mentioned ad who reminded me most strongly of that poem. Having heard me lament for it, and recite the two couplets in a public lecture in January 1994, a bohemian friend of mine among the audience called on me at my office the following day to hand me a copy of the complete text of the poem in his own handwriting, saying he had first found it quoted in full in a newspaper article about eleven years earlier (i.e. in 1983), and liked it so much that he copied it down instantly and had kept it ever since. And here is the full text of that poem entitled *'Khaniyom'* (Values), written by a virtually unknown Mr. Sakda Jintanawijit:

First thing in the morning,
grasp White Lion toothpaste and enjoy brushing teeth;
then make some tea with a National electric kettle
and smooth down hair with Tanjo pomade.

Put on Thaitorae Tetoron clothes,
wear a Seiko watch when leave home,
listen to government news broadcasts on a Sanyo radio,
drive a Toyota to pick up girlfriend.

Wonder where to do luxurious shopping?
Go to Daimaru where there are plenty
of consumer products made in Japan,
sent here from faraway Nippon.

Girlfriend buys Kanebo cosmetics
and also those of Sisedo and Pola,
Wacoal underwear for her big boobs,
Onkyo electric appliances for her ecstasy.

When back at home, switch on a Toshiba TV set,
flip through the channels looking for Gamo and Kendo.[4]
But after fighting mosquitoes for a while,
feel like visiting Sayuri massage parlour.[5]

In our modern daily life,
we begin to have self-doubt
so we ask an Asahi mirror:
'Eh, am I a Thai?'

(*Watashi wa thai yin desuka?*)[6]

To this soul-searching, nationalist question self-reflectively and rhymingly posed by a Thai consumer of Japanese goods twenty-one years earlier, the resounding answer unhesitatingly and unrhymingly proffered by a Thai consumer of un-Thai commodities today is emphatically: 'Yes, I am a Thai despite my consumption of many un-Thai things!'

Between the nationalism-above-consumerism of the 1972 'Khaniyom' poem and the consumerism-above-nationalism of the 1993 ASA's advertisement lay a text which most aptly captured the increasing commodification and de-referentialisation of the Thai signifier, namely, a Thai folk-song with the English title of 'Made in Thailand', composed and played by a highly popular folk-song group named Carabao in 1984. Owing to its economic nationalist message, the song won government approval and promotion, quickly becoming a top hit. And yet, the jacket of the Carabao cassette tape that featured this song bore the instantly recognisable trademark of the Coke soft drink in red and straightforwardly declared in print the following assuring message:

'Coke and Carabao jointly promote the value of Thainess'!?![7]

Freedom of consumption and liberation of national identity

I would argue that this affirmative answer signifies, in present-day Thailand, manifest cultural liberation from the nationalist regimes of the past, be it radical leftist or right-wing authoritarian. On the one hand, it is the liberation of consumption in which the consumption of commodities is no longer limited or constrained by the consumers' own national identity. One can consume commodities of whatever nationality or ethnicity regardless of one's own national identity with no nationalist angst, guilt or remorse. Or, to parody a well-known *cri d'extase à la* American civil rights movement of the 1960s, the Thai consumers are now 'free, free at last (to consume whatever they desire)!'

But it also suggests, on the other hand, the liberation of national identity as signifier from the control of specific national or ethnic commodity-referents. Thus Thainess becomes unanchored, uprooted, liberated or freed from the regime of reference to national or ethnic Thai commodities. Thainess is now able, as it were, to roam freely around the commodified globe, to coexist and copulate with Italian ear-rings, American fragrance, English wool, a Swiss-made watch, Seiko, Sanyo, Toyota, Wacoal, etc., or any other un-Thai commodities and sundries, and still to refer as such to the consumer of these products. Its referential essence is limited to mere spectral, amorphous, incorporeal, intangible, hollowed-out and undefined Thai-Thai feelings in the spirit. Once liberated, Thainess takes wing and turns into a free-wheeling, free-floating signifier.

Would a rose, by any other brand names, smell as sweet?

And yet, come to think of it, on the third hand (the promo world is such a complex place, and we have only two hands), is it the products themselves or their representations, i.e. brand names, that are at issue here? From the point of view of our lady with un-Thai bodywear, and her fellow consuming compatriots, will it still be 'not strange', 'not wrong' or 'not unusual' if the brand names of the bread and coffee, as well as Western dresses and Japanese cars which they consume daily, are changed from fashionable foreign to commonplace Thai ones (for example, from Sony to *Seni*, or from Hitachi to *Hatthachai*)? Or, if Thai products assume exotic foreign brand names or even generic names, will they become more or less palatable to the Thai national spirit?

Numerous examples spring to mind in this connection. For instance, not long ago, the Thai manufacturer of a popular but controversial stimulant drink called *Krating Daeng* (meaning Red Bull) launched a new product line, which is a sterilised refreshing tissue, under the English brand name of Red Bull. Also, during the annual Chinese Buddhist *kin ce* (a Thai term for going vegetarian) festival in October 1994, a long-established Thai manufacturer of a variety of canned food products bearing the *Tra Nok Phirap* (or Pigeon Brand) trademark launched a line of canned, ready-cooked Chinese vegetarian food under the brand name of J-Foods, which is a fantastic linguistic hybrid, consisting of the abbreviated English transliteration of a Thai word whose origin is Teochiu Chinese plus an English word.[8] In addition, there are Regency brandy, Cute Press and Oriental Princess cosmetics, etc., all locally produced by Thai manufacturers. As to generic names, during the 1994 Chinese lunar festival, the traditional Chinese cakes seasonally made and consumed at that time, whose generic name in Thai is *khanom wai phracan,* were widely advertised for the first time ever in Thailand as simply 'moon cake'.

The foregoing questions are posed against the background of a distinct and growing trend among Thai business companies, manufactured products, film and TV stars, singers, musicians and entertainers to adopt foreign (that is, Western and Chinese) names, brand names, or stage names. A recent survey by Associate Professor Dr. Wilaiwan Khanisthanan of the Faculty of Liberal Arts, Thammasat University, shows that over 90% of the brand names of products advertised on Thai television are in English.[9] This is readily understandable in the case of those companies, products and individuals that plan to go global and are targeted at foreign export market. But even when they are clearly for domestic consumption, foreign names are still widely adopted. Thus, most shopping centres in Bangkok and major provinces in Thailand now have such names as Central, The Mall, Robinson, Pata, Welco, Wonder, Safco, Cathay, etc.; the bigger and better-known among Thai companies adopt such names as

Telecom Asia, Jasmine International, Bangkok Land and Houses, IBC, Thai Sky TV, Media of Medias, etc.; and singers of Thai songs call themselves such foreign-sounding stage names as Tik Chiro, Chen Chen Bunsungnoen, Honey Sri-isan, etc.[10] As for business establishments with original names in Thai, a convenient ploy is to use the abbreviations of their English transliterations along with them. Hence, DK for Duang Kamol Bookstore, MBK for Mabunkhrong Shopping Centre, and CP for the Charoen Phokphand Group. Interestingly, the nominal metamorphosis of the Charoen Phokphand multinational conglomerate from Chia Tai through Charoen Phokphand into CP is indicative of the cultural and economic transformations of Sino-Thai businesses in general.[11]

The reason for this, as told by Mr. Thiraphol Phongphana-ngam, the general manager of a newly-opened Thai fast-seafood restaurant located in the midst of cut-throat competition from nearby McDonald's, Popeye's, Kentucky Fried Chicken franchised fast-food restaurants and the like in a huge shopping mall in an affluent residential area in Bangkok, is presumably fairly typical. Here he explained why, having pondered over more than 200 possible names, he finally chose to name his restaurant in English as Calico Jack:

> Although we set up our restaurant for Thai customers, it would be risky to use a Thai name. That's why we decided to use an English name in order to create an inter (sic) image as well as to compete with ourselves.[12] (My translation)

The last part of the final sentence in Mr. Thiraphol's statement is worth pondering. So, in order 'to compete with ourselves' or, in other words, to drive our Thai selves harder, we need an inter(national) image created by a foreign brand name to prod us and prick our Thai conscience. Thus, in the case of Calico Jack, what remains of Thainess (the Thai id) is being contested right there in its last refuge in the psyche by the more competitive and dynamic un-Thai superego and, hopefully, will be overcome someday.

Adoption of foreign brand names by Thai products aside, it has become increasingly difficult and even pointless to try to determine the Thai/un-Thai nationality of a consumer product in the Thai market through its original brand name in this present age of economic globalisation. As it is now 'possible', according to Milton Friedman, 'to produce a product anywhere, using resources from anywhere, by a company located anywhere, to be sold anywhere', so, unsurprisingly, Thailand has become, in recent years, a favourite overseas investment site and production base for the export of many a Japanese, Asian Nics', and Western multinational corporation, owing to its comparatively lower labour costs and strategic geo-economic location as a gateway to Indochina and South China.[13] Therefore, not only Toyota but also Mitsubishi, Isuzu, Honda, Nissan, Volvo, BMW, etc., cars, not only National but also Sony, Sharp, Sanyo, Saijo Denki, Nordmende, etc., electrical appliances are now being manufactured and/or assembled in Thailand by Thai workers and technicians with increasing local contents. In this strictly economic sense, be it with regard to the production site, manufacturing labour, component parts, or export earnings and balance of trade, these products are already getting more and more Thai despite their foreign brand names. Consequently, what is actually liberated to copulate with Thainess may not be so much the products themselves as their foreign representations or brand names.

Freedom from Thainess

The liberation of consumption, national identity, and brand names leads to the next logical step, i.e., the liberation of identity from the national. Since the exclusive power of Thainess as a signifier to refer to only Thai things is loosened, the signified of Thainess also changes, from the supposed embodiment of the inherent essence of all things Thai into just one identity option among many others, national, ethnic or otherwise, which anyone can partake of and indulge in through the purchase and consumption of commodities as identity signs. To put it another way, the manifold freedom from the barriers imposed by national or ethnic self-identity simultaneously allows Thai consumers the possibility to consume commodities as identity commodities, i.e., the consumption of consumer products not for their intrinsic use value or socio-economic exchange value, but for their cultural value as signs of desired identity.[14] And the objects of desire in question may vary from national or ethnic to mere brand-name identities as provocatively and succinctly put by Mark C. Taylor and Esa Saarinen in their recent iconoclastic work:

'i am what I buy'.[15]

The Desire to be Thai in the age of globalisation

The alienation of Thais from Thainess, the distance they subconsciously assume between themselves and their supposed national/ethnic essence, the manner in which they regard Thainess as other than, and separate from, their own individual identities, and treat it as reified 'thingness', are evidently the underlying premises in the following excerpts from the interviews of four rising young stars in the Thai entertainment industry. First, Miss. Angkhana Thimdi, or simply Ann, a sexy film and TV star, fashion model, and occasional singer, well-known for her voluptuous body and her often tight and skimpy dresses, was reported to have commented on her attitude towards Thainess, just before the New Year's eve and the beginning of the government's designated *pi ronnarong watthanatham Thai* (or Year to Campaign for Thai Culture) of 1994,[16] as follows:

Does anyone know that, even though she likes to wear extremely provocative dresses, actually Ann-Angkhana Thimdi is very strict in observing Thai traditional customs, to the point of always saying a Buddhist prayer before going to sleep ... She also likes to give alms to Buddhist monks regularly. Moreover, she is a very old-fashioned lady who *likes to preserve Thainess* ... However, that Ann-Angkhana must wear such provocative dresses, says the reporter, is due to the fact that she has a good figure and wants to show off what she has ... And having learned a lot about the teachings of Buddha lately, Ann-Angkhana would like to take vows as a Brahmin nun sometime next year.[17] (My translation, emphasis added)

In the same vein, Mr. Billy Ogan, a popular, half-Filipino half-Thai, young singer and film and TV star, explained the concept of his new music album in relation to the official Year to Campaign for Thai Culture as follows:

Although the songs that will be produced are songs for teenagers, Thai cultural issues will also be stressed. This is because next year will be the Year to Campaign for Thai Culture, therefore, in regard to the new songs, Thai cultural issues must be mixed in. And personally speaking, I also *like Thainess* a lot but haven't had much chance so far to express that. So, when there is a chance of producing songs according to my own ideas, I would like to bring out what I myself am.[18] (My translation, emphasis added)

And last but not least, Kop – Paphassara Chutanuphong and Tui-Monreudi Yamaphai, two famous leading female TV stars, told a newspaper reporter of their special plan to celebrate the 1995 Saint Valentine's Day together in a very Thai-Thai way:

While most youngsters who are in love take today's opportunity (14 February) to celebrate the Valentine's Day or the Day of Love according to Western custom, the youngster couple, Kop – Paphassara Chutanuphong and Tui – Monreudi Yamaphai, *choose instead to observe the Thai Buddhist festival of Magha Puja* [a Buddhist festival on the day of the full moon in the third lunar month to commemorate the spontaneous great assembly of the Buddha's disciples], which falls on the same date. Kop states that actually she and Tui had already celebrated their Day of Love festival late last year by touring round the U.S. for two full weeks with Tui's elder sister. 'Both of us work hard and intend to save ten-thousand baht a month. When October and November come, we will spend our savings on a tour to refresh ourselves. This year, we plan to go to Italy'. However, *it so happens that this year's*

209

> *Valentine's Day coincides with the Magha Puja Day. So, Kop decided on doing something special* even though they have already celebrated the Day of Love. Kop says that on the 14 February, she and Tui will fly to the province of Kalasin to make merit by buying a bookcase for the Tipitaka and Pali texts for a Buddhist temple as well as wearing white frocks and observing the Buddhist precepts in that temple for a day. On the following day, they will come back to work.[19] (My translation, emphases added)

Cultural schizophrenia

So, professedly, all four of them – Ann, Billy, Kop and Tui – like Thainess, love Thainess, and desire to be Thai, to remain Thai and, better still, to become even more Thai. The actuality, even possibility, of their professed common desire is premised upon the existence, on the one hand, of Thainess as the object of desire and, on the other hand, of themselves as the subjects of desire. Moreover, in the very act of pursuing their object of desire, the four subjects concurrently reveal a split in their personality and symptoms of cultural schizophrenia. Thus we have, in the case of Miss. Thimdi, the presumably un-Thai, sexy, exhibitionist Ann, and the presumably Thai traditionalist, Buddhist Angkhana. Again, in the case of Mr. Ogan, we have Billy, the embodiment of un-Thai teenage fads and Ogan, the lover of Thai culture. And in the case of Ms Chutanuphong and Yamaphai, we have, on the one hand, Kop and Tui, who crave after un-Thai tourist exotica and, on the other hand, Paphassara and Monreudi, who prefer observing Thai *Magha Puja* to Western Valentine's Day. The claims of these four young stars that their Thai self is deeper, truer or more authentic than its un-Thai counterpart can only be taken with a grain of salt, given the context in which the statements were made, namely right before and shortly after the official Year to Campaign for Thai Culture. Rather, their fragmented subjectivity seems to be a flexible artifice selectively and discreetly practised in response to the varying demands of the segmented cultural market in Thailand, which include, among others, the government, the Buddhist faithful, teenagers, soft porn fans, and so on. None of these market segments is deeper, truer, or more authentic than the others. They are just different groups, big and small, of image consumers.

Lest anyone should think that Ann, Billy, Kop and Tui are isolated individual cases, let me introduce further instances of cultural schizo-phrenia inflicted upon present-day Thailand by the widespread attempt to reconcile the overwhelming undeniability and inevitability of cultural globalisation with the nervous desire to hold on to the increasingly elusive and slippery Thainess. Thus, when the 125 students who took the Creative Copy-writing class at Ramkhamhaeng University's Department of

Advertising and Public Relations were assigned by their instructors to make a one-page ad to instil Thai cultural values into today's youth on the occasion of the Year to Campaign for Thai Culture, the best twenty among them, as picked out by the instructors, include the following samples:

Name of student	Ad picture	Ad message
Maneerat Siriwong	The back view of a boy dressed in the recognisable M-TV black rap-singer style & the front view of supposedly the same boy in a Thai traditional dress performing Thai classical dance.	'Rap dance is acceptable but Thai (classical) dance is not forgotten; though not (Thai) on the outside! ... but the heart is genuinely Thai'.
Phongmethee Saengrit	Youths making hand gestures and screaming in a pop concert & soldiers marching under the Thai national flag and the image of a national monument.	'The scream in front of a concert stage should not be different from the shout for independence; although time passes by, 'Thainess' still persists, for us to cherish, along with Thai independence'.
Jumnanja Punaret	A pair of jeans and a pair of traditional Thai trousers for males known as 'Raja Pattern' in a showcase.	'Many jeans in the market; only one (Raja Pattern pair of trousers) in the museum; who will carry on the style of dress which is Thai identity, if not you'.
Tachsanee Wongrach	A Thai male youth dressed in American teenage style skateboarding in an urban area.	'Thai-Thai games are still in (my) memory; today's world may make great progress but Thainess is never forgotten'.
Sangthian	A traditional Thai Singha (as in the logo of Singha Beer) and Walt Disney's Lion King.	'Thai Singha and Lion King; do you know the difference?'
Pongsiam Khumsoithong	A 100 baht banknote over and above a 20 baht banknote over and above a Thai citizen's ID card.	'Thainess is not only what you carry; don't let Thai culture be only an option'.

Over and over again, the same symptoms as in the cases of Ann, Billy, Kop and Tui are shown here, i.e., a split personality or fragmented subjectivity, be it individual or collective, realistic or symbolic (rap dancer vs. Thai dancer, screaming youths vs. shouting soldiers, a pair of jeans vs. Raja Pattern trousers, a skateboard vs. Thai-Thai games, Singha vs. Lion King); the submersion, subjectification, spiritualisation, interiorisation of Thainess [20] (which is evident in phrases like 'Thai (classical) dance is not forgotten', 'not (Thai) on the outside, but the heart is genuinely Thai', 'Thai-Thai games are still in (my) memory', 'but Thainess is never forgotten', 'Thainess is not only what you carry');[21] the explicit or implicit claim that the interiorised Thai self is more authentic than – or at least none the less authentic despite – the projected un-Thai self in the form of dress, behaviour or activity (thus the Thai classical dance and the genuinely Thai heart are more authentic than the rap dance and rap dress; shouting in a military parade is as authentic as screaming in a pop concert; the singularity and aura of the Raja Pattern specimen in the museum makes it more authentic than the limitlessly reproducible manufactured jeans in the market); and lastly, the irrepressible, ardent, resilient, recurrent and ever-reincarnating desire to be Thai (which is supposed to keep on haunting Thais even when they are rap dancing, screaming in a pop concert, wearing jeans, playing on a skateboard or watching a Walt Disney cartoon). Cultural schizophrenia is reaching epidemic proportions in Thailand, or so it seems.[22]

Inhaling Thainess into the psyche

After solid Thainess has been melted into air or vaporised and then inhaled or spirited into the psyche, it is then purified or purged of any elements deemed unsuitable for the urgent need to survive and succeed in the increasingly competitive economic and cultural environment of globalised Thailand. In the same manner that the manager of Calico Jack had to give his Thai fast-seafood restaurant an un-Thai name so as 'to compete with our (Thai) selves', Mr Patrick McGeown, an Australian creative group head of EURO RSCG Ball Partnership (allegedly the seventh largest advertising agency in the world) and one of the two co-instructors who assigned the above-students in their Creative Copy-writing class at Ramkhamhaeng University to make ads to instil Thai cultural values, advised his students on Thainess and their future advertising career as follows:

> It's really for the students to think that they are Thai and *never forget* it. They *don't have to drop it* when they go into the real world of advertising; it should be something that they *should always carry with them*. The things that are created in Thailand – *when creating*

an advertisement try to make it Thai, keep it Thai. It doesn't have to be Western; they don't have to copy.[23] (Emphases added)

That is, inhale Thainess, keep it in the psyche, and then proceed to create ads that are 'Thai'. So far so good. But then, he went on ...

It's because Thai people have this nature of being *kreng cai* (i.e., being considerate) and always saying *mai pen rai* (i.e., never mind). That is why I insist that my students speak up if they don't agree about anything. *This is not because I'm trying to change Thai traditional values* of always being polite and giving in, but rather I'm doing it *to improve the advertising industry,* ultimately, by standing up for one's ideas.[24] (Emphases added)

And here we have in the same person, on the one hand, Pat, a Siamophile, lover and admirer of Thai culture ('Thailand is rich in culture – so is India – but America and Australia are not', so he averred), who repeatedly urged his students to 'always carry (Thainess) with them' and, on the other hand, Mac, a world-class advertising guru, who regarded *kreng cai* and *mai pen rai* as hindering the improvement of the advertising industry, and insisted that his students had to 'drop it' and thereby become more 'un-Thai'! Alas, this proves that nationality or ethnicity not immune against the truly infectious disorder of cultural schizophrenia, induced by the desire to be Thai amidst the un-Thai exigencies of globalisation.

The case of Pat Mac offers an interesting contrast to that of Calico Jack. While Calico Jack represents an attempt to become 'un-Thai' under an un-Thai sign, Pat Mac makes the clarion call to his students to try desperately to become 'un-Thai' in their working style under the sign of 'Thainess'. One can well imagine, sometime in the near future, one of Pat Mac's former students arguing in a very 'un-Thai' style, i.e., forcefully and assertively, without *kreng cai* and *mai pen rai* , with his/her surprised, polite and submissive Thai copy-writing colleagues in a world-class advertising agency for his/her own idea of 'Thai' ads. I would like to call this process the sublimation (in the psychological sense) of un-Thainess, in which un-Thai urges are expressed under more socially acceptable Thai signs.

Cultural sublimation: psychological and pseudo-chemical

But Thainess is also sublimated, though not in the more familiar psychological sense, but in a sense analogous with the less familiar chemical one. Chemically speaking, 'sublimate' is to change a solid substance to a gas by heating it and then change it back to a solid, in order to make it pure. I have already discussed how solid Thainess is melted into air, spirited into the psyche, and then purged or purified of those elements

213

that are not conducive to un-Thai globalisation. The last step in the 'sublimation' (in the pseudo-chemical sense) of Thainess is to change it back to a solid, or solidify it with an image or a sign.

To turn vaporised Thainess into a solid sign or signifier, one needs an appropriate, readily recognisable 'Thai' form for it. That form, therefore, has to be old, venerable, immutable and hence, by the same token, rather useless, irrelevant and fossilised in present-day circumstances. Such is the standard form of almost all advertisements, official or private, related to the government's designated Year to Campaign for Thai Culture, as well as most public displays and individual expressions on this theme. This can be clearly seen in the Ramkhamhaeng students' Thai-Thai ads above. Most of the signs with which they chose to signify Thainess in their ads are of this character.

For example, television and public ads aside, the Thai traditional dress, the Thai classical dance and the Raja Pattern clothes cannot be seen anywhere else but in a museum, theatre, or Buddhist temple on special occasions only. Thai-Thai games are hardly ever played by most urban Thai youths, or they stopped playing them long ago when their parents took them away from the rural villages. Generally speaking, a Singha appears only either on a bottle of Singha Beer or on the logo of the Ministry of the Interior, 'the least just and honest government agency', according to the findings of a recent opinion poll commissioned by the Ministry itself.[25] Military parades and prowess have become less and less relevant to Thai national security and political stability since the collapse of the Thai communist rural insurgency in the early 1980s, the end of the Cold War at the end of that decade, and the middle-class uprising against military rule in May 1992. As to Thai banknotes and citizen's ID cards, they can of course be found everywhere but have become less of a necessity of late. For those 1,700,000 credit-card holders in Thailand (as of early 1995, with a 42 % annual growth rate), Thai banknotes are indeed rather cumbersome options.[26] And unless one needs to deal with government agencies (in which case a citizen's ID card is requisite), credit cards can serve the purpose of self-identification just as well. Actually, it serves that purpose even better in business establishments as it helps identify your class, income, purchasing power, lifestyle, etc., something a simple *citoyen/ne*'s ID card can never do due to its inherent egalitarian ideological bias.

Verbally and articulately symptomatic of the pseudo-chemical sublimation of Thainess is a statement made by Mr. Anand Praphaso, on behalf of a group of eight Thai painters named *Klum Nimit* (or The Creation Group), on the occasion of the opening of the exhibition of their collection of paintings called '*Thai Nimit*' ('Thai Creation') at Landmark Plaza Hotel in Bangkok on 17 March 1994. Anand wrote:

In the age of turbulent cultural currents, no one denies that *every Thai has to be able to lead his life amidst the growth and prosperity of a modern society.* Every morning, we wake up to find a confusing, chaotic and systematic (sic) way of life in which we cannot afford even a moment of mistake otherwise everything will fail. Modern Thai society has made us into a heartless robot. People's hearts become hardened day by day. We have no time to review who we are, where we come from. In the future, children will think that a home is a square box, that squids are brown strings, while *longan*s are in cans ...

All of us always accept that the comfort of present-day popular ways of life is a good thing that should not be rejected. But we call on every Thai to spend five or ten minutes daily reviewing one's own role and way of life, asking oneself what we are doing and whether we have *forgotten* what actually is the meaning of the word 'a Thai'. Is it not high time that *each and every one of us revived the spirit of being a Thai?* Is it not high time that each and every one of us refused to lead a life of a brainless robot *without any feeling for the spirit of Thainess?*

The *Nimit Group* has created the collection of their works of art called '*Thai Nimit*' partly in order to contribute towards *the arousing and awakening of the consciousness of being a Thai* so that it may *come back in the form of 'Thai Mai' (New Thai), which is in harmony with modern society.* We hope that our collection will contribute towards *linking up Thainess with technology smoothly.* We hope that the children will know what is Thai art, what is a Thai, and that a modern Thai must be 'a genuine Thai'.

Every painter of the *Nimit Group* creates his/her works of art in his/her own style based on a commonly-held concept to present *the Thai-Thai way of life* so as to communicate the rationale according to his/her own individual character. Therefore, there is no limit as to the techniques and methods of presentation.

Every painter will *project his/her mind into 'Thainess' in his/her own consciousness and then refine it into a work of art in his/her own individual style.* This is our commonly-held concept. Thus, '*Thai Nimit*' is a diversity in harmony *with the spirit of Thainess.*[27] (My translation, emphases added)

The news report features a sample of their collective effort to spiritualise, purge, subjectivise, and project Thainess back into a solid image or sign of their desire, i.e., a painting of a young Thai male in traditional northern Lanna Thai princely dress, with all the awkward trappings of ancient royalty.

215

Commodities' penetration of Thainess and other nationhoods

Thus, pseudo-chemically sublimated Thainess is returned to us in a solid but useless, irrelevant and fossilised, or mummified form, in a temple, theatre or museum. And this is as it should be for now that Thainess has been ripped away from its traditional, historical, theatrical or religious context and deprived of its aura, it becomes an empty shell, a neutral terrain, a free-floating signifier which can be entered into and 'exited' at will by commodities of whatever nationality or ethnicity. Thus, apart from Coke – the promoter of the value of Thainess – we have, in this official Year to Campaign for Thai Culture, such Thai-Thai advertising campaigns as 'Singha Beer – the pride of the nation',[28] 'Thai Life Insurance – the life insurance company of, by, and for the Thais',[29] 'Central Department Store – the Thai Store',[30] and so forth.

No matter how spurious their claims to Thainess may be seen to be under scrutiny, the fact that these commodities have indeed been turned into signs of Thainess has changed Thainess willy-nilly into one identity option among many others in the free market of a limitless plurality of commodities and/or brand names, in the same sense that Coke is just one option among many other brands of cola, Singha Beer is just one option among many other brands of beer, Thai Life Insurance is just one option among many other life insurance companies, and Central Department Store is just one option among many other department stores. By dint of association with, or signification by commodity signs, Thainess has become, alongside Chineseness, Europeanness, Englishness, etc. another choice among a variety of national/ethnic signifiers to be worn or shed according to the fluctuations of their respective cultural value.

Some more examples will help clarify, or perhaps further complicate, this point. Daewoo Corporation, a world famous South Korean automobile manufacturer, marketed its Fantasy and Espero sedan models in Thailand under the 'Daewoo sells Europeanness' concept in early 1994.[31] Coca Restaurant, a well-known chain of Teochiu 'suki' restaurants in Bangkok, which also bakes and sells Chinese cakes, released a radio spot to advertise its *CoCa Moon Cakes* (sic) during the 1994 Chinese lunar festival. It featured a bilingual conversation between a mother who speaks Thai and a son who speaks impeccable and fluent American English (with no Thai translation) about 'the best moon cake' she wants him to buy for her on this occasion.[32] Lipton, a brand of instant English tea, came up with a TV commercial in which an old bearded Chinese Kungfu master, when asked by a young disciple as to the secret of serenity, makes him a cup of Lipton tea as the answer.[33] So here we have Korean cars assuming a European identity, Chinese cakes assuming an American English identity, and English tea assuming a Chinese identity. The perfect illustration of this reduction of stature, uniqueness and aura, or this profanation of nationalities and ethnicities as they become mere commodified identity signs is the following advertisement:

Breakfast: **CHINESE.** *Lunch:* **FRENCH.** *Dinner:* **CHINESE.**
Breakfast: **ITALIAN.** *Lunch:* **CHINESE.** *Dinner:* **CHINESE.**
Breakfast: **GERMAN.** *Lunch:* **CHINESE.** *Dinner:* **JAPANESE.**
Breakfast: **ITALIAN.** *Lunch:* **CHINESE.** *Dinner:* **FRENCH.**
Breakfast: **AMERICAN.** *Lunch:* **ITALIAN.** *Dinner:* **AMER-ICAN.** *Breakfast:* **GERMAN.** *Lunch:* **JAPANESE.** *Dinner:* **FRENCH.** *Breakfast:* **JAPANESE.** *Lunch:* **GERMAN.** *Dinner:* **JAPANESE.** *Breakfast:* **AMERICAN.** *Lunch:* **CHINESE.** *Dinner:* **FRENCH.** *Breakfast:* **ITALIAN.** *Lunch:* **CHINESE.** *Dinner:* **FRENCH.** *Breakfast:* **GERMAN.** *Lunch:* **JAPANESE.** *Dinner:* **AMERICAN.** *Breakfast:* **FRENCH.** *Lunch:* **CHINESE.** *Dinner:* **AMERICAN.** *Breakfast:* **CHINESE.** *Lunch:* **FRENCH.** *Dinner:* **AMERICAN.** *Breakfast:* **ITALIAN.** *Lunch:* **CHINESE.** *Dinner:* **GERMAN.** *Breakfast:* **ITALIAN.** *Lunch:* **ITALIAN.** *Dinner:* **FRENCH**
Tired of the same old thing?

Put some spice into your life.
Tandoor
The Essence of India
Holiday Inn CROWNE PLAZA
For Reservations call 238-4300 ext. 4364[34]

One may as well say: '*Tired of the same old* **Thai** *thing?*'

But, alas, the Tandoor advertisement provides only a horizontal perspective of the profanation of nationalities/ethnicities whereas, apparently, profanation works vertically too. This point is made monetarily plain by the varieties of Chinese moon cakes on sale in Bangkok this year. Looking identical from the outside, these deep brown cubes with Chinese characters imprinted on the top are categorised according to their different inner fillings. And given the increasingly fierce competition in the 400-million baht worth moon-cake market, their filling categories have been multiplied in recent years from just a few to around a dozen so as to appeal to a wider range of consumer groups. Thus, those with traditional Chinese fillings such as *Ngo Ying* (or Five Kinds of Nuts) cost about 40–50 baht (approximately 2 US$ at 1994 exchange rate) each. The ones with Thai-Thai sweetened *durian* fruit fillings, especially of the famous *Mon Thong* (or Golden Pillow) variety, are priced a little higher at 60 baht (about 2.50 US$) each. But the most expensive of them all, fetching about 70–80 baht (or 3 US$) apiece, contain 'American' fillings, with such exotic names as *Khaeliffornia* (sic) and *Hawaii*.[35] While the comparative cultural value of Thainess *vis-à-vis* Chineseness and Americanness in this particular instance is monetarily clear, the definite national/ethnic identity of a *Khaeliffornia* or a *Mon Thong* moon cake is much harder to specify. When a greedy buyer munches on it, is it Chineseness, Thainess, or Americanness that is being consumed? Seemingly, nationality/ethnicity is now solely and arbitrarily in the eyes of the consumer.[36]

Commodities' self-penetration

Nationality and ethnicity having been loosened and unravelled thus far, it is now possible for commodities to take the next logical step, i.e., unfasten their tie with the national altogether, and create an identity of their own under the sign of their respective brand names. The following are a few examples of commodity-constituted identity being offered for prospective identity consumers to hold onto and identify themselves with amidst the flux of globalised commodity consumption.

Carlsberg Beer presents itself to Thai consumers as the globalised beer with the slogan 'the same taste all over the world', offering an imaginary world-wide identity and community of Carlsberg Beer drinkers that cut across all geopolitical barriers and cultural differences, against the Thainess advertising campaign of Singha Beer.[37] Tri Petch Isuzu Sales Co., Ltd. presents a sports utility vehicle imported from Japan as the identity sign of its prospective buyers in these words:

> You've reached the top: it's up to you to make the big decisions, the ones that count. Your achievement is the realisation of everything that people think of when they hear the word success, and your position is one that everyone aspires to attain some day. Now your life is full of new and bigger challenges. And when you move out into the world to experience the special exhilaration that comes with leadership, you drive a car that reflects **your identity** as someone who is modern, successful, and ready for anything – **an Isuzu Trooper**.[38]

To the seemingly endless and meaningless collective suffering of nameless, faceless, and powerless drivers in Bangkok's world-notorious suffocating traffic jams, Volvo offers itself as a symbolic difference and relief:

> Outside the Volvo it's hot, noisy and polluted. Inside the Volvo it's cool, very quiet and very, very comfortable. The Volvo Executive is an island of luxury and tranquillity in a sea of impatience and discomfort. Of course, everyone knows that Bangkok's traffic is getting worse by the month. And even a Volvo, with its deep leather seats, auto air-conditioning, CD player and stretch-out legroom, cannot make the traffic jams any shorter. But they certainly seem shorter. Thank goodness, I'm in a Volvo.[39]

And last but not least, the same message is said in not so many words by this advertisement, which offers a special credit card membership to prospective or actual owners of a luxurious car:

You know who I am.
Tell them who you are with the Mercedes Card.[40]

No longer a Thai, a Thai-Thai, or even an un-Thai, but simply a Mercedes person.

Conclusion: a bird's-eye view of postmodern Thainess

Since the collapse of the communist bloc, and also the May 1992 anti-military uprising in Thailand, there has been a palpably rapid and drastic change in the signification and communications of the Thai national identity, or Thainess, from the omnipotent, essentialist Subject of Thai political culture, which was created, dominated, controlled and manipulated by the conservative-royalist and later authoritarian-militarist official nationalism of the Thai state, into a changeable, malleable, reimaginable object of cultural politics in the hands of an increasingly wider range of rival, independent socio-economic and ethno-cultural groups in civil society, especially the Sino-Thai middle class.

On the basis of data drawn from popular and commercial culture in Thai mass electronic and print media, such as advertising, pop songs, TV drama, poems, etc., as well as state discourse on the issue, I detect a trend towards:

1   the unanchoring of Thainess from its racial grounding, militarist-statist grand narrative and anti-communist discourse;
2   ethnic de-essentialisation, linguistic and cultural pluralisation, and symbolic commodification of Thainess and,
3   middle-class reimagination of the Thai national community versus the state's resistance to it, and concomitant attempted conservation of the Thai state identity.

Let me outline current transformations in the essential components of Thainess, or symptoms of postmodern Thainess, I have seen:

Race: from the past dominance of the pure Thai race (*luk thai*) to the present popular cult of and infatuation with the Caucasian-Thai half-breeds (*luk khrüng*), and the coming-out-of-the-closet and celebration of the Sino-Thai (*luk cin*);

Language: from the past dominance of the standard official Thai lexicon, spelling, pronunciation, accent and script (the Royal Institute's authorised Thai language dictionary) to an infiltration, intrusion and proliferation of teenage slang, unofficial coinages, indifferent and deliberate misspellings and pronunciations, fashionable and marketable oft-feigned Western accents, self-assertive and sometimes feigned local accents, foreign Western and Chinese words, and transliterations of them in Thai scripts;

Monarchy: from the inviolable sanctity and aura of the monarchy, and the unquestionable and unspeakable taboo of *lèse majesté* to the popular profanation and commercialisation of the monarchy, and the uncontrollable, politically-motivated, underground and public, oblique and explicit reproduction of lèse majesté;

Nationalism: from the state's right-wing anti-communist imperialism and the middle-class' left-wing anti-Western imperialism to right-wing anti-Western imperialism and the middle class' unperturbed accommodation and incorporation of global commodities and culture in their non-militaristic, non-statist, non-rural reimagination of the Thai nation;

Buddhism: from anti-communist and anti-revisionist official Buddhism, and anti-capitalist radical Buddhism to the preponderance of commercial Buddhism (*phuttha phanit*) and the boom in the amulet industry and trade;

Naming: from a 50-year old decree dictating that the name of a person acceptable for official registration must not exceed three syllables, be sex-specific and spelt according to the Thai official dictionary to a recent decree allowing a name of five syllables and containing no sex-specific or spelling requirements as well as the widespread use of pseudonyms in the media and entertainment circles.

The state has responded to this change with typical stock-in-trade conservative and reactionary measures: the 'Speaking Thai Clearly' (i.e., with the standard official accent) campaign in the state media and educational bureaucracy, the designation of 1994 as the Thai Culture Promotion Year. All in all, it sticks to the mythological Thai past, invokes and parades museum and theatre culture to try to keep intact pure Thainess, and its own cultural authority.

Last question: why 'postmodernisation of Thainess' instead of simply liberalisation or pluralisation? Because I regard this transformation of Thainess as going in a postmodern direction. This is not a modernist process in which one essence, one truth, one reality, one history, one subject, one order and one language of Thainess are replaced by another set of the same kind of identity entities, but rather a decentring of these entities, an unanchoring of referential poles, a decline of cultural authority, a de-essentialisation of national identity, a clearing of ethno-ideological space, a liberation of national identity signifiers, a collapse of linguistic boundaries, an influx of commodities-as-signification units, and a resultant semiotic chaos. A growing number of well-educated and affluent Thais are busily and self-assertively asking themselves, and arguing with one another aloud in public, about who are the Thais and what is Thainess, while paying less and less heed to the standard cliché-ridden answer pushily and continually trumpeted at them by the state cultural authority via the state electronic media.

Postscript: the consumption of Thainess during economic crisis

The years 1997–1998 have witnessed the worst economic crisis in Thailand since 1929. With the collapse of the real estate, stock and financial markets, estimated 8 % economic shrinkage, up to 50 % currency depreciation, widespread business and consumer bankruptcies, at least two million unemployed workers, double-digit inflation and probably chronic stagflation, and the IMF's programme of economic austerity in place, the Thai-originated, euphemistically-called 'tomyam kung disease'[41] has spread far and wide, especially in East Asia. As a result, questions have been raised in the Thai media as to its impact on consumerist culture in general, and the commodification as well as consumption of Thainess in particular. Would instant poverty and withered purchasing power somehow help alleviate the Thai middle-class public's infatuation with global commodities and Western consumerism? After all, how can one possibly 'be' a Mercedes or a Volvo if one is not able to purchase it?

Well, not quite so. Since consumerism as a cultural phenomenon is relatively autonomous from economic production and consumption, it is possible that in times of economic crisis the latter may contract while the former still resiliently persists. There is no compelling economic reason why consumerism, as the consumption of commodities primarily for their cultural or sign value as against either their use or exchange value, should not continue to prevail even in a society made increasingly poor and unequal by an economic slump. With less money to burn in their pocket and their credit cards cancelled, our jobless and bankrupt aspirant consumers may not actually be able to afford a Mercedes or a Volvo. And yet they may go on desiring and fantasising about it while awake, remaining slavish if happy prisoners of the shopping mall, the advertising media and the consumerist dream visually virtualised there. Perhaps nothing short of the wholesale bankruptcy of the print and electronic media would release them from the sweetened shackles of consumerism, or so it seems.

It is precisely, alas, in this spirit of resilient consumerism in the face of crisis ('Let's consume, come what may!') that Thainess is now being commodified and consumed. Generally speaking, Thainess, as the all-purpose free-floating signifier, has recently had its residual nationalist signifieds and referents renewed. In response to the freshly mounted official 'Thais Help Thais' and 'Thais Buy Thai' campaigns, not a few locally-made products have suddenly metamorphosed into Thai. For example, an age-old, down-market soap bar whose brand name is *Nok Kaeo* (i.e., Parrot) has newly been advertised, in an all out, aggressive and highly successful (in terms of consequent increased sales) campaign, as a symbol of national independence against domineering and dictatorial *farang*s or Westerners (read IMF), with such catchy and striking slogans as '*Lang cai hai pen thai thae*' (Wash your heart so that it becomes genuinely Thai). However, throughout all those long years when this cheap, greenish and peculiar-smelling *Nok Kaeo* had been my parsimonious Teochiu father's choice as the family soap bar, it never struck me as having anything particularly Thai about it. And last but not least, a local whisky that adopted the English brand name of 'Black Cat' from the start is being advertised in a TV spot by a supposedly 'Scotsman' piper complete with bagpipes, traditional Scottish dress and all. After playing a brief introductory tune of pipe music, he then launches himself into a reflective and stirring monologue in Thai as follows:

> (Speaking proudly) Talking of whisky, it should come from Scotland since that was the birthplace of the popular Scotch whisky. (A sudden change of mood, now talking softly and despondently) But in the current economic condition of Thailand, I, as a whisky producer, would like to recommend those Thai drinkers of foreign whisky to turn to Thai spirits instead. (Another sudden change of mood, eyes brightened up and shouting cheerfully and enthusiastically) Black Cat, Black Thai, Hurrah!

Thus intoxicated by Thai spirits, Thai consumers drink on . . .

Notes

1 An earlier version of this paper was presented at the seminar on 'Problematising Culture: Media, Identity and the State in Southeast Asia' organised by the Institute of Southeast Asian Studies at the said institute's premises in Singapore in November 1994. The author would like to thank the ISEAS' staff, the seminar participants and other readers of this paper for their inspirational initiative and encouragement, financial support, and stimulating ideas and comments, especially Yao Souchou, Diana Wong, Chua Beng Huat, Ben Anderson and Coeli Aphornsuwan.

   As to the title of this chapter, a less elliptical and trendy if rather cumbersome alternative than the one being used here would be: 'Solid Thainess Melts into Air . . . and then Solidifies Again into Signs: National Identity and the Consumption of Identity Commodities in the Age of Cultural Globalisation'.

2 It is a long-standing and popular Thai linguistic practice to double an adjective so as to lessen the effect or intensity of its meaning. Thus, *daeng* is supposed to be redder than *daeng-daeng*, which is not very red. Likewise, whereas *Thai* implies a singular, pure, genuine, authentic, original, definite, narrow and monolithic version of Thainess, *Thai-Thai* connotes a pluralistic, mixed, mutant, altered,

simulated, indefinite, broad and differentiated version of the same. For example, one usually applies the adjective *Thai-Thai* to foods, drinks, tastes, dresses, atmosphere, etc., but never to nation, country, people, armed forces, government or king which remain *chat thai, prathet thai, khon thai, kòngthap thai, ratthaban thai, phramahakasat thai*. While *Thai* suggests a clear-cut division, disparity and even opposition between Thainess and un-Thainess both in their material existence and ideal essence, *Thai-Thai* indicates internal differentiation, blurring of external borderlines and shades of Thai-Thainess. Suffice it to say that *Thai-Thai* seems to admit a far greater and wider membership of people and things into its club than the rather exclusive *Thai* counterpart.

3 *Phucatkan raiwan* (28 April 1994: 22). The English version of this advertisement, with basically the same message but in a more concise and less colourful rendering, was published on the same day in *Bangkok Post*, p.2.

4 Being shown on Thai TV at the time, these two Japanese film series were especially popular among kids and youngsters.

5 Presumably, the name of a massage parlour in Bangkok at the time. Modern massage parlours, in contrast with traditional Thai massage, began to sprout in Bangkok during the 1960s and quickly gained popularity and notoriety as upgraded brothels. It was then a common practice among massage parlours' proprietors to give their establishments an exotic Japanese-sounding name like *Sayuri* or *Sakura* which by no means necessarily implied any Japanese ownership or connection. The actual origin of this peculiarly Thai cultural association between massage by female masseurs, on the one hand, and Japaneseness, on the other, remains doubtful.

6 Supposedly, a Japanese rendering of the question in the preceding line. The name of the bohemian friend who 'returned' this long-lost poem to me is Mr. Suphachai Jaroensakwatthana. The newspaper article in which he found it quoted is Banyat Surakanwit (1983). The poem itself was originally published in *Thairat*, 17 December 1972.

7 See cassette tape jacket information (1984).

8 '*Ce* n. food without fish or meat for Vietnamese or Chinese who observe a religious rite, also *cae*. (Chinese)' (my own translation). See *Photcananukrom ratchabandittayasathan phò sò 2525* (1987: 238).

9 See Wilaiwan (1994: 219–319).

10 In this regard, it is noteworthy that a favourite gimmick among Thai singers is to adopt a foreign stage name (e.g. Honey, Chen Chen) but keep the surname in Thai or local dialects (e.g. Sri-isan, Bunsungnoen, both of which are distinctly Laotian).

11 In this regard, see Suehiro (1992).

12 *Phucatkan raiwan* (1994, 1 November).

13 Quoted in Naisbitt (1994: 19).

14 I owe this fruitful insight to Donald M. Lowe's (1993: 280–285) perceptive analysis of the workings of the late-capitalist commodity in his 'Postmodernity and postcoloniality'.

15 See Mark C. Taylor and Esa Saarinen (1994: 4–5).

16 Although the official English rendering of *pi ronnarong watthanatham Thai* is Thai Culture Promotion Year, I prefer the Year to Campaign for Thai Culture version, coined by Professor Craig J. Reynolds of Australian National University, which is more literal (*ronnarong* = campaign) and retains the activist connotation of the original Thai.

17 *Thairat* (1993, 30 December).

18 *Thairat* (1993, 15 December).

19 *Thairat* (1995, 14 February). A not so subtle insinuation of lesbianism in their relationship by the *Thairat* reporter is distastefully evident.

20 Emphatically not 'internalisation' for reasons that will soon become apparent.

21 A superb telepathic allegory of this spiritualisation of Thainess emerged on another similar occasion, namely a TV and radio spot contest on the theme of the Year to Campaign for Thai Culture, jointly organised by Office of the National Culture Commission (a government agency under the Ministry of Education) and Robinson Department Store. The top award in the radio spot category was won by a team of five students from Chulalongkorn University whose entry was entitled *Mun khloen phit* (or Wrong Tuning). They explained the concept behind their work as follows:

> Suppose a kid turns on a radio, tries tuning in to every possible programme and then finds only Thai classical music ... That is well nigh impossible. But if we tune our mind, that is our feelings and spirit, then we can receive Thai classical music and love Thai classical music. We can be tuned in together and don't have to depend on other things around us including mass media. (My translation)

See *Siam Post* (1994, 18 May).

22 Reeya 1994, p.16–19; also see the front cover and contents page of the magazine. By the way, remember Mr. Billy Ogan, the famous pop-singer and idol of Thai teenagers quoted earlier? His new music album, in which he intended to mix in Thai cultural issues, has finally been released in mid-1994. Entitled *'Billy banloelok'* in Thai and 'Billy World Class' in English, the album features a lead song with the title *'Sawatdi rap yo'* (or 'Good Day Rap, Yo'), the most 'Thai-Thai' song in the album, whose lyrics were written by a Mr. Bunliang Angkaew and reads partly as follows:

> If you want to rap dance, let's do it but don't forget to preserve Thai-Thai things. Associate with Westerners but don't forget that you are Thais ... (My translation)

See cassette tape jacket information (1994).

23 Quoted in Reeya (1994: 18)

24 Quoted in Reeya (1994: 19).

25 The survey was conducted by Integrated Partners, a private company, among 1,200 people throughout the country from 1 to 19 November 1993. As it turned out that the overall public perception of the Ministry was strongly negative, the Ministry typically decided to suppress the findings for fear that its reputation would be further tarnished. See *Bangkok Post* (1994, 9 June: 1); and *Matichon raiwan* (1994, 9 June: 1, 13).

26 *Phucatkan raiwan* (1994, 18 July); and *Bangkok Post* (1995, 15 February).

27 *Phucatkan raiwan*, (1994, 22 February).

28 See the reports on the advertising and marketing campaign of Bunrod Brewery Company, the producer of Singha Beer in *Phucatkan raiwan*, 9 December 1993, p.25, 26; and especially the perceptive, tempting and intoxicating comparative analysis of the advertising strategies of Singha Beer vs. Carlsberg Beer by Issara Choosri (1993). It should be pointed out in this regard that Thais are well aware of the un-Thainess of beer as an alcoholic drink originally brought in from the West. There is not even a Thai coinage for the word 'beer', only a foreign-sounding transliteration. It is in this cultural context that Singha Beer chooses to present itself to the public as the pioneer in beer-brewing in Thailand, and therefore a proud sign of Thainess.

29 A TV advertising spot released in 1993 made the point that among the variety of insurance companies, Thai Life Insurance was chosen 'well, because I am after all a Thai', so said the male character in the ad to his wife. And yet, this Thai life insurance company had been founded in the 1940s by such Chinese business tycoons as Lo Tek Chuan Bulasuk, Tan Chin Ken Wanglee, etc. See Kasian (1994a).

30 Launched on 6 July 1994 by the top executives of Central Department Store themselves, all dressed up in traditional Thai style, the campaign was said to be partly an adaptive management reform in the wake of the liberalisation of Thai retail businesses as a result of GATT and AFTA, and partly a participative response to the government's Year to Campaign for Thai Culture. Needless to say, the Chirathiwat family, which owns this biggest chain of department stores in Thailand, is originally Hainanese of the Zheng clan. Also, this Thai-Thai store has adopted an English name since its founding. Of course, their Thai Store campaign has become rather problematic in the present context of global capital and multinational (Thai and un-Thai) business alliances in Thailand. See Phoemphol (1994: 29–30).

31 *Phucatkan raiwan* (1994, 28 January).

32 MCOT (Radio FM 96 MHz) 1994

33 MCOT (TV Channel 9) 1994

34 A close replica of the original advertisement in *Bangkok Post*, 8 June 1994, p.27.

35 *Phucatkan raiwan* (1994, 29 August); also see Kasian 1994b.

36 ... or of the worshipper. I distinctly remember two occasions when I found this to be the case. The first one happened in 1993 when I visited the famous Mangkorn-kamalawas or Leng Nei Yi Chinese Buddhist temple in the Chinatown area of Bangkok during the *kin ce* festival. I overheard, while viewing a religious exhibition, a Chinese Buddhist monk explaining to two Chinese women in white *kin ce* dress that originally the *Quan-yin* (*Kwan-im* in Thai) Goddess in Chinese Buddhist popular mythology had been an ethnic 'Indian' but was later Sinicised by the Chinese. One of the women looked perplexed and asked impatiently: 'Well then, is she actually Indian or Chinese after all?' To her the monk replied: 'What she is depends on the faith of the worshipper. It's the same thing with a Buddha image. The Chinese make it look Chinese while the Indians make it look Indian'. Four years before that, I had a lengthy argument with a group of Thai students in Cornell on a similar topic, i.e. the nationality/ethnicity of Jesus Christ. I suggested to them the possibility of a Jesus Christ turning black, perhaps after being Africanised by some Negroid worshippers in Africa, a possibility which they flatly denied. Alas, it's a pity that at the time I hadn't yet read page 10 of Carlos Fuentes' stupendous *Terra Nostra* (1987).

37 Issara (1993: 35)

38 *Bangkok Post*, 26 July 1994, p.15.

39 One may as well say: 'Thank goodness, I'm a Volvo'. (*Bangkok Post Economic Review* 1994: 5).

40 *Bangkok Post*, 15 August 1994, p.13.

41 *Tomyam kung* is, of course, the world-famous Thai shrimp soup flavoured with lemongrass, kaffir lime and chilli paste.

References

Newspapers

> *Bangkok Post*
> *Matichon raiwan*
> *Phucatkan raiwan* (Manager Daily)
> *Siam Post*
> *Thairat*

Works cited

Bangkok Post 1994 (Advertisement for ASA's annual seminar), p.2, 28 April.
—— 1994 (Advertisement for Tandoor Restaurant), p.27, 8 June.
—— 1994 'Opinion poll without results', p.1, 9 June.
—— 1994 (Advertisement for Isuzu Trooper), p.15, 26 July.
—— 1994 (Advertisement for Mercedes Benz), p.13, 15 August.
—— 1995 'Firms still rushing into Thai credit card market', p.19, 15 February.
Bangkok Post Economic Review (Mid-Year) 1994 'Thank goodness, I'm a Volvo', p.5, 30 June.
Banyat Surakanwit 1983 'Khwamsamphan thai-yipun: phapphot thi mai plianplaeng' (Thai-Japanese relationship: the unchanged image) in *Matichon raiwan*, 2 May.
Cassette tape jacket information 1984 *Made in Thailand*, Carabao, Bangkok: Ligo, C-27106.
Cassette tape jacket information 1994 *Billy World Class*, Billy Ogan, Bangkok: Onpa, 90-002.
Fuentes, Carlos 1987 *Terra Nostra.* (translated by Margaret Sayers Peden), New York: Farrar, Straus and Giroux, Inc.
Issara Choosri 1993 'Lokanuwat nai kaeo bia' (Globalisation in a glass of beer), p.35 in *Phucatkan raiwan*, 17 August.
Kasian Tejapira 1994a 'Comphon Plaek: phunam ratthaniyom Thai' (Field Marshal Plaek: Thai statist leader), p.56–59 in *Sinlapa watthanatham* 15(3).
—— 1994b 'Thatsana süksa watthanatham tòn pai thiao Hua Chiao' (Cultural study tour: visiting Hua Qiao)', p.8 in *Phucatkan raiwan*, 26 September.
Lowe, Donald M. 1993 'Postmodernity and postcoloniality', p.280–285 in *Positions*, 1(1).
Matichon raiwan 1994 'Poei phon wicai mahatthai, kromthidin-tò rò huai sut' (Opinion poll on Interior Ministry revealed, Lands and Police Depts. are the worst), p.1, 13, 9 June.
MCOT (Radio FM 96 MHz) 1994 'Coca Moon Cake', Bangkok, 4 September.
MCOT (TV Channel 9) 1994 'Cha Lipton, ik khan khòng khwam sukhum' (Lipton tea, a higher level of serenity), Bangkok, 4 September.
Naisbitt, John 1994 *Global Paradox: the bigger the world economy, the more powerful its smallest players*, London: Nicholas Brealey.
Phoemphol Phophoemhem 1994 'Khwam pen thai khòng senthan' (Central's Thainess), p.29–30 in *Phucatkan raiwan*, 8 July.
Phucatkan raiwan 1993 '60 pi Bunrot brewery, spirit khòng phu riroem' (Bunrot Brewery at 60, a pioneer's spirit), and 'Bunrot toem ik 600 lan' (Bunrot invests another 600 million baht to control the beer market for the next 10 years), p.25–26, 9 December.

—— 1994 'Daewu khai khwam pen yurop' (Daewoo sells Europeanness), p.36, 28 January.

—— 1994 'Nithatsakan "Thai nimit" pluk khwam pen Thai hai khün chip' (The 'Thai Nimit' exhibition: the revival of Thainess), p.10, 22 February.

—— 1994 (Advertisement for ASA's 1994 annual seminar), p.22, 28 April.

—— 1994 'Batkredit bum sutkhit, baen chi mai düng ngoenfoe' (Credit cards are booming but not causing inflation, the bank says), p.1–2, 18 July.

—— 1994 'Rao nen kanphalit baep dangdoem kap khanom wai phracan khòng rao' (We stress the traditional method in producing our moon cakes), Interview of Ms. Patchari Kesònthammakittiwut, manager of Shang Palace Restaurant, Shangrila Hotel, p.29–30, 29 August.

—— 1994 'Müa fat sifut baep Thai Thai ca su haem-kai sanchat nòk' (When Thai-Thai Fast-Seafood is going to fight ham-chicken of foreign nationality), p.29–30, 1 November.

Photchananukrom ratchabandittayasathan phò sò 2525 (1982) (The Royal Institute's Dictionary, B.E. 2525), Bangkok: The Royal Institute.

Reeya Chaicharas 1994 'The future face of Thailand's Ads?', p.16–19 in *The Sunday Magazine* (*Bangkok Post*) 20 (25 September–1 October).

Siam Post 1994 'Sü spòt thorathat lae witthayu: sing sathòn watthanatham nò sò Thai' (TV and radio spots: reflections of Thai students' culture), p.11, 18 May.

Suehiro, Akira 1992 'Capitalist development in postwar Thailand: commercial bankers, industrial elite, and agribusiness groups', p.35–64 in Ruth McVey (ed.) *Southeast Asian Capitalists*, Ithaca, NY: Cornell Southeast Asia Program.

Taylor, Mark C. and Esa Saarinen 1994 *Imagologies: media philosophy*, London: Routledge.

Thairat 1972 Sakda Jintanawijit, 'Khaniyom' (Values), p.9, 17 December.

—— 1993 '*Khita yip chin pla man khwa Billy*' (The Khita company catches a big fish, getting Billy), p.21, 15 December.

—— 1993 'Ann khan rap faetschan hit, anurak, buat chiphram (Ann responds to fashionable hit, preserve (Thainess), take vows as Brahmin nun', *Thairat*, p.21, 30 December 1993.

—— 1995 'Makha-walenthai kop-tui swit sangop khao wat tham bun nunghom khao' (On Magha Puja-Valentine's Day Kop and Tui sweetly and calmly go to the temple to make merit and wear white frocks), *Thairat*, p.14, 14 February.

Wilaiwan Khanisthanan 1994 'Laksana phasa thi chai phan sümuanchon thorathat' (The character of language used in TV mass media), p.219–319 in *Thammasat wichakan: nüang nai wara khrop ròp 60 pi haeng kansathapana mahawitthayalai thammasat* (Thammasat scholarship: on the occasion of the 60th anniversary of the founding of Thammasat University), Bangkok: Academic and Research Affairs Department, Thammasat University.

PART IV

Remembering, Social Memory, and History

■ CHAPTER NINE ■

Social Memory as it Emerges

A Consideration of the Death of a Young Convert on the West Coast in Southern Thailand

Ryoko Nishii

The objective of this chapter is to reconsider the question of the relationship between social memory and individual experience. This raises the issue of what is meant by a 'society' that can preserve social memory. I would like to approach this problem by focusing on the emergence of social memory as the memories themselves are precipitated during social processes.

Halbwachs (1950) in his work on collective memory, held that genuine individual memory does not exist. He argued that each unique individual memory occurred at intersections within the collective memory of groups. One central weakness of Halbwachs' discussion is that it is based on the premise that there is an entity called society which preserves memory. But how does society preserve a particular memory? Obviously, individuals acquire memories in the course of interaction with other people in groups to which they belong. No-one lives their life in a socio-economic vacuum. In Halbwachs' discussion, on the other hand, every memory comes out collective: the collective, or society, appears to have its own memory. Within this, individuals seem to accept passively and automatically the collective memory of the society. With this static view of memory, Halbwachs provides no means for envisaging the creative and dynamic processes through which social memory emerges in the course of social interactions among people.

In this chapter, I will try to elucidate some of the processes that lead to the emergence of social memories using the events subsequent to the death of a young convert from Buddhism to Islam. The main events of this incident occurred in October 1994 during fieldwork I was undertaking on the west coast of Southern Thailand.

The setting

According to government statistics, Muslims account for 4% of the population in a country in which 95% are Buddhists. The southern

231

provinces account for 73% of the Muslims, especially the four border provinces on the Malay peninsula, where Muslims make up 60–80% of the total population of each province (*Kromkan satsana* 1993). Most studies on Muslims in Thailand have focussed on the problems of the southern border provinces, especially on the political issues with regard to national integration. These studies tend to characterise Muslims as a minority group that speaks a different language and that possesses a different culture. Looking at the details on the ground, however, it soon becomes clear that the Muslims in Southern Thailand are not all the same. They actually fall into two broad groupings: there are the Malay-speaking Muslims on the eastern coast, Pattani, Narathivat, and Yala, where Islamic political movements are most active; and there are the Thai-speaking Muslims in the province of Satun on the west coast, where few political problems have arisen involving Muslims; these are the Muslims that the Thai government regards as a model of Thai nationals adhering to Islam, which is evidence of the co-existence of religions in a Buddhist country.

My fieldwork was conducted in a village on the west coast in which the population was about equally divided between Muslims and Buddhists, and where both groups speak the same Southern Thai dialect.[1]

In the village, about 20% of marriages are intermarriages between Muslims and Buddhists. This percentage indicates a very high rate of inter-religious marriage in comparison to other areas in the region with both Muslim and Buddhist populations. For example, in 1985 Winzeler reported that 3.1% of marriages were intermarriages between Muslims and Buddhists in a Kelantan village in Malaysia (Winzeler 1985: 116–117). Chavivun also states that there are few inter-religious marriages in Pattani on the east coast in southern Thailand (Chavivun 1982: 79–80). Besides this, intermarriages on the west coast show another extraordinary characteristic: either partner may convert to either religion because of marriage. In other words, there are cases where Buddhists convert to Islam in line with their spouses, and converse examples of Muslims converting to Buddhism may also be found. Elsewhere in the border region, such as on the east coast of Southern Thailand or Northern Malaysia, there are few cases of conversion connected with intermarriage, and, in all the reported cases, the Buddhist has converted to Islam and not the other way round.

In the intermarriages on the west coast, villagers say that 'husband and wife must be of the same religion'. In the village I studied, even after conversion due to intermarriage, converts can maintain contact with their parental families who are, subsequent to marriage and conversion, of differing religions On the other hand, Muslims also hold that conversion is a major sin in Islam. The logic of conversion in the face of this is that the prescription that 'husband and wife must be of the same religion' is more dominant in social consciousness than the idea 'conversion is a sinful deed for Muslims'. Furthermore, while Buddhists do not regard conversion as a sinful act, they also insist that, in an intermarriage, one of the conjugal pair must convert to Islam or Buddhism, so that both husband and wife share the same religion.

By analysing the events concerned with the death of a young convert to Islam, I would like to offer an explanation of behaviour which is idiosyncratic to this area. In the course of trying to cover this issue, I hope that I can shed some light on the processes by which social memory emerges, and then becomes shared among people.

Outline of the incident

During my fourth short field trip in October 1994, a young convert named Tak[2] died at the age of 29 years old. That day, he played football. In the evening, he said he had a little headache. Though it was usual for him to have headaches, his death seemed sudden to everyone around him.

He was a medical officer stationed at the public health centre and, to profess the same faith as his wife, who was a teacher of Islam, he had converted from Buddhism to Islam. Tak's death is memorable because of the religiously motivated tussle between his wife and his mother over his corpse.[3]

Tak died at about four o'clock in the morning in an official lodging on the second floor in the elementary school where his wife, Da, was a teacher. When he died, only Da was with him. By the time Tak's relatives arrived, it was nearly nine o'clock and Da had already begun preparing her husband's dead body for a Muslim burial. The first relative to get there was Tak's younger brother, Sit. Da said that because she had already bathed the corpse in the Muslim way, non-Muslims could not touch it. Sit persisted against her objections and pulled back the cloth covering his elder brother's body. Tak's mother later explained to me that Sit only did this because he loved his brother and wanted to see him. When Tak's father came, he asked Da to give Tak's corpse to Tak's mother. Tak's family felt that they could ask for the body because Da and Tak had only married three years previously and they still had no child. Da did not assent to giving up the body. She said, 'I could not let them have his corpse because he had converted to Islam and died as a Muslim. If I had let them take him away, I would have been committing a sin'.

Faced with Da's determination, the Buddhist relatives of Tak resorted to a ruse. They said that a postmortem examination should be carried out at the hospital to determine the cause of death. Da still refused to let them take the corpse away, and finally the Buddhists on Tak's side of the family removed Tak's corpse by force and put it in a car. Da also came along, and she brought 4,000 baht (about one month's salary for her) that she thought would be needed for examination expenses. On the way to the hospital, the car came to an intersection where, instead of turning right towards the

233

hospital, it turned left. The journey ended at the home of Tak's parents, and his body was carried into his mother's house. Da's Muslim relatives were late on the scene because they lived further away than Tak's relatives.

Da told me that she could not stand staying at her mother-in-law's house with all of the Buddhist relatives weeping and showing their emotions. Some of them also accused her of being somehow responsible for Tak's death.[4] Consequently, she returned to her parents' home. She was so upset that she could not work the following week. During this time, she consulted the Satun Provincial Islamic Committee, she contacted a teacher at the Islamic school that she had graduated from, and she asked her uncle in Pattani for advice. She was told that her final resort would be to bring the case before the Islamic court.[5] However, her Islamic teacher recommended she should negotiate quietly instead of taking such a forceful measure. The Provincial Islamic Committee went to Tak's mother's home to negotiate the return of the corpse, even though the weeklong Buddhist funeral rites had already proceeded about halfway through their course. Da's uncle in Pattani also telephoned the crematorium that had been booked for Tak's cremation, asking them if they dared to cremate the body of a Muslim.

Despite these efforts, Tak's body was cremated on 21 October 1994, seven days after the corpse had been forcibly taken to the maternal home. After the cremation, each side of the relatives performed rites to make merit for Tak; Tak's widow in the Islamic way and Tak's mother in the Buddhist way.

Varying accounts of the incident

There are various ways of accounting for the unusual turn of events concerning what happened after Tak's death. The determining factor lies in the different funerary practices of Muslims and Buddhists, and I will deal with these first. After that, I will examine the discourses that reveal how these religious practices are perceived. Finally, I will discuss the balance of power in the relationships around the dead person.

Burial as a Muslim or cremation as a Buddhist

The Muslim and Buddhist relatives came into direct opposition over the way of dealing with the corpse. Muslims bury dead bodies and Buddhists cremate them.[6] People contrast the different ways of dealing with a corpse as between *tham khaek*[7] (burial as a Muslim) and *tham thai* (cremation as a Buddhist). This makes it essential to determine the religious affiliation of the person after death.

Of course, it is too simple to say that Islamic and Buddhist funerary rites are solely confined to the physical method of the disposal of the body.

234

In Islamic practice, the corpse must be buried within 24 hours. Tak's mother said that Muslims do not wait for the relatives to meet the dead person for one last time, as Buddhists do. The Muslims, for their part, say that Buddhists leave the body laying around until it starts to rot and smell.

Some of the Muslim villagers have a similarly negative view of other Buddhist practices, as evidenced by their censure of the motives of Tak's mother for pursuing such drastic measures to get hold of the body: they say that she wanted to profit by conducting a Buddhist funeral. The Buddhist custom is to serve food for those who come to pay their last respects, and these callers usually make a monetary contribution towards merit-making for the dead. In the case of Tak's funeral, according to a merit-making list kept at his mother's home, during the seven days before cremation, 211 people visited and donated money totaling nearly 32,000 baht. On the other hand, this motivation was not alluded to by any Buddhist. From my investigations of other Buddhist funerals, income from contributions and the expenses incurred are generally about the same, in some cases expenses exceed the income.

Another Muslim criticism of Tak's mother is that she coveted Tak's property, such as his refrigerator and television. She denies this, saying that she did not bring anything from Tak's lodging except for some of his clothes. When they first took Tak's body home, it was covered only with a sheet of cloth around his waist. During his fatal bout of illness, Da took off Tak's clothes because he was sweating so much. Then, when he had died, Da bathed the body in the Islamic way and covered the naked corpse with a sheet of white cloth. Buddhists, on the other hand, put the deceased's finest clothes on the dead body and Tak's mother wanted to do this for the funeral. She made Sit, Tak's brother, go to Tak's lodging to get Tak's clothes. Unfortunately, as the mother tells the story, Da was so upset that she could not find her keys. Consequently, Sit had to climb up to the second floor to enter the lodging from the window. Muslim villagers who saw this started the rumour that Tak's brother broke into the house and carried everything away.

Here we can see that the difference in the ways that the two religions handle funeral arrangements and rites were an obvious source of tension between the two sets of relatives and, more broadly, how events came to be interpreted by those of different religious affiliations.

Dying as a Muslim or as a Buddhist

Tak's wife and Tak's mother hold differing opinions about his religious affiliations. Another contrast is between *tai khaek* (dying as a Muslim) and *tai thai* (dying as a Buddhist).

Da asserts Tak died as a Muslim. During his final illness, she said that he himself recited the passage of the Qur'an, 'There is no God except

Allah.' This passage is also the one recited in swearing adherence to Islam, and is typically repeated many times daily by Muslims. When Tak could not speak, Da recited it for him. Da said that although it was true that he sometimes drank alcohol and did not go to the mosque, it did not mean that he was not Muslim. It meant only that he committed sinful acts. The important thing for her is that he swore to adhere to Islam and died in the faith.

Tak's mother takes a different view. To her way of thinking, cremating Tak as a Buddhist has led to a more meritorious fate for her son. She says that because Tak did not pray at the mosque, drank alcohol, and even ate pork at her home, if he was buried as a Muslim he would be in a state of sin. That is why she insisted on cremating Tak as a Buddhist, and why she wanted to make merit for him.

These two versions correspond well with the Islamic and the Buddhist way of regarding a person's religious affiliation. When intermarriage takes place, if one of the couple swears to adhere to Islam, the couple are regarded as Muslims; if they do nothing, they are regarded as Buddhists. In Islam, a ritual is required to delineate Muslim and non-Muslim, but in Buddhism no ritual acknowledgement is necessary to demonstrate allegiance.

In daily life in the village, the distinction between Muslims and Buddhists, however, is not always an important matter. Here some explanation of the religious ideas of Muslims and Buddhists in the village will throw some light on this. I have already mentioned that Muslims and Buddhists speak the same Southern Thai dialect.

They also explain their primary religious concepts with the same terms, *bun* and *bap*. *Bun* may be translated as merit. They say that they try to enhance *bun* for a meritorious future in this life and in the afterlife. The opposite term is *bap*, which may be translated 'sin' or 'sinful deed'. The most popular phrase which people use to account for good and bad deeds is 'one will reap the fruits of one's own actions' (*tham di dai di, tham chua dai chua*).[8] Both Muslims and Buddhists say that every religion teaches what is good, and that to know religion is to know *bun* and *bap*. They say that the teachings in Islam and Buddhism are the same. The only difference between them is in the means employed to make merit. Ordinarily *bun* and *bap* are typically used in the teaching of Buddhism. But here we can find that Thai-speaking Muslims also use the same terms as Buddhists to explain their own religious acts. Muslims in the village also seem to accept these karmic ideas. Many of them also believe in reincarnation. Sometimes it is said that a Muslim is reborn as a Buddhist. So Muslims and Buddhists can be said to share the same religious concepts, which are focussed on the ideas of *bun* and *bap*.

This is not to say that the Muslims only nominally adhere to Islam, that essentially they are similar to Buddhists. They put the accent in different places in their interpretation of the same terms. For example, some Muslims think that conversion is the most sinful deed possible for Muslim, but no Buddhist thinks of conversion as sinful.[9] The attitude of the Muslims is highlighted by the explanations that Da and the Islamic committee give for their acts. They say that they tried to get back Tak's body in an effort to avoid sin. According to their Islamic beliefs, Tak was Muslim, consequently the widow and committee were obliged to bury Tak as a Muslim. If they gave up the corpse without trying, it would be a dereliction of their religious duty. They said that as long as they did as much as they could to get the body back and carry out the obligation, they would incur no sin.

The relationship with the dead

The death of Tak, a convert, threw into relief tensions latent between the relatives of differing religious affiliation. In the village, as in many other Southeast Asian societies, kinship is cognatic. There is no tendency toward either paternal or maternal descent. Where the couple live after marriage depends on the particular circumstances of each family. Usually the couple set up an independent household, but they also often set up home near the parental families and maintain close relationships during daily life. It is not unusual for children to be left under the care of grandparents. After marriage, neither set of in-laws is disregarded. Inter-religious marriages, however, do show a tendency towards closer ties with relatives of the chosen religion of the household. I have also seen cases of re-conversion, which sometimes happens when a household moves to another village where the parents of the other religion live. In other words, sometimes conversion is a social convenience to better match the relatives who live nearby (Nishii 1989).

Tak's case, however, had a number of ambiguities, including a difficulty in ascertaining which side maintained a closer relationship with the couple. This is an important aspect of the incident that ensued after Tak's death. Tak had converted to Islam following his wife, but his Buddhist relatives lived closer than the Muslim relatives, and kept in closer contact during daily life. Tak's mother often visited her son's lodging and stayed overnight two or three times a month. There was a discrepancy in the selection of religion and the balance of influence that the relatives exerted on the household.

The root of the ambiguity, however, was the couple's childlessness. Tak's mother said that if they had had a child who could make merit for Tak, she would not have taken his body away. Tak did not have a child, and if his wife married again, there would be no-one to make merit for him. The issue of whether one has a child or not points up the importance of merit-making for the dead. Both the Muslims and Buddhists mentioned this aspect, and the Buddhist villagers, even the Buddhist relatives, agreed that if the couple had had a child, the Buddhist side should not have taken the corpse. The couple's childlessness was a precondition for the mother to take the drastic measure of snatching the corpse.

This indicates the crucial importance of having a child to transfer merit to a deceased person. This relationship has priority over other relationships. In the case of Tak, the lack of this determining priority gave free rein to a power struggle between the proponents of the husband-wife and mother-child ties, each insisting on their own priority over the other.

Why do 'husband and wife have to be the same religion'?

At this point I would like to consider why 'husband and wife have to be the same religion'. In the village, they emphasize that married couples, to ensure the transfer of merit to the dead, must decide one way or the other. After the Tak incident occurred, the consensus of both the Muslims and the Buddhists was along these lines; 'Tak cannot go either way. His legs are torn in two directions; one towards Islam, the other towards Buddhism. He cannot get into either a temple or a mosque. We do not know how to make merit for him.'

From this, it can be said that securing a means to transfer merit to the dead is required to maintain the relationship between the dead and living. Among the various merit transfer relationships possible, the most important one is between the deceased and the children of the deceased, and, if the two spouses have different religions, this would cause complications and confusion. This is avoided by having household consistency in religion: parents have the same religion and children follow the religion of their parents. The question, 'Why do husband and wife have to be same religion?' could be answered, 'To ensure that their children follow the same religion and so secure a posthumous means of merit-making'.[10]

One year after the death

In October 1995, I visited the field again, one year after Tak's death. I was surprised to find out that, soon after the cremation, Tak's mother visited Tak's wife. In 1995, Tak's mother told me that she was staying with Da once or twice in a month, just as she used to do when Tak was alive.

At the anniversary of Tak's death, however, the mother made merit for Tak at the temple and the widow made merit according to Islamic tenets. Once, when Da made merit at her parents' house, Tak's mother went along and Tak's sister gave money to Da to make Islamic merit for her brother. Here it seems obvious that the Buddhist relatives of Tak are trying to mend their damaged relationship with Tak's widow. They say that any form of merit-making will enhance the merit of Tak.

A year after Tak's death, I met another young convert, this time from Islam to Buddhism, the new wife of Sit, Tak's brother.[11] The bride told me that she felt she had to make her religion clear, because otherwise, 'It might cause an incident like that after Tak's death'. At least Tak's death has become meaningful as a cautionary tale about the necessity of maintaining good Muslim-Buddhist relationships.

Concluding remarks: Tak's death as social memory

In the village there are two terms that can be translated as religion. One is *satsana*, which refers to knowing *bun* (merit) and *bap* (sin): it is a human quality that both Muslims and Buddhists share, a contrast is made here with beasts, who do not know *bun* and *bap*. Another word for religion is *phasa*,[12] which refers to the different practices peculiar to each religion. When discussing matters pertinent to the relationship between Muslims and Buddhists, villagers freely used these two terms depending on motivation, situation and occasion. Once, they used *phasa* to clarify the difference between Muslims and Buddhists. On another occasion, they used *satsana* to emphasise the commonality of Muslims and Buddhists as human beings. The relationship is not fixed: it changes according to the situations that crop up in everyday life.

We have looked at some of the various discourses surrounding the events after Tak's death. These play the defining role in creating the social memory of the events that make up the incident. During the first stage, the incident revealed the latent tension between Muslims and Buddhists concerning funerary practices, that is, the differences in *phasa*. As the incident was played out, various aspects of the events became apparent. Individual justification for her deed seems to lie behind Tak's mother's assertion that her Buddhist merit-making for Tak is somehow more meritorious. But this discourse shares the premises of the one put forward by converts, when they say that merit can be made in any religion. The logic is one that denies the difference between the religions. The Tak incident here is interpreted in the shared social discourse and emerges as a social memory about the coexistence of Muslims and Buddhists. At the third stage of the incident, villagers said that Tak's fate was such that he was torn and could not go anywhere because merit was being made in two ways. This conclusion corresponded with anxieties apparent in the discourse of Sit's new wife. The memory has come to reinforce the notion that wife and husband must share the same religion, which once again reveals the compromises made to achieve the coexistence of Muslims and Buddhists. On the one hand, Muslims and Buddhists share religious ideas focusing on *bun* and *bap*. On the other hand, there are differences in practice between Muslims and Buddhists. In a locality where inter-religious marriages are not uncommon, the best way to secure posthumous merit transfer is to ensure that children follow the same religion. In this way, conversion of one of the spouses is one of the compromises that supports the coexistence of Muslims and Buddhists sharing daily life in the same village. The memory of the Tak incident has become social memory in a society where Muslims and Buddhists are co-resident.

This incident, however, does not provide a fixed single memory. I have presented various discourses about the interpretation of the events, which taken together, form the incident: enough of the logic and interpretation of the significance of various aspects of the incident show that the memory of it is not confined to individual experience. People, by acting and by expressing their opinions about events, interact and give form to various social discourses as shared memories. If at a later date another aspect of the discourse is emphasised by an individual, and others agree with the emphasis, this aspect of the memory will be revealed. That is, the memories are multi-faceted. Different memories coexist in a way which permit ambiguity in discourse. In Tak's case, the ambiguity, while initially the source of conflict, is resolved. However, it is resolved not through the triumph of one side over another, but by the perpetuation of the ambiguity, so that both sides may remember the dead on their own terms. Remembered ambiguity is reproduced within the resolution of conflict which permits the coexistence of Muslims and Buddhists in this society without religious conflict in daily life. In this chapter, I attempted to convey some of the dynamics of the processes which lead to the emergence of social memory.

Finally, I would like to tentatively answer what is meant by a 'society' which preserves social memory. It is a society in which people who share some understanding of a discourse about the meaning of social processes interact with each other. But the society includes remembered ambiguity, which permits different memories to coexist. It cannot be a substantialised entity that is fixed and static.

Notes

1 My first fieldwork was conducted for sixteen months during 1987–88. Three subsequent two-month visits, to the same village, followed in 1989, 1991, and 1994.
2 This and all the names of villagers' that appear in this chapter are pseudonyms.
3 The cause of his death is not known because his corpse was not examined at hospital. I did ask about the cause of Tak's death and received some explanations; one of them is that Tak took *ya sang* which causes a person to die when one take specified food usually not poisonous such as banana and pineapple. At that point people were more concerned with what would happen to the corpse, and there were no other rumours that I heard about, except that there was a tug-of-war over his corpse between his wife and his mother.
4 The causal agency being witchcraft.

240

5 In the four border provinces there are Islamic courts. In these courts Muslims have the right to petition to *kadi* (a judge in Islamic court) concerning marital matters and property matters.

6 In the case of sudden death such as Tak's, Thai Budhists sometimes bury the dead temporarily (Keyes with Anusaranasasanakiarti 1980; Keyes 1987). But in this area, except for some Buddhists of Chinese descent who bury their dead, cases of sudden death such as an accident or a murder during my field research were cremated like ordinary cases.

7 *Khaek* and *Thai* are not hierarchical categories in this area. They indicate only the difference between religions. Muslims call themselves *khaek* as well as Buddhists (see Diller 1988). By contrast, the term *khaek* in Central Thailand has discriminatory (insulting) connotations, such as designating persons from India, Pakistan, the Middle East, Africa, Malaya, Java (Haas 1964).

8 In English, this is familiar as 'you reap what you sow' or 'what goes around comes around'.

9 On the other hand, most converts from Islam to Buddhism insist that because every religion teaches what is good, it does not matter in which way they make merit.

10 Of course, converts by marriage cannot make merit for their parents. In that case, they would be able to ask relatives who are of the same religion as their parents to make merit in their stead and provide them with the items and money required to do this. In fact, I have not come across any such cases. However, there are cases when parents convert following the conversion of their children. For example, there is a mother who had converted to Buddhism from Islam who converted back again when one of her children converted to Islam from Buddhism by marriage. Because she now has a Muslim child, she can secure an Islamic means of merit-making. Consequently, she was able to convert back to being a Muslim without anxiety concerning her posthumous merit-making relationship.

11 Sit had divorced his first Muslim wife who had converted to Buddhism. She later converted back to Islam.

12 *Phasa* is usually understood as 'language' and 'speech' in standard Thai. But we find another meaning of *phasa* in several dictionaries; it is identified as *prasa* (way, manner) (Bradley 1873; Haas 1964; Pallegoix 1896). In Southern Thailand, they explain the meaning of *phasa* as tradition (*prapheni*) or to do, act, perform, practice (*patibat*). *Phasa* is commonly used in the terms '*phasa khaek*' and '*phasa thai*' to designate the religious practices of Muslims and Buddhists. Usage of these terms in designating 'religion' is parallel to Burmese usage whose Pali origins are identical with Thai. Houtman (1990) discusses the two types of Buddhism as *bok-da' thathana* (the real teachings of the Buddha) and *bok-da' ba-tha* (inherited Buddhism, Buddhism-as-culture). Spiro (1970) translates these as 'the doctrine of the Buddha' and 'the worship of the Buddha' respectively. However, the meanings of these Thai terms are different from Burmese in that Thai *satsana* can be used for non-Buddhist religions, for which the Burmese *tha-tha-na* is not used.

References

Chavivun Prachuabmoh 1982 'Ethnic relations among Thai, Thai Muslim and Chinese in South Thailand: ethnicity and interpersonal interaction', p.63–83 in D. Y. H. Wu (ed.) *Ethnicity and Interpersonal Integration*, Singapore: Maruzen Asia.

Bradley, Dan B. 1873 *Dictionary of the Siamese Language*, Bangkok: Rongphim Khurusapha Latphrao.

Diller, Anthony V.N. 1988 'Islam and Southern Thai ethnic reference', p.153–167 in A.D.W. Forbes (ed.) *The Muslims of Thailand* vol.1, India: South East Asian Review Office.

Haas, Mary 1964 *Thai-English Student's Dictionary*, Stanford, Cal.: Stanford University Press.

Halbwachs, Maurice 1950 *La memoire collective*, Paris: Presses Universitaires de France.

Houtman, Gustaaf 1990 'How a foreigner invented "Buddhendom" in Burmese: from *THA-TA-NA* to *BOK-DA' BA-THA*', p.113–128 in *Journal of Anthropological Society of Oxford*.

Keyes, Charles F. 1987 'From death to birth: ritual process and Buddhist meanings in Northern Thailand', p.181–206 in *Folk* 29.

Keyes, Charles F. with Phra Khru Anusaranasasanakiarti 1980 'Funerary rites and the Buddhist meaning of death: an interpretative text from Northern Thailand', p.1–28 in *Journal of the Siam Society* 68(1).

Kromkan satsana (Department of Religious Affairs) 1993 *Raingan satsana pracampi 2536* (Annual Report on Religion in B.E. 2536), Bangkok: Kromkan Satsana.

Nishii, Ryoko 1989 'Minami tai no gyoson ni okeru musurimu to bukkyoto no tsukon' (Intermarriages between Muslims and Buddhists in a fishing village of Southern Thailand), p.51–112 in *Kikan jinruigaku* (Quarterly Journal of Anthropology) 20(4).

Pallegoix, D.J.B. 1896 *Siamese French English Dictionary*, Bangkok: Printing-Office of the Catholic Mission.

Spiro, Merford E. 1970 *Buddhism and Society: a great tradition and its Burmese vicissitudes*, New York: Harper & Row.

Winzeler, Robert L. 1985 *Ethnic Relations in Kelantan*, Singapore: Oxford University Press.

■ CHAPTER TEN ■

Remembering/Silencing the Traumatic Past

The Ambivalent Memories of the October 1976 Massacre in Bangkok[1]

Thongchai Winichakul

About two o'clock in the morning of 6 October 1976, police and raging paramilitary groups co-operatively surrounded Thammasat University, where four to five thousand people had gathered peacefully all night to protest the return of one of the former dictators ousted three years earlier by a popular uprising in 1973. Shortly afterward, gunfire from personal handguns was heard from time to time, and self-made explosive devices were thrown into campus buildings occasionally throughout the night. It was a tense morning, two weeks after two activists had been hanged while putting up protest posters, and only hours after a student theatrical skit re-enacting the hanging had been accused by the military, in a public broadcast, of staging a satire of the hanging of the Crown Prince in effigy. Students were never given an opportunity to rebut this charge by exposing the flaws in the accusation.

At 5.30 a.m. a rocket-propelled bomb was fired into the crowd inside Thammasat. It was reported that four were killed instantly and dozens injured. That bomb signalled the beginning of the non-stop discharge of military weapons which lasted until about 9 a.m.[2] Anti-tank missiles were fired into the Commerce building which by then sheltered a third of the crowd. Outside the university, after the besieging forces had stormed into the campus, they dragged some students out. Lynching began. Two were tortured, hanged and beaten even after death on the trees encircling Sanam Luang (or Phramen Ground), the huge public space that separates Thammasat from the Grand Palace by only a two minute walking distance. A female student, chased until she fell to the ground, was sexually assaulted and tortured until she died. On the street in front of the Ministry of Justice, on the other side of Sanam Luang opposite Thammasat, three bodies, alive but unconscious, were piled up with tyres, soaked with petrol, then set alight. These brutal murders took place as a public spectacle. Many of the onlookers, including young boys, clapped their hands in joy.

243

Inside the university, apart from the unknown number of casualties from weapons, more were lynched. A student leader, Jaruphong Thongsindhu, a friend of mine, was dragged along the soccer field by a piece of cloth around his neck. Later, six corpses were laid on the ground for a man to nail wooden stakes into their chests, as if they were Satan, as seen in foreign films. According to the police, forty-three people were killed, and several hundred wounded. According to other sources, the number of deaths may have been as many as a hundred. The number missing, if any, was unknown. According to the police, only two policemen were shot dead (*Khadi prawattisat* 1978: 81–83).

It was a Wednesday morning in which the deaths by gunshot seemed to be the least painful and most civilised of murders.

What happened on 6 October 1976 was the culmination of an ongoing process of political polarisation since the 1973 uprising. The increasingly radicalised student movement had expanded significantly but became more isolated from the non-radical populace, while the military and the right-wing movements, capitalising on the popular fatigue with students' relentless demand for drastic changes, became more confrontational and violent (Morell and Chai-anan 1981: 161–176, 235–252, 276). The public were first worried then scared off by the polarising politics and violence. They gradually turned away from both confronting forces. This deprived the left wing of popular support, a vital element for the radical student movement. Meanwhile, military propaganda had dehumanised the radical students, labelling them 'scum of the earth' (*nak phaendin*), the enemy of the nation, the religion and the monarchy (*sattru khòng chat, satsana, lae phra mahakasat*), or lackeys of communist aliens (mainly of Vietnam). A right-wing monk asserted killing of leftists was not considered a religious sin, since it killed the Evil One (*Mara*) (Keyes 1978: 153). In retrospect, the eradication of the radicals and the return of military rule seem to have been inevitable. Yet, that ugliest of Wednesday morning's was far beyond any Thai might have anticipated that any human could do. Our morals and political optimism had held our imagination in check. But reality is never kind. That morning's stark events remain incomprehensible to many people's minds.

A case of silenced history

The massacre at Thammasat in 1976 was a traumatic event. As this chapter will show, it was deeply disturbing but still remains unresolved, having a lasting impact on individuals and on society. It needs explanations, a resolution, or closure in some manner that will help individuals and society to come to terms with the past. Conflicting memories and politics have, however, prevented a resolution, perpetuating the self-doubts, possibly guilt, and perhaps moral dilemma among many of

244

the individuals who were involved. If the mission of history, a body of knowledge, is to recover the truth of the past, how can history deal with the traumatic past such as that of the 6 October event?

Unlike many well known traumatic incidents, for example like the holocaust or the Cambodian genocide, about which thousands of survivors have made their personal memories public, the 1976 massacre in Thailand has so traumatised our society that for twenty years there has been a silence about the event. Perhaps, given that the number of people who were personally involved was relatively small, the Thammasat massacre can be compared to the 1968 massacre in Mexico City, or the 'two-twenty-eight' 1947 incident in Taiwan, as in these cases it took decades for the silence to be broken, and full accounts of the incidents have never been compiled (see Chin 1995 for Taiwan and Poniatowska 1992 for Mexico). As for the Thai case, apart from the limited number of people who were involved, this article will argue that there are other significant factors contributing to the ambivalence of individuals, as well as of Thai society as a whole, in confronting this traumatic past, thereby perpetuating the silence. This does not mean that the event had never been discussed in public until the commemoration in 1996. As a matter of fact, it had often been mentioned in the discourse about the development of Thai democracy. Nonetheless, vague or cryptic descriptions were the norm. Only in some student literature, especially the volumes in memorial of the two October events, has the massacre been dealt with more extensively (Bandit 1983; Bandit and Preecha 1985; Bandit et al 1986; Sirot 1991). Otherwise, there are only a few narrative accounts, or analyses, of the event in the Thai language.[3] On the other hand, short stories are the form in which the tragedy of the massacre has found fullest expression.[4] Discussions of the massacre have been vague, and evasive, while many aspects have been suppressed. No depiction has emerged that would settle the meaning of the event for those involved in it. 6 October 1976 is probably still beyond the means of any historical inquiry into the Thai past to deal with, bound by the reluctance of some of the participants to speak out about their experiences. Thus still today many of the details of those events remain enshrouded in reticence.[5]

This chapter is part of an effort to break the silence and, hopefully, to take the first steps in writing a history of this traumatic past. The original draft of this chapter, both in Thai and in English, was written for the commemoration of the 1976 massacre in 1996 (Thongchai 1996a, 1996b). The commemoration was a huge success in many ways, especially in having irreversibly changed the discourse about the event. The voices of the victims were heard widely as never before, making the event twenty years earlier recognised correctly for the first time as a crime of the Thai state against its people. Despite that, the break in the silence was, at best, partial and limited. Resistance and reluctance to settle the meaning of the event remain strong; the truth of that morning is unlikely to be written in the near future.

This chapter is thus not an attempt at a full account of the tragic incident. On the contrary, it explores the limits of the discourse about the massacre, which remain in place for Thais, and the factors or reasons why the search for truth has never been attempted. Why is it extremely difficult to get to the truth of the event while evasive memories and the silence surrounding the incident remain strong? The chapter argues, first of all, that the political ramifications of truth may be literally unthinkable for Thai society, since several individuals and institutions, which command power and respect in the society, might have been involved in the killing. The main part of this chapter, however, examines the complex trauma, guilt, and remorse suffered by both the culprits and victims in different ways. Moreover, the chapter argues the massacre does not fit the normative ideology in Thailand for the memorable past. In the context of this ideology, it resists comprehensibility and remembering. In other words, at least three forms of domination are at work in silencing this past: first, the threat of political repercussions; second, the sense of guilt whether of the perpetrators or the survivors; and third, the ideology of national history, which suppresses the 'anomalies', or pushes them into silence, leading to ambivalent memories, reflected in the handling of the controversial memorial of the 1973 and 1976 events. This chapter differs from the original version presented in 1996. There are substantial changes in light of the 1996 commemoration, which it integrates into the discussion, particularly its impact on the discourses and memories of the massacre.

I myself was a key participant in the incident as one of the student leaders who organised the demonstration. I witnessed those hours of carnage. I saw friends fall before my eyes. I was arrested on that Wednesday morning and was imprisoned for two years. I also initiated the 1996 commemoration and was involved throughout. Therefore, I may be one of the most appropriate persons, as a witness of history and a historian myself, to write a full account, at least from my own viewpoint and memory, of that morning. Contrariwise, I may be the least appropriate person to evaluate the event objectively. I pledge no impartiality in discussing the matters of this remembering/silencing of the traumatic past. But at the same time, as a historian, I strongly believe that the end of this silencing of the memory of this traumatic past can best be accomplished through the fullest telling of what happened from all sides and perspectives. What I intend to do to some extent in this chapter is possibly as much as any Thai can do in the near future. What follows draws on scholarly research, but will serve also as a commemorative writing from recollections, personal knowledge and information from contacts, and my own reflections.

The politically unspeakable

More than twenty years after the massacre, what happened on that brutal Wednesday morning and the whole conspiracy leading to it remain unclear. The massacre itself, and the right-wing regime that took office soon afterward, suppressed the discourse right away. As will be shown in more detail below, the public desire for reconciliation following the take-over of that repressive regime in essence has helped in perpetuating the silence as well. Curiosity and attempts to revive the issue, or any efforts to clear up the mystery, from this standpoint, are subversive attempts to undermine social unity. Even the commemoration in 1996 caused some concerns about being divisive.[6] The truth about October 1976 remains a sensitive issue for the Thai state.[7] Nonetheless, as we shall see, controversies have erupted from time to time concerning the massacre and the associated conspiracies. Those occasions, including the commemoration, however, only succeed in recognising that there were ugly murders by the state on that day, an obvious fact that has been difficult to speak out about for years, and which has not yet been admitted publicly by anyone in authority. Those altercations also expanded the limits of the discourse a little further every time, especially so in the case of the commemoration. Yet a lot remains unknown and beyond discussion. Limits remain.

The bottom line is the fact that many people in power over the past twenty years, along with some of the most important national institutions, could be implicated in one way or another with the massacre and the conspiracies surrounding the event. Here I will describe only a few immediate incidents that led to the killing in order to point to a number of unresolved mysteries and unsayable facts about who might have been involved in some way with the crime.[8]

After the last dictatorial regime was ousted by the popular uprising in 1973, from mid-1975 to September 1976 there were several incidents that signalled the conspiratorial attempts of the military to return to power. Then on 19 September 1976, Thanom Kittikachon, the ousted dictator who had fled to and taken exile in Boston since 1973, was brought back to the country. Thanom himself was in the yellow robes of a Buddhist novice, and pleaded in public that he had decided to become a Buddhist monk, abandoning the secular world of wealth and power, in order to show his sincerity in return to visit his dying father. There was, he claimed, no hidden political agenda. In retrospect, there is no question that Thanom's return was a well-planned conspiracy, one stone for two grandly prized birds, namely the end of the radical student movement and the fall of the elected civilian government. His father, in the event, died ten years later, while his renunciation of secular life lasted only for three months after the massacre. He left the monkhood in January 1977 and requested the return of his assets, which had been confiscated on corruption charges (*Sayam rat*

1977, news, 8–17 January). Who was involved in orchestrating Thanom's return? No investigation has ever taken place; no questions have ever been asked since then.

A security motorcade took Thanom directly from the airport to the Bowornniwes Royal Monastery, a widely respected temple where every king of the present dynasty since King Mongkut in the nineteenth century has been ordained. Being a novice upon arrival, Thanom was immediately ordained as a Buddhist monk by the abbot, one of the most respected monks in the country, who was the teacher of the present King while the latter was a monk in 1956. Later in 1987, moreover, this abbot was appointed the supreme patriarch of the Thai *sangha*. The monk who facilitated Thanom's ordination, known as Phra Maha Rabaep, was the abbot's secretary, and was an outspoken leader of an ultra-conservative Buddhist group, Pariantham Samakhom. One day after Thanom's ordination, the King and the Queen took a direct flight from the Southern Palace to Bangkok, and went straight to the Bowornniwes temple for a hasty private visit to the abbot and the new monk. In an unscheduled media interview at the temple, the Queen alleged that there were some people trying to destroy Buddhism in Thailand. She urged people to protect the religion and the Bowornniwes temple in particular. Although she did not name the enemy of Buddhism, there was no doubt that the radicals were in deep trouble.

It was a special ordination, one that was protected and legitimised by the highest possible moral powers in the land. In retrospect, it seems almost incredible that the two most important institutions of the country, the monarchy and the *sangha*, were part of this scheme. The involvement of the monarchy, especially the queen, in the pretext for the massacre has rarely been mentioned, and then only in a few publications in English (Morell and Chai-anan 1981: 270–273). But there was not, and probably could not be, an investigation into this matter. Nobody has asked about or raised this issue, or even mentioned these facts, since then. It remains a taboo in Thailand. During the commemoration in 1996, every organiser and participant fully realised that in order to preserve everyone's neck, one had to be aware of this limitation, and the likely consequences of violating it.

The special legitimation of Thanom's return was undoubtedly expressly intended to undermine the justification for the protest led by radical students. Despite that, several protests erupted in many provinces. The legitimation for Thanom's return also pre-empted the attempts by the elected government of Prime Minister Seni Pramoj who, given the unpredictable consequences if widespread confrontation erupted, were trying to solve the crisis resulting from the conspiracy by forcing Thanom out of the country again before a confrontation took place. On 24 September, two activists were hung while putting up posters against

Thanom's return in a provincial town near Bangkok. There was evidence of police involvement in the hangings. On 4 October, a student's skit re-enacted the hanging as a protest against police brutality, and against any attempted coup to return to military authoritarianism.

The immediate pretext for the massacre was a picture on the front page of the 5 October issue of a right-wing newspaper, *Dao sayam*, asserting that radical students had staged a mock hanging of the Crown Prince in effigy. *Dao sayam* was a tabloid mouthpiece of the extreme right-wing movement, and this newspaper had been calling for the crushing of the student movement all along. Its front page of that day stated unequivocally that the radicals were eager to destroy the monarchy. In a single stroke, the confrontation was transmuted: it was no longer about the return of dictatorship but had turned into a communist attempt to destroy the monarchy and the nation.

The truth of the photo remains unclear even up till today. Many people, including Seni and some of his cabinet members, believed that the photo had been doctored (*Matichon* 1979, news, 16 February). Seni noted very specifically that it was not simply a case of film doctoring, but a photo make-up that had then been re-photographed (*Khadi prawattisat* 1979: 429). If so, who did it? Did they anticipate the deadly consequences? A similar picture from the skit was also published on the same day in the *Bangkok Post*, a local English daily, which did not hint at lèse majesté at all. There were suspicions that the *Bangkok Post* and *Dao sayam* were participants in the same conspiracy involving the photo. Seni himself mentioned the photo he had seen in the *Bangkok Post*, not *Dao sayam*. It was to be twenty years before the editors of *Bangkok Post* finally spoke out in its 6 October 1996 issue, the day of commemoration, saying that they regretted the consequences of the photo but denying any conspiracy on their part. The photo was not doctored, they insisted, and the Post editors in 1976 did not detect anything unusual in that photo; thereby they had it published as a dramatic news piece ('Front page editorial'). It remains a mystery if the photo was an element in a well-planned conspiracy or was a starkly tragic accident.[9] In any case, the ways it was exploited as a pretext for the violent suppression of the students movement was definitely a well-executed scheme.

In the evening of 5 October, a massive number of the picture from *Dao sayam* was distributed throughout Bangkok, along with a polemical calling on the Village Scouts and other right-wing groups to rally against the students. They surrounded Thammasat in the middle of the night, and never allowed students any opportunity to disperse. According to Police Captain Akas Chompuchak, who was a prosecutor's witness in the 6 October trial in 1978, the Border Patrol Police (BPP) stationed at Hua Hin, about three hundred kilometres Southwest of Bangkok, received an order without explanation at 2 a.m. to rush to Bangkok. His regiment of

50–60 police, fully equipped with HK33s and 70–80 bullets each, travelling by a truck and jeeps, arrived in Bangkok around 6 a.m. (*Khadi prawattisat* 1979: 345–346). It is still not known who gave the order to the BPP since the government did not.[10] By 2 o'clock that night, so far as I can recall, the situation at Thammasat was tense, but there was no indication of a need for a troop showdown. Besides, there were no reasons for a particular force four hours away by road to be called in to operate in Bangkok. The BPP and the Village Scouts turned out to be the most deadly forces in the massacre (Bowie 1997: 28–29). Although there is no evidence, as there has never been an investigation, of the involvement of the monarchy in the massacre, it is well known that the BPP have a close relationship with the royal family (Lobe and Morell 1978: 169). The BPP was also instrumental in the creation of the Village Scouts (Bowie 1997: chapters 2 and 3). In fact every member of the royal family themselves was very active in the mobilisation of the Village Scout movement during that time (Bowie 1997: 82–86, 97–99, 108; Morell and Chai-anan 1981: 242–244).

It was not clear if, or how much, the Seni Pramoj government still had power at sunrise on 14 October. A group of student leaders including Sutham Saengprathum, the General Secretary of the National Student Centre of Thailand, agreed with a government mediator on a meeting with the prime minister to avert the tragedy. According to Sutham, they were temporarily obstructed by the police, then taken to the Prime Minister's residence. Upon arriving there, they were not allowed to get out of the cars. After some hesitation, probably due to changing politics, the police in these cars eventually took the student negotiators straight into custody. The meeting never took place (Sutham 1979: 37–43). What remains unclear is on just whose authority these critical negotiations were aborted.

Apparently, the government was slow in responding to the killing a few kilometres away because the development caught them by surprise, and they had their own crisis to solve. According to a cabinet member of the Seni government, the prime minister called for a special meeting that morning to declare a state of emergency (Surin 1986: 126). The purpose was to disperse all the gatherings, namely the students inside Thammasat, the right-wing groups outside it, and the Village Scouts and other groups who were demonstrating at the Equestrian Plaza in an attempt to dislodge the government. The cabinet members who opposed such a measure were the leaders of the Chat Thai party, Chatichai Choonhavan (the prime minister in 1988–1991) and Praman Adireksan (deputy prime minister in many governments from 1975–1987) (Surin 1986: 126; Wattanachai 1988: 144–145). They were against such a measure precisely because they wanted the Village Scout demonstration to proceed. Chatichai brought in Police General Charoenrit Chamratromran, Deputy Chief of the BPP and the co-founder of Village Scouts, to support his argument. Another police general, Chumpol Lohachala, came in tears to report to the cabinet that students were heavily armed, resulting in heavy casualties among the police. Charoenrit and Praman urged that it was the opportunity to eradicate the students and 'erase the name of the National Student Centre of Thailand', the leading student organisation. On the other hand, the National Police Chief, apparently not being part of the conspiracy, reported to the cabinet that no police were dead, and only a few were injured. The cabinet also learned that police had found only three light pistols among the demonstrators (Surin 1986: 126–127). Yet the government was indecisive. Even though they knew that the report of police casualties was false, the government issued a statement putting the blame on the students for the violence.[11] It did nothing else. Later that afternoon, the Village Scouts marched to Government House in order to demand the resignation of the alleged three 'communists' in the cabinet, among them Chuan Leekphai, who would become the prime minister in 1992–1995 and 1997–1999. The Village Scout demonstration was finally dispersed after the coup by the appearance of the Crown Prince at the Equestrian Plaza urging them to return home.

The military coup was formally announced at 6 p.m. Although the full story of the coup has not become public, it is believed that a faction in the military was involved in the scheme that led to the massacre, but the actual coup itself was led by another faction. It is still not clear if the latter faction was involved in the massacre, or if and how other co-conspirators in the morning massacre, like the people behind the Village Scouts and the BPP, were also party to, and benefited from, the evening coup. Nonetheless, the important fact is that many of these same people remained very powerful in Thai politics in the 1990s.

Last, but very importantly, so far there has been no official account of how the brutality occurred. Did the situation get out of hand? Were the police and right-wing groups in confusion, the right-wing crowd out of control, and the brutality unexpected? Or was it anticipated and planned? Did anybody try to stop it?

There is also an allegation that the Communist Party of Thailand (CPT) might have had its own conspiracy to end the urban radicalism abruptly in order to force students to join the armed struggle in the jungles. According to this hypothesis, the hanging skit and the photo might not have been accidental (Zimmerman 1976: 66–67).

> ... [T]he CPT had infiltrated the [student movement] leadership and chose to employ such an incident to engender just the kind of emotional reaction from the right that did occur on October 6. Party leaders could have reasoned that massive violence against the students rallying at Thammasat was exactly what was required to induce a sizeable number of potential student cadres finally to

reject parliamentary reform and join the party's revolution in the hills. This was indeed the result, though it need not imply that the hanging incident had been consciously staged by the CPT as a calculated move to anger the rightists.

(Morell and Chai-anan 1981: 282)

Furthermore, it was alleged that student leaders refused to disperse the crowd in order to let the killing happen.[12] It became common knowledge, which was even conceded by the military, that the CPT was the eventual beneficiary of the massacre. According to many student leaders who later met with the CPT leaders, the CPT acknowledged this and expressed satisfaction with what had happened. The alleged CPT conspiracy is, in my view, a wishful projection without substantial basis. It assumes the ability of the CPT to foresee and manipulate every step of the situation, which was otherwise unpredictable; such as that the skit that did not cause a single member of the audience to suspect that the act involved lèse-majesté (Puey 1977: 5) until the photo was published by newspapers, which were beyond the CPT's control; the siege by the police who were unable (or not assigned) to control the Village Scouts; the angry crowd which got out of control; the level of brutality which was unprecedented, and so on. In a sense, the allegation gives too much credit to the CPT for the success and/or failure of the radical movement during that period.

In retrospect, the CPT definitely played a crucial role in the increasingly uncompromising radicalism of the student movement, which contributed in terms of how the student leadership thought and made decisions in those sensitive situations. In the crucial moments, as far as I can recall, none of the student leaders had any way of foreseeing what was going to happen. A massacre remained theoretical, as they had learned from reading about the experiences of other student movements; any anticipation of a massacre was, at most though, very abstract. When it erupted, all of them were profoundly shocked and knew nothing of what lay ahead, let alone being participants in the alleged grand strategy of boosting the CPT's armed struggles.

It should be clear by now that the facts about the October 1976 massacre are abundant. They are definitely recoverable. Despite that, so far there has been no effort to investigate the incident and it is hard to place the blame precisely. First, there is unlikely to be sufficient evidence because it is unlikely that those who were involved will speak out. Second, suppose that sufficient evidence were gathered, the truth could be devastating to many individuals and institutions – the military, the *sangha*, and the monarchy – which command respect and control power in Thai society. Truth could lead to a political and social disaster, thereby also devastating those who try to get to the truth themselves. Silence is therefore mostly self-imposed, either out of fear or out of concern for the unthinkable consequences to the country. The traumatic events of 1976 lie in the realm of the unsayable. Its full history is impossible to write under the present system of 'Democracy with the Monarch as the Head of the State'.

But the reasons for silence are not the politically undiscussable ones alone. Over the years, given the changing political situation and the shifting discourses about the massacre, both the perpetrators and the victims of the event have become ambivalent and traumatised in different ways, which makes it difficult for them to break their self-imposed silence.

The perpetrators' ambivalence: from jubilation to shame

On the afternoon of 6 October 1976, 'Yan-krò', the radio station of the Armoured Division which on that day took control over the radio airwaves throughout the country, broadcast live interviews with a number of policemen who had stormed into Thammasat in the morning.[13] Police Commander Salang Bunnag of the Crime Suppression Police, one of the high-ranking officers who led the force into Thammasat, described the successful execution of the raid with jubilation. He and the programme host made fun of those students who had been beaten until they could not speak. They said those students must have been the 'Yuan' (the derogatory term in Thai for Vietnamese), otherwise they would have been able to speak. Then they laughed. The anti-Communist mania and the jubilation over the success on that morning blinded them and their audience, darkened their hearts, and dehumanised themselves as much as they had dehumanised the radical students by their repeated propaganda for more than a year.

After the massacre, in newspapers articles from October 1976 to January 1977, the event was usually called a 'riot' or 'disturbance', but never a massacre. The victims were further victimised; they were called rioters (*phu kò kan calacon*), rabble-rousers (*phu kò khwam wunwai*), communists, rebels (*kabot*), the deceived (*phu long phit*), or enemies of the Nation-Religion-Monarchy – the three pillars of Thai identity. They were criminals who had killed policemen at Thammasat, even though in fact the light police casualties might have been the results of self-defence or retaliation against the carnage. Apparently, they were both victims and criminals.

Over the years, however, the discourse on the incident shifted significantly in such a way that an involvement with the operation on that morning became grounds for utmost shame. Apart from several minor remarks, this was clearly reflected in two controversies relating to the massacre: first, the 6 October trial in 1977–78, and second, the Chamlong Srimuang case in 1988.

The 6 October trial

Among the three thousand students arrested at Thammasat on 6 October, nineteen of them were charged and put on trial in a court martial in September 1977, almost a year after their arrest.[14] I was one of them. After a year under the totalitarian government led by a staunch royalist judge, Thanin Kraivichien, the 6 October trial in 1977–78 gave the student supporters an opportunity to show their force, for it became a legitimate occasion for political gathering to attend the trial inside the military compound where the court was located. Several foreign governments sent their representatives to observe and assure the fairness of the trial. This increasing domestic and international pressure gave the opportunity for a counter discourse of the incident, in which the students were not rioters and definitely not criminals.

The political atmosphere had slightly opened up after the Thanin government was ousted by another coup in October 1977. A month later, a number of academics and civic leaders signed a petition calling for the amnesty of those on trial, followed by a similar action on the part of a hundred leading lawyers in the country, by Thais in the US and Europe, and by international governments and organisations. The main reason cited in calling for the amnesty was for national reconciliation (*Khadi prawattisat* 1978: 302–321; daily newspapers in 1978 from 23 November to 31 December). Meanwhile, the ongoing trial turned out to be a political threat to those who had been involved in the conspiracy, rather than implicating the accused. Not only did several prosecution witnesses fail to indicate any wrongdoing by the defendants, but the court martial also became the site where facts and truth emerged that pointed to the conspiracy, and the mystery surrounding the massacre. The public perception of the massacre had obviously shifted. As the trial went on, I remember the feeling among us, the defendants, that we were part of a judicial fiasco, which ironically had put the state on trial.

In September 1978, the government rushed through the amnesty bill, absolving everyone of any wrongdoing related to the incident on 6 October 1976. The purpose of the bill, as stated, was to close the rift in Thai society. Despite the immediate result of the release of all defendants of the 6 October trial, it was not hard to see that the real benefits of the amnesty went to the state, the police, and all the perpetrators, since the bill ruled out any possible trial in the future. The official announcement, as well as the amnesty bill, stated that the defendants had committed wrongdoing due to their inexperience but they had been detained long enough (*Khadi prawattisat* 1979: 415). The prime minister at the time, Kriangsak Chomanan, emphasised that the amnesty was granted by His Majesty and the Crown Prince. The released defendants should take to heart their royal kindness. He lectured us, and warned us 'not to repeat the mistakes' (*Matichon* 1978, news, 22 September).

In response to this official address, Sutham Saengprathum, the leader of the defendants, declared, 'We are innocent', a tacit implication that the real criminals had never yet been brought to trial. The released student leaders, who symbolically represented the student movement as a whole, were no longer outcasts, rioters, criminals, betrayers, or enemies of the nation. There were several celebrations for the released students at various campuses. In a sense, these celebrations propagated the counter discourse. The government intervened, ordering universities to cancel them, arguing that the celebrations might have led to confrontation with opposing groups, and that reconciliation could not begin to take place unless all sides and the public stopped talking about the incident, thus letting the 6 October case fade away (*Matichon* 1988, news, 22–27 September). This reflected a major discursive shift about the massacre. In the spirit of reconciliation, nevertheless, the government urged the public to forget and let the massacre melt away, with no fingers being pointed at the criminals. Like the amnesty bill, the government's stance ignored the perpetrators of the massacre and encouraged forgetting the whole affair.

After the amnesty, the discourse on the 6 October event was mixed. In general, the state tried to suppress any extensive exposure or discussion about it. Police confiscated and closed a newsmagazine, *Lok mai*, which published several pictures of the massacre for the first time in Thailand in 1979. Whenever the incident resurfaced in public, the authorities urged people to forget it in order to avoid social divisiveness (*Sayam mai* 1982, news, p.21, 16 October). Only in a few university communities was the massacre remembered differently (see the words by Thammasat's Rector, *Matichon* 1983, news, 7 October).

The Chamlong Srimuang case

Chamlong Srimuang was a retired army general and a former leader of the Thai 'Young Turks', a small group of powerful military officers who commanded crucial army divisions during the coups in 1976, 1977 and the failed coup in 1981 (Chai-anan 1982: 22–29). As a loyal follower of the Santi-Asoke, a Buddhist sect antagonistic to the *sangha* establishment, Chamlong later became highly popular for his reputation as an honest, uncorrupt, and moral politician. He was elected the Governor of Bangkok in 1986 in a landslide victory. Riding on his popularity, in 1988 he founded a political party, Phalang Dhamma (literally, the power of righteousness), whose platform was to clean up the corrupt politics. It was during the election campaign in July 1988 that the controversy erupted.

One of the candidates of Chamlong's party, Jongkol Srikanchana, stated in a public interview that while she had been the leader of a right-wing group at the demonstration at the Equestrian Plaza on 6 October 1976, Chamlong in disguise had been the person who had directed action on the stage and made suggestions to speakers on what to say to the anti-Communist crowd (*Lak thai* 1988, p.26–28, 30 June). Apparently, she meant to boast of her long political association with Chamlong, but this naive revelation backfired. The disclosure came to be seen as a shocking allegation, given Chamlong's reputation as a religious person. Chamlong denied any involvement in the massacre. Meanwhile, the candidate who still considered that her role in 1976 had been heroic[15] was silenced by the party's order.

Many people came forward both to confirm and refute Chamlong's denial. Among them, one of his former friends alleged that Chamlong had been an army intelligence officer who had been active in organising the right-wing demonstration (*Khaophiset* 1988, news summary, p.16–17, 27 July–2 August). On the other hand, Professor Chai-anan Samudavanija came out as Chamlong's best defender, quoting from his own research that although Chamlong had been actively against student radicals he had not had any part in the massacre (Chai-anan 1982: 32–33). Chamlong's denial, including one in front of tens of thousands of people before the election day, was at best evasive. He categorically denied that he had been anywhere near Thammasat that morning. But he admitted having participated in the right-wing movement during that period, and also in the demonstration on 6 October 1976 at the Equestrian Plaza, a few miles from Thammasat, as an ordinary citizen who was upset about the students' *lèse majesté* and the apparent disorder in the country. Arguing that the situation at the demonstration had been very confusing, he had merely been one among many who had tried to make suggestions to people on stage. He denied any authority or special service in that gathering. Besides, he argued that the right-wing demonstration had nothing to do with the killing on the morning of the same day (*Matichon* 1988, 'Full text of Chamlong's speech', 18 July).

During the controversy, several political leaders from1976, including Chatichai, were questioned by the media. As if complicity in the massacre had to occur at or near Thammasat and the only crime had to be the actual shooting with their own hands, all denied having been near Thammasat on that day. But they were evasive about their roles, or about having any relation with the right-wing movement (*Khaophiset* 1988, news, 27 July–2 August). They sang in chorus that the controversy was a dirty political ploy for immediate gains in the election. Students who urged more disclosure were accused of being political pawns in the election. There was no investigation into whether or how these political leaders had been involved in the atrocity in 1976. Their excuse was indeed a cheap political evasion to avoid trouble in the short and long terms. It seems likely that these political leaders, including Chatichai and Chamlong, considered their action within the right-wing movement to have been a justified one. By 1988, however, they tried to hide their past, while scrambling to save their immediate political stakes by evasion and unconvincing excuses. They did not even condemn the killing in 1976. Instead, by charging that the attempts at disclosure were dirty political ploys and that the 1976 event should be left to rest to avoid societal rift, they continued trying to bury the past in the realm of silence.

On a brighter note, however, the controversy clearly indicated that the discourse on the 6 October event had shifted dramatically. The story of Chamlong's role on that day, no matter how truthful it is, could have featured as a record of honour had it been told ten years earlier, like Salang's interview broadcast on Yan-krò. By 1988, an involvement with the right-wing's activities on that day was still thought of by some, like Jongkol, as heroism, but was seen as a disgrace by the media and a large number in the political public. The crime was more properly admonished, even though no attempt had been made to go after individual perpetrators. Victims were recognised more as victims, and no longer as criminals. Despite the fact that silence eventually returned, in my view at least, this was a saner impression of the massacre.

In 1994, Manas Sattayarak, a Police Captain and a famous writer, wrote a short memoir reflecting on what had happened on Wednesday, 6 October 1976. Manas woke up that morning, he recalled, with grave concern for the students at Thammasat. He disagreed with the order of his superior, allowing the police to use weapons to defend themselves. He had been in Thammasat the night before the killing and knew, he said, that the student demonstrators were unarmed. Once he arrived at the scene in the morning, he tried in vain to stop the police shooting. Either the police were in disarray, Manas speculated, or they were under strict instructions to follow the orders of only their own commanders. Either way, they did not stop firing into the campus. Manas saved a man from being lynched by throwing his own body in front of him to protect him. As a consequence, he was almost shot, presumably by those invading Thammasat, although Manas did not make this clear. He urged his fellow policemen to treat the arrested students with civility, until an unidentified man nearby became upset and threatened him verbally. He then led a few busloads of students to the place of custody at Nakhon Pathom, Southwest of Bangkok. Upon arrival, he found that one 'captive' had been shot dead while attempting to escape. As ambivalent as he was, Manas decided to make an excuse for his young officer. 'His [the student's] complexion is so white', he said out loud in front of the media onlookers, 'perhaps he is a *Yuan* [Vietnamese]'. At dusk of that dark day, he wrote, 'The situation was calm. Only ruins remained, materially and spiritually' (Manas 1994).

This narrative voiced sympathy for the victims of the massacre. Admirable as it is, one may wonder if this courageous police narrative could have spoken out earlier. It would have been unthinkable, or could have resulted in the author becoming another casualty, had it been written a few years after the incident. Times have changed: the triumphant police narrative about the massacre like Salang's have given way to an apologetic one like Manas'. Both Salang's and Manas' accounts reflect personal views of two police commanders, of course. Yet, they also represent a drastic change in the discursive conditions, which determined their reversed moments of public utterance.

Time changes public discourses. Apparently, it changes memories and histories, too. Time is not an empty passage of orbiting celestial bodies. Nor is it homogeneous. It has subjects, whose memories are caught up in complex contention. Guilt and shame are often only felt retroactively. It is not uncommon for one to feel guilt only after deep reflections on the views of the present. For those involved in the killing, the October 1976 incident might not have become a matter for shame had the anti-Communist phobia not subsided to such an extent that nowadays the fear of communism twenty years ago seems absurd. Had the right-wing totalitarian regime remained in power, had the Cold War gone on propagating the strategy of the diabolic anti-Communist dehumanisation, and had the communist threat remained real, the culprits and their supporters might not have had the opportunity to reflect on their thoughts and actions, and the October 1976 victims could have remained stigmatised as criminals. Being prisoners of time, the criminals turn out to be the victims of their past deeds.

The commemoration in 1996 marked another turning point in the discourse about the massacre. Before looking at it, let us consider the victims of the massacre who, too, were ambivalent about their past and were caught up in even more complex traumas.

The victims' ambivalence: from revenge to remorse

The ambivalence among former radical students is more complex and harder to evaluate. In most cases, their trauma has not been publicly registered anywhere. I partly share their ambivalence, and for many years I learned from them personally. Their suffering, then disillusionment with the radical and communist movements, eventually leached away their pride, and their confidence in, or feelings of justification for, their past activism. Without such pride, suffering and grief due to the loss of friends in the massacre, and after, became a spectre of moral ambivalence which may never entirely clear. This traumatic memory does not concern shame; it has had a harder time to find expression.

After the killing at Thammasat, more than three thousand people, mostly students, sought refuge in the jungles with the CPT. Although many of them had had no connection with the CPT before, the massacre and the subsequent witch-hunt left the student activists with no other obvious sanctuary. At the same time, it appeared to them that the CPT's denial of the viability of the parliamentary channel for popular democracy had proved to be correct. The massacre pushed these young radicals into the embrace of the CPT, whose operation among students became stronger and more efficient despite the more dangerous conditions after the massacre. For many of them, the brutality and the loss of their friends only left bitterness and anger in their hearts and minds. The communist alternative seemed to offer as much an ideal political and economic system as the possibility for revenge. Inspired by the sacrifice of their friends on that Wednesday, it was said that many students-turned-insurgents fought bravely and died heroically in the revolutionary war.

Within the revolutionary movement, those who died in the massacre were regarded as martyrs (*wirachon*) who had sacrificed their lives for the revolutionary future. One after another, former student leaders who joined the armed struggle made broadcasts on the CPT's underground radio charging the Thai state and the monarchy for their crime at Thammasat and denouncing them. They promised revenge when the revolutionary victory arrived in Bangkok in the future. As one of the songs written and sung by student revolutionaries announced,

We'll revenge our brave comrades.
We'll fight for people, forever.
So the ideal society will be made.
Soon, the red flag will be planted at the city's centre.

('Sahai' [Comrade] by Kanmachon)

Had the communist party won the revolutionary war, those who died in the massacre would definitely have been glorified as the 'Martyrs of 6 October'. The massacre, as was said by the CPT, proved to the students the truth of the party line that the CPT had advocated all along, and led them to join the revolution. The martyrs, it could be said, inspired the revolutionary youth even more than the events of October 1973, since October 1976 was such a turning point for the revolutionary youth, while the 1973 event was merely a bourgeois victory. Had the red flag been planted at Thammasat, the revenge would have been gained and the debt of gratitude to those who had sacrificed their own lives would have been paid.

In reality, the CPT and the entire radical movement collapsed in the early 1980s.

This was due to three major factors. First, the Sino-Vietnamese conflict led to an alliance between the Thai and Chinese governments against the perceived Vietnamese threat. The CPT, which had been tagging along behind the Chinese regime for decades and regarded Maoism as the true socialism, suddenly fell into ideological and political disarray, since their patron and their enemy were now on the same side. They also found their logistical support from China cut off (Gawin 1990: 37–41).

Second, the Thai government changed their view and strategy toward communism. After the coup in 1977, the Thai state started to depart from the military-oriented anti-communism and its old counterinsurgency strategy. They learned from their past failures that military means increased the number of communists (Chai-anan et al 1990). The turning point was perhaps the use of force against students, which only resulted in a stronger and more legitimate seeming CPT than ever. Meanwhile, the public discourse on communism had changed, too. For decades during the Cold War, the Thai state depicted the communist insurgency as an evil, alien terrorism, which was aimed at colonising and destroying the country. They were definitely not Thai. In 1973–1976, this discourse was challenged. It emerged that many communists were rural villagers who had been neglected, or suppressed, and were the victims of the abuse of power (Morell and Chai-anan 1981: 169–172, 213–228). Thus, the more abuse, the more communists. The October 1976 onslaught was thus simultaneously the culmination of the old strategy, and the beginning of its end. Most urban communists were children of the bourgeoisie who were attracted to communism by its idealism, in contrast with the dictatorial state. Many became communists because of the worst abuse of power on 6 October 1976. Definitely they were not aliens. Suddenly, the CPT was not such an alien power either. The amnesty for the 6 October trial and the rhetoric of reconciliation reflected the new counterinsurgency strategy. It was crystallised in the document known as the Prime Minister's Order Number 66/2523 in 1980 (Suchit 1987: 49–76, 90–104). The order set out new principles and guidelines based on the recognition that the communist 'problem' was primarily domestic and political, not a military one. Most importantly, the government issued an amnesty for the students who had joined the CPT, allowing them to return to their studies without either conditions or interrogation.

Thirdly, meanwhile inside the CPT, the radical students were becoming increasingly frustrated with the party. They had found that the revolutionary movement was both dogmatic and totalitarian. The party, from the top down to local commanders, tried to control their lives and behaviour in every matter. Students were forced to conform with the party directives even if it meant the crushing of their creativity and enthusiasm. Above all, the party's directives in ideological and practical matters were out of kilter, since many of them were from textbooks of their Chinese mentors' experience. Many students challenged the party's rigid adherence to Maoism and this Chinese guidance: from its analysis of Thai society, its revolutionary strategy, to the inefficiency and lack of democracy within the party. From top to bottom of the party structure, these students proposed changes, only to be met with indifference and, to the outspoken ones, distrust, and malicious smears by the party leadership. The conflicts between the students and the CPT leadership at all levels almost led to mutinies in many camps. Like a wild fire, dissatisfaction spread. The CPT's response was too slow, and resulted only in cosmetic changes, not unlike the usual reactions of the Thai state (Gawin 1990: 27–33, 43–64, 70–76). It could have been even more disastrous, most students finally concluded, had the CPT come to power. Disillusioned with the communist party and its ideology, almost all the students took the opportunity offered by the government's amnesty, leaving the jungle camps individually and en bloc.

But it was a home-coming in total defeat. These students had denounced the Thai state with the intention of not returning until the revolution succeeded. The jungle, despite hardship, initially meant new hope, strong idealism, and the expectation of a just revenge. Now they returned to the embrace of the state, denouncing the CPT's revolution from absolute disillusionment, while feeling totally humiliated. One of the common sentiments shared among them after returning from the jungle was their feelings of uncertainty and insecurity about how people – friends, family, colleagues and future employers – would react to their past. After dedicating years of their youthful life to a historic mission which, they believed, was correct, inevitable, and which would bring lasting happiness to all people, most of them now felt completely lost and thoroughly dejected about their own mistakes. Many felt they had dedicated years of their lives to an eventually hopeless cause. Their lives had become a void. They brought home only stigma and malaria. They were only in their middle twenties, but they had already lost two historic wars: one in the city ending with the slaughter of their friends, the other in the jungles ending with disenchantment. How couldn't they help feeling disgusted, humiliated, and ashamed for the catastrophic mistakes they had made, and then for having to beg for clemency from the state they had previously denounced? Many considered committing suicide. 'I am a historical ruin', declared Seksan Prasertkul, one of the best known student leaders, shortly after he left the jungle in 1981. This saying became the catch phrase of the returnees.

Less severe, but in a similar vein, those who had remained in the city working underground, only to witness the gradual collapse of the CPT, had similar experiences. Like their friends in the jungles, they had lost the same two wars. At times, they tried in vain to defend their socialist idealism. Toward the end of the debacle, some refused to accept defeat, trying to launch new rounds of debates, studies, and activism.[16] Eventually, these urban radicals, too, turned to questioning and challenging the once revered party and its ideology. When their friends started abandoning the jungle camps, they, too, abandoned the lost cause. Some turned to other radical causes, including the ones once criticised by them, such as radical Buddhism and populist NGOs. In any case, like their comrades from the jungles, they could never view the past in the same way again.

261

For these former radicals, it was not so difficult to consider the past politics rationally. But rationality had no answer to their ambivalence about their moral responsibility stemming from their disenchantment. For the losers of two wars, the loss of friends on 6 October 1976, and in the revolutionary war, became personal traumas that are very hard to come to terms with. The price of sacrifice suddenly looked too steep. For all their naive idealism, their sufferings for unclear political benefits had all perhaps been for nothing. From their disillusioned perspective, the losses appeared empty of all meaning, and the high price was without any justification. It should never have happened.

Many former radicals did not feel that they could completely exonerate themselves from being responsible for the loss, no matter how indirectly or remotely. Many of them, not only the well-known leaders, had been active in this movement that led to polarisation and death. Many were active in recruitment for the CPT, or in despatching people to the jungle, many of whom never returned. The ambivalence of responsibility falls heavier on these people. The fact that the sacrifice, as seen in its time, was for a noble cause, and no matter how beautiful the idealism might be, cannot outweigh another fact: had those friends survived that Wednesday morning they could have had another chance in life like most surviving former radicals have today. Their families would not have had to endure their sufferings. The burden of surviving while they perished will stick with those still living, myself included, perhaps forever. Given such a trauma and ambivalence, the massacre was not a subject they could talk about without troubled reflections on this moral dilemma.

Lastly, it cannot be denied that the degree of violence was the outcome of the tense animosity sustained by both sides in the confrontation over a long period. While the right-wing propaganda machine and their anti-communist discourse dehumanised the radicals, the latter were no less hostile and even somewhat threatening, although only ideologically, verbally, and never in actual practice. That is to say, many former radicals still feel partly responsible for what happened, even though in the event they were the victims, not the criminals.

The moral torments of the victims had never surfaced publicly until the commemoration in 1996. As a way of revisiting the past, to be discussed later in this chapter, it was among the first and most significant occasions that provided a forum for many former radicals to come to terms with their painful past.

Historical incomprehensibility

In both the cases of ambivalence discussed above, the present invalidates the past. The past and its meanings are framed and comprehended from present perspectives. The lapse of time, all the happenings between the massacre and the moment of remembering, altered perspectives and memory. Memory, in other words, is always the projection from the present moment of remembering onto the past. But the perspectives in the present are normally formed and informed by historical discourses, which allow an incident to be understood and discussed in certain ways, and without which such an incident may not find a voice or may not be comprehensible at all. In other words, historical knowledge provides prior texts that also determine and shape what and how we remember past events in the present.

Whether or not the present leaders of the Thai state have the courage to confront the past crime is one question. Here, another cultural and ideological question, which has direct effects on memory, is whether or not state crime is a comprehensible concept, and how it fits into the narrative of Thai history. What makes the 6 October event so difficult to understand is the lack of Thai historical discourse about the state massacre of its own people, regardless of the fact of whether or not the Thai state has committed such violence against people in the past.

As argued elsewhere (Thongchai 1994: 159–161), modern Thai historiography is a saga of the unity of Thai people under benevolent rulers, mostly the monarchy, in confronting the threats, and consequent sufferings, posed by foreign countries, in the course of which the nation survived and prospered. The customary master narrative always begins with the peaceful and independent Thai kingdom facing danger from colonising aliens. Troubles and sufferings ensue. Fortunately, a heroic and benevolent warrior always emerges to protect or restore independence. Under his righteous leadership, the country prospers in peace. According to this master narrative, the rulers were normatively kind and caring about the people. Mass destruction took the form either of a justified battle against the enemy, or in the suppression of malicious rebels, and thus was not a state crime. If a ruler turned despot, he would soon be challenged and deposed by a righteous successor. A massacre by the state is, therefore, an alien concept, usually heard about in an international news report, or described in histories of other countries.

All the recent incidents of popular struggle, namely, the October 1973 uprising, the October 1976 massacre, and the May 1992 bloodshed, deviated sharply from the normative historical discourse.

First of all, in these incidents the country's independence was not at stake, and no foreign threat was involved. Despite a temporary public acceptance that the 1976 massacre was a measure against an alien threat, this rationalisation by the state eventually failed. What happened cannot be written as a narrative of a struggle against an alien intruder, or a factional dispute among the elite. It can only be described as a state crime against its own people.

Secondly, the three incidents were mass revolts against the despots and their abuse of power, without any role for a righteous challenger arising from among the elite leaders. There have also been sceptical discourses that downplayed the significance of popular struggle to the level of being merely a power struggle among ruling factions, with crowds being manipulated as pawns. Despite that, the significance of people's power cannot be discounted.

Thirdly, the incidents show repeatedly that Thailand is anything but peaceful. Violence and brutality visited by Thais on Thais erupted three times on a broad scale in less than twenty years. Especially in the case of October 1976, it was executed in the cause of being Thai in order to protect the triple pillars of the Thai identity – the Nation, Religion and the Monarchy.

These three occurrences of bloodshed are impossible to include in the master narrative of Thai history. They do not fit into the spirit of the national saga of prospering through unity under a benevolent ruler. They taint the noble biography of the country. Above all, there exists no prior historical discourse that would allow them to be understood properly. Yet at the same time, so many people participated and the events' impacts were too significant for them to be simply forgotten. Popular struggles, therefore, can only exist on the margins of the domain of the memorable past, where they will always pose challenges to the normative national history. Even though it has been over twenty years since they occurred, these events have not been forgotten, but the discourses about them are limited; the truth about what happened has never been fully recounted; and their place in history remains unclear.

Among the three, the massacre of 1976 is probably the most difficult to fathom. As the master narrative of Thai history also contains the theme of an ever-advancing country, development and progress are always implied. The October 1973 and May 1992 incidents were major developments toward democracy in Thailand, since in both cases the military regimes were brought down by popular participation. This is widely recognised among the public, even though the military may view the incidents differently. From this perspective, could the October 1976 event count as a case of political development too? What positive contributions did it make to democracy? Or was October 1976 a loss for everybody concerned? Compared to the 1973 and 1992 events, the 1976 massacre seems to be on the edge of the domain of the comprehensible past, or possibly falls within the adjacent domain of ambivalence and silence. It was uneasiness about the misfit of these events, their incompatibility with the accepted historical narrative that exposed the fallibility and the limitations of the national history. What Mary Steedly has written about the public memory of the 1965 bloodshed in Indonesia could be applied here, 'The monument unbuilt, the story unspoken, is no more than an invisible inscription along history's silent edge, marking an official limit placed upon the past by the present' (Steedly 1993: 238).

Last but not least, the brutality of that morning, particularly the methods of killing and the fact that the crowd, including many youngsters, enjoyed the horrific carnage, was a shock to many Thais. Moreover, while people may be willing to believe that the right-wing crowd went berserk because they had been incited to it by propaganda, the possibility of an anticipated or planned carnage cannot be ruled out.[17] Thais generally take pride in their history, as much as they know of it, of the record of relatively not-so-violent political conflicts. The massacre crushed their pride, invalidating their belief, confidence, or trust that such carnage could not happen in their country. So far, there has not yet been any attempt to explain, or rationalise, how such brutality could happen. What they experienced and their perceptions of Thai history are grievous to reconcile. This may be another reason for avoidance and silence.

A happening without words looms still in the past but has not yet found its way into history. The commemoration in 1996, four years after another mass killing, was an occasion for public remembrance, and a reminder of past brutality. Those mass killings in themselves form a counter-history, which can no longer be written out of the biography of the nation.

Sites of contesting memories: a monument of ambivalence

Probably the clearest evidence of the evasive public memories about the uprisings and massacre are the names the events have come to be known by, and the most conspicuous site of contested memories is the controversy over the memorial for the events.

All the three recent popular struggles have names that are known to the public. How awkward they are to the normative historical narrative, however, can be seen precisely from the names. The 14 October 1973 was called the 'Day of Extreme Grief' (*wan maha wippayok*) by the king in the evening when the turmoil subsided. Shortly after, it was challenged by the jubilant students at the time as the 'Day of Great Joy' (*wan maha piti*). Obviously, both names represented opposing political stances, perspectives, and implications. Trying to avoid any commitment to such a polarisation, most people opted for a more neutral name, that is, simply the '14 October event'. The massacre in 1976, as mentioned earlier, was known as the 'riot', and students as the 'rioters', or the 'deceived' at first, and thereafter by other names depending on the shifting discourses about it. Meanwhile, the CPT promoted an opposing analysis calling the same incident, the 'suppression of people', and those who died the 'martyrs'. Newsmagazines sometimes used more sensational descriptions like the 'brutal murder' (*kan sanghan hot*). But the best known label until now is much less clear and less committed to any standpoint, namely the '6 October event'. Among the most imaginative and most evasive mention of

265

the 1976 massacre I have come across was an indirect reference without any specific angle by a former prime minister, Anand Punyarachun, who once referred to it simply as 'an abrupt end' (Anand 1996).[18]

We might say such a non-committal name carries no meaning. On the contrary, I would argue, it is loaded with many unsettled meanings, which imply the absence of any commitment. The unsayable words and snarling voices are implied by such an avoidance, and in this silence the naming occurs (Trouillot 1995: 114–115). Anand's evasive allusion is an example (Kasian 1996). Such a designation, therefore, obscures the past because it is too heavily loaded with contesting voices. The dates and months cloak the sufferings, and also the mysteries, as well as ever. As it turns out, the non-committal naming situates these episodes on the edge between recognisability and anonymity, between history and the silenced past, and between memory and forgetfulness.

The most prominent and most heated contest surrounding the ambivalent memory is the case of the monument for the 'October Martyrs'. At the end of the uprising in 1973, the victory was hailed by all political camps, excepting only perhaps the military, and those who died were recognised as the 'October 14 martyrs' (wirachon sipsi tula). In October 1974, Their Majesties presided over the cremations in a state ceremony. The government at the time also agreed to be partner with the students in building a memorial for the event and the martyrs.[19] The former headquarters of one of the ousted junta members, which had been burnt down during the uprising, was chosen as the site for the monument. In 1975, the government at the time agreed to buy the land, which was the property of the Crown Property Bureau (CPB) who, in 1974, indicated there would be no problems, apart from some minor technicalities. In October 1975, the prime minister and the supreme patriarch at that time laid the foundation stone at the site. Political uncertainty, however, led to changes of government, while political polarisation and the increasing propaganda against radical students led to the shelving of the monument project. By October 1976, the uprising three years earlier had come to be judged in a different light, as a communist-influenced disorder. The martyrs of 1973 were soon ignored, and no longer even classed as martyrs. Build a monument for them? For the rabble-rousers?

Soon after the Thanin government assumed power, the project was officially abandoned. Early in 1978, the government confiscated the account of the National Student Centre of Thailand, including the funds raised and allocated for the monument. Like the ambivalent memory behind it, however, the project could not be stifled.

Several years later, when the anti-Communist sentiment subsided, student organisations began to hold annual ceremonies to celebrate the 1973 victory. The public were reminded annually about the promised memorial.[20] Despite that, there was no progress until 1988. Behind the stalled project during that period was in fact the stalemate of contested memories. First, in 1978, the CPB adopted a project to develop the monument site for commercial purposes. An officer of the Bureau argued that they had never given permission to students to lay the foundation stone in that place (*Athit* 1978, p.27, 11 October). For unknown reasons, the project had never been realised. Astonishingly, it was claimed that the bureau dared not do so for fear of risking political repercussions. Instead, the site was leased to the Thai army, which leased it to the Lottery Sellers Association. This was a slap in the face of the 14 October Martyrs, and an offence to the spirit of the 1973 uprising, since one of the buildings burnt down in the uprising had been the headquarters of the government lottery bureau. As if recognising that they were participants in a historical tug-of-war, nonetheless, the lottery sellers only dared to set up temporary shelters for their lottery sales around the edges of the site. The foundation stone was left at the centre of the site under the open sky as if it were no part of the leased area. Despite that, the stone was venerated every day as a locus of good fortune by the lottery ticket sellers and buyers. Nobody cared apparently about its original political meanings. Even so, every year on 14 October, the lottery people would stop their business in the morning as students held the annual commemoration. The lottery people always stood by, watching, uninvolved, allowing it to go on as long as the ceremony lasted.

In 1989, the issue of the memorial for the October Martyrs erupted once more as a consequence of the Chamlong controversy. This time, the civilian government, ironically led by Chatichai Choonhavan who had supported the right-wing demonstration on 6 October 1976, agreed to resume the project. Over four million baht of the fund for the monument project, confiscated in 1978, was returned to a special committee to oversee the project. To everybody's surprise, the site was not available yet. The obstacles concerning the leases by the CPB to the army, which had leased it on to the lottery sellers remained unresolved. There was no progress until the May 1992 uprising took place, ending with another victory for popular struggle. Suddenly, the monument for the martyrs of democracy became even more legitimate. But this time, the proposal was that the memorial was to inclusively honour all the sacrifices in 1973, 1976 and 1992. The opposition to the monument, especially among the military and some right-wing politicians, immediately voiced protest. They considered all the three incidents to have been occasions of riot, chaos, and lawlessness, and thus that none of these should be memorialised. The military warned that the monument would be divisive.

Despite the renewed outbreak of controversy, a new site was selected in order to circumvent the perennial obstacles at the old one. It was on the same road at the former building of the Department of Public Relations, which had been burnt down in the 1992 event in protest against its role in misinforming the public, and telling lies in support of the military regime. The plan for a new memorial to represent both the October 1973 and the May 1992 events was drawn up and the chosen site declared rid of all legal obstacles. The supreme patriarch at the time gave the name to the proposed memorial park as the Peace Garden (*suan santipòn*). Despite some progress on the new memorial, in 1995, while the plan for the memorial was under way with reserved support from the government, His Majesty the King proposed a plan to relieve the traffic congestion in the area, which was truly one of the worst affected in Bangkok. Under His Majesty's proposal, the site of the planned memorial would be turned into diverting streets and roadsides. As this happened in Thailand, no controversy was possible. The new memorial project was quietly but abruptly discarded. The monument project had to return to the drawing board, and the old site was once again on the table.

A contest of memories also took place on an opposing issue, namely how the ousted junta of 1973 were to be treated. After they had left the country in 1973, they were found to be 'unusually rich'. It is widely believed that their wealth was the result of corruption and abuse of power. Without due process, the interim government in 1974 used their executive power in confiscating the junta's assets. After the 1976 massacre, given the swing of political momentum to the right, all of them returned to Thailand and demanded the return of their assets. The right-wing government, while branding students as enemies and a threat to the country, eagerly worked to meet the demands of the former dictators. Yet they did not have enough time before being turfed out in their turn. Since then, every government has been reluctant to respond to the repeated demands for the return of the junta's confiscated assets. There are always public voices protesting the demands.

In early 1997, the government at the time restored his army rank, and thereby pensions and benefits, to Colonel Narong Kittikachon, Thanom's son, one of the three tyrants who had been ousted in the 1973 incident. The strength of the pro-democracy reaction had been underestimated by the government, which was finally pressured to rescind its decision. In early 1999, another government made a similar mistake. Citing Thanom's contributions to the army and the country, the prime minister appointed Thanom as an Honorary Officer of Royal Guard, a highly prestigious award for a retired military officer. The protests led to a political crisis that almost brought down the government. Like the monument for the October Martyrs, the issues of the confiscated assets and the recognition of former dictators were entangled within the sphere of contested memories.

The monument issue was raised again during the commemoration in 1996. As has become only too familiar, there were no signs of forward progress, despite the success of the event and the publicity accorded it. The monument seems to be an impossible project. It cannot be built. Yet it will not be forgotten either, perhaps for as long as the contesting memories, and the resultant stalemate, last. The foundation stone remained surrounded by lottery booths, as if the memory of violent popular struggles and state crimes would remain under siege beneath the open sky.

Then in 1998, while I was writing this chapter, the commemoration of the 1973 uprising produced an unexpected result: the monument for the October Martyrs would after all be erected. Ironically, the force behind this success was not popular pressure but personal connections between the leader of the 1973 uprising, Thirayuth Boonmi, and the former Prime Minister, Anand Punyarachun, who had personally negotiated the agreement with the Director of the CPB. The CPB finally agreed with Anand, who delivered the good news and the monument to the public. More importantly, as it happens, the monument was for the October 1973 Martyrs only. The events and names of the victims of the massacre 1976 or the May 1992 bloodshed were not to be included. The speeches and discussions during the commemoration of the 1973 victory, according to news reports, did not devote much attention to the other two events either. In the view of many of my friends from that generation, it is the first step toward the recognition of the other two events. In my view, that may not be the case. I have been arguing in this chapter that all three events were anomalies of Thai history. In fact, as we shall see below, they were not equally subversive. The monument for 1973 is possible, I would argue, partly because of the exclusion of the 1976 massacre in particular from the memorial project.

The 1976 massacre in narratives of Thai democracy

The story of the monument above focuses primarily on the 1973 uprising, since it was the event the monument was originally to solemnise. But the memory and perspectives of the 1973 event were shaped by subsequent events, namely the following three years of radicalism that ended with the massacre, and the rise and collapse of the socialist movement. The 1973 and 1976 events in particular were not generally perceived separately.[21] The unsettling memory of the 1976 massacre could have seemed to soil the memory of the glorious road to democracy. Had its memory and meanings been brought to the forefront of the debate about the monument, the proposed project might have been even more controversial. As we shall see below, the place of the massacre in the history of democracy has been awkward to assess, and has generally been simply lumped in with the other two victorious events.

Historical knowledge is always a narrative of the textualised past. That is to say, a story becomes intelligible or meaningful in certain ways by breaking up the flow of events in undifferentiated time by marking off the beginning and the close of such a story at more or less arbitrary moments in time. In this manner, the historical narratives of Thai democracy have attempted to deal, rather awkwardly, with the 1976 incident. Even among the former radicals and the sympathisers with the victims, to place the 1976 massacre within the discursive narratives of Thai democracy has not been an easy task.

For the many conservatives who consider the popular struggles for democracy as threats to national security, the 1976 massacre is easily understood as the justified suppression of the danger from urban communism. A former leader of the Red Guars, the right-wing paramilitary group that led the police into Thammasat that morning, and the infamous army general behind the group, Sutsai Hatsadin, were still proud of what they had done to save the country in 1976 (*Sarakhadi* 1996, October, p.159–161, 166–169). Interestingly, however, for Sutsai the 1973 uprising was a great historic event (*Sarakhadi* 1996: October, p.169). Conservative students groups held similar views that separated the two October events: one was for democracy, the other to suppress the leftists (see Controversy at Ramkhamhaeng University in October 1982, *Matichon*, news, 14–15 October). It must be noted here that in the 1973 uprising the three members of the junta were ousted after the intervention by the palace. The royal family came out in public to receive students who were fleeing from the beating into the palace ground. They went to visit the injured and the live telecast of the king's speech virtually stopped the chaos. A year later, they presided over the cremation of the martyrs. Things only went wrong, it seems, after the uprising.

For those who recognised the 1973–1976 period as a democratic process, the victory of 1973 was memorable, and so worth celebrating, since it had made a great progressive contribution. They regarded the 1976 massacre as a tragic setback, the closure of three years of democratic experiment. From this point of view, then, the historical questions relating to the 1976 event were not merely the massacre and its enigmas, but more importantly what went wrong with the student movement after 1973. It is generally agreed that the massacre was the inevitable consequence of the isolation of leftist students from the middle class public. Radical students, in other words, were the victims of their own making to the extent that their activities gave the right-wing the pretext to strike back. This is probably the most widely held view regarding the 1973–1976 period after the collapse of the radical movement (Morell and Chai-anan 1981 and Khanungnit 1987 represent this view). This interpretation of the two inseparable October incidents is therefore a tragedy, beginning with a glorious hero who kills a giant in a highly celebrated battle but ending with the fall of the hero, who has apparently lost his virtue and magic. It is a like the Star Wars trio, without the last section. In this sense, October 1973 represents success, while the other October, the 1976 massacre, represents failure. Although most people holding this view support the notion that the monument should recognise both events, and that the term the 'October Martyrs' should be an inclusive one for both the October 1973 and October 1976 casualties, the latter clause seems to be included only because it was seen as indivisively linked, the bleak ending to a sequence that had opened with such promise. The value of the October 1976 event in itself was dubious, definitely not on a par with the 1973 one. There was nothing positive to commemorate, and only negatives to reflect on: mistakes, failure, and the sacrifices to extremism. This remains the accepted interpretation of the history of radicalism in Thailand.

Since the May 1992 uprising, however, the past has begun to be textualised differently, thanks to this other celebrated democratic victory. The 1976 massacre was no longer construed as a denouement to the story of democratic struggles. Instead, a new narrative of the democratic struggles emerged, taking the May 1992 event as a continuation of the process beginning in 1973. Some argued that the democratic process started even earlier, with the 1932 overthrow of the absolute monarchy. The 1973 spirit, it is said, was handed down to descendants nineteen years later. The interesting point here is not whether or not the narrative is true, but how the past is being retextualised and plotted. The new version is a historical scheme of popular struggles for democracy that started in 1932, but subsided or were suppressed by the continuous military rule until the breakthrough in 1973, which, despite the 1976 massacre, resumed in 1992. Although the May 1992 uprising was not a true beginning, it was another important milestone in the history of the development of Thai democracy, for which no full realisation is as yet in sight. This is a rejuvenated discourse about democracy, which is good for the country. But where is the place of the October 1976 massacre in this scheme?

Since May 1992, the proposed monument for 'Democracy Martyrs' project, much like the Peace Garden plan, has become even more inclusive, with the intention of honouring the sacrifices not only of the two October events but that of May 1992 as well. It appears that the memory and meanings of the 1976 massacre have now been parcelled in with the two popular victories. Set in a historical perspective, the event of 1976 was perhaps one of the roadblocks encountered, unfortunately resulting in excessive bloodshed, on the long and bumpy road to democracy (Charnvit 1996). It is relatively marginal in relation to the victories celebrated by the pro-democracy people themselves. As it happened, while the annual commemoration of the 1973 uprising has been organised and relatively well attended every year, a small annual commemoration of the massacre, originating in 1978 after the release of the October 6 defendants, became smaller by the mid-1980s, and had faded away by the early 1990s. This, I would argue, was due to the ambiguous place of the massacre in the history of Thai democracy.

Had the construction of a memorial been possible, how should it have paid tribute to the victims of the 1976 massacres who, unlike the 1973 and 1992 martyrs, were regarded as radicals and not as heroes by the public? What should be the grounds for including them? It seems impossible to leave them out, simply by virtue of the fact that they were the offshoots of the 1973 generation, and their deaths seemed to point the moral of the tale. The scenario that has emerged is to ask the martyrs of 1973 and 1992 to carry their 1976 comrades along with them in the memory and narrative of democracy. The flaw in such a story line is that it marginalises, if not obliterates, the history of Thai radicalism represented by the 1976 massacre. To put it in another way, the memory of the massacre may survive, ironically, only by being minimalised in the narrative of Thai democracy. In a country and culture which does not recognise the abstract concept of the 'noble cause', for which idealistic people sacrifice themselves for the happiness and benefits of the community at large, there are no obvious grounds for a proper commemoration of the 1976 massacre and Thai radicalism.

The uneasy place of the massacre in the narrative of Thai democracy surfaced as an issue in 1998, as I was writing this chapter, for the 25th anniversary of the 1973 uprising. There was a movement calling for the official recognition of 14 October every year as the 'Day of Freedom' (*wan seriphap*). This led to a debate among the former radicals about the historical meaning of the events in 1973, or to be more precise, what is implied by the proposed name of the day. On one side, the 1973 uprising was seen primarily as a major breakthrough in the history of democracy as described above. On the other side of the debate, it was argued that the name did not give due recognition to the elements of radical idealism, such as socialism, egalitarianism and popular nationalism (as opposed to elitist nationalism), which formed the basis for the growth of radicalism during the subsequent three years. As is apparent, the issue here is not exactly the day of the uprising twenty-five years earlier in itself, but the day in the perspective of the historical unfolding after that. In other words, the name and historical meaning of the 14 October day depend on how they reconcile, or fail to do so, the subsequent years including the massacre.

The unexpected realisation of the monument for the 14 October 1973 is therefore less surprising. As long as the 1976 massacre is excluded or marginalised as a sombre finale after a glorious beginning, definitely not as an unresolved state crime, and as long as the glorious story of the 1973 uprising dominates the meaning of the monument, the October 1973 memorial is perhaps acceptable as the first step toward the recognition of popular democracy. This is a great step forward, in my opinion. But it is by no means an indication that the 1976 massacre will ever be recognised for what it was. Above all, the roles of the monarchy in the two events were completely opposite. The memorial for 1973 will definitely enhance the monarchy's reputation and legitimacy. An honest and truthful memorial for the massacre might lead to contrary effects.

The real significance of the 1976 massacre can nevertheless perhaps be best evaluated in a different context, such as a history of Thai NGOs. After the massacre, and especially during the collapse of the urban radical movement in the early 1980s, a fair number of student activists refused to follow the CPT and its armed struggle. Instead, quite a few civic groups advocating human, children and women's rights, or working for rural development, and many other causes, had flourished in spite of, or because of, the failure of the Marxist radicalism. As it turned out, these NGOs have become influential and a noteworthy feature of the Thai political landscape since the late 1980s. The massacre, in this case, marked their disillusionenment with both the state and the movement of left radicalism, and the beginning of the search for alternatives. It was, as Charles Keyes put it, 'an end of innocence' (personal communication).

The 1996 commemoration of the October 1976 massacre

The commemoration in 1996 was perhaps a significant break in the silence surrounding the 6 October massacre. The event, unprecedented in Thai history, was highly successful due to a number of converging factors. Nonetheless, it may be too early to assess its effects on the memory of the Wednesday massacre. In this section, I would like to offer a few opinions regarding the factors for its success, and a preliminary evaluation of what has been accomplished, what has not, and the limitations to any attempts to dispel the mystery and silence.

In retrospect, the commemoration was conceived in 1995 at the right moment, after most former radicals of that generation had worked through the phases of uncertainty in their lives and settled down economically. Most of them now had the opportunity and resources for returning to political activism. Indeed, it is believed that the large contingent of the politically committed of the 1973–1976 generation played active parts in the demonstration against the military in 1992 (Anek 1993: 87–88, 127). The commemoration might not have been possible had the economic crisis hit Thailand sooner. On the other hand, the political situation in Thailand in 1995 was much more open to a fresh critical view of an ugly blemish on Thai history. In particular, as explained earlier, the discourse about the massacre itself has shifted dramatically in favour of the victims.

During the year leading to October 1996, quite a few former radicals organised several commemorative activities. The project, initially conceived as a merit-making for the dead, evolved into a huge event. There were discussions, talks, and meetings to record oral histories of the radical

Plate 10.1 An exhibit at Thammasat University, Bangkok, at the 1996 commemoration of the October 1976 massacre.

movement in the 1970s, and in the jungle. Media attention was unexpectedly high for several weeks prior to and during these. What happened twenty years earlier was retold innumerable times, though, unsurprisingly, without any reference to the undiscussable parts of that history. By way of contrast, any reaction or attempt at disruption from the right-wing was conspicuously absent. Apart from a few flyers handed out by an obscure group, there was no reaction, not even any comments, from the military or any conservative organisations. The two-day commemoration included academic discussions, public speeches, music and performances, an art exhibition, publications, an exhibition of an account of the massacre, and many others. They took place without instigating even minor resistance.

Unlike earlier annual commemorations by students, the discourse of the 1976 event was not about the history of Thai democracy. The commemoration was able to locate the massacre in the forefront by confronting the issue of state crime, while relegating the history of democracy to a secondary role. A video recording of the morning of the massacre was shown repeatedly for two days.[22] Several thousand copies of it were sold. It was made clear, nonetheless, that the commemoration had no interest, and would not be involved, in any talk of revenge. The denunciation of this state crime avoided imputing blame to any specific

274

individuals. In addition, instead of focusing on any of the movements' accomplishments or contributions to Thai society, the victims' self-sacrifice for society's sake, even if this had taken the form of communist idealism, was honoured. In this manner, the traumatic experience of the former radicals during the jungle years was also understood sympathetically. For many among them had become politically engaged only after October 1973, and the 1976 massacre had significantly reoriented their beliefs, while their commitment had eventually evaporated due to their total disillusionment with the CPT. The history they were thus finally able to commemorate and honour was not the history of Thai democracy, but that of the radicals of the 1970s.

The most significant accomplishment, in my opinion, had not been foreseen, nor was it realised until the end of the event, namely, the opportunity to start coming to terms with their painful recollections. Healing obviously took place in various degrees among the participants. Several activities before and during the commemoration gradually brought these former radicals to revisit the painful past they had struggled to cope with privately for years. For the first time, they could talk about it and tell their stories in public. And this time people listened with understanding. One common comment from these former radicals was the fact that it was the first time they had been able to publicly share their painful personal and collective memories of a unique generation of activists who had played roles in a history, which has been neglected. Several memoirs by former radicals were published during that year, 1996, and thereafter. Many more public commemorations and cremations at former CPT camps in the jungle were organised. Public reactions, if the media can be taken as representative of them, were overwhelmingly sympathetic. For many of them, the stigma – fear of being denied – was finally over. Their painful past was exorcised; indeed, many could now talk about their past with pride and confidence. In a culture which normally does not recognise this means of coming to terms with the past by speaking out or sharing their stories as a way of healing, what happened during the commemoration was unprecedented.

The most memorable activity was perhaps the symbolic cremation for those who had died twenty years earlier. Unlike the martyrs of the other two incidents, who had received special cremations and whose families had been honoured by the public, among the official forty-three deaths recorded in the 1976 massacre, only half a dozen corpses had been claimed by their families or relatives for cremations. The rest had never received any kind of cremation. Nobody knows what happened to those remains. A few of them have not yet been identified even after twenty years. In the case of Jaruphong – the friend mentioned at the beginning of this chapter – his parents had not known or been informed about their son's death until mid-1996, after keeping their hopes alive of seeing their son again for twenty years (*Sarakhadi* 1996: 137–140). On the morning of 6 October 1996, a symbolic cremation was given to all forty-three at the soccer field where the massacre had taken place. In the absence of their bodies, each of them was represented by their names written on separate sheets of paper. Some had pictures; most had none. All were honoured as individuals who had faces, names and families like everybody else, but whose lives had ended abruptly due to their idealism. The symbolic cremation was performed by Buddhist monks and spiritual leaders of other religions. It was solemn but graceful. Twenty years later, in my opinion, former radicals of the 1970s had accomplished one of the most important missions in their lives: to publicly cremate and say farewell to friends who had forfeited their lives in the event that shaped thousand of lives of their whole generation forever. This brought more peace of mind than any other previous deed. Tears in public over their past radicalism was perhaps a sign that none of the survivors would any longer have to grapple alone with their personal traumas. Collectively and individually, the cremation epitomised the commemoration in 1996 and its accomplishments.

It remains to be seen if, and in what ways, the memories of the massacre in the broader context of recent Thai history have really changed, and in what ways ambivalence remains among the culprits and victims. The commemoration was definitely a major break in the silence, another major shift in the discourse on the massacre, a turn-around in which the victims were recognised and honoured while the culprits were condemned to silence. The crimes and suffering were, finally, properly understood. The commemoration was, however, no magic rite effective in dispelling all ambivalence. Despite more political openness than at any earlier period, it took place under many conditions of political circumspection, which have changed little. The exhibition on the massacre and every other item on the programme carefully observed such limits to avoid unwanted troubles. As a result, despite the focus on state crime and the noble sacrifice, mysteries remained. Nor did it try to resolve the uneasy fit of the massacre in the narrative of Thai democracy. The issue of the memorial for the Democracy Martyrs was raised many times during the commemoration. But there was no debate about how the massacre should be memorialised in the proposed monument.[23]

While efforts to seek out the whole truth, and to locate the proper place of the massacre in the national narrative, will always remain inconclusive, it was clearly suggested by the commemoration that there are multiple ways individuals can revisit the traumatic past and find ways of healing. Even collective acts were possible within limits. Personal histories, either written out, or being created within as individuals engaged in the collective commemorative events, have the potential to help cope with the past trauma and the present domination.

Plate 10.2 A symbolic cremation held on 6 October 1996 at Thammasat University, Bangkok. At the centre was a specifically crafted urn containing sheets of paper. The names of the individuals who has died were written on each sheet, representing their body. The named sheets were then cremated.

A national ambivalence

The massacre of 6 October 1976 is an example of a past that becomes a spectral presence. Even though all the souls may now rest in the other-world, the memory of the event still haunts thousands of people. Unlike the holocaust or the Cambodian genocide, this is not because the number of deaths was astronomical, or that the entire nation feels responsible for the crime. As this chapter has explained, the memories of the massacre are, still, contested, unsettled, and disturbing. The complexity of such contested memories was added to by the subsequent unfolding of political situations, which reflected dramatic changes in the country, not only politically but in other aspects as well. It is quite clear, too, that the changing contested memories were in many ways a consequence of the mutating global politics. The ambivalence is likely to remain for years to come, because fundamentally the subjects of these memories are very much in contention. And our society is trying to foster harmony by avoidance, rather than by an inquiry into the truth.

Given the fact that only a few thousand people were directly involved in the massacre in one way or another, this strategy of avoidance may have time on its side. The ambivalence may last with those people over decades

277

Plate 10.3 On 6 October 1996, hundreds of civic groups marched with wreaths around the soccer field of Thammasat University in Bangkok where the killing took place twenty years earlier.

to come. Unlike the martyrdom at Tienanmen Square in China, or the 8888 event in Burma, which will be remembered because the ideals of those struggles remain unfulfilled, Thai radicalism has already proved to be a failure. Perhaps those who do not want to recognise the history of radicalism and the traumatic past are buying time, in hopes that this national ambivalence may simply fade away.

I believe that the monument for the Democracy Martyrs will eventually come to fruition as the country progresses, and becomes more open and democratic. I doubt, however, if this state crime will ever be officially condemned, or that the history of Thai radicalism ever be fully acknowledged. The October 1976 massacre is likely to remain in the shadows of Thai history for years to come. In the meantime, the unfinished monument, or a monument exclusively commemorating the 1973 uprising, is the most fitting memorial to this national ambivalence.

Notes

1 The research for this project was partly funded by the Graduate School of University of Wisconsin-Madison in 1996. The Institute for Research in the Humanities at the University of Wisconsin was generous enough to allow me to work on this project, and present it in Thailand during the fall of 1996 when I was a fellow at the Institute. During 1995–1996, I presented several drafts of this article in many places in Thailand and in the US, and received valuable suggestions and support, especially from Charnvit Kasetsiri, Chaiwat Satha-anand, Chaiyan Rajchagool, Jamaree Pitakwong, Charles Keyes, Shigeharu Tanabe, Mary Steedly, Hue-tam Ho Tai, and graduate students in my seminar class in Spring 1996 on the 'Traumatic Past in Thailand'.

2 The brief account up to this point is from my own recollection of that morning. The specific chronology may not be the same as in other sources, such as Puey 1977: 5–7. The rest of the account is drawn from conversations with other detainees while we were in prison, and confirmed by photos that became available in later years (Wattanachai 1988).

3 Although there are a number of them in English, namely Anderson 1977, Puey 1977, Mallet 1978, and Morell and Chai-anan 1981, only the translation of Puey 1977 and his testimony to the US Congress are available in Thai (in Puey 1981). Apart from student publications, another well known account in Thai was the collection of interviews, and some writings, by those student leaders who were arrested and sent on trial, *Rao khü phu borisut* 1978 (reprinted several times by various publishers). Most of these publications in Thai, I may say, were activist literature written as part of political campaigns to expose the massacre and to support those students in prison. The extensive analysis, like Morell and Chai-anan's (never been translated) and Anderson's (translated), are relatively unknown in Thailand. This relative silence about the 1976 massacre was once noted by a Thai scholar as a limit of academic discourse in the country (Chaiwat 1986).

4 Among the famous ones is Atsiri Thammachot's, *Khunthòng cao ca klapma müa fasang* (Khunthòng will return when the sun rises), which was awarded the Southeast Asian Writer Award (SEA Write) in 1981.

5 The idea of how history is produced and always sustained by silencing certain pasts is from Trouillot 1995.

6 Internally, the commemoration committee was full of personal and political conflicts. Among them, the most serious political issue was the concern that the commemoration would be seen as causing divisiveness again. One faction tried to avoid sensitive issues, such as confronting the massacre as state crime and reconsidering the past radicalism. They tried to make the commemoration an occasion for social harmony. Others wanted to confront the past head on.

7 The US State Department report on human rights in Thailand in 1994 listed the forbidden issues Thai films cannot address, among them corrupt police and

monks, and the 1976 incident. The last item does not appear in the previous reports. Is it an error of the 1994 report?

8 Information for the following description, if not stated otherwise, are from daily newspapers in Thailand such as *Prachathippatai, Prachachat* (in Thai) and *The Nation Review* and *Bangkok Post* in English. Commentaries are mine. See Morell and Chai-anan 1981: 257–277 for the broader political context of the massacre, especially about the military, government and parliament.

9 Morell and Chai-anan (1981: 274, 281–282) suggested four scenarios: an accident; a design by the students to poke fun at the monarchy; a conspiracy by the right wing movement; and a conspiracy by the Communist Party of Thailand. They seem to pay more attention to the last one, although they denied any indication that the drama was a conscious move by the CPT. If I am allowed to speak as a source, there was definitely no intention of referring to the monarchy. Later in the text, I discuss at length the unlikeliness of the fourth scenario.

10 Apparently trying to distance himself and his government from responsibility over the killing, Seni said in the afternoon of 6 October 1976, according to a recording of the government's public announcements over the Radio Thailand that day, that his government ordered only the arrest of students involved with the alleged skit of the hanging of the Crown Prince in effigy. They made no other order regarding the shooting at Thammasat. He repeated this several times in later years, adding that even the arrest itself was not by his government's order (*Sayam rat* 1977, Seni's public statement, 9 September; Wattanachai 1988: 145).

11 According to the statements read over the Radio Thailand that afternoon, it appears that the government accepted the false report about arms stockpiles in Thammasat, even though it was denied by the Police Chief, and challenged by some cabinet members. This shows how indecisive the Democrat government was and how far it would go to reach a compromise with its rivals.

12 As the person in charge of the gathering in Thammasat, I was questioned about whether I received an order from the CPT and was part of its conspiracy (*Su anakhot*, 1988, p.1–3, July 17). The hypothesis that the hanging drama was part of the CPT's scheme appears to be an absurd allegation in light of the revelation by people who were involved in it (*Tulakan* 1996: 34–36). The allegation also refers to many false items of information. For example, it was said that the extremist faction among the students refused to end the demonstration, while the moderate faction led by Sutham tried to ease the situation by negotiation with the government. Sutham denied the existence of such a split (Sutham 1979: 42–43).

13 That section of the broadcast turned out to be a historic one. Most of the police officers on that programme were later in the top list of the prosecution witnesses for the 6 October trial. The broadcast of Yan-krò that afternoon, and those of Radio Thailand before and after the coup in the evening, were recorded by a source who does not wish to be named. He gave a copy to me in 1982.

14 The defendants were civilians. But as the result of one of the orders by the coup group, all the cases involving communist and lèse-majesté charges had to go on trial in a military court. In the 6 October case, all but one were charged as communists, and seven of them also with lèse-majesté.

15 It should be noted that in 1978 there was a flyer signed by 'Village Scouts and the Housekeepers Club of 6 October 1976' attacking the amnesty for the case. The flyer called their actions on the day of the massacre 'heroic acts of the 6 October'. Chamlong's candidate was an outspoken leader of the Housekeepers Club in 1976.

16 The magazine *Parithatsan* was one of these major attempts. It was at this time that many former radicals had turned to the grassroots NGO works which later proved to be so successful.

17 A careful look at pictures of the hanging, burning, and torture (and rape?) of the woman reveals the same man at all the three sites. Was he temporarily insane? Or was he an agent provocateur whose job was to incite others to commit such atrocities?

18 I am grateful to Kasian Tejapira (Faculty of Political Science, Thammasat University) who informed me about Anand's keynote address.

19 Unless stated otherwise, the information below regarding the monument project is gathered from three sources: *Bangkok Post* 1997, 6 April; *The Nation* 1998, 13 October; and *Sai than düan tula* 1990.

20 The massacre of 1976 was always mentioned in passing in these commemorations of October 1973. Separate commemorations to the tragedy in 1976 were held on a much smaller scale on 6 October almost every year. It gradually faded away in the early 1990s. This reflects the relative significance in the social memory of the two October events.

21 Because both events happened in October (*tulakhom*), and the year 1973 is known in Thai as B.E. '2516', the names '14 tula 2516' and '6 tula 2519' are sometimes mixed up and become '16 tula'.

22 Several years ago, a video of the event was circulated in a small circle. I never watched it but was told that it was a collection of news clippings by foreign journalists from several sources. The quality of the pictures was unfortunately poor. In mid-1996, a better quality recording of the events that morning was discovered. It was said to have come from the archives of the army television station (Channel 5) for a propaganda documentary about the incident produced, and had been circulated throughout the country shortly after the event. I did not investigate this information, nor do I know how it was discovered or reproduced. A brief section that I watched shows the police operations outside Thammasat with military marching music in the background. Ironically, it was this version of which thousands of copies were sold at the commemoration as evidence of the atrocity.

23 I wrote about this point in the official volume of the event (Thongchai 1996c). I did not intend to stir up debate, however.

References

Daily Newspapers and Weekly News Magazines

Athit, 11 October 1978.
Bangkok Post, several issues in October 1976, October 1996, October 1998; 26 May 1996, 6 April 1997.
Khaophiset, 27 July–2 August 1988.
Krungthep trurakit, several issues in 1996.
Lak thai, 30 June 1988.
Matichon, several issues in 1978, 1979, 1982, 1983, 1988 and 1996.
The Nation, several issues in 1976–78, October 1996, October 1998.
Phucatkan raiwan (Manager Daily), 27 May 1996.
Sayam mai, 16 October 1892.
Sayam rat, several issues in 1976–1978.
Su anakhot, 17 July 1988.

Books and Articles

Anand Punyarachun 1996 'Long Live His Majesty', p.4–5, in *Bangkok Post*, 26 May.

Anek Laothammatas 1993 *Mop müthoe: chonchan klang kap kan phatthana prachathippatai* (The mobile-phone demonstrators: middle class and democratic development), Bangkok: Matichon Publishing.

Anderson, Benedict 1977 'Withdrawal symptoms: social and cultural aspects of the October 6 Coup', p.13–30 in *Bulletin of Concerned Asian Scholars* 9 (3).

Bandit Thamtrirat (ed.) 1983 *Khlun haeng thotsawat* (Waves of the Decade), Bangkok: Thammasat Student Government.

Bandit Thamtrirat and Preecha Thamwinthorn (eds.) 1985 *Wiphak thorarat* (Critiques of the Tyrant State), Bangkok: Thammasat Student Government and the Students Federation of Thailand.

Bandit Thamtrirat et al (eds.) 1986 *Satcha thorayuk* (Truth in Tyrannical Era), Bangkok: Thammasat Student Government and the Students Federation of Thailand.

Bowie, Katherine A. 1997 *Rituals of National Loyalty: an anthropology of the state and Village Scouts movement in Thailand*, New York: Columbia University Press.

Chai-anan Samudavanija 1982 *The Thai Young Turks*, Singapore: Institute of Southeast Asian Studies.

Chai-anan Samudavanija et al 1990 *From Armed Suppression to Political Offensive: attitudinal transformation of Thai military officers since 1976*, Bangkok: Institute of Security and International Studies, Chulalongkorn University.

Chaiwat Satha-anan 1986 'Ròi dang kap khwam ngiap' (Stain and silence) p.151–154 in Bandit Thamtrirat et al (eds.) 1986, *Satca thorayuk* (Truth in Tyrannical Era), Bangkok: Thammasat Student Government and the Students Federation of Thailand.

Charnvit Kasetsiri 1996 'Hetkan hok tula yu thinai nai prawattisat' (Where is the place of the 6 October event in history?), p.313–328 in *Tulakan* (In October), Bangkok: The Co-ordinating Committee for the 20th Anniversary of the 6 October Event.

Chin, Chui-Liang 1995 *Democratizing Oriental Despotism: China from 4 May 1919 to 4 June 1989 and Taiwan from 28 February 1947 to 28 June 1990*, New York: St. Martin.

Gawin Chutima 1990 'The rise and fall of the Communist Party of Thailand (1973–1987)', University of Kent at Canterbury, Centre for South East Asian Studies, Occasional Paper, no.12.

Kasian Tejapira 1996 'Nüng prayok kao kham' (One sentence, nine words), p.8 in *Phucatkan raiwan* (Manager Daily), 27 May.

Keyes, Charles F. 1978 'Political crisis and militant Buddhism in contemporary Thailand', p.147–164 in B. L. Smith (ed.) *Religion and Legitimation of Power in Thailand, Laos and Burma*, Chambersburg, Pa.: Anima Books.

Khadi prawattisat: khadi hok tulakhom (The Historic Trial: the 6 October Trial) 1978 (vol.1) and 1979 (vol.2), Bangkok: Bophit.

Khanungnit Tangchaitrong 1987 'Khwamkhit rüang kanplianplaeng sangkhom khòng khabuankan naksüksa thai phò sò 2516–2519' (The ideas of social transformation of Thai student movement 1973–1976), MA thesis (History), Chulalongkorn University.

Lobe, Thomas, and David Morell 1978 'Thailand's Border Patrol Police: paramilitary political power', p.153–178 in L.A. Zurcher and G. Harris-Jenkins (eds.) *Supplementary Military Forces: reserves, militia and auxiliaries*, Beverly Hill, Ca.: Sage Publications.

Mallet, Marian 1978 'Causes and consequences of the October '76 Coup', p.80–103 in Andrew Turton et al (eds.) *Thailand: roots of conflict*, Nottingham: Spokesman

Manas Sattayarak 1994 'Ramlük hok tula wan wangweng' (Commemorating 6 October: the saddest day), p.79–80 in *Matichon Weekly*, 7–13 October.

Morell, David, and Chai-anan Samudavanija 1981 *Political Conflicts in Thailand*, Cambridge, Mass.: Oelgeschalager, Gunn & Hain.

Puey Ungphakorn 1977 'Violence and the military coup in Thailand', p.4-12 in *Bulletin of Concerned Asian Scholars* 9 (3).

—— 1981 *Khamhaikan khòng Dr. Puey Ungphakorn karani hetkan hok tulakhom 2519* (The Testimony of Dr. Puey Ungphakorn Regarding the 6 October 1976 Event), Bangkok: The Komol Keemthong Foundation.

Poniatowska, Elena 1992 *Massacre in Mexico* (translated from Spanish by Helen R. Lane), Columbia, Mo.: University of Missouri Press.

Rao khü phu borisut (We are Innocent Defendants) 1978, Bangkok: Klum Naksüksa Kotmai (reprinted many times by various publishers).

Saithan düan tula (Streams of the Octobers) 1990, Bangkok: The Committee for the Construction of the October Memorial.

Sarakhadi (Feature Magazine) 1996 'Khamhaikan khòng khon run hok tula sipkao' (Testimonies of people of the 6 October 1976 generation), p.133–174 in *Sarakhadi* 140.

Sirot Klamphaibul (ed.) 1991 *Laepai khangna prachathippatai* (Looking Forward toward Democracy), Bangkok: Thammasat Student Government and the Student Federation of Thailand.

Steedly, Mary 1993 *Hanging without a Rope*, Princeton: Princeton University Press.

Suchit Bunbongkarn 1987 *The Military in Thai Politics, 1981–1986*, Singapore: Institute of Southeast Asian Studies.

Surin Matsadit 1986 'Cotmai phra surin' (Letter from Phra Surin), p.125–128 in Bandit Thamtrirat et al (eds.) *Satca thorayuk* (Truth in Tyrannical Era), Bangkok: Thammasat Student Government and the Student Federation of Thailand (reprinted from *Khadi prawattisat* 1979, p.434–459).

Sutham Saengprathum 1979 *Phom phan hetkan hok tulakhom ma dai yangrai* (How I Have Been through the 6 October Event), Bangkok: Daohang Publishing.

Thongchai Winichakul 1994 *Siam Mapped: a history of the geo-body of a nation*, Honolulu: University of Hawaii Press.

—— 1996a 'Remembering/silencing the traumatic past: the ambivalent narratives of the October 1976 massacre in Bangkok', paper presented at the Sixth International Conference on Thai Studies, Chiang Mai, October.

—— 1996b 'Khwamsongcam kap prawattisat batphlae karani kan prappram nònglüat hok tula 2519' (Memory and traumatic past, the case of the bloodshed suppression on 6 October 1976), p.181–194 in *Sarakhadi* 140.

—— 1996c 'Khwam ilak ilüa haeng chat nüangmacak hok tula 2519' (The national ambivalence because of the 6 October 1976), p.242–289, in *Tulakan* (In October), Bangkok: The Co-ordinating Committee for the 20th Anniversary of the 6 October Event.

Trouillot, Michel-Rolph 1995 *Silencing the Past*, Boston: Beacon Press.

Tulakan (In October) 1996, Bangkok: The Co-ordinating Committee for the 20th Anniversary of the 6 October Event.

Wattanachai Winichagoon (ed.) 1988 *Samutphap düan tula* (Photo Collections of the October Events), Bangkok: The Student Federation of Thailand.

Zimmerman, Robert 1976 *Reflections on the Collapse of Democracy in Thailand*, Singapore: Institute of Southeast Asian Studies, Occasional Paper, no.50.

PART V

Reflections

■ CHAPTER ELEVEN ■

Social Memory Reconsidered

Masato Fukushima

Memory: its various forms

A well-known Russian neuropsychologist, Alexandre Romanovich Luria, has left a very interesting record of a man who incurred heavy brain damage caused by a bullet which penetrated near the top of his head, destroying the parietal lobe of the left hemisphere of his brain. This injury caused a systematic destruction of his faculty of memory, perception and understanding, though he somehow had recovered the ability to write down primitive sentences. For the patient, named Zassetsky, everyday life after the incident was, in brief, a series of enormous confusions, with incessant efforts to recreate a sense of order out of endless chaos. However, rather surprisingly, the patient has left two volumes of diaries, in which these ceaseless struggles are minutely described, full of primitive sentences and a variety of childlike drawings to show this seemingly endless ordeal due to his destroyed memory and abnormal perception of things (Levitin 1982; Luria 1979: 184–187).

Obviously, this is fascinating material for analysing the everyday workings of the psychological faculty of memory, and its dysfunction within its ecologically natural setting, but what also attracts our attention is that this case study may symbolise the very phenomena we are confronted with collectively: the role of remembrance and forgetting under the name of social memory discussed in this volume.

Psychological studies of memory have been, as Tanabe and Keyes have already indicated in their Introduction, limited to the model of individual information processing: input of the information into the mental database, in the forms of short term memory (STM), long term memory (LTM), and of other different classifications; the act of remembrance is compared to the way such stocked memory in the mental database is retrieved as in the functioning of a computer (cf. Stillings et al 1989: 73–85). This model obviously imitates the internal structure of a computer's software, and as

287

such, it has produced a number of interesting scientific facts, in contrast with the barren efforts of the behaviourists, who, while refusing to hypothesise on the internal structure of mental activity, tried to establish psychology without resort to concepts such as memory, thought, and consciousness.

The euphoria among the so-called cognitive psychologists, who welcomed the return of such scientific themes as memory as one of the central subjects in psychology[1] soon waned, however, when this model of memory was increasingly criticised, even by the same psychologists, as being not pertinent to the study of the functioning of memory in its ecologically valid environment (cf. Neisser 1982; Neisser and Winograd 1988). A new school of scholars, called social constructivists, have proposed the model of collective remembrance, in which memory is described not as something stocked in the mental database and retrieved directly from it, but as a result of social collaboration through which it is reconstituted and recreated collectively.[2] In this sense, the social scientists who deal with the problem of memory are, by definition, social constructivists, and in fact, the chapters in this volume are more or less concerned with a similar leitmotif, i.e. the collective reconstruction and recreation of particular memory in the process of social interaction. So, what is the use of talking about social memory in a particular setting such as the rapidly changing Thai society?

Simply collectivising the analysis of memory from something individual to something social does not add anything particularly new to the understanding of the problem. That said, however, it seems that there are at least three areas of theoretical interest where the social scientific approach could make a novel contribution to the subject matter. The first is the particular type of memory which has a character of embodiedness; the second is the study of the nature of social mediation and remediation through which the memory is constructed; and finally, there is the wider setting where such reconstructed social memory is used and abused in political manoeuvres or as part of a more general collective social formation. The following sections will deal with the above-mentioned areas separately.

The embodiment of memory: ritual

A few years ago, a fascinating Japanese TV programme was made about a patient who, like Zassetsky, had lost the capacity of memory due to localised brain damage caused by a faulty prescription of medication for a disease he was suffering that was unrelated to problems with his brain. The brain damage that occurred seemed to be more localised than in the case of Zassetsky, so that, though he could not sustain memory for more than thirty minutes, his memory from before the medical accident and his other mental capacities remained undamaged. The TV programme described, in a calm and restrained tone, details of the daily difficulties he encountered, and a series of failed attempts to retrieve the lost capacity for memorising; for instance, he went out shopping with one of his children, seemingly quite normally, but after returning home, his memory was completely blank, without any trace remaining of what had happened in his mind. But as was shown near the end of the programme, he found that, after a certain period of unemployment due to his disability, he could indeed learn technical skills like typing or weaving, despite his lack of memory of when and how he learned them. The memory of a skill, as the TV programme showed, is carried by a different part of the brain, which in his case was undamaged, so he could indeed learn something, or more precisely, his body could remember what he had learned.

Psychologists of memory have long realised that our capacity to memorise facts or events is different from that of remembering physical skills. This kind of embodied memory has been an important component of anthropological concern with the theme, without any clear realisation of the fact. For example, Marcel Mauss's original theory of habitus, which he believed was the central notion of the 'techniques of the body', is undoubtedly related to this type of embodied memory (Mauss 1950).

Among the miscellaneous kinds of skills and techniques of the body illustrated by Mauss, little objection will be raised if we choose ritual as one of the exemplars of such socially shared techniques of the body. In fact, anthropologists have accumulated piles of ethnographies around the world, and, as a result, a wide variety of theories, from functionalist, semiotic, performative to anti-semiotic, and so forth, have flourished from among them. Among such theoretical variations, here we consider both the formalised and embodied character of ritual action; one of the conspicuous features of ritual is its rigid adherence to a particular sequence, which is usually thought not to be changeable at the practitioners' will. This formality entails at least two very important consequences. One is the unreflectability of ritual action. Ritual, in its ordinary setting, is not something to think about, but something that should be followed rigorously. In this sense, the performance of ritual action is unrelated to the practitioners' understanding of the details of its meaning. The reason why the so-called tradition of the symbolist theory – which presupposes the ritual action as symbol, expressing something particular in the form of, say, metaphor or metonymy – has begun to be disputed[3] is because much ethnographic data shows that the actual practitioners usually do not care much about the meaning of what they perform. They usually carry it out because it is either their custom or tradition, or something their ancestors have decreed.

This lack of reflection entails the other important feature of ritual, i.e. its historical sustainability. The very fact that ritual is a series of formal procedures which cannot be changed at will guarantees the sustenance of the whole sequence against the arbitrary manoeuvres of its practitioners. Right procedure, or if you like orthopraxy, as Geertz put it (Geertz 1973b), is the essence of ritual action, and if something ominous, such as drought or collective misfortune, happens after the execution of a certain ritual, it is often attributed to mistakes in carrying out the procedure, rather than to the utter failure of ritual itself to prevent such misfortune. This orthopraxy systematically guarantees its historical sustainability, unless it is overtly challenged, for instance, by a different type of ritual system. The sustainability of ritual creates a sense of historical continuity: the generalised feeling that ritual is a pool of traditional memory and knowledge, though its full meaning is rather unintelligible to the ordinary practitioners.

But there is a caveat to this: this generalised understanding of ritual as a pool of embodied memory can be somewhat misleading. If the ritual is wholly embedded in the sequences of the social practices, the practitioners may not even believe that there is something worthy of preserving in the ritual itself. It may be conceived of as a sort of routine work that should be finished quickly, without noticing its importance to the society, as I observed in the case of Javanese *slametan* rituals. What Bourdieu wanted to explain with the use of the term 'doxa' (Bourdieu 1977: 164–172; Bourdieu and Eagleton 1994) is this kind of transparency of social fact: if ritual is totally embedded within the sequence of social practices, ritual itself can be transparent to the practitioners. You do it because it is supposed to be done so. The meaning of the embodiedness of ritual derives from this observation: just as one is usually not aware of one's bodily skills, one usually does not reflect upon what is there in ritual practice. What is left is not a kind of memory as we imagine when we use the word, like a reconnaissance of a particular event, but a sort of unnoticed, unmentioned skill of embodiment, which has been repeated historically. In this sense, the embodied memory in ritual practice is a particular kind of memory, similar to that of the patient in the aforementioned TV programme, without particularly remembering any historical facts or events.

Then there is a second caveat: the supposed transparency of ritual can be challenged by a number of social conditions, and this book gives ample examples of such confrontations. But before proceeding to make comment on them, we have to take a side trip to the notion of 'mediation'.

Mediation: signs, tools, and spirits

The problem of mediation is critical in the study of memory, both individual and social. As Zassetsky's case indicates, a person who had lost the system of memory could somehow manage to survive in everyday life through the constant use of notebooks and other tools as a substitute for memory. The aforementioned patient on TV actually tried to do the same thing to regain his memory, but in vain. But this is not an idiosyncratic case solely concerning patients with heavy brain damage. As Luria's mentor Lev Vygotsky correctly showed, our mental activity is thoroughly mediated by various kind of tools, both material and psychological, and being a human means being mediated by such tools (Vygotsky 1978; 1986). In this sense, Zassetsky's case is not an exception but only an exaggerated example of the very workings of mental functions in our everyday life, which is thoroughly mediated by various kinds of signs and tools.

Thus the approach to social memory should pay attention to the nature of the medium through which our memory is constituted collectively. And indeed, Vygotsky and his socio-historical psychologist followers were very conscious of how, for instance, children made use of various tools such as pictures, letters, and so on to enhance their powers of memorising. Through those experimental results, Vygotsky and his disciples enriched the notion of mediation, and what they call the higher mental function (cf. Bakhurst 1990).

But the Vygotskyan school would be amazed to find that there is the third type of medium, which is neither semiotic nor instrumental: spirit mediums. Indeed, spirit mediumship as described mainly in Tanabe (chapter 1) and Morris (chapter 2), challenges some of the assumptions of both the above-mentioned embodiedness of ritual, and the theory of mediation by the Vygotskyan school.

One of the difficulties of situating spirit mediumship in the context of ritual theory is its apparent dramaturgicality and interactivity. While an ordinary ritual action is an ensemble of collective formal actions, spirit mediumship evolves around the notion of a particular individual being possessed by a spirit, of whatever kind. For this particular phenomenon to unfold, a number of conditions are prerequired; first, the medium should be able to convince clients that what is possessing him/her is a real entity existing in the world, and second, the medium should be sensitive to the clients' requirements, and should react to them appropriately. The first point highlights the contrasting concept of embodied memory, between that of ritual as vaguely understood as the ancestral custom, and that of mediumship with the focused and reified image of a particular deity or spirit. Mediumship, then, is capable of becoming a very effective apparatus for reifying the unmentionable feeling of the past into something quite concrete, and possibly extremely contentious, due to its very pseudo-historicality. I remember witnessing a case in Java in which there was a heated debate among a number of followers of Javanese mysticism (*kebatinan*) as to whether the spirit which possessed a medium was the real spirit of Sunan Kalijaga, one of the leading Muslim saints who had converted the Javanese to Islam, or was simply a fake, pretending to be so (Fukushima 1987).

In addition, the possessing spirits are not limited to historical figures: as Tanabe indicates in chapter 1, the point of spirit mediumship is its mimetic capacity, by means of which mediums may copy whatever they like, as long as they can discover a source of power in it. The plasticity of the mimetic capacity turns mediumship into something exceedingly adaptive to the changing environment, while rigidly formalised rituals usually cannot be so. This contrast explains why, as Morris points out in chapter 2, that mediumship is not thought to be part of the repertoire of the national identity policy: the plasticity of mediumship contains something more than the traditional memory embedded in the formal action of ritual. There is something excessive in it. But this excessive character ironically fits better with the capitalistic transformation of society, in which Tanabe observes 'the recent explosive proliferation of spirit mediumship'.

Embodied memory challenged

As mentioned above the transparency of embodied ritual action can be guaranteed if, and only if, the environment which supports the ritual practice is relatively stable, so that the unreflective character of its formality is not challenged by external elements. The recent rapid capitalistic transformation of Thai society, however, presents an unrelenting challenge to the very embodiedness of such ritual action, and, in fact, the proliferation of spirit mediumship mentioned previously is one such minatory sign of the increasing threat to unreflectivity of ritual action.

Nonetheless, there are cases where the threat to ritual is tactically averted: Hirai's description of the housewarming ceremony (chapter 7) shows a kind of habitat segregation between the traditional rite and the newly emerging 'party', which is an ostentatious symbol of the factory women's newly acquired wealth. The structure of the double concentric circles of two types of ceremonies conceals the very fact of immanent antagonism between the two. But a clash may occur, with apparent political conflict. One of the classic cases of such direct confrontation around ritual is Geertz's account of a clash between orthodox Muslims and the followers of a nativistic, Javanist organisation called Permai soon after the independence of Indonesia. Permai advocated the total abolition of foreign customs, which was mainly targeted at Islamic elements in Java, but when one of its members died, they automatically thought he could be buried with the traditional, i.e., Islamic funeral. But the religious officer in the village refused to bury him because he was anti-Islam (Geertz 1973a). It is clear from this incident that despite its conscious anti-Islamic ideology, Permai was not yet ready to create its own ritual for burying the dead, preferring to resort to the traditional ritual, which was re-interpreted by the officer, antagonistic to the Permai movement, as 'purely Islamic', thus unsuitable for burying the Permai member. In spite of the very reflective reorganisation of daily ideology by Permai, the funeral occupied a blind spot, since they believed there was no bar to their being buried according to its rites.[4]

Nishii's description of the case of the funeral of a young convert (chapter 9) shows structurally the same kind of problem as Geertz's Permai case, though the co-existence of two religious systems, Islam and Buddhism, has a longer, more intertwined history than Permai's, which was of very short duration. What impresses me here, however, is not the clash itself, because it is possibly inevitable in such cases, but a kind of latent tug-of-war between the momentum which may develop into explosive conflict, and the constraint which restrains such conflict from breaking out. Nishii criticises Halbwachs by underscoring 'the multifaceted nature of memories', but Halbwachs' definition of social memory, which obviously recapitulates the Durkheimian notion of collective representation, is more suitably applied to the unreflective environment of ritual action, rather than the case of co-existence of two different religious systems, which may give way to open conflict. Whether it is a question of a party, or Permai, or religious intermarriage, these are things that the Durkheim-Halbwachsian notion of collective representation cannot deal with, because the source of conflict is already inherent, and there is a fluctuating equilibrium between the two poles of conflict and stability.

The kind of expansion of social traffic, as Marx put it (Marx 1970), in the process of capitalistic transformation, has a conspicuous tendency to leave the embodiedness of ritual behind, inserting a reflective regard to the historically repeated practice. The encounter with what has never been experienced before creates a sense of self-reflection and a search for self-identity. In more neo-functionalist terms, the very complex function of ritual is usually simplified, or utterly changed from the silent practice of embodied repetitive actions into a spectacle meant for foreign spectators. Kunio Yanagita, a prominent founder of Japanese ethnology, observed the systemic transformation of ritual from the silent practice of ancestor worship to the pompous spectacles in the centre of a city, and he pointed out that the presence of outside spectators contributed to the transformation of the nature of the ritual performance (Yanagita 1956; cf. Fukushima 1993b; 1995; Tanabe 1993). In other cases, the ritual system may be replaced with something else, as in conversions from tribal rituals to world religions.

Ritual conveys memory, but as indicated above, memory of a particular type, i.e. skill-memory, and this kind of ritual can be considered ahistorical in nature, with repetitiousness as its essence. Ritual thus gives shape to doxa. But the social transformations described throughout this book are eloquent testimonies of transition from embodied memory, which is never talked about among its practitioners, to one of historical consciousness, in which ritual's original authenticity can be contested, challenged, or even negated. Once such embodied knowledge transmutes into something contestable, we gradually shift to the realm of what Bourdieu calls the field of opinion, i.e. the area where the very orthodoxy of certain versions of memory can be contended or even counter-argued (Bourdieu 1977: 167–171). The medium for memory changes from repetitive bodily practice to various forms of discussion, writing, and argument, wherein contention and contradiction are ordinary phenomena. And now, we come to the notion of history, and its *problematiques*.

Social synaesthesia of memory: history

Let us go back to Zassetsky's case. He struggled among evaporating memories to find the 'right' memory for himself in order to sustain his personal identity. Being without memory thus means being without a personal identity, unable to know who one is. In the attempt to achieve such awareness, he made use of various media, such as notes and drawings. But there is another contrasting case, which Luria documented, that of an extraordinary mnemonist, Sherashevsky. He had an unheard-of capacity for memorising, and Luria's thirty-year-long observation showed that Shera-shevsky could memorise massive amounts of unrelated signs and numbers very quickly, and could recall them even fifteen years after the experiment without forgetting any of them. The secret of such exceptional capacity was his ability to transform every sign and number into concrete visual images, with the other four senses added to it due to his synaesthesia. In other words he could see, hear, feel, and taste such abstract signs as a, b, c or 1, 2, 3, and this led to huge and elaborate constructions of images when he attempted to remember particular numbers or nonsensical syllables.

His enormous capacity for memory, in contrast to that of Zassetsky's, had its own defects, however. One of the problems was that as he could visualise things so vividly that often he could no longer tell what he actually saw from what he conjured up in his memory. His perception and his own construction of images were so often mixed that it caused him problems from time to time: for instance, he was often late for school during childhood as he imagined the clock to be showing 7.30 in the morning, though in reality it was already nine o'clock.

Zassetsky and Sherashevsky can be situated at the two extremes of an axis of co-ordinates, i.e. scarcity of memory vs. its excess. But what is revealing in these cases is that both men suffered from the lack of the right amount of memory necessary for them to live their lives normally. And, on reflection, these two cases shed light upon our everyday faculty of keeping our memory in balance between scarcity and overabundance. By adequately remembering and forgetting, we can manage our everyday lives.

The pursuit of the mechanism that facilitates such balancing is a challenging theme for psychologists of memory, but for anthropologists and historians, the pursuit of an optimum social memory, of the balancing act between scarcity and excess, is one of the central themes of the rest of this volume. What complicates the schema for analysing such a process as the pursuit of an apposite social memory is the fact that there are a number of agencies, or if you prefer system theorist terminology, of subsystems, engaged in this search. Here our analytical approach has been to leave the familiar examples of villages and their customary rituals behind, and to observe instead the macroscopic social system at large.

It is almost a truism to maintain that history is the very battleground of the struggle for orthodoxy, and, in such struggles, you may find a variety of historiographies, of royalist, historical materialist, nationalist, populist, revisionist modes, or whatever you like, competing with each other. The proliferation of various 'isms' is the result of our capacity to reflect on the interpretation of historical fact. But this does not mean that, as a matter of course, every kind of interpretation of history is allowed to circulate: the battle for orthodoxy does not imply that everything could be orthodox; if anything, there have been winners and losers, and many of the chapters unmentioned so far, are about the games played in search of orthodoxy.

But there is a substantial difference, I believe, in studying contemporary historiography, compared with, say, the ancient chronicles of a royal court. The merit of studying the contemporary formation of history is the possibility of witnessing the very techniques of manipulation, exclusion, and inclusion in the process of the establishment of mainstream historical narratives. The analysis of political mechanisms is by far the most conspicuously lacking element in psychological studies of social memory. Contemporary historiography evolves from a mix of influences between very complex multiple agents, or subsystems, i.e. state apparatuses like the ministry of education and political parties; left- and right-wing intellectuals and mass media; teachers, schoolboys and girls, and then rather ambiguously, those who, sometimes clamorously, assert their beliefs in folk-history.

Tannenbaum (chapter 5) and Evans (chapter 6) both deal with statues and monuments as particular tools of social memory which are manipulated with a certain political intention; but it is Keyes' chapter (chapter 4) that illustrates more systematically a number of the main subsystems in such a contest over orthodoxy, i.e. academic historians, politicians, the general public who raised objections to Saipin's new interpretation of Grandma Mo, the mass media, and then a spirit-medium. As Luhmann put it, each subsystem of society has a particular self-referential autonomy (which he calls the autopoiesis of the social system), and each subsystem creates its reality rather independently from other subsystems.[5] According to him, there is no clear cut input-output relationship between inside and outside of the system, there is only 'perturbation' from the outside of the system into the inside. So the relatively independent academic system creates, according to its code, a historical debate, which has quite a different perturbing affect on other systems like politics, the mass media, and especially folk-historiography. While Keyes describes the particular event which was created within the academic system, and how its impact perturbed the other systems quite differently, Thongchai painfully shows (chapter 10) the mechanisms by which such a traumatic event as the student massacre of 1976 was silenced, kept apart from any subsystems of societal response to it.

The macro-theory of social memory, in contrast with its micro-theory, should deal with a variety of social systems, which are concerned with historical formation at large. And, in this sense, its itinerary is a non-linear, almost chaotic process in the sense of the complexity theory (cf. Gleick 1987), caused by the multiple interferences from various subsystems of society, which are all more or less related to the construction of social memory. If we adopt the metaphor of the afore-mentioned Sherashevsky, it is a kind of social synaesthesia of memory, i.e. the co-construction of memory through the different subsystems of society simultaneously, and thus comparable to Sherashevsky's way of memory co-constructed through the use of different senses at the same time, synaesthetically.

As for building a comprehensive theory of social memory at large, we will be obliged to assimilate the results of the above described autonomous interference of a number of subsystems, with what has been characterised as embodied memory in the previous sections, and then attempt a new synthesis. In other words, the relationship between the roles of various institutions at the national level of history formation, and those of the more localised, more embodied type of historical consciousness, should be examined in much greater detail. This is a problem of micro-macro linkage of the study of social memory. Or, if you like, a combination of Zassetsky and the TV patient model of social memory as embodiment, marked by its scarcity, and the Sherashevsky model of synaesthetic co-construction of memory marked by its overabundance.

By way of illustration, during the process of curriculum formation for schools, whether or not a certain event is described in a history textbook as a result of multiple interference of social subsystems is one thing to study, as the macro-sociological subject of memory, but how teachers teach and how particular pupils interpret them is a different though related area of research. Or the same type of contrast can be detected in the relation between how the mass media describe a certain event, and how the audience interpret it idiosyncratically. So, in this sense, we have to proceed further in order to synthesise the study of everyday historical (un)consciousness, and that of systemic formation of mainstream historical narrative, which, in a sense, amounts to a synthesis between the psychological approach of social constructivism and the mainly systems-theoretical approach to the study of history formation. The study of social memory requires us to cross over the disciplinary boundaries, and, though so far as I know, such attempts have still been limited, they are also less than successful.

However, among the chapters in this book more or less related to the notion of social memory, I begin to sense that we can detect auspicious signs of attempts towards such a synthesis, though I confess I am a bit puzzled about whether such signs really exist, or are simply due to my own misperceptions, just as Sherashevsky was often at a loss to tell the difference between reality and his own self-made illusions.

Notes

1 This transition of behaviourism to computer-modelled cognitivism is sometimes described as a 'cognitive revolution'. See Gardner (1985) for the history of the alleged revolution, though this revolutionary history seems to be losing its relevance as the computer model is losing its pertinence these days as a model of mental activity.

2 Among others, Halbwachs (1992) is a precursor of this tradition. Middleton and Edwards (1990) is a representative collection of articles by social constructivists; Fentress & Wickham (1992) and Connerton (1989) deal with the theme from an anthropological perspective rather different than mine.

3 One of the pioneers of such anti-symbolist interpretation of ritual is Dan Sperber. See Sperber (1975; 1985) and Fukushima (1993a; 1993b) for the consequence of what happens if you abandon the symbolist assumption for the analysis of ritual.

4 In the 1980s, when I conducted research in Java, groups like Permai, which overtly advocated an anti-Islamic ideology, had been wiped out after the coup of 30 September 1965, and the subsequent political turmoil. There were a number of what they call the *kebatinan*, or Javanist sects, though, which tried to invent their own way of burying the dead. But there was a further twist to this story. These Javanist sects were not admitted as one of the official religions (*agama*) of Indonesia, but were regarded as part of its culture, officially called 'belief' (*kepercayaan*), and their invention of new rituals was forbidden by the Government because it is only the official religions that can have their own ritual, but not 'belief' sects. See Fukushima (1991) for a detailed analysis of this issue.

5 As to the social system theory of Niklas Luhmann, see Luhmann (1982; 1984; 1990); its introductory outline can be seen in Kneer and Nassehi (1993). The original notions of autopoiesis, operational closure, and perturbation to the system, etc. derive from the seminal argument as to the essence of living entities, by Maturana and Varela (1982). The notion of social differentiation is also argued collectively in Alexander and Colomy (1990).

References

Alexander, Jeffrey and Paul Colomy (eds.) 1990 *Differentiation Theory and Social Change: comparative and historical perspectives*, New York: Columbia University Press.

Aoki, Tamotsu 1984 *Girei no shochosei* (The Symbolism of Ritual), Tokyo: Iwanami Shoten.

Bakhurst, David 1990 'Social memory in Soviet thought', p.203–226 in D. Middleton and D. Edwards (eds.) 1990 *Collective Remembering: inquiries in social construction*, London: Sage Publications.

Bourdieu, Pierre 1977 *Outline of a Theory of Practice* (translated by Richard Nice), Cambridge: Cambridge University Press.

—— 1990 *The Logic of Practice* (translated by Richard Nice), Stanford: Stanford University Press.

Bourdieu, Pierre and Terry Eagleton 1994 'Doxa and common life: an interview', in S. Zizek (ed.) 1994 *Mapping Ideology*, London: Verso.

Callinicos, Alex 1987 *Making History: agency, structure and change in social theory*, Cambridge: Polity Press.

Connerton, Paul 1989 *How Societies Remember*, Cambridge: Cambridge University Press.

Fentress, James and Chris Wickham 1992 *Social Memory: new perspectives of the past*, Oxford: Blackwell.

Fukushima, Masato 1987 '*Kebatinan* mystical sects and the meaning of spirit possession in Javanese culture', p.29–46 in *Man and Culture in Oceania* 3.

—— 1991 'Shinko no tanjo: indoneshia ni okeru maina shukyo no tousou (The birth of belief: the struggle of minority religions in Indonesia)', p.97–210 in *Toyobunka kenkyujo kiyoo* (The Bulletin of the Institute of Oriental Culture) 113.

—— 1993a 'Girei, hatsuwa, jokyo-ninchi: bunka to ninchi no interface (Ritual, utterance and situated cognition: the interface between culture and cognition)', in *Sobun* 384.

—— 1993b 'Girei to sono shakugi: keishiki-teki kodo to kaishaku no seisei (Ritual and its exegesis: formal action and the generation of interpretation)', in Daiichi minzoku-geinou gakkai (eds.) *Kadai to shiteno minzoku-geinou kenkyu* (Towards the Study of Folk-Performing Arts), Tokyo: Hituzi Shobo.

—— 1995 'Girei kara geinou he (From ritual to performing arts)', in M. Fukushima (ed.) *Shintai no kochiku-gaku* (The Architectonics of the Body), Tokyo: Hituzi Shobo.

Gardner, Howard 1985 *The Mind's New Science: a history of the cognitive revolution*, New York: Basic Books.

Geertz, Clifford 1964 *The Religion of Java*, New York: The Free Press.

—— 1973a 'Ritual and social change: a Javanese example', p.142–169 in C. Geertz *The Interpretation of Cultures*, New York: Basic Books.

—— 1973b "Internal conversion" in contemporary Bali', p.170–189 in C. Geertz *The Interpretation of Cultures*, New York: Basic Books.

Gleick, James 1987 *Chaos: making a new science*, New York: Viking.

Halbwachs, Maurice 1992 *On Collective Memory* (translated by Lewis A. Coser), Chicago: University of Chicago Press.

Johnson, Richard et al (eds.) 1982 *Making Histories: studies in history-writing and politics*, Minneapolis: University of Minnesota Press.

Kneer, Georg and Armin Nassehi 1993 *Niklas Luhmanns Theorie Sozialer Systeme*, München: Wilhelm Fink Verlag.

Levitin, Karl 1982 *One is Not Born a Personality: profiles of Soviet education psychologists* (translated by Yevgeni Filippov), Moscow: Progress Publishers.

Luhmann, Niklas 1982 *The Differentiation of Society* (translated by Stephen Holmes and Charles Lamore), New York: Columbia University Press.

—— 1984 *Soziale Systeme: Grundriss einer allgemeinen Theorie*, Frankfurt am Main: Suhrkamp Verlag.

—— 1990 *Essays on Self-reference*, New York: Columbia University Press.

Luria, A.R. 1979 *The Making of Mind: a personal account of soviet psychology* (translated by Michael and Sheila Cole), Cambridge, Mass.: Harvard University Press.

—— 1987 *The Mind of a Mnemonist: a little book about a vast memory* (translated by Lynn Solotaroff), Cambridge, Mass.: Harvard University Press.

Marx, Karl 1970 *The German Ideology* (translated by C.J. Arthur), New York: International Publishers.

Maturana, Humberto and Fransisco Varela 1972 *Autopoiesis and Cognition*, Boston: D. Reidel Publishing Company.

Mauss, Marcel 1950 *Sociologie et anthropologie*, Paris: Presses universaires de France.

Neisser, Ulrich 1982 *Memory Observed*, Oxford: W.H. Freeman.

Neisser, Ulrich and E. Winograd (eds.) 1988 *Remembering Reconsidered: ecological and traditional approaches to the study of memory*, Cambridge: Cambridge University Press.

Sperber, Dan 1975 *Rethinking Symbolism* (translated by Alice L. Morton), Cambridge: Cambridge University Press.

—— 1985 *On Anthropological Knowledge*, Cambridge: Cambridge University Press.

Stillings, Neil et al 1989 *Cognitive Science: an introduction*, Cambridge, Mass.: The MIT Press.

Tanabe, Shigeharu 1993 'Kugi to bukkyo-teki gensetsu: kita tai no pu se ya se seirei saishi (Sacrifice and Buddhist discourse: the Pu Sae Ña Sae spirit cult of Northern Thailand)', p.35–70 in S. Tanabe (ed.) *Jissen shukyo no jinruigaku: jozabu bukkyo no sekai* (The Anthropology of Practical Religion: the world of Theravada Buddhism), Kyoto: Kyoto University Press.

Vygotsky, L.S. 1978 *Mind in Society: the development of higher mental psychological processes* (translated by Michael Cole et al), Cambridge, Mass.: Harvard University Press.

—— 1986 *Thought and Language* (translated by Alex Kozulin), Cambridge, Mass.: MIT Press.

Yanagita, Kunio 1956 *Nihon no matsuri* (The Japanese Rites), Tokyo: Kadokawa Shoten.

Index